D1239444

Science, Culture, and Modern State Formation

Science, Culture, and Modern State Formation

PATRICK CARROLL

University of California Press

BERKELEY   LOS ANGELES   LONDON

(CUD)
Q
125
.C3835
2006

University of California Press, one of the most distinguished university presses in the United States, enriches lives around the world by advancing scholarship in the humanities, social sciences, and natural sciences. Its activities are supported by the UC Press Foundation and by philanthropic contributions from individuals and institutions. For more information, visit www.ucpress.edu.

University of California Press
Berkeley and Los Angeles, California

University of California Press, Ltd.
London, England

© 2006 by The Regents of the University of California

Library of Congress Cataloging-in-Publication Data

Carroll, Patrick, 1961–
    Science, culture, and modern state formation / Patrick Carroll.
        p.   cm.
    Includes bibliographical references and index.
    ISBN-13: 978-0-520-24753-6 (cloth : alk. paper);
    ISBN-10: 0-520-24753-1 (alk. paper)
    1. Science and state—Europe, Western—History—Philosophy.
2. Science—Social aspects—Europe, Western—History—Philosophy.
3. Science and industry—Europe, Western—History—Philosophy.
4. Engineering and state—Europe, Western—History—Philosophy.
5. Engineering—Social aspects—Europe, Western—History—
Philosophy.   6. Science and state—Ireland—History—Philosophy.
7. Science—Social aspects—Ireland—History—Philosophy.   8. Science
and industry—Ireland—History—Philosophy.   9. Engineering and
state—Ireland—History—Philosophy.   10. Engineering—Social
aspects—Ireland—History—Philosophy.   I. Title.

    Q125.C3835   2006
    338.9'406—dc22   2005026929

Manufactured in the United States of America

15   14   13   12   11   10   09   08   07   06
10   9   8   7   6   5   4   3   2   1

This book is printed on New Leaf EcoBook 60, containing 60% post-consumer waste, processed chlorine free; 30% de-inked recycled fiber, elemental chlorine free; and 10% FSC-certified virgin fiber, totally chlorine free. EcoBook 60 is acid-free and meets the minimum requirements of ANSI/ASTM D5634–01 (Permanence of Paper).

WITHDRAWN
Loyola University Library

*To my mother, Aileen Cleary, for showing me
the meaning of determination and perseverance*

Contents

Illustrations

Acknowledgments

Through the writing of this book, and through all my time in the academy, I have benefited from the support and inspiration of many great advisers and scholars. Chandra Mukerji influenced my thinking more than anyone, particularly with respect to the fruits of studying material culture. Thank you, Chandra, for guiding me and at the same time giving me the space to go my own way. Steve Epstein, Martha Lampland, Bob Westman, and Gerry Doppelt deepened my appreciation of the social, historical, and philosophical dimensions of science. Thanks, Bob, for constantly urging me to historicize actors' categories and to use the *Oxford English Dictionary on Historical Principles* as a tool to do so. It was good advice for an aspiring sociologist-historian, and you'll be happy to know that I am an avid user-owner of the complete first edition of this great dictionary. Without your advice I might never have thought to probe the complex historical meanings of words such as *engine* and *police*.

There was not a single member of the Science Studies Program at UCSD who did not broaden my interdisciplinary horizons and enrich my intellectual development. Special thanks to Steve Shapin, Martin Rudwick, Philip Kitcher, Adrian Cussins, and Roddy Reid (who was always a program member in spirit). I was also fortunate to benefit from program visitors such as Mike Lynch, Harry Collins, David Bloor, and Bruno Latour, and the excellent colloquium series that defined my Mondays for four years. My fellow students, however, made my introduction to science and technology studies (STS) truly memorable. We really had something special, uniting the best of comradeship with spirited intellectual exploration. Special thanks to Bart Simon, who sustained me through shared woodwork and theoretical debates on the culture of science (the universe and everything). Thanks also to Andrew Wayne, Ernie Hamm, Alan Richardson, Tim Shanahan,

Margaret Garber, Jane Camerini, Charis Thompson, Cris Philips, Chris Henke, Charlie Thorp, Josh Dunsby, and every one of my fellow students and postdocs, who made science studies at UCSD so rich and inventive.

Conversations with colleagues in the UC Davis Department of Sociology, the STS Program, the Center for History, Society, and Culture, and the Cultural Studies Program shaped my thinking as I revised and better defined my analysis. Special thanks to Jim Griesemer, who always insisted on talking about the "real stuff," that is, science studies, and who has been a constant source of inspiration to me. I greatly appreciate John Hall and Jack Goldstone for their openness to my ideas and for helping me to better appreciate the sociological dimensions of my research. Thanks to Joan Cadden, Susan Kaiser, Ryken Grattet, Vicki Smith, Laura Grindstaff, Jenny Broom, Kathy Kudlick, Diane Wolf, Marisol de le Cadena, Ben Orlove, David Kyle, Carolyn de la Pena, Bruce Haynes, Tom Beamish, and Deb Harkness for their support, particularly as personal troubles threw my work off course. Thanks also to Sean Ó'Riain, Pat Joyce, Philip Corrigan, Derek Sayer, Bruce Curtis, Lyn Lofland, Paul Teller, Clarence Walker, Ming-Cheng Lo, Sergio Sismondo, John Walton, and Vincent Comerford. I also wish to express my genuine appreciation to the three reviewers for the University of California Press for the time they took with my work and for their helpful suggestions and constructive criticism. In this context, my warm thanks are due to Stan Holwitz, my editor at UC Press, for seeing value in this book from the outset, but especially for sticking with me despite my delays along the way. Thanks to my copy editor, Robin Whitaker, for her exacting work on the manuscript, and also to Jacqueline Volin, for moving it swiftly and smoothly through the production process.

I am grateful to the staffs of the National Library of Ireland, the National Archives of Ireland, the Ordnance Survey of Ireland, the Bodleian Library, the British Library, and the National Library of Scotland for their assistance. Special thanks to the staff of the National Library of Ireland for the genuine warmth that developed over the long days and months that I spent there.

The research was supported by grants from the University of California, San Diego, and the University of California, Davis, and was presented at conferences of the American Sociological Association, the Society for Social Studies of Science, the Pacific Sociological Association, the West Coast Society for the History of Science, MEPHISTOS, the Council of European Studies, and the Workshop on State Formation in Comparative, Historical, and Cultural Perspectives at St. Peter's College, Oxford. I appreciate all the feedback I received at these venues and would like to thank especially Philip Corrigan for inviting me to the Oxford workshop. Parts of chapter 2 appeared in an earlier version in Patrick Carroll-Burke, "Tools, Instruments, and Engines: Getting a Handle on the Specificity of Engine Science," *Social Studies of Science* 31, no. 4 (2001): 593–625, © Sage Publications Ltd., 2001, and are reprinted by permission. Parts of chapter 5 appeared in an earlier version in Patrick Carroll, "Medical Police and the History of Public Health," *Medical History* 46 (2002): 461–94, and are reprinted courtesy of the editors of *Medical History*. Parts of chapter 6 appeared in an earlier version in Patrick Carroll-Burke, "Material Designs: Engineering Cultures and Engineering States—Ireland 1650–1900," *Theory and Society* 31 (2002): 75–114, and are reprinted with kind permission of Springer Science and Business Media.

Finally, thanks to Veronique Remulla for helping me through turbulent times with care and love.

Introduction

Speaking coherently about the state is far more tricky than it might at first appear. From Hobbes to Weber and beyond, numerous theoretical arguments have attempted to explain the state's ontological status and ideological claims, its proper limits and appropriate actions, and its relations to the people. In sociology the state is often conceived of as a social relationship, a bureaucratic or technically rationalized organization, an ideological project that masks real social conditions, a discourse of governmentality, a cultural and cognitive institution, an executive, actor, or entire country. States are said to be places that people live in, that they enter or exit, influence, protest, or smash. States and nations are sometimes thought to be entirely distinct—the latter, sovereign peoples; the former, sovereign governments. (Native American nations exist as sovereign peoples within the territory of the sovereign United States.) On other occasions states and nations seem almost inseparable, particularly in the idea of the nation-state. The state is viewed as a coercive structure of armies, police, and prisons, and sometimes also as an ideological apparatus that extends beyond the state itself, reaching deep into civil society through religion, media, education, and so on.

While some sociologists speak of the relationship between state and society, others suggest that states are in fact particular types of society, questioning the very idea of a (civil) society set apart from the state. For many, theory is centered on the concept of a state-society relationship, especially on the question of whether the state is autonomous from or structurally integrated with the capitalist organization of production. Almost everyone currently agrees that the modern state is no mere executive committee of the capitalist class, the task of theorists being one of establishing the degree of autonomy between state and society. Talk of relative autonomy suggests a high degree of separation between the two; talk of embeddedness, a lesser degree. Differentiation of state forms produces a nomenclature in which generic talk of the state shifts to talk of city-states, federal states, premodern states, modern states, postindustrial states, welfare states, communist states, feudal states, fascist states, military states, bureaucratic states, republican states, democratic states, racial states, confessional states, and so on.

Despite its complexity, the historical sociology of state formation has made tremendous advances in the last quarter century. There can now be little doubt, as Charles Tilly has most forcefully demonstrated, that the military-fiscal model captures what is common to all states across history.[1] States are, at the most basic level, coercive organizations sustained by revenue extraction and the political alliances, scheming, and war that such extraction implies. The engagement with Marxist questions by Weberian sociologists such as Theda Skocpol has, in addition, established a model of the modern liberal state as an organizational actor with varying degrees of autonomy from the interests, if not quite from the logic, of capital. This tradition has also generated a great deal of knowledge on the breakdown of states through revolutions. Another wave of research, informed by feminist and postcolonial questions, as well as by traditional concerns with ideology, moral economy, and religion, is revealing the role of culture in state formation.[2] A crucial early example of the cultural approach is Corrigan and Sayer's *The Great Arch: English State Formation as Cultural Revolution.*

While each of these approaches adds to our understanding of the state, sociologists have paid surprisingly little attention to the role of science, particularly natural science, in modern state formation.[3] Because historical sociology has been focused on macro-issues such as state formation, and science studies have focused on knowledge production in local contexts, there has not been much interaction between the two fields. The result is that advances made in understandings of science, particularly by treating science as a form of practice and culture, have not significantly affected studies of the historical sociology of the state. Historical sociologists have paid some attention to science in terms of social policy,[4] and some science studies scholars have addressed issues related to state formation,[5] but the traffic of ideas between the two fields has been thin at best. However, a budding interest in science studies among historical sociologists[6] is currently being paralleled by greater attention to the state by those who study the production of scientific knowledge. Indeed, a major new volume from the perspective of science studies argues that "states are made of knowledge, just as knowledge is constituted by states."[7] I seek to show precisely this, by detailing how, in the context of England's colonial ambitions in Ireland, the modern state was materially engineered through the networked practices of modern science and government.

The image of the state that emerges from this analysis is one in which governed and governing forms are ubiquitous. The idea of ubiquity should not, however, be confused with the idea of coextensive, for state and state power are not, despite the best efforts of some actors, everywhere. There are, as there must be in any system as complex and extensive as modern government, numerous spaces that cannot be continuously occupied, that can be reached only by agents that enter and exit them temporally. Some of these spaces are restricted by the political culture itself, whether through tradition, refusal, resistance, or formal constitutional or legal constraint. There are, in addition, redundancies of government, unfunded mandates, unenforced directives, and tolerated illegalities, and while they often are patterned with respect to socioeconomic power, status hierarchies, and geo-resourceful location, they are also sometimes statewide. There are broken links, paths begun but left unfinished, historical residues of earlier projects, overlapping and incoherent agencies, dysfunctional corruption and incompetence, and ceremoniously reenacted discourses that are decoupled from organizational and experiential outcomes. State governing forms are not coextensive with the totality of social life. Indeed, other than in the visions of state engineers, design ideologues, and technical rationalizers, they probably never will be. But it is equally implausible to suggest that a neat line can be drawn between the two, the state on one side and society—the economy, the private, the people—on the other.

By drawing on, and driving the development of, medicine, public health, sanitary engineering, natural history, geology, structural mechanics, soil science, toxicology, cartography, and so on, government extends into the plumbing beneath our feet; the food, water, and drugs within our bodies; the roofs above our heads; and the landscape within which we live. The social, political, economic, and natural are engineered together over centuries, increasingly integrated until they appear more and more like a *plexus*. This word is not as obscure as it might at first appear. In the field of anatomy it describes a dense and minutely interwoven structure of intercommunicating fibers or tissues. More generally it denotes any intertwined or entangled mass forming a complex web or network. Its close etymological cousins are *nexus, complexity,* and *perplexing,* though the last two tend to denote cognitive categories, while *nexus* and *plexus* are unambiguously object categories. Unlike *nexus,* however, *plexus* does not imply a single or central point of connection. That is, while *nexus* may describe a series of connections established through one primary entity, in the sense that Marx used the idiom *cash nexus, plexus* implies multiple discrete forms connected together in complex ways. I conceive of the relationship between science and the state, and therefore science and society, through the idea of a "science-state plexus": the ontologically dense, interwoven, multifaceted, heterogeneous, and yet intercommunicating nature of modern science and modern government. The plexus subsists in three *boundary objects* that are key to how science and government intersect and network in the modern period. These objects are land, people, and the built environment. The question is how the networking of science and government transforms them into the modern forms of "techno-territoriality," "bio-population," and "infrastructural jurisdiction." What that means is what this book is about.

Figure 1 illustrates, probably as well as any single image can, something of the character of the plexus. It depicts the baseline measurement (1825) that served the principal triangulation and ground survey of the first modern map of the entire island of Ireland. Conducted by the Royal Engineers of the British army, the Ordnance Survey of Ireland produced perhaps the most accurate of all national maps at that time (1846). The baseline was measured near the shore of Lough Foyle in Ulster, to the east of which is illustrated the colonized and known land of Derry, to the west the relatively uncharted lands of Donegal. Good cartographic reasons for choosing the location were articulated by the scientists, but the wider symbolism the site furnished was also significant, visualizing as it did the link between modern scientific England on the one hand and traditional Ireland on the other. To the west a blank page or great unknown, to the east a great engineering culture, plotting its ingenious and probing protraction. The illustration captures the designs of a modern scientific endeavor, the truth of a modern form of government, and the image of a modern colonizing power.

The triangulation operations at the heart of the cartography illustrate the role of the most abstract form of knowledge—mathematics, specifically geometry—in the formation of the modern state. The accuracy achieved by the triangulation method is reflected in the detailed knowledge it produced of the lay of the land, showing not only the natural and civil boundaries—the provinces, counties, towns, baronies, rivers, mountains, bogs, and so on—but also the size and shape of individual fields and the precise meandering of ditches and streams. Not revealed in the map itself, but necessarily implied by it, are the army of engineers who moved methodically across the land for two decades, equipped with the mundane baggage of tents, chains, and provisions, and the more esoteric technologies of the time, at the heart of which were telescopes, microscopes, compasses, and so on. Nor

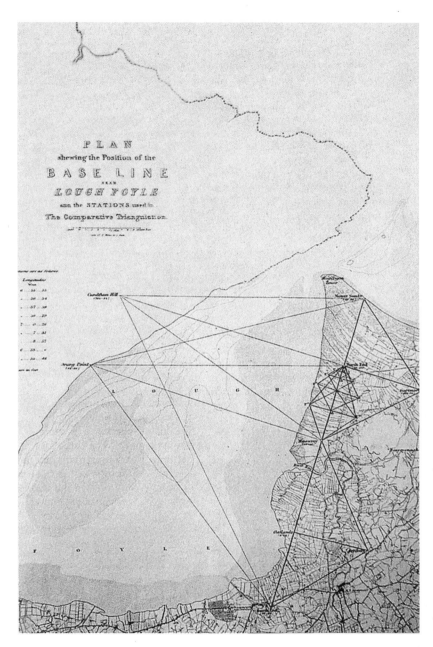

FIGURE 1. Ordnance Survey, baseline measurement, 1825. Ordnance Survey Ireland Permit No. MP 004805 © Ordnance Survey Ireland and Government of Ireland.

does the image record the spirit-leveling that rendered the rise and fall of the land, producing a map that facilitated a more effective prosecution of roads and railways into the interior. Geological, zoological, botanical, and natural historical inquiries helped to value the land as a commodity and establish its potential for economic development. All manner of samples were collected and analyzed in government museums and laboratories. Archaeological research reconstructed the ancient face of the island, complicating and making intellectual the question of who could legitimately lay claim to it. Historical, statistical, political-economic, and "social-economic" studies rounded out the map as a statement not simply of place but also of the people and their economy, society, and culture. Lexicographic and orthographic inquiries documented possible place-names and their spelling, clearing the way for the wholesale translation of the country into the English language.

The survey was an interrogatory of the broadest scope and most minute detail. Data was inscribed in reports and maps, delivered to the government, integrated with other representational forms such as the census and the land valuation, and made to stand for the real Ireland, that which was demonstrated by science and enshrined in law. Almost every sinew of the body of the country, both natural and political, was displayed, collated, compared, marked, numbered, named, classified, indexed, and filed. The country was quantified, illustrated, squared, and triangulated. A dense web of intercommunicating elements was discovered and invented. This is what the image of figure 1 captures, but as I hope to show in the chapters that follow, the map was, as they say in Ireland, only the half of it.

PLAN OF THE BOOK

Chapter 1 poses the problem of the relationship between science and state formation in terms of culture. By viewing science and the state as cultural formations, I seek to contribute to recent third-wave research in historical sociology. The point is not to set third-wave research in opposition to earlier work, but rather to add to that research by revealing the cultural uniqueness of the modern state when viewed from the perspective of technoscientific development and the rise of modern engineering. Indeed, a cultural explanation of modern state formation was developed by Weber, who argued that local religious culture shaped organizational practices, practices that in turn helped to spawn modernity and, with it, modern capitalism and the modern bureaucratic state-system.

In order to avoid the dualisms of the modern episteme and also the tendency toward monism in postmodern analysis (which sometimes seems to implode all social reality into discourse), I adopt a strategy of triangulating culture in terms of discourse, practice, and materiality. The approach permits a conceptualization of the state with respect to the state-idea, the state-system, and the state-country. The state-idea captures the state as a discourse and institution; the state-system refers to the state as an organization of administrative practices. Both of these aspects of the state are well understood in the literature, but my focus is primarily on the state-country. The concept of the state-country directs analysis to the ways that land, people, and the built environment are materially incorporated into the state.

State-idea, -system, and -country are not ontologically bounded realities. I present them rather as useful analytic categories that are best understood through the metaphor of centers of gravity. The idea is to capture distinctions and connections, to think through the issue of state formation from a perspective that lies somewhere between rigidly bounded dualistic categories on the one hand and post-structuralist tendencies toward monist implosion on the other. The approach should not, however, be read to mean that everything equally co-constructs everything else. Rather, I suggest that the co-construction of science and government can be understood as a specific causal mechanism that explains the peculiar form of the modern state compared with other states in history.

To understand how the mechanism of co-construction works, I conceive of science as culture and extend the analytic strategy of triangulation. Chapter 2 develops an analysis of the cultural integration—in practice—of natural philosophy, mathematics, and engineering in the second half of the seventeenth century. I describe this integration with the term *engine science*. The chapter conceptualizes engine science as a culture of inquiry characterized (among other things) by a discourse of ingenuity; by practices of measuring, scoping, graphing, and manipulating; and by a material culture of tools, instruments, and engines. I single out scopes, meters, graphs, and chambers as key among the array of material culture found in engine science. Scopes augment human senses, meters render objects in numbers so they can be handled mathematically, graphs extend the capacity of inscription, and chambers capture material entities so that they can be manipulated. The practices associated with these technologies cut across the activities of statecraft and experimental inquiry. That is, while engine science became one of the crucial forces driving the development of England's engineering culture, the engineering culture was also driven by statecraft itself. The analysis is centered on the writings of Robert Boyle and concludes with the question of how this new form of science related to political philosophy and the modern state-idea.

Chapter 3 focuses on the relationship between engine science and government with respect to philosophy, colonial statecraft, and the civilizing mission. Hobbes was among the first to raise alarm about the prospect of "experimental politics," a politics he believed to be implied by Boyle's agenda for natural philosophy. I situate Hobbes's *Leviathan* in relation to Machiavelli's *Prince* and William Petty's *Political Anatomy of Ireland*, arguing that Petty's work represents a key shift in the science and art of government. I use Petty to demonstrate the role of engine science in the designs of English government in Ireland, particularly in terms of cartography, surveying, censuses, political arithmetic, and political economy.

Chapter 4 develops the concept of the "data state," by which I mean a condition of being governed by number. Government by number emerges from "political anatomy" and "political arithmetic." My focus in this chapter is on the emergence of these political forms as engines for counting and calculating natural and political objects. The chapter begins with a discussion of Samuel Hartlib and William Petty's designs and concludes with the great innovations in censuses and cartography developed in Ireland in the first half of the nineteenth century. The modern census, I argue, is a political technology engineered by bringing metering and graphing into a simultaneously practiced and representational relationship. It is through such engines, of which the census is exemplary, that the data state was crafted. Though the subtlety of the census lay in its literary form, its special power derived from its character as a *sociometer*. In chapter 4 I also discuss the concept of graphing, particularly the graphing of people, the built environment, and land. I analyze Petty's geometric cartography, the Ordnance Survey, and the survey's integration with the census and the land valuation. In all the complexities of its ingenuity, the Ordnance Survey made a land, a built environment, and a people legible[8] with a geographic, orthographic, and ethnographic detail never before realized. It was, in the late 1840s, a science and state graph and *socioscope* without parallel anywhere in the world.

Ireland was not only a site for the deployment of experimental government meters and graphs. It was also a laboratory for the government of natural and political bodies through medical institutions and public health. In chapter 5 I draw out the links between "public health" and "medical police,"[9] demonstrating the inaccuracy of the widely held belief that public health displaced medical police in the nineteenth century. The essentialist association of medical police with the Continent (particularly Germany) and the idea that it constituted an "opposite model" to that of English public health are not supported by the historical record. Beginning with Petty's "political medicine," I show how medical police became one of the most powerful engines of government for scoping out people and integrating them into engineered social spaces. The complexity of police cannot be grasped, I suggest, by the singular idea of the repressive hypothesis. The point is, as Foucault suggested, that the state develops as an *administration of life*, with government constantly seeking to arrest disease and extend longevity. Medical police is, therefore, a positive power, productive to health, safety, and population security.

A central thesis of this book is that the character of the modern state and its relations with science can be fully appreciated only when careful attention is paid to material culture. In chapter 6 I show how the civilizing mission was expressed in a discourse that linked moral improvement with material engineering. The chapter covers agriculture and land management, public buildings, roads, town improvement, and sanitary engineering. It discusses how "natural bodies" became "political objects" through the culture of engine science, and how land, bodies, and the built environment were engineered into the forms of techno-territoriality, bio-population, and infrastructural jurisdiction.

The analysis concludes with some general implications that I believe merit consideration, discussing the arts of government in relation to the practices of engine science and suggesting that a form of "engineering governmentality" develops that cuts across and undergirds different manifestations of the modern state. I draw out the implications of the analysis in relation to the specific case of Ireland and the broader question of the character of the modern state. With respect to Ireland, for instance, the legacy of English science and statecraft led to an ambivalent (at times cynical) attitude toward the powers of engineering culture, an attitude only recently replaced by an apparently insatiable appetite for technoscience. With respect to more general issues, I question the somewhat taken-for-granted coupling of nation and state in the modern period, suggesting that the relationship between the two is by no means essential. On this question I follow Tilly, who pointed out some time ago that "nation-states" have rarely existed in modern or premodern times.[10] I also discuss the growing expansiveness of the government of nature, its continued modern character, and the implications with respect to freedom and police power, especially in terms of public health and safety, that is, biosecurity. Like James Scott, I conclude that our freedoms are inextricably bound up with the modern state and that there is little chance of life-security absent scientifically informed government. This is not to suggest that scientifically informed statecraft is necessarily benign. History provides plentiful evidence of the disastrous effects of the intersection of social and other forms of science and engineering. In addition, there is little question that science helped to secure colonial expansion and the modern capitalist order. Nonetheless, scientifically informed statecraft is qualitatively distinct from Machiavellian regime-craft, a difference recognized in the late seventeenth century by leading figures of the new science, such as William Petty. In the Foucaultian sense, scientifically informed statecraft realizes a productive form of power, a power that augments life and combats abjection.

1 Science, Culture, and Modern State Formation

Theory and Analysis

A newly invigorated synthesis is under way in science and technology studies (STS), one that gives as much attention to broad sociological questions concerning organizational, institutional, and state forms of power as it does to more micro-issues raised by the focus on epistemological questions. The effort has been evident for some time in the work of a wide range of STS scholars, such as Bruno Latour, John Law, Steven Shapin, Karen Knorr Cetina, and Donald McKenzie. It is currently reflected in organizational studies (for instance, the work of Diane Vaughan),[1] in the sociology of science (for instance, the work of Thomas Gieryn),[2] and in analyses of socio-technical networks.[3] More recently, Sheila Jasanoff and others have laid out an expansive research agenda around the theme of the "co-production of science and social order." Such work is not only forging productive dialogue between STS and broader sociological traditions but also opening up opportunities to reconnect with earlier research that has much to offer contemporary social scientists.

As well as Merton's early work on the institutionalization of a new technology-centered science in seventeenth-century England, and Boris Hessen's work on the relationship between Newtonian mechanics and industrial capitalism, Edgar Zilsel's "The Sociological Roots of Science" has generated a great deal of renewed interest.[4] Originally published in 1942, Zilsel's article was reprinted in 2000, with commentary, in *Social Studies of Science*. Zilsel linked the development of capitalism directly to the birth of the new experimental science in the sixteenth and seventeenth centuries, suggesting that the rise of craft knowledge with respect to literary knowledge created a new synthesis of theory and practice. Zilsel's analysis centrally informs my elaboration of the concept of engine science, since it shows the importance of the *integration* of practical mathematics (mechanics), engineering, and theory in the development of a specifically modern and crucially Baconian science. The idiom *engine science* foregrounds ingenuity and design, material technologies of inquiry, and power and control as key to the success of the new science. Zilsel suggested that the new synthesis resulted from a "breakdown of social barriers,"[5] but an aristocracy of the intellect eventually subordinated engineering to theory, viewing the latter as the wellspring of scientific knowledge and the former as its "mere application." STS has shown that abstract theory and practical engineering stand in a dynamic and dialectical relationship in modern scientific practice, that the power and success of modern science lies in this relationship, and that it is a relationship crucially mediated by the language of mathematics. Science is no longer conceived in terms of purity (the idea of "pure science") and is not reducible to any one of these three key elements, each of which at any moment in history is a specific and semiautonomous cultural formation. The conceptualization of science as "impure" opens up new ways of thinking about the question of the relationship between science and the state.[6] The purpose of this chapter is to introduce my conceptualization of that relationship, explain how a cultural analysis of science reveals the unique character of *modern* states, and discuss the implications for how we think about the state.

Charles Tilly has developed one of the most influential general theories of state formation.[7] For Tilly, the crucial activity of states is coercion, but they must make concessions to groups in order to raise the capital required for both building their coercive structures and waging their coercive campaigns.[8] The theoretical beauty of Tilly's model lies in its empirical reach. It is practically universal in scope, covering some ten thousand years of state history across all regions of Europe (perhaps even the world). At the same time it orders all the diversity of state forms (which Tilly readily acknowledges and documents copiously) into three basic types: coercion-intensive, capital-intensive, and capitalized-coercion.[9] Tilly's model readily explains key aspects of state formation in Ireland. War making and resource mobilization were without question the basic grounds for what John Walton calls "conquest and incorporation."[10] My own analysis is consistent with this general model but aims at a more particularized explanation of the specificity, and indeed uniqueness, of the modern Western state. Just as Walton turns to culture and ideology as a way of providing a more historically grounded explanation of local collective action and its relationship to broad societal forces and change, so I argue that by conceptualizing science in cultural terms we can fully appreciate its significance for the formation of the modern state. While reference to science is not required for the kind of general theory that Tilly has developed, it is crucial with respect to the particularity of the modern Western state. The rise of modern science, at the center of which is a special form of experimental and engineering practice, became institutionalized only within a limited area of Europe between the seventeenth and nineteenth centuries. This new science, I suggest, transformed the activities of governing, the processes of capital accumulation, and the relationship between the two. Government and capital accumulation, in turn, shaped the development of science in a process of coproduction.[11]

SCIENCE, CULTURE, AND CAUSALITY

Science is a transformative collective activity rooted in local communities of meaning and extended over time through various strategies and technologies to the level of a social movement and social institution. Collective action in the domain of science confronts the same difficulties identified by Walton with respect to more explicitly political organizations, unfolding within a moral economy that constantly reconstructs its past in the face of immediate obstacles. In this process science constructs an ideology of legend, remembering its past in terms of heroic and stoic individuals struggling against irrationality, ignorance, and obfuscation. Local articulations of what science is and what it offers emerge in relation to wider social conditions, not least of which are the demands and expectations of statecraft and the need for any particular vision of science to secure the blessing of government (no matter how begrudgingly). As political power was centralized in the early modern state, scientific practitioners were confronted by new limitations and opportunities. Experimentalists were forced to defend their natural philosophy against philosophical, political, and religious enemies, but they did not do so simply in the negative sense of resistance. The early experimental philosophers actively pursued new opportunities to align their designs with religious precepts and political realities. They spoke of mathematics as the language of God, and of God himself as a designing engineer. They offered up scheme after scheme for the "Empire of Man over Nature," and more specifically for the aggrandizement of the state and the invigoration of economic development. Their capacity to deliver on these claims in the short term is not the issue here: the point, rather, is to explain how the culture of the new science moved from a local form of collective action to an institutionalized culture that caused the emergence of a state form that was without precedent in world history.

The key theoretical issue is how to conceive of culture,[12] and a useful way of introducing my approach is by comparing how Walton and Tilly theorize the concept. Both conceive of culture in broadly cognitive terms, but their emphases are sufficiently different that they lead to divergent arguments concerning culture's efficacy as an *explanatory* category with respect to social (or collective) action. Drawing upon Clifford Geertz, Walton defines culture as "the meanings that people construct for their lives and their environment."[13] Tilly defines it in a similarly cognitive fashion, as "shared understandings and their representations."[14] The emphasis for Walton, however, is on the *active construction* of meaning rather than simply the fact that such meanings are shared. Walton seeks to establish culture as an explanatory category with respect to "collective action," whereas Tilly argues that we should start with "social interaction" and from that point of departure explain culture.[15]

Like Walton, I seek to advance a conceptualization of culture as a causal explanatory category, one that can explain historical change. However, I wish to advance a concept of culture that goes beyond the realm of symbolic meaning. With Stuart Hall and Chandra Mukerji, I suggest that we should also view culture as belonging to the realms of practice and materiality. Hall, for instance, argues that culture encompasses "both the meanings and values which arise amongst distinctive social groups and classes . . . [and] the lived traditions and practices through which those 'understandings' are expressed and in which they are embodied."[16] Mukerji shows how culture becomes embodied in the material world, acting back on cognitive meanings and organizational practices in uniquely powerful ways.[17] As George Steinmetz points out, this broader concept of culture is distinctively "socioanthropological," and its elements can be traced back, if somewhat vaguely, to the late eighteenth century.[18] John Hall, Mary Jo Neitz, and Marshall Battani have recently affirmed that all three elements should be included in the concept of culture, placing particular emphasis on the need to theorize the material dimension.[19] What I wish to do is articulate these three elements in a more explicit and theoretically symmetrical way and elaborate on each as a crucially structural pillar in the "architecture of culture."[20]

TRIANGULATING CULTURE: DISCOURSE, PRACTICE, AND MATERIALITY

All three dimensions of cultural formation—discourse, practice, materiality—can be granted their peculiar agential power, though in a manner, and this is a crucial point, that does not theoretically subordinate one dimension to

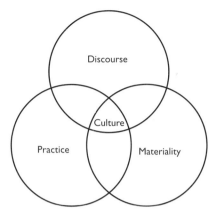

FIGURE 2. Triangulating culture.

the other. The relative agency of discourse (symbolic meaning, representation, and cognitive structure), practice (social activity variously organized), and materiality (constructed environments, spaces, and technologies) in processes of cultural formation can be treated as an empirical issue to be settled in each case by research. The Royal Society of London (1660), for instance, was an organizational form of collective action that mobilizes resources and becomes a powerful catalyst of new webs of discursive meaning. But in the approach I am proposing, culture does not thereby become secondary to organized action and resource mobilization. Rather, organizational culture becomes the primary agent with respect to the growth and institutionalization of meaning in a particular context and at a particular moment in history, as, for example, it did in England in the 1660s. The collective action that led to the organization of the Dublin Society (1683), on the other hand, can be better understood as an organizational instantiation born of meanings that were already becoming institutionalized. In the English case, the organization was the forcing house of meaning; in the Irish case, the organization was established more through what DiMaggio and Powell call "mimetic processes."[21] As I hope will become clear, these distinctions are particularly important if one wishes to understand the material dimensions of science and the state. Figure 2 seeks to illustrate the distinctions in terms of *centers of gravity*, an analytic concept that maintains reference to embeddedness and internal relatedness.

I should perhaps anticipate a likely criticism: that by expanding the concept of culture beyond the bounds of the cognitive or discursive in order to include practice and materiality, I have drained it of any specific theoretical efficacy. Or to put it another way, making culture embrace everything ensures that it can explain nothing. The solution cannot avoid either ontological or epistemological issues. Ontologically, it seems impossible to conceive of practices (variously organized) as anything but cultural. Skill, and the tacit knowledge that goes along with it, is a revealing example. Developing an observation made by both Michael Polanyi and Thomas Kuhn, Harry Collins has demonstrated that not only is tacit knowledge distinct from abstract knowledge in that it is acquired in practice rather than through formal communication, but also in many cases it is in principle impossible to communicate other than through practice.[22] One cannot learn, for instance, to be a carpenter or surgeon from a book. Knowing how much pressure to put on a knife in order to cut through the skin of a body without cutting too deep and causing damage to organs is a knowledge that can be gained only by practicing with actual materials. Thus, practice must have its own cultural agency; it must be a form of communication that is embodied and tactile, experiential in the most material sense of the term.

With respect to the material world a similar argument can be made. The material world created and transformed by cultural discourses and practices (institutionalized and organized)—tools, instruments, engines, buildings, landscapes, and so on—is indisputably cultural, not simply in the meanings such a world has for social actors, but also because humanly transformed materiality embodies cultural designs, aspirations, and objectives, materializing and structuring discourses and practices. Lyn Lofland, for instance, illustrates how the materiality of an urbanscape exerts power over social interaction, structuring action in ways that could not be achieved by purely symbolic means.[23] Similarly, Chandra Mukerji has demonstrated the importance of the material culture of Versailles in the construction of Louis XIV as the Sun King and indeed of France as a new Rome.[24] It was not simply that the gardens functioned as a symbol but also that they served as forces that structured interaction in a manner that served symbolic articulation. And Susan Davis has shown how the great thoroughfares of modern cities provided the material conditions of possibility for the development of disciplined "parades" and "demonstrations" as new forms of political action.[25]

The point I wish to make here, however, is that I do not advocate a conceptualization of culture that uniformly and homogeneously applies to "everything." While from an ontological perspective it is impossible to deny the internality of culture with respect to practice and humanly transformed materiality, analytically useful distinctions can still be maintained. Applied to the state, the triangulation method results in distinctions/connections

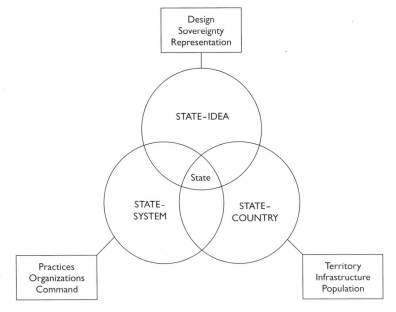

FIGURE 3. Triangulating the state.

among the state-idea, the state-system, and the state-country. Figure 3 does not attempt to capture all aspects of the state. Its purpose, rather, is to illustrate how some of the aspects of the state with which this study is concerned map onto the analysis of culture outlined above.

STATE-IDEA, STATE-SYSTEM, AND STATE-COUNTRY

The idea of the modern state is variously institutionalized, ideological, philosophical, and scientific. In the context of these wider discourses, the modern state-idea is articulated with respect to at least six key centers of gravity: discourses of legitimacy (e.g., Hume's concept of "natural liberty"); discourses of political representation (who should be represented and by what mechanism); discourses of nation (the "nation-state" idea); discourses regarding the proper scope of government authority (e.g., with respect to the economy, political liberties, etc.); discourses of security (including generalized health and safety); and discourses of design (schemes for governing land, the built environment, and the population). The focus of this study is on discourses of design, for it is there that ideas in science and government most clearly intersect. But it should be noted that a focus on design necessarily provides a route to discussions of the other five centers of gravity, for most matters concerning the modern state-idea ultimately become matters of design and craft, social and political engineering, and security. In terms of practice and materiality, my focus is on scientific and governing activities that targeted land, people, and the built environment. The aim is to explain how these materialities were transformed into techno-territoriality, bio-population, and infrastructural jurisdiction.

DESIGNING STATES

The French revolutionaries of the late eighteenth century were among the first to suppose that one could wipe the political slate clean and engineer a state from the bottom up on the basis of an entirely new and abstract design. Their attempt, like that of the Bolsheviks in the early twentieth century, stumbled and failed, partly because the inertia of the existing conditions called forth the application of brute force, a strategy that from the outset betrayed and corrupted the very values the revolutionaries claimed their designs sought to realize. The English took a somewhat different approach, in which a strong tradition of localism, an ideology of self-government, a peculiarly modern worship of indigenous antiquities, and a more empirically oriented idea of science than one finds in Cartesian France shaped an engineering culture that sought to build into what already existed rather than erase older forms in the name of an overly abstract rational plan.

When Ireland was completely mapped in the second quarter of the nineteenth century, enormous effort was made to research the oldest and most "authentic" civic boundaries and place-names, and their inscription on the new map affirmed continuity with the past. The English and French cases demonstrate how the business of engineering the modern state in different contexts drew upon divergent designing ideas, sometimes highly abstract and "rational," other times resembling those of the *bricoleur*. These ideas about the state were, one might say, "internal" to its construction. There were others who sought to understand the state from the "outside," from the perspective, in particular, of the social, political, and economic sciences. The distinction, once again, involves a center of gravity rather than an absolute or categorical separation, but the point of the distinction is to make possible a reflexive stance, one that places social-scientific conceptualizations of the state on the same level as those articulated by the state engineers. The interests of social scientists are generally quite different from those of state engineers, but that is not sufficient reason to treat the two asymmetrically. Indeed, as discursive formations, academic constructions of meaning oftentimes exhibit an easily identifiable traffic with the ideas of state engineers. In this context an important effect of a critical reflexive stance is to question the idea of the state as an *actor*, an idea first fully elaborated by Hobbes and still central to discourses of state that emerge from both within and without the offices and chambers of government.

THE LIMITS OF THE ACTOR-STATE IDEA

While it makes sense to speak of the state as an actor in some contexts, the idiom has its limitations, because, as I hope to show, states are complex and historically changing configurations of meanings and institutions; agencies, technologies and practices; and land, built environment, and people. While sovereign governments act in the name of states, they are not coterminous with states. Indeed, to conflate "the state" with the "government" or its bureaucratic agencies is in effect to rob a people of a body politic that is importantly constituted through that people's very corporeal being, bestowing on a particular government or regime, at a particular moment in time, the image of the universally representative state-as-actor, philosophically conceived by Hobbes as the sovereign. When social scientists uncritically adopt the idiom *the actor-state*, they do not so much describe a political reality as become agents in the construction and institutionalization of the Hobbesian state-idea, the idea that when the head of state acts, the state itself acts. John Meyer has noted the problem, acknowledging that states "are by no means really actors,"[26] despite the deeply institutionalized idea that they are.

Questioning the idea of the actor-state is not an idle academic exercise. Philip Abrams, one of the founders of historical sociology in Britain, has suggested that one of the crucial ways through which organized political subjection is effected in modern societies is by a particular and interested government presenting itself as the universal and disinterested organization of the society as a whole.[27] A particular political organization thus presents itself as a unitary entity, speaking and acting in a unitary manner and in a highly personified form. Abrams alerted sociologists to this state-supporting discursive strategy in order to warn about the ease with which social-scientific discourses might unwittingly serve it. Yet his remedy, that sociologists reject the notion of the state as a "real" object and instead focus on the ways the state-idea is constructed and legitimized, directs analysis toward ideology rather than material forms. Problematizing the personified actor state-idea need not, however, lead analysis in this idealist direction. While accepting that such a state-idea is central to the ideological project of legitimizing organized political subjection, one need not be diverted from the ways the material environment is itself constituted as a force of moral and political governance. Like Abrams's analysis, Meyer's analysis of the state does not get us there, because he reduces the state to its "tendentious" culture, suggesting that its real foundation is a series of discursive "myths."[28]

If treating the state-idea as *the* center of gravity of *the state* leads us into idealism, an exclusive focus on the state-system is also problematic. Treating the state-system as though it is coextensive with the state as a whole[29] circumvents analysis of the material forms of state power that do not reside in the apparatus of governing bureaucratic agencies. Foucault rejected such an analysis precisely because it implied the existence of another domain, that of civil society, which was set in opposition to the state, and this is one of the reasons he was "led to raise the question of power by grasping it where it is exercised and manifested, . . . without considering, for example, the presence of a state which would exercise its sovereignty upon a civil society which itself would not be the depository of analogous processes of power."[30] Foucault suggested that we should cut off the king's head in political theory, and work inspired by Foucault has seriously questioned the value of talking about the state as an actor.[31] Such work has not generally done so, however, on the basis of an analysis of ideology. Rejecting the idea that power and ideology stop at the water's edge of knowledge, the work focuses on discourses of knowledge-power and the discursive rationalities of governance. Though centrally concerned with issues of science and power, "governmentality studies" largely remain at the level of discursive "mentalities." This is true even though governmentality studies emphasize the importance of science and technology in politics. As Mitchell Dean acknowledges, "thought" rather than practice is the center of gravity of governmentality studies.[32]

DISCOURSE, PRACTICE, AND IDEOLOGY

Without an analysis of the ideological aspects of discourse, maintaining an efficacious analytic distinction between discourse and practice is difficult. For instance, by presenting "medical police" as an essentially German or Continental phenomenon inherently at odds with English political discourse, Thomas Osborne dispatches it as irrelevant to English history. "Britain," he declares, "was a country without a tradition of police."[33] Osborne arrives at this conclusion because his theoretical orientation takes discursive formations at face value. Accepting the central premise of English liberal discourse, that is, the idea of self-government, as a sufficient measure of social reality, he precludes empirical analysis of the role of government through police in eighteenth-century England. Yet as Karl Polanyi has demonstrated, the discourse of classical liberalism was crucially ideological, because there was "nothing natural about laissez faire."[34] On the contrary, the "road to the free market was opened and kept open by an enormous increase in continuous, centrally organized and controlled interventionism."[35]

This mismatch between discourse and practice is difficult to grasp without acknowledging the ideological aspects of discourse. Polanyi's insight is readily applicable to the history of the relationship between police and public health in England. Though the liberal discourse of nonintervention and self-regulation with respect to markets was extended into the domain of public health, that domain was, in fact, secured (to the extent that it was) by the expansion of the police power of government.[36] This is an important point, because it counters the claim that medical police was a feature of English colonial government but not of English domestic government. Such arguments tend to downplay the role of police in modern liberal state formation. Thus, while governmentality studies provide a rich resource for understanding the development of liberal rationalities of government, much greater attention needs to be paid to actual practices of government. This is beginning to happen. Patrick Joyce, in his remarkable book *The Rule of Freedom*, navigates the dis/continuities across discourses and practices with respect to liberalism and the modern English city, noting that liberal ideas of self-government have never fully displaced practices of police government.[37]

Others inspired by Foucault, most notably Timothy Mitchell, have confronted the ideological problem head on, approaching the state as an "object of analysis that appears to exist simultaneously as material force and as ideological construct."[38] Mitchell interrogates this and a range of other contradictions, such as that between the coherence of the analytical/popular state-idea and the incoherence of state practices, and the distinction between the state and the economy/society. He provides a much needed problematization of the basic concepts through which the state is understood, but I suggest that we need to move beyond the deconstruction of dualisms and begin instead with a single triangulated distinction among state discourses, state practices, and state materialities. The actor state-idea, because it is centered in discourse, reaches well beyond the state-system in precisely the way Foucault suggests, and by virtue of being believed it structures a whole range of apparently nonstate practices and oppositional politics. The state-system, however, can be viewed as well-bounded once it is analytically distinguished from the state-idea. The state-system is the organizational apparatus of governing organizations, from courts, legislatures, and executives to government departments, police organizations, postal systems, census offices, and so on. It is through the state-system that governing *practices materially incorporate* land, bodies, and built environment into the state-country.

STS AND HISTORICAL SOCIOLOGY

Trying to speak to many disciplines, and especially across STS and historical sociology of state formation, I sometimes make observations that are news to one paradigm but not in the least to the other. The effort to integrate the theoretical and methodological strategies of historical sociology with those of STS has, however, great potential for advancing explanation in both areas. The scientific, engineering, and technological culture that facilitated the Western takeover of the world is now being recognized for the power that it has been. Jack Goldstone, for instance, explains why the technological "effervescence" of modern Europe did not give way, as in other regions and at other historical moments, to a period of technological stagnation.[39] Goldstone's emphasis on the significance of the steam engine, and the science and engineering culture that fostered its invention and development, provides a more specific explanation of the rise of the West than more general theories of rationalization, bureaucratization, institutionalization, capitalization, or modernization. Indeed, Goldstone demonstrates that much of what is cited as unique to the West can be found in many regions of the world at different points in history. The steam engine, however, was the first really powerful technology in that it transduced fire into mechanical motion, a dream pursued by a number of engine scientists in the seventeenth century, including William Petty. Though the steam engine represented a departure from previous technologies, its invention is not surprising when viewed in the context of over a century of experimental engine science, the engineering culture it fostered, and the material technologies it spawned.

One of the aims of this book is to further advance the emerging dialogue between STS and historical sociology by revealing the intimate relationship between science and statecraft. This relationship is evident when viewed in the context of the rise of modern engineering culture, the coproduction of this culture in both scientific and governing practices, and the proliferation of institutional, organizational, and material relations between science and government. Modern statecraft is science-based as well as coercion-based. Developments in scientific statecraft are, of course, importantly related to the rise of modern political economy (in its various forms) and the social sciences generally. Equally important, however, is the reconceptualization of political objects in terms of the natural ontology attributed to them by the new experimental science in the seventeenth century. This reconceptualization resulted in land, built environment, and people becoming "boundary objects"[40] that linked science and governance together. On the basis of the concepts of "engine science" and "engineering cultures," I seek to show that the relationship between science and state formation is profound and that a modern state is, by definition, an "engineering state."

TRIANGULATING SCIENCE AS CULTURE

The post-foundationalist question of how to distinguish science from other domains of culture is a critical problem in current science studies.[41] Once again I triangulate the question, distinguishing among the idea of science, the practices of science, and the material culture of science. (See figure 4.) Three crucial dimensions of the modern science idea can be distinguished: mechanical philosophy (the grand unifying concept), ingenuity (a cognitive culture of intellectual and technological inventiveness), and experimentalism (the concept of how to practice natural philosophy). I suggest that experimentalism implies an overarching engine science that places material technologies at the heart of natural scientific inquiry. Engine science requires the integration of natural philosophy, engineering, and mathematics *in practice*. The result is a culture of inquiry[42] in which the conceptualizations of theory are tied to the manipulations of engineering and the operations of mathematics.

This new culture of inquiry is importantly defined by the role of material engines in the key epistemic practices of measuring, scoping, graphing, and manipulating. The four forms of material engine that correlate with these practices are meters (barometer, hydrometer, etc.), scopes (telescopes, stethoscopes, etc.), graphing technologies (cartographic instruments), and chambers (e.g., hydraulic and pneumatic technologies). I conceive of these as *epistemic engines,* because they generate objects of inquiry, institutionalize and structure practices of inquiry, and drive the research agenda.

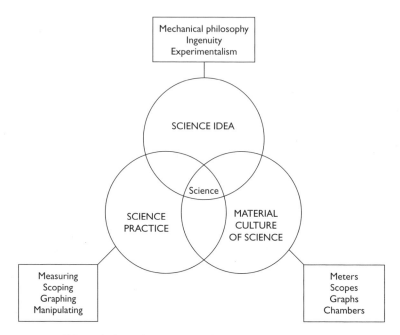

FIGURE 4. Triangulating science.

In doing so, they become what Latour calls "obligatory passage points" in scientific inquiry.[43] Attention to these technologies facilitates a comprehensive and naturalistic understanding of science as a very specific cultural complex of discourses, practices, and material culture. And though the specific technologies employed in statecraft may differ from those in natural inquiry, analogous practices of scoping, metering, graphing, and manipulating can be identified. Geological surveys and censuses, for instance, can be understood as terrascopes and sociometers. The point is to view the specific technologies in terms of the wider practices of engineering culture that straddle science and government in the modern period. Practices are the lynchpin between discourses and materiality, because they participate in both.

TRIANGULATING THE SCIENCE–STATE RELATIONSHIP

My conceptualization of the relationship between state and science follows the same analytic strategy. The relationship is conceived from the three angles of discourse, practice, and material culture. (See figure 5.) In this context I investigate discourses that sought to orient government practice toward experimental intervention. I connect the theological "argument

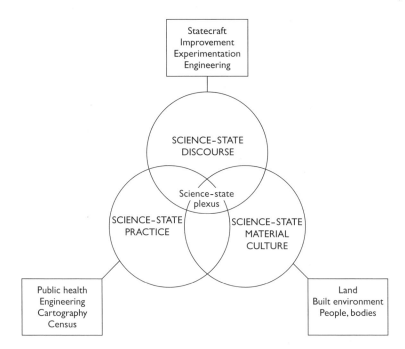

FIGURE 5. Triangulating the science-state plexus.

from design"—the conceptualization of God as the "Contriver and Maker of the Whole World"—to the emergence of engine science. I draw connections between engine science and ideas about the virtue of labor, the idea that civility and grace were signified by a cultivated nature, and show how the supposed absence of culture among "barbarous nations" legitimated colonization as a civilizing mission. The ideology of "improvement," at the heart of the civilizing mission, served the construction of colonies as spaces of experimental statecraft and social engineering.

Viewed from the angle of practice, the period of modern state formation (1650–1900) is one of continual proliferation of the relations between government and science, resulting in what I call the science-state plexus: a dense web of heterogeneous connections among scientific and governing practices. From public health and geology to cartography and censuses, the land, built environment, and people were targeted as natural and artificial objects whose cultural, political, and economic capital could be augmented. Land, people, and the built environment, as I hope to show in the following pages, were materially incorporated into forms of governing through the practices and knowledge of science and were transformed into a socio-technical network of techno-territory, bio-population, and infrastructural jurisdiction.

THE CASE

The case of Ireland might strike some readers as an unlikely one to illustrate the rise of the engineering state, since that country is so often associated with the worst poverty in all of Europe. There is, however, no reason to believe that the rise of the engineering state implies a prosperous and just social system. Beyond this, Ireland is not simply one case among others. A crucial site for experimental statecraft, constructed as such on behalf of one of the greatest modern engineering cultures, Ireland is as revealing to historians and social scientists now as it was to those who treated it as an experimental field between 1650 and 1900. Ireland was the first and greatest "living laboratory" of English science and government and as such reveals the emergence of modern state forms at the very point of their experimental development. As William Nassau Sr. put it in conversation with Alexis de Tocqueville, "Experiments are made in that country, and pushed to their extreme consequences . . . [such] that they give us results as precious as those of Majendie."[44] I argue that Ireland provides an especially revealing case of the way modern institutions of science and government were forged through the experimental designs and practices of an engineering culture.

As well as analyzing the ideas that informed the science-state relationship, I investigate how science and government networked in cultural practices that constituted new objects of inquiry and intervention, particularly those where Ireland led the research frontier, such as in cartography, public health, medical institutions, censuses, and police. The Irish case demonstrates that while it makes sense in one context to speak about a relationship between science and the state, in another it is more appropriate to speak of a complicated entanglement of things material and immaterial, human and nonhuman, in an elaborate socio-technical network.[45] The generalizability of the Irish case will depend on research into other modern cases, particularly Western cases. Yet the modern Irish state was so successfully engineered in the English and European image that it provides a revealing window on both European state formation and European colonialism.[46]

While the triangulation of culture in terms of discourse, practice, and materiality allows me to capture and hold together a diverse set of objects, my presentation of the empirical material follows a narrative approach. In chapter 2, I develop the concept of engine science through a narrative that traces the *discursive* meaning of mechanics, mechanical philosophy, engines, and experimentalism in the writings of some seventeenth-century English philosophers, particularly Robert Boyle. I develop an understanding of engine science that draws together the discourses of ingenuity, the practices of experimentation, and the *material culture of inquiry.* By focusing on the material culture of inquiry, the scopes, meters, graphs, and chambers, I place emphasis on the *practices* of sensing, measuring, writing, and manipulating, practices at the heart of engineering culture—a specifically *modern* engineering culture that was immanent in the activity of both modern statecraft and experimental scientific inquiry.

2 Understanding Engine Science

*Robert Boyle and the
New Experimentalism*

Whereas all writings ought to be descriptions of things, they are
now onely of words, notions, opinions, theories—because the
writers of books know little of things, and the practical men have
not language nor method enough to describe [things] by words.

SIR WILLIAM PETTY, *son of a textile dyer*

. . . the experiments of our engine [are] themselves sufficient to hint
such notions we build upon them.

SIR ROBERT BOYLE, *son of the First Earl of Cork*

The history of science and government in Ireland largely begins in seventeenth-
century England. Among the many reasons for this fact, three in particular
are crucial. First, England during the seventeenth century was one of the
most important European centers for the development of experimental science. This set the stage for England to become one of the great modern
engineering cultures. Second, the English conquest of Ireland that began
with the Tudor regime in the 1530s was finalized under William of Orange
at the end of the seventeenth century. Subsequently, a century of relative
peace brought a period of enduring state development and the rise of the
ideology of civilization through material improvement. Finally, the middle
of the seventeenth century marks the English civil war and its prosecution
in Ireland under the command of Cromwell and his "New Model Army,"
an event that brought William Petty to Ireland for the first time.
Midcentury also brought the Interregnum, the Restoration, and the foundation of the Royal Society of London. It is in the context of these conditions and events that the new experimental science was introduced into
Ireland. Chapter 3, which focuses on William Petty, discusses the new
experimentalism in Ireland, but first it is necessary to get a handle on what
the experimental philosophy involved and why it is fruitfully understood
as engine science.

An initial clue about the nature of the new science comes from the
philosophical dispute between Robert Boyle and Thomas Hobbes. In their

groundbreaking book *Leviathan and the Air-Pump*, Shapin and Schaffer reveal the full complexity of the dispute, but one aspect of it is particularly important to my argument about engine science: the issue of the role of technology in experimental philosophy. In this context, Hobbes discredited Boyle's claims regarding pneumatic "matters of fact" by construing his entire enterprise as one dependent on the rude and vulgar contrivances of mechanics and artificers. The implication, as Shapin and Schaffer have shown, is that Hobbes considered Boyle's practice to be, "as it were, 'engine philosophy.'"[1] There is little doubt that Hobbes's purpose was to disparage Boyle's program for natural philosophy, to represent the knowledge it produced as inferior to that attained by the philosopher alone with his reason and his method, untainted by the trickery of "enginery" and "natural magic." Yet his construal of Boyle's program as engine philosophy merits attention for reasons other than those he intended. Hobbes, I suggest, was correct in his characterization. Regardless of the negative evaluation he sought to place on Boyle's claims, the "new science" did involve an integration in practice of natural philosophy, understood as a search for natural causes and the elaboration of theory, with engineering understood as the systematic intervention in, and manipulation and mobilization of, natural forces and bodies.

CONCEPTUALIZING ENGINE SCIENCE

The term *engine science* is meant to circumvent the separation and opposition of science and engineering. Unlike the term *technoscience*, which assumes a process that tied "science and technology" together in the late nineteenth century, the term *engine science* suggests that the marriage of the practices of natural philosophy, mathematics, and engineering in the seventeenth century is what created the conditions of possibility for the growth of one of the most successful and powerful forms of modern science. Like the opposition between work of the head (intellect) and that of the hand (body), the purification of science with respect to engineering explains more about the politics of class and status than it does about the character of modern science.[2] Though the division of labor in science and the attribution of differential status that goes with it are real enough, both "science" and "engineering" can be viewed sociologically as parts of one collective practice and culture. Viewing experimentalism as engine science suggests that Hobbes was right about the marriage of the new philosophy's proposed natural causes to effects that in significant epistemic ways were engineered.

While the term *engine science* was not used by actors in the second half of the seventeenth century, it was implied, beyond Hobbes's complaints, in multiple sources from the period that express a wide-ranging idiom of engines and "enginery," particularly in Boyle's writings on the experimental program in natural philosophy.[3] An immediate temptation is perhaps to think that reference to engines in the seventeenth century was simply part of the idiom of mechanics and mechanical philosophy, and thus is not in itself worthy of special attention. Yet whatever the connections between the idiom of mechanics and engines, understanding the new science is disadvantaged by equating the two.

Mechanics and Mechanical Philosophy

The term *mechanics* had a number of distinct if related meanings in seventeenth-century Europe. First, it referred to the "doctrine of the moving powers," which was derived from antiquity and was expressed in the six "simple machines": the balance, lever, wheel, pulley, wedge, and screw. Second, and more specifically in the context of early mechanical philosophy, it had a "larger sense," comprising "not only the vulgar staticks, but divers other disciplines, such as the centrobaricks, hydraulicks, pneumaticks, hydrostaticks, balisticks, &c."[4] In the latter sense, mechanics could also be understood as the branch of "mixed [applied] mathematicks," which dealt with the formal expression of mechanical motions or tendencies. Thus the mechanical philosophy involved the elaboration of a mechanical theory of nature, in which the same kinds of causes and calculations posited for mechanical motions could be ascribed to nature. Finally, it referred to those whose art was the design and construction of machines, a practice pertaining to manual labor or skill, and thus often qualified in the seventeenth century by adjectives such as *mean* (in a later sense of average) and *vulgar* (i.e., common).

Engines and Ingenuity

The word *engine*, though having its root in the Latin *ingenium*, was part of the vernacular and did not have a contemporary Latin counterpart in the way that *mechanics* had. Whereas *mechanics* survived from antiquity in scholarly Latin, *engine* emerged historically from "low culture," entering the English language around the fourteenth century, first via the French *engin*, the primary reference of which appears to have been a mill, one of the quintessential engines of the early modern period. Boyle's *pneumatick engine*, when translated into Latin, was thus rendered as the *machina Boyleana* rather than the *ingenium Boyleana*. Before the mid-seventeenth century, however, when signified and signifier had not yet been fully wrenched apart,[5] and when the spellings of words could vary considerably, *ingyn* could designate ingenuity, in the sense of "native wit or mother wisdom," as well as material contrivance, which expressed such ingenuity. Thus it had both a subjective meaning and an object reference, designating an intellectual or cognitive activity as well as a material thing in the world. This double meaning indicated that ingenuity was a cognitive category quite distinct from contemplation. Whereas the latter term implied, from Greek times, an activity entirely of the mind, an activity set in opposition to action in the world or practice on things, *engine* and *ingenuity* implied a way of thinking that was intimately related to skillful practice. Among the many connotations of *engine* were art, craft, design, scheming, plotting, and contriving, which could also be expressed in negative terms, as artfulness, cunning, and trickery. *Engine* could refer to a trap or wile, a crafty or deceitful trick, an underhanded artifice or stratagem.[6] Thus a poem published in 1628 spoke of "Monuments of Praise, that Art, or Engine, or Strength can raise,"[7] while a history of Scotland spoke of the "malicious ingyns" of conspirators "against Kirk, King, and Country."[8]

These meanings indicate the specific usage the word enjoyed in the early modern period. In the military, for instance, it referred to any weapon, especially those of large scale, such as battering rams, catapults, and artillery, and in the business of catching game it could designate a net, snare, or decoy. Thus it is easy to understand why two of the earliest uses of the word *engineer* referred to a person who laid snares or who designed, constructed, and handled ordnance. As a verb *engine* meant to contrive, plan, frame, or fit parts together, to take by craft, ensnare, or deceive. Finally, the word came to be used in reference to any mechanical contrivance or machine, including the new microscopes and telescopes. In the second half of the seventeenth century, however, it began to center on its modern meaning, becoming more associated with material forms of more or less complicated and differentiated parts that worked together to produce a desired effect, especially a powerful material effect. The connotation of power is the sense with which *engine* has become most associated, though in the early modern period it had this coinage in a rather different sense, in the practice of judicial torture, torture directed at extracting truth in the form of a confession. It referred generically to the rack, where "words," "by engin," were "wrested" from subjects. The reference to power meant that it was generically applied to the new pumps, such as Boyle's vacuum engine, and it is this connection that gave us the terms *fire engine* and *beer engine*. Even the notion of a "search engine" expresses this history of meaning. In this little word, then, lies a broad array of cultural meaning and significance, of intervention and manipulation, design, contrivance and art, ingenuity and engineering, head and hand united in material practice, the deployment of force, and the realization of power.

It is in the new science that this cultural configuration finds one of its primary places of sustenance and growth. Thus, it is not insignificant that Boyle's pneumatic engine was a central emblem of the new science in England and Ireland in the latter part of the seventeenth century, a science for which Boyle was a preeminent spokesperson, or that distinguished visitors to the Royal Society were always entertained by engine experiments.[9] As a powerful contrivance through which to capture nature and force it to behave in particular ways, Boyle's pump symbolized the place of engines in the new science. Since the word *engine* was part of a vernacular linking the world of engineering with the creativity of genius and ingenuity, it is understandable that members of the Royal Society "enjoyed addressing each other as ingenious: the ingenious Mr. Boyle, the ingenious Mr. Wren," and so on.[10]

INGENIOUS ENGINES FOR KNOWING
AND ALTERING NATURE

Boyle presented his pneumatic engine not simply as the means through which to exhibit natural phenomena[11] but also as the material condition of possibility for conducting experiments that revealed the nature of air, "the experiments of our engine being themselves sufficient to hint such notions we build upon them."[12] He constantly emphasized the power of engine science to intervene in nature, to "alter nature," and to produce "changes in the creatures."[13] The purpose of such manipulation was to "increase the Empire of Man." Power was at the heart of this vision of science. As Boyle explained, "I should not have near so high a value as I now cherish for physiology, if I thought it could only teach a man to discourse of nature, but not at all to master her; and served only, with pleasing speculations to entertain his understanding, without at all increasing his power."[14] Nature's abhorrence of a vacuum indicated the need to *force* "her" to admit of such. The engine, by doing so, epistemically gave warrant to the claim that it was possible to have "place without body." Indeed, engine and art populated the world with a whole array of new forms:

> And sure it is a great honour, that the indulgent Creator vouchsafes to naturalists, that though he gives them not the power to produce one atom of matter, yet he allows them the power to introduce so many forms (which philosophers teach to be nobler than matter) and work

such changes among the creatures, that if *Adam* were now alive, and should survey the great variety of man's productions, that is to be found in the shops of artificers, the laboratories of chymists, and other well furnished magazines of art, he would admire to see what a *new world*, as it were, or set of things has been added to the primitive creatures by the industry of his posterity.[15]

Boyle's conceptualization of the new science is Baconian. Nature is gendered female, and philosophers bring their engine to bear to extract through force the truth that she has secreted from them.[16] In the *New Atlantis*, Bacon described the "engine-houses" in which were "prepared engines and instruments for all sorts of motions." In these houses the engines were designed, built, and "multiplied," made "stronger, and more violent than yours are; exceeding your greatest cannons and basilisks . . . ordnance and instruments of war, and engines of all kinds."[17] And in the mathematical, perspective, and sound houses, engines and instruments were mobilized for making natural philosophical demonstrations.

William Petty, a founding member of both the Royal Society and its sister organization, the Dublin Society for the Improvement of Natural Knowledge, Mathematicks, and Mechanicks, also advocated the development of engines and instruments in the service of the new science. For Petty, one could not practice experimentalism without instruments and engines, and he complained of the difficulty of obtaining such in Ireland.[18] He designed an "engine for planting corne"[19] and displayed to the Dublin Society "an engine for trying experiments relating to land carriages."[20] Like Boyle, Petty expressed great interest in pumps and water engines. In response to a paper on "hydraulic engins" by William King (presented to the Dublin Society) and the work they might perform in sewage disposal and land drainage,[21] Petty attempted to contrive an engine "moved by fire."[22] In his unpublished papers there are plans for essays on the making of "modells for Engines of strength"[23] and for "Engines strengthening nature."[24] In one of his more theoretical papers, which nonetheless was framed around matters "tending to profit and palpable Advantages," Petty articulated his principles of "duplicate proportion" in relation to the "Strength of Timbers or other homogeneous materials applied to Buildings, to Carts, or any other Machinaments intended for strength."[25]

Robert Hooke was one of the great early engine scientists. Among the many experimental apparatus that he prepared for the Royal Society were his "engine . . . for . . . trying experiments of condensation," his "whale-shooting engine," his "turning engine," his "arithmetical engine," his "lens-grinding engine," and his "engine for determining the force of gunpowder."

In 1664 his microscope was described as a "modern engine."[26] Hooke, it may be suggested, was one of the first great engineers of natural knowledge (at least in Britain and Ireland). While Boyle could finance a laboratory and division of labor such that he rarely put his hand on his engine, Hooke constituted in a single practitioner both the engineer and the philosopher.[27] Hooke expressed these connections in his admiration for Christopher Wren, who perfected in one person "such a *Mechanical Hand,* and so *Philosophical a Mind.*"[28] Michael Hunter, who defines science as an intellectual enterprise, points out that the Hartlib Circle (of experimentalists)[29] advocated the integration of science and technology, defining "'science' and 'technology' so close together that it is difficult to disentangle them."[30] However, one can simply acknowledge that the new philosophy, rather than trying to effect disentanglement retroactively, *was* inextricably bound up in engineering practices and technological forms.

ARTIST-ENGINEERS AND IMPURE SCIENCE

Edgar Zilsel was one of the first sociologists to recognize that modern science was born not of purity but of mixture.[31] Zilsel identified three "strata of intellectual activity" in the early modern period (c. 1300–1600): university scholars, humanists, and artisans. From among the artisans he identified five groups who developed their practice to the level of "high art." Surveyors and navigators became representatives of the mechanical arts and were crucial to the development of techniques of measurement and observation. Makers of nautical and astronomical instruments formed another group, and they also made compasses and astrolabes, cross-staffs and quadrants, and invented the declinometer and inclinometer in the sixteenth century.[32] Some were retired navigators or gunners. Two other groups were the artificers of musical instruments and the surgeons. But perhaps the most important group in terms of the early development of engine science is the one whom he called the "artist-engineers, . . . for not only did they paint pictures, cast statues, and build cathedrals, but they also constructed lifting engines, canals and sluices, guns and fortresses. They invented new pigments, detected the geometrical laws of perspective, and constructed new measuring tools for engineering and gunnery."[33] Zilsel suggested that the artist-engineers, perhaps the most famous of whom was Leonardo da Vinci, were not yet fully scientists but were their immediate predecessors. It was not until "the social barrier" between the "superior craftsmen" and the "academically trained scholars" was broken down that "real science was born," an event Zilsel locates around 1600 and identifies with William Gilbert, Francis Bacon, and Galileo.[34] Shapin and Schaffer have shown that the social barrier was not broken down, even though we can identify specific individuals who united the engineering with the philosophical art, such as Hooke. And Jim Bennett criticizes the social division as deployed in the historiography of science, for it assumes, as Zilsel explicitly does, that "the 'mechanic' or 'craftsman' was someone unconcerned with higher science."[35] Zilsel must, however, be credited with the insight that, in general terms, "the rise of the methods of the manual workers to the ranks of academically trained scholars at the end of the sixteenth century" was a "decisive event in the genesis of science."[36] A little fine tuning of his insight would acknowledge the emergence of literate "hands" who became conversant with natural philosophy and sought themselves to express their engineering practice theoretically and with respect to natural causes. Robert Norton described himself as one of his majesty's "Gunners and Enginiers," and, like the new philosophers, he expressed a preference for a "few experimental truths" over "many Rhetorical imbellishments of words."[37] Gunnery, the art of designing, contriving and handling the most complex engines of war, was for Norton "euen able to spose the knowne parts of Naturall Philosophy, Arithmetick, Geometry, and Perspectiue."[38]

As Bennett notes, the actual relationship was more ambiguous than Norton implied, "but the fact that this aspect of practical geometry raised questions pertinent to natural philosophy may be relevant to the emergence of a new relationship between the two—one where mathematics, experiment and instruments are all recruited to a reformed explanatory programme for the natural world."[39] It was precisely through this kind of integration of otherwise relatively autonomous practices that conditions of knowledge production conducive to the development of engine science were created. Zilsel's framing of the question in terms of the dualist opposition of scholar and craftsman led him to neglect the importance of mathematical practitioners as an additional bridge between natural philosophy and engineering. Bennett addresses this problem, mobilizing the early modern distinction between natural philosophy, "concerned with causal and theoretical understanding of the natural world," and the mathematical sciences, "engaged in the development of mathematical techniques which, if applied, were rather to useful ends than to enlightened understanding of nature."[40] He argues that the use of "instruments," even if for the purpose of mathematical problem solving rather than theoretical and causal investigation of nature, was established first in the mathematical sciences, in which it was "initially the trademark" of the practice of mathematics.[41]

MATHEMATICAL MECHANICS AND NATURAL PHILOSOPHY

In England, practical mathematics emerged as a practice of a significant number of people only in the second half of the sixteenth century, though its growth was substantial thereafter.[42] It is here that Bennett identifies the basis for the development of a more intimate relation between the mathematical sciences and the mechanical philosophy, a relation for which the use of instruments is the bridge. One example (from Bennett's many) of how mathematical instruments were deployed for natural philosophical purposes is the navigational problem of finding longitude at sea. The problem focused the attention of mechanical mathematicians on the issue of the earth's magnetism, an issue engaged by "practical men, whose business was to make, sell, teach and use instruments designed to solve practical problems."[43] Robert Norman began the scientific study of the earth's magnetism in England.[44] Norman appealed to experience and experiment over authority and book learning, particularly in relation to the practical problem of the magnetic inclination, or "dip," of the compass needle. Bennett demonstrates how Norman, as a result of his investigation of this problem, contributed to the design of a "very early example of an instrument of natural philosophy."[45] Norman's "dip circle"—adapted from an astrolabe and contrived with a magnetic needle—was an instrument specifically designed to investigate the nature of geomagnetism. Though his immediate objective was the solution of a practical navigational problem, he also sought to elaborate "Theorik with Hypotheses, and rules for the saluyng of the apparant irregularitie of the Variation." This was "a genuine natural philosophical investigation, using the tools of the mathematical sciences."[46] It was, according to Bennett, a clear and early example of what would soon become a "cycle of influence between the practical and the natural philosophy" and an example of the growing intersections between experimental natural philosophy and the mathematical sciences in England, where the former was institutionally secured at Gresham College, the center of "practical mathematical professionalism" in England.[47]

The mathematical connection is thus particularly significant in the context of the institutionalization of the social movement for experimental natural philosophy. Bennett identifies John Wilkins and Robert Hooke as two leading figures in these developments. Wilkins's *Mathematical Magick*, of 1648, was entirely concerned with practical mechanics. It was addressed to those philosophers prejudiced against the works of artisans and artificers, which he defended both in terms of "nobility and importance."[48] But more than anyone else it is Hooke who, for Bennett, represents the integration of the mathematical sciences into the practice of natural philosophy:

> A Professor of Gresham College, a surveyor and architect, a mathematical practitioner in his own right and an intimate of opticians and instrument makers, he also officially represented the methodology of the Royal Society's natural philosophy, through his position as Curator of Experiments, and he vigorously practised its natural philosophical mechanism. He was the designer of a great many instruments and mechanical contrivances, and he provided demonstrations for Royal Society meetings, both of mechanical improvements in the mathematical sciences and of experiments in natural philosophy. The instrument of natural philosophy, seen in its classic expression in Hooke's air-pump, was now central to the study of nature.[49]

NEGOTIATING INEXACTNESS AND CONTRIVED EFFECTS

Though the mathematical sciences ranged from "pure" to "mixed" (or applied), the distinction was not, in the seventeenth century, considered to be one of kind. The distinction was significant enough, however, that it called for negotiation by the practitioners of engine science, particularly those engaged in optics, who sought to express in mathematical terms what they viewed as material forms, such as rays of light. William Molyneux, for instance, explained that he could not always achieve "Geometrical Strictness," since his aim was to achieve knowledge useful "in practice." It was thus necessary to suppose many lines to be equal, and many angles proportional, "which strictly taken are not." He insisted, however, that this was not to be understood to "prejudice any Demonstration," for "Dioptricks being a part of mixt Mathematicks, conversant about material Lines (or Rays of Light) and the refractive Power of a corporeal Glass, cannot be delivered with that . . . Geometrica requisite in abstracted Mathematicks."[50] Pure mathematics, then, was associated with geometrical abstraction and exactness, while mixed mathematics traded some exactness in return for a mathematized natural philosophy. As Peter Dear explains, mixed mathematics was "physico-mathematics," a branch of mathematics "applicable to all areas of natural philosophy, insofar as all parts of physics implicated considerations of quantity."[51] Consideration of quantity was not, however, natural to seventeenth-century experimental philosophy. Like the movement to integrate theory with engineering practice, the application of mathematics to the material world depended on a social movement toward that end. Thus William Petty admonished the Royal Society to "apply your

Mathematicks to Matter,"[52] and he campaigned tirelessly to have represen-tations of natural and political phenomena expressed, where useful, in "number, weight and measure."[53] Newton reconciled the pure and mixed mathematics with the mechanical philosophy as a whole by representing the geometrical as "nothing but the perfectly mechanical."[54] According to Newton, if abstract geometry was superior in precision to the geometry of mechanical contrivances, this was to be attributed not to inexactness in the art of mechanics but to the failures of artificers.[55] Thus the low status of the artificers became a positive asset to the new push for experimental science. Artificers and engineers could be held responsible both for the errors that led experiments to fail and for the mathematical impurities embodied in engineering practice.

CONTRIVANCE, ARTIFICE, AND THE ART VS. NATURE DISTINCTION

The language of "contrivance," a central connotation of the word *engine*, is important in this regard, since it problematized the distinction between art and nature found in Aristotelian natural philosophy. The interventions of art and artifice imposed human purposes on nature and as such could not, from an Aristotelian perspective, be the basis of natural philosophy.[56] Such interventions were, however, the mark of engine science, which intention-ally forced nature to behave in particular ways.[57] Bacon was among the first to philosophically defend the method of intervention, arguing that "art was only a matter of setting up situations in which nature will produce a desired result—so that art is the human exploitation of nature rather than an activity outside of nature."[58] Contrived effects were not funda-mentally different from natural effects, or at least could not be if they were to provide the basis for experimental practice, since experimental knowl-edge was extracted from precisely such situations.[59]

As a natural philosophy rooted in artifice, Boyle's practice exemplified engine science. He explained, for instance, that when he placed small ani-mals in the vacuum chamber of his pneumatic engine and then sucked out the air, they died. The artifice and contrivance of the engine thus created an entirely artificial situation through which Boyle proposed natural causes with respect to air and respiration.[60] The influence of the distinction between products of art and those of nature remained forceful, however, and Boyle found it necessary to explicitly reject this distinction if he was to save the epistemic significance of his artificially contrived effects.

While proposing to show that the tradesman and naturalist could benefit from each other's knowledge, he dealt with the prejudice toward the former, which was in part based on the nature/art distinction, the argument that "the things exhibited [by mechanics] are works of art, and not of nature."[61] Boyle argued that the difference held by the "generality of learned men" to exist between "all natural things and factitious ones" was unreasonable. The difference was one not of "essence" but of "efficients,: . . . and scarce any man will think, that when a pear is grafted upon a white thorn, the fruit it bears is not a natural one, though it be produced by a coalition of two bodies of distant natures put together by the industry of man, and would not have been produced without the manual and artificial operation of the gardener."[62] Thus Boyle ascribed a naturalistic ontology to the products of art, arguing that "the things made by tradesmen," as much as the effects contrived in his pneumatic engine, were legitimate objects of natural philosophy. Such objects were prime targets for the attention of engine science, since they presented "nature in motion, and that too, when she is (as it were) put out of her course, by the strength or skill of man."[63] Nature "vexed and disturbed," to use Petty's words, was nature subject to ingenious capture and manipulation, the "most instructive condition, wherein we can behold her."[64] Boyle and Petty argued that the history of trades was "also an History of Nature" and that some of the "phenomena" of artifice "may be reckoned among its more noble and useful parts." Engineered effects projected a "great deal of light to divers theories, especially by affording instances, wherein we see by what means things may be affected by art, and consequently by nature, that work mechanically."[65]

TRADES, MUNDANE EXPERIMENTS, AND THE PUBLIC RIDICULE OF ENGINE SCIENCE

Petty, in his plan for a paper on the history of trades, included everything from metalwork, rigging, masting, digging, smelting, and refining to wedges, pulleys, engines, and "wheele works of all kinds." He planned to include all that was known about watering and draining of lands, the building of houses, the distilling and compounding of forms, and of "changing the nature [of] soyles and adapting it to beare other plants."[66] Indeed, hardly an instance of artifice was left out of Petty's list for his "history of nature vexed and disturbed." Arts and trades had an affinity with engine science precisely in terms of the manipulation and alteration of nature that they both involved. The connections among engine science, trades, and mundane worldly experiments could, however, result in public ridicule, as is well illustrated in Thomas Shadwell's satire *The Virtuoso*.

The virtuoso, cast as "Sir Nicholas Gimcrack," is possibly none other than Boyle himself. The name chosen is of more than passing interest. In the seventeenth century, *gimcrack* had a number of related meanings: it could designate a mechanical contrivance, especially in the context of showy and worthless trumpery, and could stand for a fop, dodge, or fanciful notion. Boyle, as the great spokesman for engine science, could easily be portrayed as the practitioner par excellence of gimcrackery. The "ingenious" virtuoso is presented throughout the play as a senseless fop, flashy wit, and dull villain. Words were "no more to him than breaking wind, they onely give him vent; they serve not with him to express thoughts, for he does not think."[67] The critique of thinking capacity is important. The Greshamite is presented as being too busy dealing with "engineers, glassmakers" and "Mechanic gross fellows" to study Alexander and the ancients or the "wisdom" and "knowledge" of "mankind." The virtuoso "sot" is found instead to be spending "2000 *l*. [pounds] in Microscopes, to find out the Nature of Eels in Vinegar, Mites in a Cheese, and the Blue of Plums."[68]

The virtue of the ancients is contrasted with the foolhardiness of the moderns. At a gathering at the gimcrack's house, a "gentleman of sense and wit"[69] inquires about the virtuoso's trip to Italy and whether he had observed the people's "Wisdom, Policies, and Customs." Gimcrack retorts, "By no means! 'Tis below a Virtuoso to trouble himself with Men and Manners. I study Insects."[70] After dinner the guests are not enlightened by readings of polite literature, but audience to "a Lecture concerning the Nature of Insects" and to a survey of "Microscopes, Tellescopes, Thermometers, Barometers, Pneumatick Engines, Strentrophonical Tubes, and the like."[71] On another occasion, "Sir Formal Trifle" (Hooke?), "orator," "coxcomb," and friend, admirer, and "shadow" of the virtuoso, lectures guests on the ingenuity of mouse traps and the nature of mice: "After I had contemplated a while upon the no little curiosity of the Engine, and the subtilty of its Inventor; I began to reflect upon the inticement which so fatally betray'd the uncautious Animal to its sudden ruine, and found it to be . . . alas! Specious bait of Cheshire-Cheese, which seems to be a great delicate to the pallet of this Animal, who, in seeking to preserve its life, O misfortune, took the certain means to death."[72] Shadwell is not generally remembered, prolific though he was, for literary greatness, but throughout the satire the connections he makes between the engines of mechanical contrivance and the philosophy identified with Gresham College are revealing. Shadwell not only identifies the central place of engines and instruments in experimental practice on mundane worldly phenomena; he also sets such practice in opposition to the more noble study of the ancients and to authentic sense and wit.[73] In a similar manner to that of Hobbes, he denigrates engine science by associating it with mechanical trickery. The same politics of nobility and philosophy is displayed. The ingenious manipulations of the virtuoso are represented as senseless foppery, hardly able to claim the mantle of true philosophy.

If Shadwell is to be believed, the play was well received by the king and other members of the royal family, and among a wider audience had "few profest Enemies." There is no need to doubt his claims in this respect, because the play drew upon generally held criticisms of engine science, that it was both ignoble and useless. When a character in the play inquires rhetorically in relation to the weighing of air, "Is that all the use you make of these Pneumatick Engines?" he was mouthing an often-expressed sentiment, so much so that Petty felt compelled to confront it directly: "For as much as this Society has been censured (though without much cause) for spending too much time in matters not directly tending to profit and palpable Advantages (as the Weighting of Air and the like) I have therefore, to streighten this crooked stick, bent it and my present Discourse the quite contrary way, viz. to the Sails and Shapes of Ships; to Carpentry and Carriages; to Mills, Mill-dams, Bulwarks; to the Labour of Horses, and to several other particulars."[74] It is in the context of the dismissal of the experimental philosophy that one must, in part, understand this and other attempts to represent it as inherently useful to trade and government. But it would be wrong to believe that overtures of practical usefulness were simply rhetoric. Engine science had an inherent affinity with profitable and power-augmenting engagements with nature. Thus Boyle's essays on the "usefulness of experimental philosophy" are as serious as any of his philosophical works. The value placed in these essays on the knowledge of artificers, tradesmen, mechanics, and engineers is both epistemological and political. Engine science was presented as the ally of trade and, by implication, of capitalism. Attempts at alliances with the vulgar world of trade and artifice could, however, backfire. Shadwell was shrewd enough in this regard, constructing a Luddite-like scene (a century ahead of the famous King Ludd) that orchestrated both the enginery of the new experimental philosophy and the dangers of too close a conversation with it for tradesmen. The scene begins with the virtuoso's house under siege from a "Rabble of People." The virtuoso's servant calls to the crowd across the door to see what they want; they reply, "You Son of a Whore, the Engine, and the Rogues that invented it."[75] On inquiring of the ruckus, the virtuoso is told by his servant, "They are Ribbon-weavers; who have been informed, that you are he that invented the Engine-loom, which has provok'd 'em to rise up in Arms."[76] The virtuoso protests that he never invented anything of any use in his life.

The scene, like others in Shadwell's satire, was cut from readily available fabric, and expressed suspicions regarding the activities of the Royal Society, in relation to both trades and "reason of state."[77] Indeed, the dangers raised by the campaign to integrate the knowledge of trades with that of natural philosophy are explicitly addressed by Boyle in his "Considerations Touching the Usefulness of Experimental Natural Philosophy." These essays made reference to many aspects of trade knowledge, and Boyle was careful not to "injure tradesmen" by divulging their secrets. Nonetheless, he defended putting such knowledge in print, noting that others, such as Antonio Neri, had done so before him without injury to trades. He also noted that many French and Italian works had been "published about several arts by the artificers themselves," such as that by the goldsmith Benvenuto Cellini and the mineralogist Georgius Agricola. Indeed, he argued that throughout Europe, including England, a "notorious" number of books were published on "the arts of gunnery, distillation, painting, gardening, &c." by persons who "professed those callings."[78]

Boyle suggested that the cost of procuring the material means to carry on trades was sufficient to ensure that virtuosi would not become competitors with tradesmen. Similarly, a few experiments could not hope to provide the virtuosi with the "manual dexterity" necessary to conduct handicrafts, a skill "not to be learned by books, but to be obtained by imitation and use."[79] Finally, he argued that while some inconveniences might accrue to some tradesmen, for the most part it would "prove more advantageous than prejudicial to tradesmen themselves, that many of their practices should be known to experimental philosophers."[80] Despite these arguments, Boyle still felt compelled to assure readers that his descriptions of the manipulations of nature by art were kept to a minimum so as not to "defraud those others, to which they were more proper, and some of them necessary."[81] All these precautions against offending the mechanics, artificers, and handicraft workers were crucial for a manifesto that openly sought to "carry philosophical materials from the shops to the schools, and divulge the experiments of artificers, both to the improvement of trades themselves, and to the great inriching of the history of arts and nature."[82] There was a degree of truth to the proto-Luddite concerns raised by Shadwell, however, since Boyle's interest in engines often did align more precisely with those of the master and the capitalist than with those of the worker. Commenting on "silk-stockings woven by an engine," he pondered, "What handy work it is, that mechanical contrivances may not enable men to perform by engines?"[83] Boyle was a harbinger of engine-powered production, and Shadwell rightly anticipated the de-skilling and redundancy that this would involve.

"an union between parts of learning": boyle's philosophical manifesto

Among the arts and trades Boyle discussed in his manifesto were brewing, baking, fishing, fowling, and building. He gave special attention to husbandry, where the philosopher, through his knowledge of generation, nutrition, and accretion in plants and animals, could aid the farmer in the altering of soils and the forms of culture, particularly through chemistry. The farmer could also be aided by hydrostatics and hydraulics "that teach us to make engines and contrivances for the lifting up, and for the conveying of water."[84] The naturalist's knowledge was also presented as valuable to the manual trades, such as stonecutting and the making of cement. At one point Boyle practically describes the philosopher as a mechanic: the "philosopher may, as a mineralist, and a mechanician, improve the ways of making iron and steel."[85]

Boyle goes much further than was necessary for the purpose of constructing a rhetoric of utility as a defense against charges that engine science was a waste of time, arguing that in many cases "a trade differs from an experiment, not so much in the nature of the thing, as in its having had the luck to be applied to human uses, or by a company of artificers made their business, in order to their profit; which are things extrinsically, and accidental to the experiment itself."[86] It was precisely this idea that bothered Hobbes, for if art could be fully experimental, how could experiment be fully philosophical? Boyle did not reply by adding some extra criteria so as to distinguish experimental philosophy in an essentialist manner from arts and engineering. He did not even employ the readily available, and still to this day pervasive, distinction between pure science, whose aim we are assured is pure knowledge (light), and practical application, whose aim we are told is mere utility (fruit). Indeed, he explicitly rejected that proposition, for though "that famous distinction, introduced by the lord *Verulam* [Bacon], whereby experiments are sorted into luciferous and fructiferous, may be (if rightly understood) of commendable use; yet it would much mislead those, that should so understand it, as if fructiferous experiments did so merely advantage our interests, as not to promote our knowledge; or, the experiments called luciferous, did so barely enrich our understandings, as to be in no otherways useful."[87]

While Boyle advertised the value of experimentalism for trades and mechanics, he rarely used the word *engineer,* which in the seventeenth century enjoyed the widest coinage in the military. Thus Boyle used the term mostly in relation to ballistics, surveying, and fortification, noting that it was already "taken for granted by divers geometricians and engineers, that the excellent Galileo, and his not degenerate disciple Torricellius, had demonstrated the line, which a heavy body, projected, and even the bullet, shot out of a cannon, describes, to be parabolical."[88] Boyle could easily connect his program for engine science with the work of Galileo, because Galileo elaborated a geometrica of "fortification and the destruction of fortification" based on "propositions" and "demonstrations" as to the "resistance of bodies to be broken, and the weights requisite to break them, and the lengths at which they may be broken by their own weight."[89] Petty sought to build on this knowledge through his work on "engines that strengthen nature," advocating a proto-material science through inquiries into elasticity. The vision was one in which engineering could learn from philosophy, just as philosophy could learn from engineering. Boyle illustrated a number of ways through which the naturalist could benefit from engines and how better engines could be designed. One good mechanical contrivance might be "equivalent to, and may perhaps actually produce many good experiments." Thus by "frequenting the shops and workhouses of mechanicians," the naturalist might see "a variety of engines and instruments to compass different things."[90] Engines such as the air-pump were particularly important because they acted with such force upon nature. As Boyle put it, "When she is as it were vexed by art, and roughly handled by ways unusual, and sometimes extravagant enough, [one] may discover to a heedful and rational man divers luciferous things not to be met with in books."[91]

Engine science cannot be expected to have had immediate wholesale consequences. But Boyle's manifesto is clear enough and extremely relevant to the subsequent development of science and engineering. He sought to provide "materials for the history of nature," an account of the methods and knowledge of artifice, and of the states of nature when vexed and disturbed. He sought to advance the "practical or operative part of natural philosophy" and to "enable gentlemen and scholars to converse with tradesmen," because the latter were "men that converse[d] with things."

Experiments with things provided a common ground for science and business, and he hoped to facilitate an exchange of experiments between philosophers and artificers. He believed he was "rescuing natural philosophy from that unhappy inputation of barrenness" that it had gained in the hands of a scholastic elite without ties to either "men or things." As such he sought not to establish "pure knowledge" but to "beget a confederacy, and an union between parts of learning, whose possessors have hitherto kept their respective skills strangers to one another."[92] Just as Bacon had stated that neither "the naked hand nor the understanding left to itself can effect much," so Boyle sought to bring into conversation the knowledge and skills of "shop-men" and "book-men."[93] These were the basic ideas that informed the development of engine science.

Although engine science drew on a vast range of techniques and technologies in agriculture and industry, it remained distinct because it was primarily a culture of *inquiry.* It developed a specific array of engines of inquiry that correlated with a core set of inquisitorial and representational practices. Understanding engine science requires sorting out these technologies in relation to the practices they both supported and powered.[94] Such sorting indicates how engine science maintained its original integrity as it developed over the following two and half centuries and how its core technologies and practices were employed, proliferated, and perfected in industry, medicine and public health, and statecraft.

ANALYSIS OF THE MATERIAL CULTURE
OF INQUIRY IN ENGINE SCIENCE

Four core technologies have been central to the practice of engine science: meters, scopes, graphs, and chambers. I call these technologies "epistemic engines," because they were crucially generative in the practice of making scientific knowledge. Epistemic engines can be objects of knowledge in their own right, or they can be surrogates (or models) for other "epistemic things."[95] They can be isomorphic with natural things, or they can consist of the key components of an "experimental system."[96] Indeed, they can be all these things at once. Their epistemic quality lies in the way they focus activities, channel research, pose and help to solve questions, and generate both objects of knowledge and strategies for knowing them. Epistemic engines crucially embed the discourses of knowing *what* in the practices of knowing *how.* Figure 6 shows the centers of gravity of the practices associated with each of the four epistemic engines.

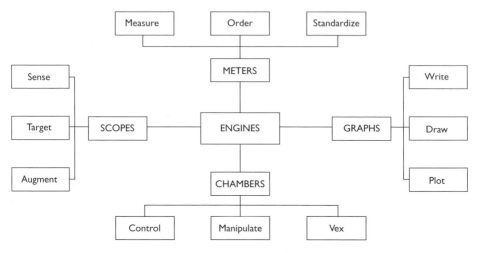

FIGURE 6. The material culture of engine science.

Meters

Barometers and thermometers are two early examples of meters, a form of material culture that became a trademark of engine science. The importance of meters lies in their transduction of phenomena into number so that they can be abstracted, formalized, and handled mathematically. Meters facilitate the standardization and material institutionalization of measurement practices and units. Indeed, meters order phenomena through regulation in the same sense that the musical-beat meter orders time (hence tempo). And since standardized measures are repeated over time, serial quantitative records are created, whether with respect to rainfall, population levels, or mortality. Meter engines are, therefore, the material condition of possibility for the development of statistical analysis. Their growing centrality in scientific inquiry since the seventeenth century is indicated by the scores of variously complex devices that contain the word *meter* in their names (such as the inclinometer, spectrometer, galvanometer, and micrometer, etc.).[97] The word itself, however, is just a clue. It is important to recognize that censuses or numeric "gauges" are no less meters than are barometers.

Thermometers and barometers were early boundary objects linking engine science to the drive for a new scientific statecraft. Petty, Locke, Boyle, and many others began keeping records of the weather, often keeping notes on unusual events such as famines and epidemics. But it was Petty more than anyone who sought to apply this metering practice to statecraft. As I hope to show in chapter 3, Petty's work placed the practice of metering phenomena central to what he perceived as a new "peaceful" and post-Machiavellian form of statecraft. His was a new discourse of state, the center of gravity of which was "design" rather than "sovereignty." Here, as in other respects, Petty united the concerns, while moving beyond the disagreements, of Hobbes and Boyle.

Scopes

Like meters, scopes are engineered forms that embody a stable purpose in engine science. Scopes frame, target, and augment phenomena for the senses, whether it is hearing in the case of the stethoscope, seeing in the case of microscopes and telescopes, or the sense of dynamic orientation in the case of the gyroscope. Dozens of engines bear the suffix *-scope* in their names, but once again the actual name is but a clue, since radar, sonar, and various probes and scanners can also be understood as scopes, as various forms of survey.[98] The practice of scoping has been central to the history of engine science, particularly in relation to seeing. Vision reigns as the supreme sense in science, linking the practice of scoping with diagrammatic and other visualization technologies.[99] Yet the idea of scoping extends the meaning of "observation" beyond visual perception. Scopes may vary considerably depending on context, but they materially express a basic design and purpose that remain relatively stable across different spatial and temporal localities. As a form of material culture, they embody the designs of a sensitive practice, engineering gaze, attentive ear, and tactile orientation.

While surveys had long existed, engine scientists such as Petty developed them as new and more penetrating scopes for sensing the body politic. Petty's *Down Survey* of Ireland rendered both land and people sensible to government in a manner that facilitated the differentiation of resources and their more effective exploitation. Employing an innovative division of labor and specially designed and standardized instruments, plotting paper, and field books, Petty perambulated the country so as to "survey down" cadastral and topographical data onto scaled maps showing both civil and natural boundaries. As I show in chapter 4, surveying became, in its many forms, the preeminent scope on land and people. In the nineteenth century, with the development of new theodolites and compensation devices, the use of trigonometry to triangulate and proof the ground measures, and the integration of the cartography with geological, natural history, and social surveys, this great engine of scientific statecraft became a key marker of modern governing and engineering practices. It is not surprising that political surveying increasingly integrated the scopes of natural science, such as microscopes and telescopes, into the practice, because all scope work expresses a common strategy aimed at rendering the world to the senses. The anatomy of Ireland was brought within the increasingly surveillance-based activities of state government through the deployment of surveys, which can be understood as terrascopes and socioscopes.

Highlighting the stability and worldly orientation of scoping does not, however, detract from the findings of scientific studies concerning the "theory-ladenness" of observation, the importance of perspective, and the disciplined (by schooling as well as by conceptual framework) character of scientific perception. Scopes have been viewed as evidence for a raw empiricist epistemology, but the questions of what is being sensed, what is to be targeted, what is seen or heard, always remain and are always embedded in social and historical contexts. Perceptions become knowledge only through technologies of representation. Michael Dennis has demonstrated how the first microscopes, though generating immediate interest among experimental natural philosophers, caused problems concerning what was actually being perceived. It was not sufficient simply to see; one had to *represent* what was seen, to write and draw it so it could be "re-viewed" by members of the experimental community.[100] Only then could "virtual witnessing" occur.[101] Until written, that which is sensed can have little epistemic sway within the community of practitioners. Hence Hooke's *writing,* his *Micrographia,* is as important to the history of microscopy as the material scope itself.

Graphs

The word *graph,* at root, is a verb that designates the act of writing and drawing. While the term has become more narrowly associated with axial data plots, there are good analytic reasons for reclaiming the more general meaning.[102] Given the importance of the linguistic turn in social theory and the need for broad (e.g., discourse)[103] as well as narrow (e.g., idiom or pidgin) categories of representational analysis, it is useful to view various strategies for formally writing phenomena through a single lens. Hydrographs, cartographs, spectrographs, ethnographs, orthographs, cardiographs, geographs, and so on, can be viewed together as so many strategies and technologies for generating formalized "inscriptions."[104] To do ethnography is to write a people, as orthography involves writing their words and names. Thus there is analytic value in conceiving of graphing in a manner that embraces all scientific writing and drawing, the strategies of elevation and projection, of translating the complexity that is everything into the formal expressions of discrete selections. Literary graphing need not be viewed as necessarily less scientific than other kinds of graphing. On the contrary, literary forms are powerful precisely because of their capacity to graph complex and subtle relationships and advance novel reconceptualizations, and are crucially integrated with other—generally visual—forms.

The detail of mapmaking reveals an array of graphic strategies and technologies that were crucial to modern statecraft. The reports of government investigations can be viewed in a similar way. And the scoping activities of government have produced not only literary graphs but also exquisite visual graphs of territory, cities, and the geology of the land. As with the microscopists' micrographs, so too with the surveyors' cartographs. Graphic technologies of representation were key to the development of both engine science and the modern state.

Chambers

One final kind of epistemic engine that needs to be distinguished is that, like the pump or steam engine, whose crucial component is a mechanism for physically capturing and manipulating phenomena. The power of chambers is different from the power of graphing. For instance, it is the very special power of the steam engine, its capacity to generate mechanical motion from fire, that not only distinguishes it from all previous technologies in history but also partly explains how England and Europe came to dominate the world.[105] Chambers are closest to what W. D. Hackmann calls "active instruments," and might justifiably be given the eponym "Baconian." Boyle's pneumatic engine, for instance, physically captured and restrained natural phenomena, often bringing great force to bear upon them. Seals and valves blew, parts imploded, and birds suffocated. Chamber engines, more than any other kind of engine, have facilitated the vexing of phenomena, their systematic physical manipulation. This is one of the reasons why the humble pump is so emblematic of late seventeenth-century experimental philosophy. In the Baconian sense, knowledge is gained not by contemplation but by intervention, by putting nature out of its natural course. Chamber engines include pneumatic, hydraulic, steam, and later internal combustion and jet engines, but also centrifuges and all manner of target, containment, compression, and vacuum chambers, engines that are ubiquitous in scientific practice. In the case of the steam engine (and many chamber engines), valves are crucial components that permit manipulation, a fact recognized by Boyle, who hoped for a "history of valves." Chambers made it possible to manipulate phenomena materially with great force and precision. They are the quintessential modern engines—the power-generating engines. Chamber engines signal a matrix of values of work, ingenuity, and power that sustain their centrality in scientific inquiry at least as far back as the seventeenth century.[106] The importance of chamber engines lies in their material capacity to bring force to bear on phenomena in ways that graphs, meters, and scopes cannot. Schools, hospitals, workhouses, and prisons are like chambers in that they are not simply buildings but, rather, controlled spaces designed to permit the material manipulation of bodies.

Meters, scopes, graphs, and chambers are isomorphic with the integrated practices of scoping out the world so as to make it available to the senses, of transducing the world into number so that it can be handled mathematically, of representing the world by methodologically writing it, and of intervening in the world in forceful ways that materially manipulate phenomena with powerful and revealing effect. They are engines of sensing and perceiving, measuring and mathematizing, writing and representing, and forcing and controlling. Engine science is sustained by its cognitive culture of ingenuity, its metric, its inscriptions, and its engineering praxis. The power, and thus the political significance, of engine science derives directly from the specificity of its practice rather than from the uses to which it might be put by particular political constituencies. Rather than simply being a tool of power, engine science is generative of power.

It is difficult to imagine how such a culture could have been successful if it did not in some sense align with religion. For Boyle, engines were proof that God was an "ingenious contriver,"[107] and "living engines" were proof of his "plastic skill."[108] Boyle regularly referred to God as the "ingenious architect," an "omnificient artist" through which the "admirable architecture and skillful contrivance" of nature is realized. The "design" of nature demonstrates that "she is skilled in the mechanicks, not only as a mathematician, that understands the powers of distance, weight, proportion, motion and figure; but as an artificer, or handicrafts man, who knows by dexterous contrivances to furnish the more endangered parts of his work."[109] Boyle's move to make God, as it were, an engineer magnificently skilled in the arts of contrivance and design had the important function of ennobling all engines, his own included, since the latter expressed in human artifice what nature exhibited of divine artifice. Ironically, the "argument from design" was first articulated by agents of the scientific revolution.

The ideas of engine science could easily traffic with those of religion. But the center of gravity of the discourse of engine science was ingenuity, experimentalism, improvement, profit, and power over nature. The practices of engine science were crucially interventionist and sought to alter nature and effect "changes in the creatures." I have suggested that the most important practices were those associated with the material culture of engine science, with scopes, meters, graphs, and chambers. These technologies correlated with the practices of probing, measuring, graphing, and manipulating, practices at the center of an emerging engineering culture that would become central to modern statecraft. I am not claiming to have written an account of experimental philosophy in seventeenth-century England, much less an account of natural philosophy generally. Rather, I have attempted to show that the experimental program represented by Boyle, Petty, Hooke, Wren, and others tied natural scientific inquiry to engineering practice and material technology.

Petty agreed with Boyle on the idea that industry and experimental inquiry could only mutually benefit each other. But Petty took this belief to a higher level by considering it in terms of the economic development of a state. In so doing he was one of the key founders, as Marx later noted, of the science of political economy.[110] As I show in chapter 3, Petty extended experimentalism and the practices of engine science into politics and statecraft by conceiving of land, people, and the built environment as simultaneously natural and political objects. It was not, however, only the practices of engine science that translated into the political realm, since specific technologies of natural scientific inquiry were also integrated into political projects. For instance, microscopes and telescopes were crucial for accurate mapmaking, pumping engines were necessary elements of land drainage and sanitary engineering, and thermometers and barometers became instruments of political medicine.

3 Engineering Culture and the Civilizing Mission

William Petty and the
New Science in Ireland

God send me the use of things, and notions, whose foundations are
sense & the superstructures mathematical reasoning; for want of
such props so many Governments doe reel & stagger, and crush the
honest subjects that live under them.

WILLIAM PETTY

Just as Robert Boyle argued that the objects of trades were proper objects
of natural philosophy (by rejecting the ontological opposition between
things natural and things artificial), so William Petty made similar arguments with respect to the objects of government: that they were no less
"natural" for being "political." As such he presented, in a single text,
"Natural and Political Observations," "some concerning Trade and
Government, others [concerning] the Air, Countries, Seasons, Fruitfulness,
Health, Diseases, Longevity, and the proportions between the Sex and Ages
of Mankind," all of which he considered to be "Natural History."[1] He
addressed his observations both to the king, the "Prince of Philosophers"
and "Physico-Mathematical Learning," and to the Royal Society, which he
called the king's "Parliament of Nature" and "Privy Council for Philosophy."
The Royal Society, he suggested, was composed of "three Estates, viz. the
Mathematical, Mechanical, and Physical."[2]

Petty was clearly as able as any of his contemporaries when it came to
rhetoric, but as this chapter seeks to show, his vision of political science represented a genuine elaboration of engine science in the context of statecraft,
and this vision was subsequently institutionalized in eighteenth-century
Ireland through organizations such as the Royal Dublin Society and the
Royal Irish Academy. Before discussing Petty's political science, however, I
would like to introduce the man and explain how he came to Ireland in the
mid-seventeenth century.

WILLIAM PETTY

Petty's biography is relatively well accounted for, but a brief account of his life will help provide the context for understanding the influences that helped to shape the formation of his natural and political philosophy, his advocacy of arts and engineering, his taste for adventure, and his hostility to book learning and the academic schools.[3] Petty was born in 1623 in the town of Romsey, in Hampshire, England. His father was a textile dyer in that town, which was known as a seat of the woolen industry and a center of arts and crafts. According to John Aubrey, the young Petty took delight in watching the "smyths, the watchmakers, carpenters, joiners, &c.: and at twelve years old, he could have worked at any of these trades."[4] He attended school and had a smattering of Latin by age twelve, and at about fifteen bound himself by apprenticeship to the master of a vessel. It was apparently in this context that the "most remarkable accident of life" befell him, an accident that formed, he later said, the "foundation of all the rest of his greatness and acquiring riches."[5] Petty was not well treated by the sailors, and after ten months at sea was abandoned on the French coast near Caen, apparently with a broken leg. In Caen he worked at various jobs, gaining an early acumen for making money by collecting stones and crafting jewelry and hawking it on the streets. He explained to his cousin how he got sixpence for showing a squire a card trick, doubled it in a card game, and then through other transactions, the "shilling came to bee 4s 6d."[6]

Through such business adventures and by enrolling himself in a local school, he learned French. Setting his sights on attending the Jesuit College in Caen, he got to know the students by hanging out where they bathed, and was eventually admitted. There he added some Greek to his language skills and learned, according to his own account, "the whole body of common arithmetic; the practical geometry and astronomy; conducing to navigation, dialling, &c.; with the knowledge of several mathematical trades."[7] These skills earned him a position in the British navy and thus his first job working for the government. However, when the Civil War (1641–49) broke out, he left the navy and returned to the Continent. He spent three years in France and the Netherlands, becoming acquainted with Hobbes, whom he assisted with drawings for his treatise on optics. Through Hobbes he was introduced to other English exiles associated with the Mersenne Circle. With these connections and upon his return to England at the end of the Civil War, Petty's rise was truly meteoric. In 1649 he secured a doctorate in medicine and soon after became a professor of music at Gresham College. At Gresham he cemented his ties to experimental philosophers such as John Wilkins, John Wallis, Robert Boyle, and Christopher Wren. He also became intimately connected to the New English adventurers and planters, especially through his involvement in the Invisible College and the Hartlib Circle. He subsequently became a founding member of the Royal Society of London, and in 1683 he cofounded, with William Molyneux, the Dublin Society for the Improvement of Natural Knowledge, Mathematics, and Mechanics.[8]

During a two-year leave of absence from Gresham (with an annual stipend of thirty pounds), Petty secured the position of physician-general to Cromwell's forces in Ireland, landing in Waterford in 1652. So began his enduring connection, and that of his family, to Ireland. As part of the payment for his survey of Ireland he acquired an estate of some 270,000 acres in Kerry. He was sometime secretary to Henry Cromwell and was knighted less than two years into the Restoration. He even became a member of Parliament, though he faired less well in government circles in his later years, and the suggestion that he was at one stage surveyor general of Ireland is unconfirmed.[9] Petty's failure to secure a position of government authority after the Restoration says more about the powerful interests that opposed his plans than it does about the plans themselves. He subsequently became an enduring "Father" of science and government in Ireland, and was regularly cited in the eighteenth and nineteenth centuries as an inspiration and guiding light.

DISTINGUISHING PETTY'S POLITICAL SCIENCE
FROM THAT OF MACHIAVELLI AND HOBBES

The *Natural and Political Observations . . . upon the Bills of Mortality* is widely credited as the first text of modern statistical analysis. I emphasize that it is, in addition, an early example of efforts to bring the experimental philosophy to bear on political bodies in terms of their natural ontologies. In this respect, Petty's political science marked a break with that of Machiavelli. Rather than a science of human affairs in political regimes, Petty's design was for a political science of wealth that could serve to strengthen the state for the benefit of all. His political science did not involve advising the prince on how he might best secure his principality from the challenges of others. Rather, it was a matter of how to secure land and people as economic resources and measures of state power. Though the idiom is anachronistic, Petty did in substance invent the science of "political economy." It was, however, a political economy quite distinct from that of classical economics, in that it posited government as a key agent of economic development. Petty's political science, or more precisely his science of statecraft, also represented a break with the political science of Hobbes, the central concern of which was to solidify sovereign power, to found the "mutuall Relation between Protection and Obedience"[10] on immutable "Laws of Nature." As Shapin and Schaffer show, Hobbes's desire for certainty in natural philosophy was inseparable from his desire for certainty in political philosophy. Indeed, Hobbes's opposition to the experimental natural philosophy was importantly informed by his fear that it would necessarily result in experimental politics. As Hobbes himself put it, paraphrasing Boyle, "You are quite right about [our] politics. For like our physics, that [too] is experimental."[11]

Unlike Hobbes, Petty sought to describe and explain by "sense" rather than "law" all the complex elements and relations of the state. These elements and relations embraced "things" as well as people. Only after such objects had been revealed to the senses could they be made subject to mathematical operations. In addition, Petty was less interested in justifying the balance of civil and ecclesiastical power than in using experiment and mathematics to effectively intervene in and improve the state. In order to understand the state, one had to probe it, to scope it out with specially designed tools, instruments, and engines. In this way it could be made "legible" and thereby amenable to the designs of statecraft.[12] There was, however, no avoiding the engines of regime-craft in seventeenth-century Ireland, and Petty was always ready to contribute to those designs when the situation demanded. For instance, when the monarchy was restored after Cromwell's death, Petty helped to draft the "acts of Settlement and Explanation" that secured the Cromwellian land confiscation largely intact, and therefore also Petty's own holdings in Kerry.[13] In addition, Petty was an "adventurer" (i.e., a colonial venture capitalist) in Ireland, ready to take great risk in order to gain great reward. These colonial regime-building activities should not, however, distract from his wider experimental engine science and its employment in every form of inquiry, from shipbuilding and carriage design to political, economic, medical, and social science.

"Lands and Hands" were at the center of Petty's political-economic science. These could be understood either politically, as territory and population, or economically, as capital and labor. Petty stitched the political and economic together precisely by pursuing schemes that increased the wealth of the state. Like the cameralists on the Continent, he believed that population (labor power) was the key to a wealthy and powerful state, though he also argued that nature was itself a source of wealth. Population could be calculated by "political arithmetic" (see chapter 4) and augmented by "political medicine" (see chapter 5). Land was the indispensable basis of power and independence, but could not be known and exploited without cartography and natural history. Petty proposed all sorts of experiments in government and designed numerous instruments for conducting them. He was exemplary among his contemporaries when it came to the government of natural bodies through experiment and political engineering.

EXPERIMENTAL GOVERNMENT

Experimental government, with its schemes, plans, and innovations, raised suspicion and was circumvented at every turn. For this reason Petty viewed Ireland as an ideal laboratory for experimental statecraft. His proposal for a "registry of lands, commodities, and inhabitants," in a tract of that title, was first addressed to England, but it met such stiff opposition, particularly from the legal profession, that he proposed instead, as one of his admiring progeny later put it, that "the experiment should be made upon the corpus vile of Ireland."[14] Such schemes were resisted because they envisioned the contrivance of powerful government scopes and meters, engines of government perception and measurement designed to render "a cleere view of all persons and things, with their powers & familyes." The reason for scoping out these phenomena was to make them available to government intervention and statecraft, to "methodize and regulate them to the best advantage of the publiq and of particular persons."[15] Petty's scheme for a "new instrument of government," the office of "Surveyor General of the Lands, People, Trade, and Revenue," was thus restricted to Ireland, as an "experiment of this nature, may be better tryed upon poor Ireland than upon proud England." Ireland was a practical site for conducting experiments precisely because "the King's Government is somewhat more absolute in Ireland than in England."[16] On another occasion he provided a different rationale, describing Ireland as a "political animal" analogous to the "cheap and common" animals on which students of medicine practiced. Being "scarce twenty years old" and without "confusion and perplexure of the parts," Ireland provided an ideal field for experiments in statecraft.[17]

Petty's work is exemplary for exploring the beginnings of a new relationship, forged largely between the seventeenth and nineteenth centuries, among engine science, material culture, and state power.[18] His vision of statecraft followed logically from the application of engine science to political objects. It was a statecraft of intervention, mobilization, contrivance, and material transformation, of integrated techniques for capturing, forcing, scoping, and metering the phenomena of society. The designs of such were realized over the *longue durée*. The result, rather than the "artificial society" complained of by Edmund Burke,[19] is better captured by the concept of a "skein" of networks, as suggested by Latour,[20] the hybridization of nature and culture in a Leviathan realized by the combined action of a science and a government, which, for all the denials, were (and are) cultural siblings. Across the vicissitudes of party, the material effects of engineering constituted a powerful continuity in the history of state formation. Petty was ahead of his time, and though he complained, "I have no luck with my Politics," and "the solid study of other men's peace & plenty ruins me," he would no doubt have been pleased to witness how many subsequent innovations in government in Ireland resembled his early designs. In the contemporary history of science, Petty is less well remembered than Boyle, but he was at least as important a figure in the foundation of engine science, because he systematically employed it in the development of a new, definitively modern form of statecraft.

POLITICAL ANATOMY

A crucial work, published posthumously, is Petty's *Political Anatomy of Ireland*. He introduced the work by noting that Francis Bacon made a "judicious parallel in many particulars, between the Body Natural, and the Body Politic, and between the arts of preserving both in health and strength."[21] While his use of the political metaphor of the body was not in itself particularly unusual—the body natural had long served as a metaphorical resource for representing social and political organization—Petty put the metaphor to work in the service of preserving the body natural and the body politic in health and strength. His interest in the relation between the natural and the political body lay less with its discursive power to produce a universal representation embracing, for instance, microcosm and macrocosm, than in its strategic capacity to facilitate the fabrication of specific ways of intervening materially yet "safely" in the body politic. Given the turbulent period in which Petty lived, a capacity to intervene safely in the body politic was of no small importance. These were revolutionary times, in politics as much as in science, "the present condition of men . . . like a field where a battle hath beene lately fought, . . . [had] want of a union and a soule to quicken and enliven them."[22] About a decade earlier Cromwell's body had been dug up, his corpse dragged through the streets, hung in chains, and buried finally in a criminal's grave. Petty had his own political problems, not least of which arose from charges of fraud in his cartographic survey of Ireland.[23]

Since anatomy, Petty explained, was the best foundation for securing the body natural in health and strength, so political anatomy might equally serve these ends for the body politic. As anatomy was practiced using instruments to intervene in the materiality of the body natural, so political anatomy was a "practice upon the politic" that looked to forging instruments for the material manipulation "of lands and hands." Yet practice on the body politic, as with that on the body natural, required knowledge of its "symmetry, fabrick, and proportion." Thus, Petty set out to describe, in the "first Essay of Political Anatomy," the symmetry, fabric, and proportion of the Irish body politic. The main categories he used were land, people, houses, produce, government, defense, weather, trade, and money. In respect to land he documented its extent (location, acreage) and nature (whether arable, forest, bog, mountain, etc.) and its holders, value of leases, and rental income. He investigated hands in terms of population, number of families (particularly titular), and national and religious identity. He made further distinctions by age, rank, fitness for labor or trades, and occupation. Note was made of the infirm and blind, the unemployed, and the number and causes of death. As with land, he computed a monetary value for hands, settling on seventy pounds a head for laborers and fifteen for slaves. His scope on the Irish people was broad in the sense of nineteenth-century "social economy." Thus, he included comparisons of the diets of different sections of the population, their "manners," language, and so on. All these phenomena were further probed in the eighteenth and nineteenth centuries.

By "houses" he meant all forms of building, which he distinguished first on the basis of the number of hearths and chimneys they possessed. From these criteria he estimated monetary values, arriving at a valuation of the entire stock of buildings in the state. He also distinguished among types of building, such as "ale-houses" and "transcendental houses" (churches), and sought to document who owned what. Types of trades practiced, products grown or manufactured, and the amount of money in the economy were either documented or estimated. On this basis he suggested that the "whole substance of Ireland" was worth about sixteen million pounds.[24] With respect to government and defense, he identified both the type and number of offices and the material infrastructure of castles and fortresses. He described the government as consisting of the king, lord lieutenant, twenty-one bishops (among them four archbishops), and 270 members of the House of Commons of the Irish parliament (being knights, citizens, and burgesses). These MPs and burgesses represented about three thousand freeholders and about one hundred corporations, respectively. There were forty sheriffs and about four hundred bailiffs. The lord lieutenant was the "chief governor," ruling by prerogative with the assistance of a council of about fifty "lords justice." The judicial branch consisted of five courts (chancery, king's bench, common pleas, prerogative, and palatinate) and also an admiralty court, martial court, and a number of bishop's courts. Law enforcement consisted of 950 justices of the peace, 252 head constables, and 2,278 petty constables.[25] The joining of the natural and political in Petty's political anatomy is illustrated by his inclusion of the "coelum" (sky or atmosphere) as an important part of the fabric of the country, and thus object of political economic science. Petty described the "heat, coldness, drowth, moisture, weight and susceptions of air, and the impressions made upon it, viz. the state of the winds, as whether the wind blows in Ireland in comparison with, or differently from other places; as from what points of the compass the wind blows most frequently or fiercely, and what proportion of the whole year from each point."[26] Petty summed up his vision in the *Natural and Political Observations:*

> Whereas the Art of Governing, and the true Politics, is how to preserve
> the subject in Peace and Plenty, . . . men study only that part of it
> which teacheth how to supplant and overreach one another, and how,
> not by fair out-running, but by tripping up each other's heels, to win
> the Prize. Now, the Foundation or Elements of this [his own] honest
> harmless Policy is to understand the Land, and the hands of the
> Territory, to be governed according to all their intrinsick and accidental
> differences: As for example; It were good to know the Geometrical
> Content, Figure, and Situation of all the Lands of a Kingdom, especially
> according to its most natural, permanent, and conspicuous Bounds. It
> were good to know how much Hay an Acre of every sort of meadow
> will bear; how many Cattle the same weight of each sort of Hay will
> feed and fatten; what quantity of Grain and other Commodities the
> same Acre will bear in one, three, or seven years, *communibus Annis;*
> unto what use such soil is most proper. All which particulars I call the
> intrinsick value: for there is also another value meerly accidental, or
> extrinsick, consisting of the Causes why a parcel of Land, lying near a
> good Market, may be worth double to another parcel, though but of
> the same intrinsick goodness; which answers the Queries, why Lands in
> the North of England are worth but sixteen years purchase, and those
> of the West above eight and twenty. It is no less necessary to know how
> many People there be of each Sex, State, Age, Religion, Trade, Rank, or
> Degree, &c. by the knowledge whereof, Trade and Government may be

made more certain and Regular; for, if men knew the People, as afore-said, they might know the consumption they would make, so as Trade might not be hoped for where it is impossible.[27]

Thus Petty concluded, as Thomas Newenham would a century later, that a "clear knowledge of all these particulars . . . is necessary, in order to good, certain, and easie Government."[28] It is in this context, also, that one can understand Petty's hostility to bookish philosophy, and his preference for the manipulation of "Objects and Actions, whether they be Naturall or Artificiall," and the study of "things" over the "rabble of words."[29] In response, for instance, to a publisher who complained that one of his man-uscripts lacked bulk, he explained, "I could assure you that I wish the bulk of all books were less."[30] His commitment to practice on "the world" demanded instruments, however, and in his understanding these were not confined to tools one might hold in one's hand or even to more complex apparatus such as Boyle's vacuum engine. Organizations like the Dublin Society and the Dublin College of Physicians were "the instruments under God, of reforming the practice of physick" in Ireland. Designs such as these were as much instruments, for Petty, as the chains, pins, magnetic needles, protractors, "tyme scales," and "compasse-cards" he used in his geograph-ical survey of Ireland. Instruments in the broadest sense were the "helpes" which permitted perception, measurement, and material manipulation of nature.[31] His tendency to use the idiom *instruments* rather than *engines* is explained by his training in medicine, anatomy, music, and surveying, where the language of instruments was well established. His understand-ing of political instruments, however, drew on all the connotations that the word *engine* held at the time: they were "ingeniously contrived" and designed, and they served the art of government and statecraft. Instruments of government were the means to cut into the body politic and act on its constitutive parts. They aimed to alter its fabric and to aug-ment government agency and state power. When applied with "authority" they could be used to "bend the present state."[32]

THE ADVICE TO SAMUEL HARTLIB

The extent of Petty's philosophy of transformation can be gleaned from a closer look at his first publication, *The Advice of W. P. to Samuel Hartlib for the Advancement of . . . Learning* (1648). It was directed toward those he called the "Reall Friends to the Designs of Realities, not those who are tick-led only with Rhetorical Prefaces, Transitions, & Epilogues, & charmed with fine Allusions and Metaphors (all which I do not condemn)." Condemnation was not Petty's way. For instance, he did not condemn astrology, which in the seventeenth century was philosophically questioned, as long as it was subject to the same "experimental tests" as other claims. And in his design for a model hospital he advocated having a mathematician as one of four curators, who as well as serving as a steward and accountant, was to "be skill'd in the best Rules of Judiciall Astrology, which he may apply to calculate the Events of diseases, and Prognosticate the Weather; to the end that by his judicious and careful Experiments, the Wheat may be separated from the Chaffe in that Faculty likewise; and what is good therein may be applyed to good uses, and the rest exploded."[33]

In the advice to Hartlib, Petty presented a number of educational and promotional instruments, both mechanical and institutional, for the advancement of experimental philosophy. Acknowledging Hartlib's call for the creation of the "Office of Common Address" (a centralized data base), Petty enumerated proposals for the creation of *"ergastula literaria,"* or literary workhouses; the "Gymnasium Mechanicum," or college of trades and technology; and the "Nosocomium Academicum," or model hospital, for teaching and research. Petty's concept of workhouses was quite different from what they would eventually become. Indeed, the plan was more akin to a national system of literary, mathematical, and technical education. *All* children over seven were to receive education suitable for making a living, in addition to acquiring reading and writing skills. No child was to be excluded on the basis of poverty, for there were many "now holding the Plough, which might have beene made fit to steere the State."[34] The poor children were to be trained such that they could perform tasks normally the preserve of "elder and abler persons, *viz.* attending Engines, &c." They were to be educated regarding all sensible objects and actions, natural and artificial. The "Art of Drawing and designing" was included because in many cases it "performeth what by words is impossible." All children, including those of the highest rank, were to be "taught some gentile Manufacture," such as turning curious figures, making mathematical instruments and dials, painting on glass, engraving and etching, grinding glasses, and making musical instruments. They were to be taught "Navarchy and making Modells for buildings and rigging of Ships"; architecture and building; the confectioner's, perfumer's, and dyer's arts; chemistry and anatomy; the making of magnetic devices, and the elements of arithmetic and geometry, "they being the best grounded parts of Speculative knowledge."[35]

Petty proposed the Gymnasium Mechanicum as the means to advance mechanical arts and manufactures and encourage new inventions. It was to contain a botanical theater with stalls and cages for all the animals, plants, and rarities of the "ancient world." It was to house "Modells of all great and noble Engines, with Designes and Platformes of Gardens and Buildings," as well as the "most Artificiall Fountaines and Water-works."[36] There was also to be a gallery of the rarest paintings and statues, with the best globes and "Geographicall Maps." Only the most "ingenious" workmen were to be employed.

His plan for a model hospital, to cure the "Infirmities both of the Physician and [the] Patient," was to have a garden, library, chemical laboratory, anatomical theater, apothecaries, and all the instruments and furniture required. The design of its administration and economy is particularly interesting. The plan of the hospital united the action of stewards, physicians, surgeons, and apothecaries in a single house, each with specific duties relating to his special skills. In this sense the plan prefigured Petty's later designs of division of labor and his broader schemes for the "government of the society." It was an important model for the organization of administration generally. As Petty's first publication (at age twenty-four), the *Advice* provided a blueprint of his later works relative to both government and the new learning.

PETTY'S RULES FOR THE DUBLIN SOCIETY

Further insight into Petty's scientific agenda can be gathered from his rules for the Dublin Society. Members of the society were to address themselves chiefly to making experiments, which Petty suggested they should prefer to the "best Discourses, Letters and Books they can make or read, even concerning experiments."[37] This attitude toward reading, that is, a radical rejection of the value of such for learning, is characteristic of Petty. He contrasted the "wit" of "letters" with the "skill" of drawing and painting, the latter embodying "exactness" in contrast to the "extravagance" of the former.[38] Aubrey noted that Petty positively boasted in his later years that he had read little since he was a young man. He even stated that had he been distracted by reading, he would not have "known as much as he does, nor should he have made such discoveries and improvements."[39] Thus it is not surprising that he admonished members of the Dublin Society not to exhibit contempt for any experiment, no matter how trivial, common, or vulgar. In addition, his commitment to the mathematization of the world was expressed in his requirement that members "provide themselves with the Rules of number, weight and measure; not onely how to measure the

plus & minus of the quality and Schemes of matter, but to provide themselves with Scales and Tables, whereby to measure and compute such qualitys and Schemes in their exact proportions."[40]

Petty exhorted members to "bee always ready with Instruments and
other Aperatus," so that observations could be made of rarely occurring
phenomena. Indeed, he never tired of emphasizing the need for tools,
instruments, and engines, and in 1684 "brought in a paper, *Supellex
Philosphica*, containing 40 Instruments requisite to carry on the designs of
the Society."[41] Petty extended this aspect of his natural philosophy to
policy just as he did with mathematics, describing the Dublin bills of mortality as an "Instrument of Government."[42] His designs for the internal
political economy of the Dublin Society were similar to his schemes for the
government of nations, involving "registers," "records," and "accounts"
through which to keep stock of happenings.[43]

The Dublin Society did not fare well in the turbulent years of the
Williamite wars and settlement. Having begun meeting in 1684, it was
interrupted by the "Glorious Revolution" and did not meet at all between
1687 and 1693. Petty's death in 1687 was a major blow to the society, and
Molyneux, after the Williamite settlement, became more occupied by political analysis focused on issues of representation and rights.[44] The society
ceased meeting again in 1697, and Molyneux died the following year. His
son, Samuel Molyneux, revived it in 1707, but it collapsed again the following year. Nonetheless, the spirit of Petty's vision survived, and engine
science was eventually institutionalized in Ireland.

THE INSTITUTIONALIZATION OF ENGINE
SCIENCE IN THE EIGHTEENTH CENTURY

Almost twenty-five years subsequently passed before the new Dublin
Society was established in 1731. The second Dublin Society in many ways
carried forward the tradition of practical experimental philosophy in
Ireland, particularly in relation to agriculture.[45] Indeed, the second Dublin
Society was eminently practical and experimental in precisely the manner
advocated by Petty. It was even more concerned with practical matters than
its predecessor, which is indicated by its name, the Dublin Society for the
Improving of Husbandry, Manufactures, and other Useful Arts and
Sciences.[46] It fully embraced and promoted experimentalism and forwarded
the culture of "improvement" through ingenious interventions and manipulations. The original code of rules mandated that "all the works, journals,

and transactions which shall for the future be published by other societies and private persons, which shall contain any useful improvement or discovery in Nature or Art, be purchased by the order of and at the charge of the Society."[47] Similar in principle to Petty's plan for a history of trades, a catalog was compiled the following year, which aimed to include all works on husbandry and mechanical arts in English, French, Latin, and Greek. Every member of the society was expected on admission to choose "some particular subject either in Natural History or in Husbandry, Agriculture or Gardening, or some species of manufacture or other branch of improvement, and make it his business by reading what had been printed on that subject, by conversing with those who made it their profession or by making his own experiments to make himself master thereof and to report in writing the best account they can get by experiment or enquiry relating thereunto."[48] Thus the second Dublin Society, very much in the spirit of the first, was intended not to amuse the public with "laboured speculations" but to promote "improvement" through "experiment."[49] Its vision as such was somewhat captured in a poem by James Arbuckle in 1737:

> Thus if th' endeavours of the good and wise
> Can aught avail to make a Nation rise,
> Soon shall Hibernia see her broken state,
> Repaired by Arts and Industry, grow great.[50]

The second society, hereafter the *Royal* Dublin Society,[51] was one of a range of scientific, literary, medical, and professional societies established in eighteenth-century Ireland. All animated the culture of experiment and improvement and served as crucial institutional supports for the emerging ideology of "patriotism" associated with figures such as Samuel Madden, Charles Lucas, and Henry Grattan. Equally crucial is these institutions' creation of a powerful node in the relationship between landed and urban Protestant populations in Ireland, the latter having only recently been recognized as central to the course of Irish history.[52] An early example of the intersection of experimentalism, moral improvement through material engineering, and the emerging Irish patriotism of the Anglo-Irish is Samuel Madden's famous letter to the Royal Dublin Society. Madden called on the "gentlemen" of the country to become the "principle engine" for "making experiments and attempting new improvements" in arts and agriculture, and thus for making the "good designs of the Society successful."[53] Madden complained of those gentlemen who spent the wealth of Ireland in England (the "absentee" landlords), condemned luxury and extravagance, and called on "all Men [to] unite in the Service of *Ireland.*"[54]

He described the wealth leaving the country through absentees as a crime and treachery and called Ireland his "Native kingdom." It was in this way that a constituency of the planters led the transition from "New English" to "Anglo-Irish." They constructed Ireland as their own nation, not a nation consisting of all the people that made up the material body politic, but rather a political nation consisting of those who by property and religion belonged to "civil society." Indeed, as early as 1698, William Molyneux had expressed precisely this view in his claim that "the present people of Ireland are the progeny of the English and Britons that from time to time have come over into this kingdom, and there remains but a mere handful of the ancient Irish at this day."[55]

This image of the origins of the nation informed, throughout the eighteenth century, the "Protestant Ascendancy's" ideology of patriotism, which culminated in 1782 with the establishment of "Grattan's Parliament." It was precisely these patriot Protestant gentlemen who constantly called for the "improvement" of the country through building, drainage, reclamation, forest management, inland navigation, and so on. Building was meant not only to add wealth and value, thus increasing the "National Treasure," but also to "beautify the Face of our Country" and give "Hearth and Life and Spirit to our People." Improved housing would provide a broader security for the "nation" than could be achieved through fortifications, since the weakness of the mud cabins rendered their inhabitants "fearful" and "emboldened Thieves."[56] "We should therefore improve their Buildings as well as our own Houses, and see them more snug, warm and decent, to give them a Taste and Desire for the reasonable Satisfactions of Life, and this will be the best way to spur them onto Industry and Labour."[57]

This new patriotic and improving spirit required a distancing from the policies of the past. Madden complained that the forests of Ireland had been laid waste by the early colonists and armies, who had viewed them "as the main Shelter and lurking Places for Rebels, Thieves, &c." Landlords had forced their tenants to burn only wood and to cut down a certain acreage per year. More was consumed by building and in the ironworks set up by the planters. In order to arrest the destruction, the forests required management as part of an overall strategy of "Planting and making Drains and Enclosures and Hedge-rows, with all the Arts of good Husbandry."[58] Madden called for legislation that would force landlords to replant, and proposed experiments with various species of tree in different parts of the country. The famous "Irish Linen," according to Madden the "great Stay, and Support of this Island," was made an industry in Ireland by the planters.

Ulster was the heart of linen production by the 1730s and, for Madden, stood as proof of how such industry might be made the basis for securing the nation in peace and plenty. Indeed, Ulster, in all the dimensions of material engineering and the culturing of nature, early stood as a testament to the colonial project. On entering Ulster in 1756, Wesley noted how the "ground was cultivated as in England, and the cottages not only neat, but with doors, chimneys and windows."[59]

That Madden believed gentlemen to be the "engines" of improvement and civilization demonstrates how forms of government stemmed not simply from officials of state but from a certain constituency of the political nation, which was in important respects the cultural wellspring of such officials. Thus, one should not confine the history of government to the history of official agencies. Colonial government initially developed in Ireland through the forging of cooperative linkages between "private" and "public" forces. Thus, official government funded the wider constituency that produced the culture of scientific government. During the eighteenth century the Royal Dublin Society received a generous endowment of three hundred pounds from the Irish parliament for the purpose of setting up a botanical garden, which could serve as an "agricultural laboratory."[60] In 1766, Parliament voted eight thousand pounds to the society for encouraging trades and manufacture, in addition to the relatively regular grants for agricultural improvement.[61] A chemical laboratory with a dispensary for paupers was established with grants of 250 pounds from both the government and the society.[62] Arthur Young claimed that the government, by late century, was regularly granting ten thousand pounds a session to the Royal Dublin Society.[63]

LESS SUCCESSFUL SOCIETIES OF LEARNING IN EIGHTEENTH-CENTURY IRELAND

Other societies were also established in the eighteenth century, such as the Physico-historical Society of Ireland and the Medico-philosophical Society. The former was established in 1744 by twenty-three "Lords and Gentlemen" who wished to promote inquiries into the "ancient and present state of several counties of Ireland." The members planned to establish county committees that would collect information on local weather conditions, geology, plant life, and agriculture, as well as ancient monuments, estates, charities, and public buildings. The information was to be communicated to the Royal Dublin Society, but the plan was never realized.

Though surviving less than a decade, the society did manage to collect various plant and fossil samples, and it assisted Charles Smith's work on the surveys of Waterford and Cork. The Medico-philosophical Society was founded in 1756 by another group of gentlemen with interests in natural and philosophical inquiries "and all such improving and entertaining subjects as happened to fall in their way."[64] John Rutty, remembered for his pioneering work on the relations between meteorological conditions and disease, was active in the new society and dedicated his famous *Chronological History of the Weather and Seasons, and of the Prevailing Diseases in Dublin* to its members.[65] It remained for the most part, however, a medical society and ceased meeting in 1784. All of these efforts show, nonetheless, the nexus of engine science and planter ideology, a nexus that stretched back as far as the mid-seventeenth century.

PETTY, THE NEW ENGLISH PLANTERS, AND THE IDEOLOGY OF CIVILIZING THROUGH IMPROVEMENT

That Petty's advice was addressed to Samuel Hartlib, who indeed published it, is evidence of his early connection to the Hartlib Circle and the Invisible College. The Invisible College, as Charles Webster convincingly argues, emerged out of the intimately connected families of New English planters who fled to London when the "Old English" aligned with the king during the Civil War. Webster suggests that the context for the emergence of the Invisible College was provided by Lady Ranelagh (Boyle's sister) and the Anglo-Irish exiles who met at her house in London. The Invisible College was initiated around 1646 by Boyle and Benjamin Worsley (surveyor general of Ireland c. 1650s), "as a means to propagate their conception of experimental philosophy."[66] Two other important members of the group in the Irish context were the brothers Gerard and Arnold Boate, authors of the *Natural History of Ireland*. The significance of these early associations lies in their important influence on the young Boyle and also the link they established among capitalism, colonialism, and engine science. The Invisible College and the Hartlib Circle championed a very similar experimental philosophy to that of the Royal Society of London, though with an even greater emphasis on technology. They also illustrate how the ideology of "improvement" figured in the civilizing mission in Ireland avowed by the New English and how that was related to the new science. As with engine science, here too Bacon is the harbinger, writing in 1603 of Ireland and Scotland: "[We shall] reclaim them from their barbarous manners . . . [and]

populate plant and make civil all the provinces of that kingdom . . . as we are persuaded that it is one of the chief causes for which God hath brought us to the imperial crown of these Kingdoms."[67]

The New English planters and adventurers began arriving in Ireland in the sixteenth century. As Protestants and bearers of plans for the reformation of Ireland, they were quite distinct from the Old English, or Anglo-Normans, who from the twelfth century had integrated in significant ways with the Gaelic lords, the result of a combination of strategy and necessity, given the failure to wholly conquer beyond the Pale (Dublin and its hinterlands). Robert Boyle was born of such a New English family, reputedly the richest in the kingdom. His father, the first Earl of Cork, "placed an emphasis on 'public works' or 'commonwealth work', which encompassed English tenant settlement, the erection of fortified towns, churches, bridges and castles, and the sponsorship of preachers, schools and almshouses."[68] Cork, like many New English planters, brought the philosophy of Bacon to Ireland. Thus, Cork saw to it that Robert was educated in "mathematics, surveying and fortification studies," a curriculum becoming more common for the nobility, though perhaps with an added urgency in Ireland, where the security of the New English was still precarious.[69]

The connection among commonwealth work, laborious work on wild nature, and thus the nobility of the hand as much as the mind signified important strands in the New English conception of their civilizing mission in Ireland. A worldly mission that would continue into the eighteenth and nineteenth centuries, the civilizing mission was expressed in an idiom that linked "physical" conditions to "moral" standards. As Toby Barnard demonstrates, improvement "was in the air in the early eighteenth century, and nowhere more strongly than in Ireland."[70] In the context of the schemes and interventions of the New English, improvement meant "making Ireland more like [lowland] England."[71] The discourse of improvement in Ireland was thus bound to the project of colonization, but it also animated a wider theology of "works" that stimulated engineering culture. The theology and culture of improvement ennobled the practice of transforming the material world and celebrated the experiments through which such transformation was to be achieved. The projects it implied included draining bogs, clearing brush, introducing new crops, enclosing lands, erecting permanent buildings, and extending roads and canals. These were projects that in every case could be promoted through the tripartite objective of taming and civilizing wild Ireland, strengthening the (planter) nation, and augmenting private profit—a new trinity animated by a quest for redemption and for the glory of God.

Barnard links gardening and developments in Irish horticulture directly to the newcomers' determination to "tame the menacing environment."[72] The effort was fueled by a theology that viewed nature "left to its own devices" as a source of weeds and pests, and thus a sign of the fall from grace: "By regaining control over unruly nature, man in some measure atoned."[73] The "native" Irish, by simply taking what nature offered, were necessarily reduced to slovenly habits and indolence. The Irish were construed as constituting a blurring between man and beast.[74] The theology of the new planters united with a colonizing and civilizing mission and with the underlying philosophy of engine science. Nature was to be intervened in, manipulated, and made subject to culture. Even the language of agriculture and horticulture expresses this philosophy. It was not sufficient to "husband" nature; one also had to culture "her." This is precisely the language of the Royal Dublin Society, which constantly promoted new and experimental ways to "culture" plants.[75] Samuel Madden expressed this interventionist philosophy when he noted that what "Plato said of Government, we may very properly apply to Agriculture, and maintain that it can never be rightly managed till Plowmen turn Philosophers, or Philosophers Plowmen."[76]

These linkages among improvement in agriculture, transformation of the material environment, and experimental natural philosophy continued throughout the eighteenth and into the nineteenth century. For instance, a pamphlet published in 1790 noted the numerous works on the improvement of agriculture and asserted that the "only source of knowledge in agriculture, that can be relied on [is] *experiment*."[77] Walter Wade's *Sketch of Lectures on Artificial or Sown Grasses* continued the tradition and signaled the extent of the connections that had been established among agriculture, botany, and medicine. Wade was a member of the Queen's College of Physicians in Ireland, physician to the Dublin General Dispensary, and honorary member of the Royal Dublin Society, Apothecary's Hall, and the Farming Society, as well as a professor and lecturer on botany at the Royal College of Surgeons. He argued that every person engaged in agriculture required competence in chemistry, which supplied knowledge of how best to nourish crops; in natural philosophy, which permitted the farmer to "judge of the most proper instruments he should employ in dividing and loosening the soil"; in veterinary art, which provided the grounds for raising healthy animals; and in botany, a science on which successful agriculture depended.[78] Joshua Trimmer, in 1809, explained that after spending some time in Ireland he changed his mind with respect to the view that the Irish were by nature depraved. Lauding what had already been achieved, he advocated further improvements in agriculture as the basis for moral improvement.[79] Thus, both the very conception of nature articulated by experimentalism and the interventionist and transformative culture of engine science united a program for the cultivation of natural bodies with a mission for moral redemption. The trope of material and moral improvement is one that survived the vicissitudes of two centuries of Irish history. By the mid-nineteenth century, "town improvement," "sewerage improvement," "road improvement," and "estate improvement" were advocated partly on the basis of their civilizing and moralizing capacities. It was precisely this belief, that the Irish could be improved through material works, which set William Petty apart from some members of the Hartlib Circle, such as the Boate brothers. The Boates were more in the tradition of Edmund Spenser, viewing the Irish as inherently barbarous, but their *Natural History of Ireland* indicates precisely the cultural configuration in which a historically specific mode of rule was founded on the government and exploitation of natural bodies. References to the *Natural History* rarely supply the reader with the complete title, which alone goes far toward capturing the various strands that came together with the importation of engine science into Ireland:

> *Ireland's Natural History. Being a true and ample Description of its Situation, Greatness, Shape, and Nature; Of its Hills, Woods, Heaths, Bogs; Of its Fruitfull Parts and profitable Grounds, with the Severall ways of Manuring and Improving the same: With its Heads or Promontories, Harbours, Roads and Bays; Of its Springs and Fountains, Brooks, Rivers, Loghs; Of its Metalls, Mineralls, Freestone, Marble, Sea-coal, Turf, and other things that are taken out of the ground. And lastly, of the Nature and temperature of its Air and Season, and what diseases it is free from, or subject unto. Conducing to the Advancement of Navigation, Husbandry, and other profitable Arts and Professions. For the Common Good of Ireland, and more especially, for the benefit of the Adventurers and Planters therein.*[80]

Regardless of the immediate successes and failures of the projects implied by the *Natural History*, it marks a particular form taken by the new science in the context of colonialism. As Patricia Coughlan has pointed out, though the *Natural History* contained a "new full and empirically based description of Ireland," it was also crucially a political document in the narrowest sense of the term.[81] The Boates pepper their *Natural History* with "expressions of violent revulsion against the native Irish," "a nation extremely barbarous in all the parts of their life," who have resisted all the "great pains taken by the English, ever since the Conquest, for to civilize them, and to improve the

Countrie."[82] The failure of the Irish to exploit mineral resources was provided as evidence that they constituted "one of the most barbarous Nations of the whole Earth."[83] In the context of the rebellion, the notion that the Irish were barbaric by virtue of their *passivity* in the face of nature (they simply took what nature gave them) was expanded by the claim that they *actively* destroyed the products of English cultivation:

> the naturall inhabitants of Ireland, who not content to have murthered or expelled their English neighbours (upon whom with an unheard-of and treacherous cruelty they fell in the midst of a deep Peace, without any the least provations) endeavoured quite to extinguish the memory of them, and of all the civility and good things by them introduced amongst that wild Nation; and consequently in most places they did not only demolish the houses built by the English, the Gardens and Enclosures made by them, the Orchards and Hedges by them planted, but destroyed whole droves and flocks at once of English Cowes and Sheep, so as they were not able with all their unsatiable gluttony to devour the tenth part thereof, but let the rest lye rotting and stinking in the fields.[84]

This view of the Irish as naturally barbaric had plenty of coinage and was most famously expressed by Spenser in his *View of the State of Ireland* (c. 1598). In the first sentence Spenser asked why, if Ireland was of "so goodly and commodious soyle," it had not been put to "good uses" and "to better government and civility."[85] His answer, provided immediately and throughout the book, was that the problem lay in the ancient Brehon law, the customs and manners of the people, and their religion, which, having resisted all attempts at reformation, might be better eradicated than reformed. The important point about the *Natural History* is not, however, the continuity it exhibits with Spenser's forsaken view of the Irish, but rather how it constructed Ireland as a *natural object* to be both known and exploited through the practices of engine science. As had long been articulated, gardens and enclosures represented a culturing of nature, an eradication of natural wildness through "civilizing" government; now a new science was to be mobilized in order to know the land scientifically and to effect these changes through more ambitious experiments and engineering schemes.

It is Petty again who fully expresses this philosophy in relation to both land and people, since he viewed the failures of the people as something to be corrected by ingenious schemes for governing population. It is crucial to note in this respect that Petty takes a view of the native Irish quite different from Spenser's or the Boates', rejecting the argument that the Irish were inherently barbaric. He explained how he "deduced" Irish "manners" from multiple bases: their "original constitutions of body," their air and food, their "condition of estate and liberty," the influence of their governors and teachers, and their customs, "which affect as well their consciences as their nature."[86] In their "shape, stature, colour, and complexion," he saw "nothing in them inferior to any other people, nor any enormous predominancy of any humour." He did not question the claimed laziness of the Irish, but he explained it at any rate as stemming "rather from want of employment and encouragement to work, than from the natural abundance of flegm in their bowels and blood."[87] In this sense Petty expressed an understanding that would become, in the eighteenth and nineteenth centuries, one of the central ideas of reformative morality, the idea that work was virtuous in itself and that industry was the road to both material improvement and moral salvation.[88] Thus, he rejected the notion that the Irish were "naturally" inclined to "treachery, falseness, and thievery":

> For as to treachery, they are made believe, that they all shall flourish again, after some time; wherefore they will not really submit to those whom they hope to have their servants; nor will they declare so much, but say the contrary, for their present ease, which is all the treachery I have observed; for they have in their hearts, not only a grudging to see their old properties enjoyed by foreigners, but a persuasion they shall be shortly restored. As for thievery, it is affixt to all thin-peopled countries, such as Ireland is, where there cannot be many eyes to prevent such crimes; and where what is stolen, is easily hidden and eaten, and where 'tis easy to burn the house, or violate the persons of those who prosecute these crimes, and where thin-peopled countries are governed by the laws that were made and first fitted to thick-peopled countries; . . . In this case there must be thieving, where is withal neither encouragement, nor method, nor means for labouring, nor provision for impotents.[89]

One sees, in the views of Petty and Spenser, the opposing sides of an enduring debate between those who viewed the Irish as having fixed and inferior natures and those who located the "problem" in environment, culture, economics, and government. It was also possible to have both ideas expressed together. In the eighteenth century, for instance, Berkeley made the not unusual argument that Irish vices stemmed from both "race" and culture, suggesting (as Spenser had) that the Irish were descended from the Scythians:

> The Scythians were noted for wandering, and the Spaniards for sloth and pride; our Irish are behind neither of these nations from which they descend in their respective characteristics. . . . Never was there a

more monstrous conjunction than that of pride and beggary; and yet this prodigy is seen every day in almost every part of this kingdom. At the same time these proud people are more destitute than *savages,* and more abject than *negroes.* The *negroes* in our plantations have a saying, *If negro was not negro, Irishman would be negro.* And it may be affirmed with truth, that the very *savages* of *America* are better clad and better lodged than the *Irish cottagers* throughout the fine fertile counties of *Limerick* and *Tipperary.*[90]

Berkeley, describing the Irish as his "countrymen," made his remarks in the context of an admonition to the Catholic clergy to exhort the impoverished Irish "to labor" so that they might be civilized.[91] James Tyrrell, in the seventeenth century, speculated that the Irish originated in Scotland and, though expressing the view that they were "very much given to sollenesse & stealing & fornification," thought this was bound to be the case with all people who had "few or no trades [or] manufactures."[92] Thomas Newenham, at the beginning of the nineteenth century, noted the still widespread opinion of many in England that the Irish peasant was barely more than a savage, but argued that bad government, particularly a failure to promote tillage, was the culprit and that "the Irish peasant will be found, at least as far above the level of the savage man, as the well-housed, well-clad, and well accommodated peasant of England."[93] Gervase Bushe, in a letter to the Earl of Charlemont, made a similar argument in 1789, contradicting the "opinions of others as to the nature of the Irish peasantry." In places where tillage had taken root, "no peasantry can be more industrious; and the continued frugality of those who have grown rich is perfectly astonishing."[94] Thus, during the eighteenth century the views of Petty were kept alive, and they gained ground in the nineteenth century before the emergence of "racial science" and eugenics, when the middle-class belief in the cultural formability—and, indeed, reformability—of "character" was at its strongest.[95] Though the view that the Irish were naturally depraved has a tradition going as far back as Spenser, and though it was a view that gathered particular strength in the second half of the nineteenth century, the eighteenth and nineteenth centuries saw the growth of what today is called the environmental viewpoint. It is in this context that one can grasp how the material work-over of Ireland was so crucially bound to the ideology of a civilizing mission. What makes Petty important, however, is not simply that he is one of the earliest observers who attributed the alleged Irish brutishness to a lack of culture rather than a defective nature, but also the range of his schemes for bringing culture to bear upon Ireland and the breadth of his engineering mind in respect to such schemes.

ENGINE SCIENCE IN THE NINETEENTH CENTURY

In the nineteenth century the Royal Dublin Society succeeded in having the government establish the Museum of Irish Industry, which was later enlarged under the supplementary title of Government School of Science Applied to Mining and the Arts.[96] Members were required to give their time equally to the society and to the museum. The museum remained under direct government control but in 1865 became the Royal College of Science for Ireland under the administration of the newly established Science and Art Department of South Kensington.[97] The Royal Dublin Society initiated many of its own industrial improvements. A society factory was established in Dublin, manufacturing agricultural technologies and implements and establishing an extensive store of both past and innovative agricultural machinery.[98] Indeed, the Royal Dublin Society was the pioneer of technical education in Ireland and was also the first industrial development agency. One of its main objects was the promotion of education in drawing and design, particularly as related to crafts. As such it carried out, if in a much more limited way, Petty's proposal in the *Advice*. Premiums were awarded for painting and sculpture, lacework, embroidery, tapestry, carpet design, and the invention of enamels. Fifteen years after the establishment of the Royal Dublin Society, an academy specializing in drawing and painting was created, becoming the first School of Art in Ireland, later the Metropolitan School of Art. Instruction, free for the first hundred years of the school, was centered on industrial work, and the school was divided into four departments: figure drawing, landscape and ornament, architecture, and modeling. Eventually it, too, was brought under the direct control of the government, becoming in 1849 the Government School of Design in connection with the Royal Dublin Society.[99]

While the Royal Dublin Society embodied the spirit and animated the culture of the new science, there is no doubt that the areas in which it did so were limited, and this perhaps partly explains the formation of a number of other associations of learning in Ireland during the eighteenth century. Also, the discursive opposition between pure science and mere technology intensified during the eighteenth and subsequent centuries (hardly challenged until the late twentieth). Thus, these ancient oppositions were reinscribed in discourse even while science as a practice increasingly developed toward its modern technoscientific form.[100] After the Royal Dublin Society, the Royal Irish Academy was the most important and influential of the new scientific societies established in eighteenth-century Ireland. However, the same opposition between pure science and impure technology that obscured the continuity between the two incarnations of the Dublin Society has equally distorted the history of the Royal Irish Academy.[101]

The academy had three sections: science, polite literature, and antiquities. In the first eight volumes of the transactions, published between 1785 and 1803, 106 papers were published in the science section, compared with 25 in literature and 32 in antiquities. The papers in the science section ran the entire range of engine science, from telescopic astronomy to political arithmetic. Papers were published on pendulum design, the manufacture of gunpowder, principles of shipbuilding, new steam engines, "a telegram," signal engines, geometrical measurements, and social surveys.[102] William Preston published a program for Irish industrial development in 1803; John Templeton, a paper on the introduction and naturalization of new species of plant; Richardson wrote a paper on grasses for farmers. Richard Kirwan, the chemist, mineralogist, geologist, and meteorologist, wrote on coal mining, manures, bleaching, mineral waters, and mineralogy. After one thousand pounds was bequeathed to the academy for the "improvement of natural knowledge and other subjects of their institution," a system of premiums and awards was set up.[103] The first premium, of twenty pounds, was offered for an "experimental investigation of any subject, with a particular tendency to the improvement of arts and manufactures."[104] Two premiums of fifty pounds each were offered for "the best system of education and the best means of providing for the employment of the people."[105] In 1795, the question for the competition was, "To what manufactures are the natural advantages of Ireland best suited?"[106]

During the nineteenth century, academy competitions continued to express the practical dimensions of engine science. In the science section, for instance, competitions were held on the subject of advantageously matching specific manures to different soils and "on the effects of the discovery of galvanism [battery capacity] both as regards the theory of chemistry and as an experimental agency."[107] Even in the sections on antiquities and polite literature, investigations were sponsored among natural forms, engineering and mechanics, and social and moral improvement. In natural forms, for instance, a competition was held "on the means of rendering the sources of natural wealth possessed by Ireland most available for the employment of the population"; and in social and moral improvement a competition was held on the subject of "the influence of the extension of mechanical improvements on the character and happiness of a nation."[108] In the preface to the first volume of the transactions, the standard defense of engine science was made against the charge of "barren and speculative" learning. Natural philosophy, the author explained, was crucial to advances in arts and manufactures. All manufactures could be understood in terms of basic chemistry and mechanical engineering and thus advanced through basic research. Even the section on polite literature was promoted in practical terms, as a mechanism that would "civilize the manners and refine the tastes" of the people. Neither the art for art's sake nor the science for science's sake argument was made.[109]

Thus, there is an unmistakable continuity between the aims and works of the two Dublin Societies and the Royal Irish Academy. All three express the ideology of the colonial civilizing mission, propose projects of moral and material improvement, and animate a philosophy of engineering through the scoping out, measuring, and manipulation of natural and political forms. These societies of learning were clearly institutions of the New English–cum–Anglo-Irish. While the first Dublin Society had but one Catholic member, the Royal Irish Academy had two among its eighty-eight founding members. The second Dublin Society's founders were all Anglo-Irish. Like the Royal Dublin Society, the Royal Irish Academy received both the blessing and the financial support of central government. The academy received free accommodation in government buildings even before it obtained its royal charter. In 1788, the lease on the old headquarters of the Inland Navigation Board was vested by king's letter in the organization. On the eve of the nineteenth century the academy secured a grant from Parliament and, in 1816, consolidated this with an annual grant of three hundred pounds, later raised to five hundred, seven hundred, and in 1866 fifteen hundred.

ENGINE SCIENCE AND THE LEGACY OF THE IMPROVEMENT IDEOLOGY

All of these institutions, from the Dublin Society founded in the 1680s to the Royal Irish Academy established a century later, animated a very specific cultural configuration. They represented the projects of a particular constituency of the Anglo-Irish who came to adopt Ireland as their own country even as they distinguished themselves from the native Irish. They were committed to a patriotism that viewed the "improvement" of Ireland as a moral duty. And most significantly, they were the heirs to the experimental science pioneered by Boyle and Petty. They desired to know their new country's natural history, geography, resources, ancient history, and, in the words of Petty, its political and economic "symmetry, fabrick, and proportion." They believed that the country and people could be improved and made prosperous through experimental programs in material transformation. In order to improve it, however, they needed knowledge of the country, and this explains the advanced state of surveying in Ireland, from Petty's geometrical cartography to the Royal Engineers' Ordnance Survey. Petty apparently never secured the position of surveyor general, but he set the practice in Ireland on a sound foundation. His cofounder of the Dublin Society, William Molyneux, did become "surveyor-general and chief engineer," as did Thomas Dobbs, a leading member of the Royal Dublin Society. Lord Mountjoy, the master general of the ordnance, succeeded Petty as president of the Dublin Society.

Throughout the eighteenth and into the nineteenth century, the culture of improvement, experiment, measurement, intervention, and transformation was extended such that everything from cowsheds to school routines came within its scope. These practices constituted a mode of government that remained largely absent from the famous political treatises of the period, much as the practices have remained absent from most contemporary political theory and history. Works such as Hobbes's *Leviathan* or Locke's *Second Treatise of Civil Government* were framed by questions of representation, rights, and the limits or legitimacy of sovereign authority. They were very different from the discourse of government articulated by Petty. Rather than offer a theory of representation or sovereignty, Petty designed a range of tools, instruments, and engines for the practice of scientific government. And while his designs in political arithmetic, medicine, and anatomy met with opposition within the political nation, they substantially survived and were proved by the test of time. By the end of the nineteenth century, every aspect of the body politic was rendered in number, weight, and measure, the relations between doctors and patients and the provision of medicines made subject to government, and the land worked over and made to yield new species of plant. The relationship between the arts of maintaining a powerful state and the promotion of healthy bodies was made intimate. While the theorists, from Voltaire to Marx, argued about what constituted a legitimate and just government, the engineers, cartographers, surveyors, medical police officers, and statisticians continued to work the materiality of the land, the built environment, and the bodies of the people, never ceasing the practice of scoping out, classifying and differentiating, measuring, metering and regulating, intervening, forcing, and transforming. These practices were almost always wrapped in the discourse of improvement, a discourse that trafficked with ease across the domains of government, engine science, and colonial ideology.

RESISTING EXPERIMENTAL GOVERNMENT

Edmund Burke was perhaps the first to rail against the melding of Petty's style of designing statecraft with the machinations of the more conventional forms of Machiavellian regime-craft. In his first publication (1756), he sought to defend and vindicate "natural society" and, with that, "natural religion," "natural rights," "natural justice," and "natural reason" against the instruments, engines, arts, and ingenuity of policy, police, and "Reason of State." The last was, he said, "a Reason, which I own I cannot penetrate."[110] Burke condemned the "Mysteries of State-freemasonry" and all forms of "artificial society." "Despotism" was the most basic and slavish form of artificial society. "Aristocracy" was even worse, precisely because it was more regularized than arbitrary: "The regular and methodological Proceedings of an *Aristocracy,* are more intolerable than the very Excesses of a *Despotism,* and in general, much further from any Remedy."[111] The form of "democracy," however, was worse again, since it constituted a more refined contrivance of subjection. And "mixed government" was worst of all, since it not only engineered all the evils of the other forms into a "very complex, nice, and intricate machine," but also ensured through the centrality of "party" that the society would be frequently subject to "Cabals, Tumults, and Revolutions."[112] Art and ingenuity and the science of artificial society only intensified in "mixed government," and the "more deeply we penetrate into the Labyrinth of Art, the further we find ourselves from those ends for which we entered it."[113] It is sometimes suggested that the language of the *Vindication* is so outlandish that the book can be read only as satire. There are passages in the text that would lead to that conclusion, such as the section attacking the jurists, the "learned Sages, these Priests of the sacred Temple of Justice."[114] Yet satire, among other things, is designed to convey greater truths than those immediately obvious on the page, and there is little doubt that Burke's contempt for the inefficiencies and conceits of artful statecraft was genuine and deeply held. Indeed, his oft-cited embodiment of contradiction—sometimes Whig, other times conservative—perhaps derived in part from his inability to ever find comfort in any political "party," particularly in the context of Irish-English politics. Though he does not say so explicitly, he implies that his caustic criticism derived from his experience of the mistreatment of the Irish ruling class by the "parties" of the English parliament:

> We have some of us *felt,* such Oppression from Party Government as
> no other Tyranny can parallel. We behold daily the most important
> Rights, Rights upon which all others depend; we behold these Rights

determined in the last Resort, without least Attention even to the Appearance or Colour of Justice; we behold this without Emotion, because we have grown up in the constant View of such Practices; and we are not surprised to hear a Man requested to be a Knave and a Traitor, with as much Indifference as if the most ordinary Favour were asked; and we hear this Request refused, not because it is a most unjust and unreasonable Desire, but that this Worthy has already engaged his Injustice to another.[115]

Burke's contempt for all forms of artificial society, especially that concocted by mixing the scientist's art with the bureaucrat's craft, was confirmed over thirty years later, when he reacted to the French Revolution precisely as one would expect from reading the *Vindication*. He condemned, in horror, the designs of mathematicians, surveyors, engineers, and doctors, who without talent in legislation or honor in their designs contrived a machine "not worth the grease of its wheels." He represented the revolutionaries' erasure of "all local ideas" by the action of "geometrical policy" as a tragic blow to justice.[116] "Nothing more than an accurate land surveyor, with his chain, sight, and theodolite, is requisite for such a plan such as this."[117] In his discussion of the broader design of the revolution he identified precisely the configuration of ideas that emerged from the practices of engine science in the domain of statecraft:

> French builders, clearing away as mere rubbish whatever they found, and, like their gardeners, forming everything into an exact level, propose[d] to rest the whole local and general legislature on three bases of three different kinds; one geometrical, one arithmetical, and the third financial; the first of which they call the *basis of territory*; the second, the *basis of population*; and the third, the *basis of contribution*. For the accomplishment of the first of these purposes, they divide the area of their country into eighty-three pieces, regularly square, of eighteen leagues by eighteen. These large divisions are called *Departments*. These they portion, proceeding by square measurement, into seventeen hundred and twenty districts, called *Communes*. These again they subdivide, still proceeding by square measurement, into smaller districts called *Cantons*, making in all 6400.[118]

The metrologizing extremes of the French Revolution, exemplified in the design of the metric calendar, are well known and need not be labored here. Radical redesign of the order of things was a tendency at the heart of engineering culture, because, as Ken Adler observes, engineering viewed the "present as nothing more than the raw material from which to construct a better future."[119] In England and Ireland, however, the designs of scientific statecraft would be tamed by a certain respect for tradition and history, a respect perhaps directly fostered as a consequence of the fear induced by the destructive spectacle of the "back to the drawing board" approach of those who engineered the French Revolution.[120] Perhaps this indicates, in addition, something of the difference between the English engineering culture and that of France, the latter subordinating the practical heterogeneity of engineering practice to the dictates of "Pure Reason," or perhaps the difference is simply one of peculiar historical circumstance, engineering always inclining one way or the other depending on context. In any case, the new English graphs and meters of the nineteenth century would redefine, but not erase, old boundaries. Indeed, they would tie the abstract mathematical geometry of triangulation to an archaeology of ancient boundaries, an ethnography of the people, and an orthography of their words.

Burke's romantic vision of the state of nature, of tradition and community, of purity and freedom from artificiality, would harass the designs of an emerging engineering culture, challenging its claim to civilize and undermining its identification with reason. Nonetheless, Petty's practical vision of scientific statecraft, driven by engine science and its vast stock of experiments (both large and small), would endure the eighteenth century and triumph in the nineteenth. Yet this new state-idea would still be configured within a Hobbesian theory of sovereignty that was readily redeployed in the wake of each revolution precisely because it was a *postrevolutionary* design. In one masterful stroke it gave "a Multitude" the right to *confer* sovereign power on a single man (or body of men acting as one) and at the same time denied that multitude the right thereafter to disobey this sovereign who, in his very person, was now to be treated as the state itself, his actions none other than the actions of the state.[121] Ironic as it may seem, Hobbes, Boyle, and Petty, in their own respective ways, were each "right." "The state" would be personified as an *actor* in the manner of "the Prince." And as I seek to show in the following chapters, experimental philosophy would be powered by its epistemic engines. And through the agency of Petty's brand of political science, the land, people, and built environment would be transformed into modern territories, populations, and jurisdictions. Conquest would become less a problem of war and more a project of engineering, and domination less an imperative of sovereignty than one of material incorporation. Chapter 4 documents the role of statistics, censuses, surveys, and cartography in Irish state formation, suggesting that these political technologies can be understood as scopes, meters, and graphs, technologies that served the engineering of the modern data state.

4 Engineering the Data State

Scopes, Meters, and Graphs

By any means save the surveyor.
PHELIM O'NEILL, *during the 1641 rebellion*

Ireland is a white paper.
WILLIAM PETTY, *after the Restoration in 1662*

The period immediately following the Cromwellian conquest (1650) marked, in the form of Petty's cartographic survey, the first great intersection between government and engine science in Ireland. The Boates' *Natural History*, designed for the scientific colonization of Irish land and the exploitation of resources, was published in 1657, and in 1684 the first institution of engine science in Ireland, the Dublin Society, was established. These developments signal the new conditions out of which the modern engineering state in Ireland was born. Yet the engineering state also emerged out of the older nexus of capital and coercion, discussed by Tilly. Thus before getting to the main focus of this chapter, which is the practices of scoping, graphing, and metering land and people through the technologies of surveys and censuses, a word is necessary on the context of conquest and colonial plantation.

CONQUEST, PLANTATION, REBELLION, AND HOLY WAR

Ireland and England, in the sixteenth and seventeenth centuries, experienced profound political revolutions and unprecedented capitalist adventurism. As in other parts of Europe, much of the political turmoil grew out of the struggles that followed the Protestant Reformation. The first Protestant plantations in Ireland came during the Tudor conquest, begun in the reign of Henry VIII, and completed under Elizabeth at the turn of the seventeenth century. Though the context in Ireland was very different from that in England, both countries (as well as Scotland) experienced a meltdown of established order in the mid-seventeenth century. In England, the Civil War resulted in the execution of the king and the rise of Cromwell at the head of a "protectorate" regime. Disgruntled feudal lords in Ireland, who had witnessed their dominion gradually eroded by Protestant (particularly English but also Scottish) plantations, viewed the troubles in England as an opportunity to win back their properties. A plan to do so that began in Ulster immediately degenerated into a significantly sectarian (there were also, of course, class and other forces at work) and countrywide rebellion that brought Irish people to the brink of committing massacres like those that plagued the Continent during the religious wars.

Plantations were destroyed and livestock killed, and an attempt was made to "'destroy all records and monuments' of English rule."[1] Protestants in all four provinces were robbed, stripped, and turned out into the harsh winter without care for their survival. Rites of violence were perpetrated against Protestant objects and corpses, such as the desecration of Protestant Bibles, the parading of heads on pikes, and mutilation of the dead. Torture was also inflicted, sometimes in the form of strangling and half hanging. Whole groups of people were murdered, two of the worst cases happening in Ulster.[2] Nicholas Canny's minimization of Irish, particularly clerical, responsibility for the terror of the insurrection (calling it, emotively, an outburst of "fury") can be understood in terms of his overall objective of constructing continuity across the entire period of conquest and colonization. By downplaying the brutality of the rebels against the English Protestant planters in 1641–42, he can construct the ferocity and totality of the Cromwellian conquest as merely the final working out of Herbert Spenser's agenda in the *View*, rather than as a direct result of the character of the rebellion. Spenser was rabidly anti-Irish, representing the natives as barbarians who could never be made subject to civilized government. The rebellion, according to Canny, provided Protestants with the final proof, to a large extent "imagined," of the barbarity of the native Irish and of the need, therefore, for military conquest in the service of total subjection.

The importance of Canny's argument for this study is that he arrives at the opposite conclusion to my own, that is, that the brutality of the conquest was the final blow to visions of a civilizing mission, ensuring that the "experiment at Making Ireland British had, in every respect, proven a costly failure."[3] It is ironic that Canny evokes Petty in the context of reaching this conclusion, since Petty rejected suggestions that the Irish were inherently barbaric and continued throughout his life to look forward to a day when statecraft would genuinely serve the improvement of all classes of society. Petty's schemes of scientific improvement received no endorsement from government after the Restoration, but this is not proof that the civilizing mission was a failure or that the effort to make Ireland more like England had been forsaken. On the contrary, the Cromwellian conquest, and the Williamite settlement at the end of the century, ensured that the project of English plantation would be largely realized over the next two centuries.

The history of plantation in the wake of the Cromwellian conquest was continuous in important respects with that of the previous eighty years, especially in terms of its reliance on experimentalism in agriculture, empirical inquiry in philosophy, and the elevation of arts and trades as part of a strategy of civilizing through material improvement. The connection between plantation government and experimentalism stretches back to the 1580s, most notably in the case of Richard Boyle, first Earl of Cork. Richard Boyle is particularly important in this respect. As well as embodying these key elements of the planter strategy and ideology, he instilled this same worldview in his youngest son, Robert, perhaps the single most influential figure in the early organization of English engine science.[4] Robert Boyle's vision of engine science had been importantly shaped by his background as the son of one of the greatest early planters in Ireland, and Petty worked out his schemes for scientific government in the context of designs for postconquest Ireland. Petty suggested that the first requirement for the scientific government of a state was a good map, and it was precisely the rebellion and conquest that provided the occasion for him to produce one for Ireland.[5]

POLITICAL TABULA RASA: IRELAND AS AN EMPTIED SPACE FOR EXPERIMENTAL STATECRAFT

While Petty may not have been the first to describe Ireland as a "white paper," it was probably truer after 1650 than at any time previously. The rebellion and conquest ripped the old political nation asunder and wiped the slate in terms of the distribution of political power. The body of the country was significantly laid waste, with hundreds of thousands dead from battle and famine. The land was scorched by total war, and the plantations severely damaged by the rebels. With the transplantation of the rebel landlords west of the Shannon River to Connaught and the massive land transfer that saw about 80 percent of the country pass into new hands came a profound changing of the state regime. The idea of an emptied space, however, was more wishful than real. The idea of a universal transplantation of Catholics proved well beyond administrative capacity, and even the more limited focus on rebel leaders turned out to be less than designs would have it.

Nonetheless, it was in this context that Petty could imagine Ireland as a tabula rasa and thus conceive of starting anew in Ireland, of taking a state that was but an "embrion" and engineering it in accordance with the new science. His was a project of counting, marking, mapping, and differentiating, of rendering in the process a new cosmology.[6] It was to be a project that envisioned the contrivance of various engines of scientific government in the form of surveys, maps, censuses, registers, and reports: an apparatus of political arithmetic and information technology. Through these technologies the state would be refashioned and made visible in a process that Philip Corrigan has aptly called "commissioning cosmologies" and "setting up the seen."[7] As with scope engines, the body politic would be made sensible in all its parts and complexity. Through various -*ographies* it would be made graphic, reduced to two-dimensional immutable mobiles, transferable to the centers of political and economic calculation.[8] As with meter engines, it would be rendered in number, weight, and measure so that it could be represented and handled mathematically. All this would be done not for the purpose of contemplation but for the purpose of intervention, not so much to reflect as to engineer. As Toby Barnard has pointed out, however, "Ireland was not tabula rasa."[9] There were old bounds, indigenous cartographies, and traditional cosmologies.[10] Thus the long process of rewriting Ireland was accompanied by a project of translation, a project completed with the Ordnance Survey of Ireland in the mid-nineteenth century (see below). Of course, Petty was not alone when it came to grand designs in the seventeenth century. Samuel Hartlib had similar visions and was an important influence on Petty.

HARTLIB'S ENGINE FOR SCOPING AN ENTIRE STATE

Hartlib's scheme for an office of public address foreshadowed what was to come. Proposed as an "engine" through which to view "the frame of a whole State," it envisioned all the components of a country laid open to scoping and metering practices:[11]

> The affairs of State . . . may be infinitely improved, if they [the governors] know but how to make use of such an Engine. He that can look upon the frame of a whole State, and see the constitution of all the parts thereof, and doth know what strength is in every part, or what the weaknesse thereof is, and whence it doth proceed; and can, as in a perfect modell of a Coelestiall Globe, observe all the Motions of the Spheres thereof; or as in a Watch, see how all the wheels turn and worke one upon the another for such and such ends, he only can

fundamentally know what may and ought to be designed; or can be effected in that State for the increase of the Glory, and the settlement of the Felicity thereof with Power according to Righteousness.[12]

Hartlib spoke of "a gentleman"[13] who broke the "whole design of the House of Austria" and raised himself to a ruler of princes by bringing "great designes to passe, chiefly by the dexterity of his prudencie in making use of the Engine, which never before was set a work in any Commonwealth, to reflect upon a whole State, till he did set it afoot to that effect."[14] Hartlib proposed his engine, to be run by the "Supreme Command," as a mechanism to "reduce all into some Order which is confused."[15] The design was for a national intelligence engine, a national center of differentiation, classification, and calculation. Everything concerning the state (or society) was to be captured in the engine and revealed in its nature. The scheme was designed to record all addresses, professions, "and the Informations of things profitable." Though ruled over by the supreme command, the "Instrument" was to be available to the entire "commonwealth," and as such be a "Common Intelligencer for All." It was specifically designed for a capitalist system, to facilitate the marriage of improving ideas in philosophy with adventure capital, to allow employers to find suitable workers, and to be a "National Exchange for all desirable commodities."[16] Though "mere description" is not much valued in sociology, there is no other way to quickly capture the details of the new designs of statecraft.

Hartlib's engine was to be composed of two major registers, one for things that were "perpetually the same," and one for recording daily occurrences. The former, a "Catalogue of all Catalogues," would contain intelligences of all things extant in the world, all the boundaries and characteristics of provinces, shires, counties, towns, castles, ports, and so forth, and also Speed's maps of the kingdom. It would include information on the different trades practiced in the state, the different families, their places of employment, their "Abilities and singular Vertues," what properties they held, and whether they were born in England or abroad.

The register of daily occurrences was to contain four registers called the "Register of Necessities (or of Charity), Of Usefulness (or of Profit), Of Performance (or of Duties), and Of Delights (or of Honour)."[17] The register of necessities or charity addressed the "Accommodation of the Poor," including lists of the names of the destitute, and aimed to provide them with "certificates" proving their condition so that they might "qualify" for aid. Information on benefactors and different means for providing lodging, clothing, food, and entertainment to the poor were included. Names of physicians, apothecaries, and surgeons who served the poor were to be collected, as well as a list of "Experiments and easie Remedies of diseases."[18]

The register of usefulness or profit aimed to provide an account of money (the species of coin in use in different places), of the various articles of food grown and available at market, of all drugs and their ingredients, of various cloths for the "preservation of Life and Health," of houses providing lodgings for a fee, of the leases held on farms and manors, of household goods, wholesale shops, and libraries and booksellers. A special "chapter" would provide information on securing loans, moving commodities, currency exchange, taxes, customs, impositions and duties, terms of apprenticeships, plantations, weights and measures, rates of insurance, and the location of factories.[19]

The register of performance or duties encompassed "Persons, and Actions, in all Offices and Relations" and was to serve as a kind of employment bulletin for ministers, professors, tutors, teachers, masters, secretaries, lawyers, clerks, and servants of the crown or great noblemen, including stewards, gardeners, and the like. It was also to record individually all apprentices, manufacturers, and tradesmen, husbandmen and seamen, and soldiers of all ranks and kinds. Accounts were to be kept of lawsuits, intelligences of public affairs, and rewards made for service to the king or state.[20] As with the other registers, it was to serve as a "Common-Center of Advertisement and Intelligence," in particular to provide the hours and times of all message and small package carriers. The latter were of particular concern to engine philosophers, who were always seeking out "intelligences and interrogatories" from friends and colleagues.[21]

The register of delights or honor addressed "Ingenuities, and Matters commendable for Wit, Worth, and Rarity." It is the classic design for uniting scientific projects with venture capital. The practice of engine science and the construction of experiments were often expensive and beyond the reach of the average practitioner. Through this aspect of Hartlib's engine, new discoveries or experiments in "Physick, Mathematicks, or Mechanicks" were to be recorded. Accounts were to be compiled of all cabinets of metals, statues, pictures, coin, grains, flowers, shells, roots, plants, "and all things that come from afar." Mathematical and astronomical instruments and all manner of inventions were to be cataloged. Indeed, this was to be the office "wherein *all* things may be registered."[22] The design was for a scope and meter on the entire state and also a graph of all its various components, human and nonhuman, natural and artificial. One might say that the design was little more than a filing cabinet for everything in the state, for it involved no operations on the data such as one finds in Petty's political arithmetic. Yet as a national "search engine" it represents one of the earliest visions of the modern *data state*.

As it turned out, Hartlib's great design was not to be. Though he went to some lengths to represent the office of public address as open to all, his plan to have it under the authority of the supreme command and his occasional reference to "secret" registers made his proposal rather dangerous looking for aristocracy and capitalists alike, who were fully alert to the statecraft at work in this kind of "philosophy." William Petty's schemes for various information technologies foundered on the same rock, and it would be over a century before anything resembling the depth of his design was realized.[23] It would be wrong, however, to believe that there was no connection between Petty's early schemes and later, largely nineteenth-century, implementations. Petty's work on a registry of lands and people, his bills of mortality, and his political arithmetic more generally were regularly cited and mobilized in retrospect to give historical depth and philosophical justification to later scoping, metering, and graphing schemes.

Petty's friend and long-time confidant Sir Robert Southwell identified him as the "first man that ever brought Algebra into Human Affairs,"[24] and throughout the eighteenth and nineteenth centuries, Petty's analysis of the population of Ireland was regularly cited as the first that could be relied on.[25] Petty coined the term *political arithmetic* to refer to his method of handling economic and political matters mathematically. Political arithmetic was a form of mixed mathematics, and Petty developed it along algebraic as well as arithmetic lines. Unlike Hartlib, Petty sought to produce more than a collection of raw data. He wanted to be able to handle political and economic "things" according to "ratiocination," which he understood as the application of mathematical reasoning to matter(s).[26] Thus, he applied algebra to other than "purely mathematicall matters, viz: to policy by the name of *Political Arithmetick*, reducing many termes of matter to termes of number, weight, and measure, in order to be handled Mathematically."[27] "Reason," the engine of ratiocination, he understood as "nothing but the addition and subtraction of *Sensata*, or notions by the senses."[28] Thus, while political anatomy formed the qualitatively empirical part of Petty's political science, it was on this "foundation of sense" that he then employed the "superstructure of mathematical reasoning" (Petty may be the source of Marx's employment of·the foundations and superstructure metaphor). Beginning from a set of qualitative distinctions that could be valued by number, Petty proceeded to quantitative and comparative analysis, comparing year to year, type to type, Ireland to England, men to women and children, all the while establishing ratios through the mathematical techniques of ratiocination.

Petty was closer to Hobbes than to Boyle in terms of his commitment to ratiocination. But he was quite different from Hobbes in his commitment to mixed mathematics, and especially the expansion of its scope to include the everyday affairs of states and estates. It was less that mathematics and geometry could serve as models of perfect truth and order than that they were necessary parts of engineering in respect to the state and economy. Crucially important in this context is that he conceived of the body politic in material terms, and it was as such—as sensible matter—that it presented itself to measuring and metering and to mathematical calculation and representation. Petty, like many engine scientists, was a hybrid of Boyle and Hobbes, subjecting qualitative and substantive realities, established empirically and experimentally, to mathematical representation and analysis. But the clarity of Petty's agenda establishes him as perhaps the first social-scientific positivist. For this reason, the development of positivist social science is inextricably tied to the development of modern engineering statecraft.[29]

In his political arithmetic, as in his political medicine and political anatomy, Petty's interest was always in *both* the "Naturall, and artificiall state of Kingdoms."[30] Thus the scope of his political arithmetic could include everything from the metering of the weather and its bearing on health, and thereby population and reason of state, to the condition of lands, and thereby their economic and political value. The subtitle of one of his essays in political arithmetic demonstrates that scope: "Political Arithmetick, or a Discourse concerning The Extent and Value of Lands, People, Buildings; Husbandry, Manufacture, Commerce, Fishery, Artizans, Seamen, Soldiers; Publick Revenues, Interest, Taxes, Superlucration, Registries, Banks; Valuation of Men, Increasing of Seamen, of Militia's Harbours, Situation, Shipping, Power at Sea, &c. As the same relates to every Country in general, but more particularly to the Territories of His Majesty of Great Britain, and his Neighbours of Holland, Zealand, and France."[31] He also wrote essays in political arithmetic concerning "people, housing, hospitals, and shipping."[32] His observations on the bills of mortality were presented as exercises in political arithmetic,[33] as was his treatise on money and trade.[34] Numerous designs for registries similar to Hartlib's intelligence engine flowed from his hand.[35] These prolific productions in political arithmetic, though serving his posterity as the father of statistics and political economy, led him to be alternatively viewed with ridicule and suspicion during his own life, and he explicitly prevented the publication of much of his work for fear of the political consequences. For many there was just too much politics in his political arithmetic, too much government scrutiny of private property and the relations among gentlemen. But the term survived unchallenged until at least the late eighteenth century, before slowly being displaced by what was called the "German science of statistics" (i.e., quantitative analysis of matters of state).

POLITICAL ARITHMETIC AND SECTARIAN POLITICS

Metering land and bodies never lost its political significance, a fact that is particularly illustrated in Ireland in relation to counts based on religion. Though political representation in the early eighteenth century was not in any sense based on democratic representation, the ratio between Catholics and Protestants was symbolically important in politics. In 1736, for instance, *An Abstract of the Number of Protestants and Popish Families in the Several Counties and Provinces of Ireland* argued that Petty overstated the ratio. Petty, in his *Political Anatomy of Ireland*, had computed eight Catholics to every three Protestants, but the anonymous author of this essay in political arithmetic claimed that "the present disproportion must be much less."[36] The author did not give exact figures, but he used the technique of basing the calculation on the hearth tax returns, which in 1732–33 differentiated Catholics and Protestants, calculating the number of "heads of households" and, on that basis, the number of families. A family was defined as "a man, his wife and children," and each family was estimated at "five souls." At three children per family, this mode of calculation likely undercounted Catholics.

The question of the ratio between Catholics and Protestants became much more significant in the nineteenth century, when democratic ideals were taking hold in Ireland. In the wake of the establishment of the national education system in 1831, the "Royal Commission of Public Instruction" made an actual enumeration as part of an inquiry into "the state of religious and other instruction then existing in Ireland."[37] Though government censuses in Ireland began in 1812, it was not until 1861 that a count of religious affiliation was included. The manner through which the count was taken was truly unique. As well as using a fixed number of categories—Catholic, Established Church, Presbyterian and other dissenter (e.g., Methodist)—an "other" category was included in which respondents could write anything they chose. The write-in option resulted in about one hundred additional categories. While over four thousand chose Baptist; about thirty-five hundred, Quaker; and about four hundred, Jewish, much smaller numbers chose "Kellyites," "Arians," "Materialists," "Rationalists," and "Positivists."[38] According to this census, Ireland contained four people in 1861 who specified "socialist" as their religion.

The uniqueness of the Irish census of religion is highlighted by the absence of a like enumeration in England, Scotland, and Wales as late as 1920.[39] Indeed, the matter was an issue of dispute as to whether or not to count religious belief (not dissimilar to the debate over racial classification in the contemporary United States), and if beliefs counted, how many and what kind of categories to use. George Bisset-Smith, for instance, noted the complications, suggesting that numerous groups "would agitate in Parliament for a minuter subdivision to show their strength."[40] He discussed the difficulties facing a census of religion but made no reference to the solution found in the case of Ireland some half a century earlier. That a solution was found in Ireland as early as 1861 is probably not unrelated to the disestablishment of the Protestant Church of Ireland seven years later. In the period after the famine, the London government had to deal with an increasingly powerful Catholic Church. By making concessions to the hierarchy, the government expected that it could rely on the church to keep the flock firmly on the constitutional side of the nationalist movement in Ireland, a movement that had generated the more militant agendas of groups such as the Young Irelanders, who led the 1848 rebellion, and the Irish Republican Brotherhood (later the Irish Republican Army), who in the 1860s were conducting military drills in the mountains.

POLITICAL ARITHMETIC IN THE EIGHTEENTH CENTURY

Petty was ahead of his time, and there was only slow progress in political arithmetic during the eighteenth century. During that century the designs of taxation (only a part of Petty's scheme) and the business of life insurance drove the development of political arithmetic.[41] The hearth tax returns provided the most regular measures of the people in the eighteenth century. Counts were made in 1731, 1754, 1767, 1777, 1785, and 1791. Though Petty had, in 1672, estimated a population of 1.1 million (based on the data he had collected during his geometrical survey in 1659), an estimation published in the transactions of the Royal Dublin Society specified about a million, and the estimation of the 1731–32 tax count was more than double that, at 2.16 million. In 1731 Thomas Dobbs (onetime president of the Royal Dublin Society) computed estimates for the first half of the eighteenth century: 1712 (2.1 million), 1718 (2.17 million), and 1725–26 (2.3 million). The tax collectors counted almost 2.4 million in 1754 and estimated 2.7 million in 1777 and 2.84 million in 1785.[42] The importance of counting houses and people for tax purposes is obvious and was the main source of population estimates before the nineteenth century. There were charges, however, that the collectors were undercounting and defrauding the state of revenue. Thus in 1788 an inquiry was instituted by one of the revenue commissioners, Gervais Parker Bushe, the results of which were published by the Royal Irish Academy. Though largely relying on the hearth returns, Bushe estimated almost 1.5 million more than the hearth collectors, giving a population of over four million in Ireland at the end of the eighteenth century. The hearth collectors' enumeration subsequently increased significantly, returning 4.2 million people in 1791.[43]

"Statistical" data collection in Ireland from the late eighteenth to early nineteenth century sometimes took the form of "historical inquiries," which were generally textual graphs, though with supplementary tables of data. Two important works were published by Thomas Newenham: *A Statistical and Historical Inquiry into the Magnitude of the Population of Ireland*, and *A View of the Natural, Political, and Commercial Circumstances of Ireland*, in 1805 and 1809, respectively.[44] Newenham's work dealt with the relations among population, productive land, quality of housing, and the economic and moral condition of the country. He was particularly concerned to show that the growth of population was much greater than generally thought, and argued that the increase was occurring under "great defects of police, industry, and commerce."[45] His argument was not entirely different from that of the medical police activist Johann Frank (see chapter 5), who strongly protested that to promote an increase in population without providing security for those already alive implied a failure of policy and police. Newenham wanted government to encourage and fund the reclamation of lands, arguing that the Bog of Allen could be mined and eventually turned into meadow.[46] He estimated that about 3.5 million reclaimable acres lay "waste" and that, of the land that was reclaimed, about another 1.5 million acres were nonetheless left unproductive in any given year.[47]

Around the turn of the century the Royal Dublin Society put an ambitious intelligence engine in motion. The society's project of "statistical surveys," though not completed for every county, constituted a mass of data for scientific, economic, and governmental purposes. Like earlier statistical surveys, they were largely textual graphs, providing quantitative information but rarely organizing it in formulaic or tabular form.[48] Though not considered of much value by later statisticians, they provided a powerful scope and meter of the country that facilitated both business and government. Joseph Archer published a *Statistical Survey of the County Dublin, with Observations on the Means of Improvement*, in 1801. Charles Coote published surveys for the northern counties of Cavan, Armagh, and Monaghan, as well as the *Statistical Survey of the King's County*. Coote, in his introduction, referred to the effects of the "successful experiments" in agriculture, which had altered the "face of the country."[49] The surveys covered the widest range of subjects, divided under the heads of geographical state and circumstances, agriculture, pasture, farms, and general subjects. Geographical circumstances were described in terms of "situation and extent," "divisions," climate, soil and surface, minerals, and water. The agricultural section included the "modes of culture," the species of grain grown, the course of crops, and the nature and use of implements. Among the subjects dealing with pasture were markets and prices, modes of feeding and housing livestock, the extent of artificial and natural grasses, and the different techniques for making hay. Farms were described in terms of their size, number and type of buildings, nature of tenures and state of leases, types of fencing and hedgerows, and the modes of manuring and draining. The survey also included information on population, the number and size of villages and towns, prices of labor and provisions, the state of roads, bridges, and navigation, schools and charitable institutions, forms and "habits" of industry, and the use of the English language (to mention just some of the topics). Though without the tables that later become associated with "statistical" surveys, the investigations sponsored by the Royal Dublin Society provided a wealth of data on country and people.[50] All the statistical surveys were animated by the now familiar discourse of moral and material improvement, the duty of "every patriot, who feels the necessity of our attaining a perfect knowledge of the real state of Ireland."[51]

THE POLITICAL ARITHMETIC OF THE MODERN CENSUS: SOCIOMETERS COME OF AGE

Political arithmetic came of age with the modern census, which in 1854 was described as a "social survey," since it was concerned with both the quantitative measure *and* the qualitative condition of the people. The first attempt at a modern census of Ireland was made in 1812, though by all accounts it was an unmitigated failure. While modeled on the English census of 1810 (a reversal of experimental government that merits note), Ireland did not possess a sufficiently informed group of people to carry out the survey. In England, reliance on the poor-law officers was crucial to success, as in Scotland was the reliance on parish schoolmasters. In Ireland, however, "special agents" (with little local knowledge) were employed under the immediate supervision of the grand juries (local government outside the corporate towns). The juries met only twice a year and had little time or inclination for conducting a census. Thus, as it turned out, only ten counties secured complete returns, and four returned nothing at all. An estimate gave a return of almost six million, though it was claimed to be so unreliable that it was never presented to Parliament and thus was never recognized as an official census.[52]

A second attempt was made in 1821, this time with much greater success, because steps were taken to overcome the obstacles to the 1812 effort. The entire operation was placed under the auspices of the chief secretary (the de facto executive agent in Ireland for most of the nineteenth century), with the general supervision transferred from the grand juries to the bench of magistrates (though these could be and often were composed of the same individuals). Quite extensive measures were taken to ensure that the enumerators were qualified. For instance, candidates for the job were first required to make a preliminary return on a supplied form, specifying the names and numbers of parishes, townlands, and other subdivisions of their respective districts, the names and addresses of schoolmasters and the clergy (and their denominations), and descriptions of schools and their location. As well as screening the applicants, the process provided initial information that was used by the government such that a "wide field of communication" was opened up among clergy, schoolmasters, and officials, "which proved essential towards ultimate success."[53] The communication with the clergy, and particularly the Catholic clergy, was especially important for overcoming the widespread resistance of the people to the design. Though not mentioned in the 1821 account of the 1812 census, the people's suspicion of the census agents probably had a lot to do with its failure. In 1821 it was reported that the census agents encountered a "determined hostility to their proceedings," which often resulted in violence.[54] The common people in the early nineteenth century were no less suspicious than the aristocracy in the late seventeenth of the statecraft at work in political arithmetic. Recognizing that the hostility could be overcome only by the "most energetic measures," the government secured the assistance of the Catholic hierarchy in a manner that marked the new role the church was to have in the formation of the modern Irish state. On the basis of the information collected in the preliminary returns, a letter was sent by the government to every Catholic priest and Protestant clergyman in Ireland, explaining the intentions and design of the census and requesting their assistance "both for controlling the proceedings of the Enumerators in their respective Parish, and for removing any prejudices, or other unfavourable circumstances, that might tend to produce an unkindly feeling towards them."[55]

The strategy was apparently successful, the clergy gave their assistance, and whenever "opposition was reported" by a census agent the parish priest intervened in a manner that "immediately led to a satisfactory explanation, by which not only the obstacle was removed, but a friendly sentiment substituted in its place, so as to turn the current public opinion immediately and completely into the channel most desirable for the effectual attainment of the great objects of the Legislature under the Population Act."[56] Once again, it is impossible to make my case about the role of political meters in modern state formation without a detailed description of the content of the modern censuses, no matter how mundane and unimportant such particulars might at first appear.

Standardized notebooks and a detailed set of instructions[57] for the enumerators completed the preparations for the 1821 design, and the first reliable all-island census of Ireland by "actual enumeration" was executed. The particulars were comprehensive, though not qualitatively different from the English census, and mark this first full census of Ireland as a true "social survey." Apart from the actual enumeration of the population as a whole, the data was classified in terms of sex, age, and occupation (families were not enumerated, since it was believed this would involve judgments that would deviate from the need to deal only in "matters of fact"). Occupations were classed under the headings of agriculture, manufacturing, handicrafts, trading, liberal professions, and others, though in the published version the classification was restricted to "agriculture, manufacture, and others."

In terms of land and boundaries, information was collected on the name, situation, and acreage of every townland or subdivision of a townland or other smallest territorial district,[58] classed according to its parish, barony, and county, and the ratio of people to county acreage and to the square mile. Every "subordinate division of Land in Ireland had been analyzed," with the exception of two baronies in County Cork, the town of Belfast, part of the parish of Kilcummin in County Galway, and the island of Innismurry, off the coast of Sligo.[59] The name of every town, village, and "hamlet"[60] and the number of houses in each were itemized, as were the name and "situation" of every street, square, lane, alley, and court (or other combination of houses). The number of houses inhabited, uninhabited, and under construction was counted, as were all public buildings, including places of worship, barracks, schools (with the names of teachers and the nature of endowment), hospitals, infirmaries, lunatic asylums, prisons, gaols, bridewells, penitentiaries, mills, stores, factories, and so forth. Information was also collected on the number of inhabitants per house, their names, their families, their relations in terms of kinship, apprenticeship, or service, and the quantity of land held by each townland resident. Comparisons were also made, where possible, with the 1812 returns, but the most important innovation was that it was a nominal census. Indeed, this was one of the first national censuses in the world to collect the names of people and to relate all the other information to identifiable individuals and their addresses.[61]

It is worth noting that the censuses were also a technology through which the history of the boundaries of Ireland was officially constructed. The 1821 census stated that the country was first divided into counties, for fiscal and governmental purposes, after the Anglo-Norman invasion of the twelfth century. County status was granted only to those territories that acknowledged the government of King John. Ten counties were created, Dublin, Uriell (later Louth), Kildare, Catherlough (anglicized to Carlow), Kilkenny, Wexford, Upper Ossory, Leix, Offaly, and Ely O'Carroll. Leix, Offaly, and Ely O'Carroll, as well as some minor feudal territories, were reduced to "shire-ground" under Queen Mary and then divided into king's and queen's counties ("Laois" and Offaly were later restored; Ely was distributed among a number of counties). Connaught and Ulster were divided into counties during Elizabeth's reign. Wicklow, which had previously been divided between Carlow and Dublin, was made a county under James I.[62] Ancient Ireland had consisted of five kingdoms, Ulster, Munster, Connaught, Leinster, and Meath. Meath contained many ancient ruins, such as Newgrange (at fifty-two hundred years old widely considered the oldest free-standing building in the world), Kells (where the first Irish gospel Bible was transcribed), and Tara, where the High Kings of Ireland gathered. Indeed, the province of Meath had always been at the heart of ancient Ireland, and each new force, from the Celts to the early Christians, made it their political and religious center. Thus, it was a profound symbolic act when the province of Meath was abolished by the Anglo-Normans and incorporated into Leinster, which was dominated by Dublin, a city founded by Viking invaders in the tenth century and the center of Anglo rule in Ireland from the thirteenth to the early twentieth century.[63] It was in this context also that the first baronies were created. Meath was granted to the Anglo-Norman De Lacey, who subdivided it among his inferior feudal barons. Hence, the name *baronies,* into which the entire country was eventually divided as feudal military territories. The parishes were at first ecclesiastical divisions, which marked areas where the pagan natives had been brought under Christian influence and government, and they evolved as such into secular administrative divisions. "Townland" was the name given to areas the Irish called "baile fearainn." "Home ground" is a more direct rendering, but "baile" was also the word for town, hence the translation. As we will see below in the context of cartography, cadastral (political, civil, administrative, religious) boundary work on the land became central to nineteenth-century scientific statecraft.

The published material of 1821 filled just one volume of fewer than four hundred pages, but it became the template for the 1831 and 1841 censuses. The 1841 survey was the first to publish information on marriages, education, and the "ministering" professions. The marriage data was complemented with more detail concerning families, the education table provided information on the reading and writing ability of all children over five, and the ministering data distinguished those ministering to "moral wants" (divided into the heads of justice, education, and religion) and those ministering to "physical wants" (divided in terms of food, clothing, lodging, health, and charity).[64]

Apart from these innovations, the 1841 census is historic in that the new national police force, created in 1836, conducted the enumeration. When the agricultural census was established in 1847, the police were again enrolled, and subsequently "year by year traverse[d] the country to obtain the information."[65] The police intelligence of the country in this respect was so extensive, by the 1870s, that Sir Duncan McGregor, in testimony to a select committee of the House of Lords investigating illicit distillation, boasted that the police knew "every man who raises an acre or half an acre of oats or barley."[66] The role of the police in the censuses of Ireland was unique within the United Kingdom, and in 1841 and 1851 the three elements of census, the cartography (see below), and the police were integrated to produce a powerful government intelligence engine. The enumeration was taken according to the boundaries laid down by the cartography, and each police district was constituted as a census district under the superintendence of the subinspector or head constable, who was provided with maps by the cartographic (Ordnance Survey) department. The coast guard was also mobilized to assist in the enumeration. Using the police for the enumeration generated suspicion and resistance, and thus the legislation provided the police with "compulsory powers . . . to obtain the necessary information."[67] Steps were again taken to outmaneuver resistance. A circular letter was sent to "all persons throughout the country, whom we supposed to possess, by reason of their rank or occupation, any influence with the people—soliciting their friendly co-operation, with a view to the removal of any prejudices unfavorable to the census."[68] The press was also mobilized and was "ably assisted" by government, publishing notices and articles that explained the importance of accurate information. In order to make the enumeration "less intrusive" the police were instructed to leave the main census form at each house and have the head of the household fill it out. However, when the returns were collected the police were to "examine them carefully" and also to fill out the fifteen or so supplemental forms, unless the task was given over in the case of prisons, hospitals, workhouses, and so forth, to the master or keeper of those institutions. In all, over *1.5 million forms* were distributed throughout the country. Ireland was thus metered and quantified as never before. There was, however, much more to come.

THE 1851 CENSUS: A SOCIOMETER AND SOCIOSCOPE WITHOUT PRECEDENT

The 1851 census was the most comprehensive social, nosological, necrological, and bio-survey of Ireland to that date and perhaps also in any country in the world at that time. Executed in the immediate wake of the Great Famine, the 1851 census consisted of no fewer than seven parts, some of which contained multiple volumes, the whole amounting to thousands of pages.[69] The formatting of the information is of more than passing interest. The format of four volumes (one for each modern province) in part 1 was similar to the three previous decennial censuses. Like the earlier censuses, these volumes contained a head count and basic ratios with respect to such. For the first time, however, the data was graphed in entirely tabular form, without any textual comment. Part 1, which contained perhaps as much data as the entire 1821 meter, was but one conventional part of an otherwise enormously experimental undertaking. The head count and acreage count were "raciocinated" with respect to province, county, barony, parish, townland, and town. The area of each subdivision was provided in acres, rods, and perches (these more precise measurements derived from the Ordnance Survey; see below). The total population and sex ratios were listed, and data on houses provided.[70] Despite all this data, part 1 (which most contemporary sociologists and historians focus on when they consult the 1851 census) is the least revealing of the seven parts in terms of the advance of *sociometry* during the nineteenth century. Once again, there is no other way to convey the extent of the meter than through a relatively detailed description of its contents.

The scoping and metering of agricultural life and production are especially striking. Information collected on agricultural production, initially collected each year through an "agricultural census" (beginning in 1847, the first full year of the Great Famine), was incorporated into part 2 of the general census of 1851. At over seven hundred pages, the part on agriculture included general reports on crops and livestock, seven summary tables, and two returns of produce. Among the general tables were accounts for each county providing an estimate of the quantity of produce, with the same for each poor law union, a classification of holdings and the extent of crops for each class, a county abstract showing the number of holdings, the division of the land with its valuation and population, the number of holdings and extent of tillage in each division for the years 1847–51, and the same for the number and class of stockholders and the quantity of stock. The returns of produce were divided between crops and stocks, the data for the former arranged by poor law unions and electoral divisions, the latter by counties, baronies, and poor law unions.

One highly charged issue that emerged from these metering activities was the extent of emigration. In a review of Henry Maunsell's *Political Medicine*, published in the *Dublin University Magazine* in 1839 (see chapter 5), emigration was identified as an "engine of state policy" for the purpose of ridding the country of "superabundant population."[71] The 1851 census reported the government's view that when famine and pestilence struck, the resort to emigration was a "natural law," a law that government could only assist in its workings but never oppose. The Great Famine initiated the most massive emigration pattern the country had ever witnessed, and the government, being keen to monitor the process, stationed police officers in all the ports to officially record the level of emigration for the 1851 census.[72] All of these elements of population metering and scoping were bound up in discourses concerning the "health" of the body politic and the imperatives of "medical police" (see chapter 5).

Parts 3 and 5, containing the volumes on death, illness, and disease in the 1851 census, are truly unique. Once again, it is difficult to convey their detail other than through plain description. Part 3 is titled *Report on the Status of Disease*, and part 5 is called *Table of Deaths*, which together contain an "amount of statistical medical knowledge" that the editors of the

primary Irish journal of medical science believed had "no parallel" anywhere in the world.[73] Part 3 was divided into nine sections, with data on the
"deaf and dumb," the blind, the "lunatic and idiotic," the "lame and
decrepit," the sick in workhouses, hospitals, prisons, and asylums, and a
summary of the "total sick in Ireland."[74] This part also contained a rather
overwhelming "nosological chart of diseases," which included synonyms,
popular and local names for diseases, and their Irish-language names where
applicable.[75] The first volume of part 5 contains an unprecedented "history
of epidemic pestilences in Ireland" and a "table of cosmical phenomena,
epizootics, epiphitics, famines, and pestilences." Compiled by William Wilde
(Oscar Wilde's grandfather), who was the assistant commissioner for the
census, it drew on an extensive source base to record the history of disease,
weather, and famine from the earliest records up to 1851. Wilde also drew
on the services of the "eminent Irish scholars" John Donovan, who was
employed by the Ordnance Survey to translate place-names into English,
and Eugene Curry, whose extensive knowledge of premodern Irish manuscripts ensured that the account was as thorough a history of disease and
death in Ireland as was humanly possible to construct at that time.[76] Petty's
plan for a "history of death" was finally graphed.

The second volume of part 5 is a minutely detailed report on death and disease in hospitals and "sanitary institutions" since the previous census. It contains separate reports for every general hospital, infirmary, fever hospital,
special hospital (such as the maternity, psychiatric, venereal, etc.), and lunatic
asylums, as well as workhouses, auxiliary workhouses, and workhouse hospitals, prisons and prison hospitals, and "charitable" institutions (see chapter 5).
Abstracts on deaths where inquests were held, as well as abstracts on sudden
and violent deaths where inquests were not held, are included in the volume.
County and national tables of death are provided, as well as provincial and
general textual summaries. Tables are included on deaths, arranged by localities and causes, by diseases, sexes, and ages, by diseases, years, and seasons, and
by years, seasons, and ages. In terms of nosography and necrological analysis
in Ireland, nothing before had ever come close to the 1851 census.

It was not just death and disease, however, that was put under such an
exacting scope. The report on ages and education was radically more penetrating than what had previously been achieved. This report is mostly composed of tables but also includes an explanatory text at the beginning and
four maps showing population, education, accommodation, and livestock
distributions. The tables document the number and location of all schools
and the number of pupils in attendance. Data is presented on the number,
ages, and percentage of those (adults and children) who could read and

write, read only, or could neither read nor write, in both 1841 and 1851. Particularly interesting is the census's collection of information for the first time on the number and distribution of persons who spoke the Irish language. This collection was mandated not by the legislation but by the viceroy, who was given wide powers to extend the inquiries as he thought advantageous. The viceroy also mandated the collection of information on the names of people who were absent from the residence at the time of the census and their relation to the head of household.

The general report of the commissioners, part 6, reviewed the data and explained the manner through which it was collected, the difficulties encountered, and the measures taken to overcome those difficulties. Some very interesting observations and interpretations were presented, particularly concerning the state of the army, emigration, and the impact of the Great Famine on the population of the country according to a range of variables, from the decline in population per square mile to the effect at the provincial and county levels.[77] Interestingly, the commissioners represented the impact of the famine as greater than some contemporary historians do, since they calculated what the expected "natural increase" might have been without the effects of death and emigration. Although the population levels in 1841 and 1851 were 8.175 million and 6.552 million, respectively, representing a decline of 1.622 million (or about 20 percent), the commissioners calculated that by "natural increase" the population in 1851 would have reached just over 9 million had it not been for the famine. Thus, they concluded that a more accurate account of population loss could be "computed at the enormous amount of 2,466,414 persons."[78] The 1851 census represents the high point in the development of the engines of political arithmetic in Ireland. Not even the censuses of 1861, 1871, and 1881 come close in terms of the sheer volume of information collected or in the level of interpretation of that data. The censuses, however, were just one technology for metering and scoping land, people, and the built environment. Equally important were the efforts at cartography that began with Petty's Down Survey and culminated with the Ordnance Survey.

CARTOGRAPHY AS A PRACTICE OF SCOPING AND GRAPHING NATURAL AND POLITICAL BODIES

Most "surveys" in the seventeenth century were merely lists, though this had already begun to change with the construction of cartographic surveys. The "Gross" and "Civil" surveys were of the list type, the latter being composed by a commission created by an act in 1653 for the purpose of itemizing lands seized after the Cromwellian conquest. The Civil Survey was so called because it provided a "testified record of the facts concerning the possessions of the subjects . . . declared to on oath before courts appointed to ascertain such facts."[79] The survey contained information on "plantation acres," profitable and nonprofitable land, monetary value, whether the lands were arable or more suitable to pasture, as well as the names of the landlords and whether they were "Irish papists." It did not, however, situate the holdings precisely in relation to civil and natural boundaries. Worsley, as surveyor general and chief engineer of Ireland, sought to do this, though Petty thought his methods were very imprecise, and he thus termed this part of the survey gross in the literal sense that it provided only the gross surroundings of the lands in question.

The importance of these surveys to the practice of government is illustrated by the high status of the office of surveyor general, a position often held by military engineers, and by the oaths expected of those who held the office.[80] Molyneux and Petty both vigorously pursued the office of surveyor general and chief engineer in Ireland. Petty was unsuccessful, but Molyneux secured a share in the "patent" by paying the holder, William Robinson, 250 pounds.[81] As well as surveying, the job involved the maintenance of all government buildings in the country, particularly Dublin Castle, though Molyneux seems to have been primarily interested in using the position to further his plan of providing an Irish section for Moses Pitt's planned *English Atlas*. Molyneux put together an interrogatory with queries on the nature of the soil in different locations, agricultural uses, the plants, animals, natural resources, topography, waterways, and a range of cultural and political issues concerning customs, manners, and the government of towns.[82] Though covering many of the issues addressed by Boate, his plan was more ambitious, since it sought to incorporate the data into a geometric survey that included lines of longitude and latitude. However, as Molyneux became involved in more explicitly political activities, such as his publication arguing that Ireland was a kingdom independent of the English parliament, the atlas received less attention and, like so many lofty designs of the seventeenth century, never came to anything.[83]

PETTY'S CARTOGRAPHIC SURVEY

It was in the context of the inadequacy of list surveys that Petty proposed a "geometric" survey that involved dividing the land into parallelograms and scaling through protractions. It came to be known as the Down Survey because of Petty's constant use of the phrase "surveyed down onto maps." This was not, however, the first time that such a survey was conducted in Ireland. The Strafford Survey, for instance, though limited to County Tipperary, was also plotted onto maps, though Petty examined it and after many "experiments" concluded that it "did not yield much advantage."[84] The coordination between the cartographic information in the Down Survey and the legal titles through which the land was distributed to individual conquerors and colonizers was made in the form of the *Books of Survey and Distribution*.[85] A complete set of the books of survey belonged to the auditor general, and they became useful to government for one of the very reasons that Petty's general registry was defeated, that is, the more effective collection of taxes.[86]

The scope of Petty's cartographic plan was truly exceptional, and its feasibility was initially questioned. Worsley, who at the time was surveyor general and was using the Civil Survey based on the gross surrounds of estates, claimed that Petty's scheme would take close to twenty years to accomplish. Petty in return offered to conduct the survey under contract in the space of thirteen months for an "extraordinary fee." The army agreed to pay whatever additional sum was required over and above what had been allocated by the Council of State, and the project began. He completed the survey at least a month ahead of time, primarily by adopting a system of employment and division of labor generally credited to Adam Smith. In his account of the "most material passages relatinge to the Survey," he criticized the pretentiousness of surveyors, noting how they were commonly persons of "gentile and liberall education" who represented their work as a "mistery and intricate matter, farr exceedinge the most parte of mechanical trades."[87] He also commented on how the making of surveyor's instruments was considered a matter of "much art and nicety, if performed with that truth and beauty as is usuall and requisite."[88] With little respect for such pretensions, Petty explained how he instead "thought of dividinge both the art of makeinge instruments, as alsoe that of using them into many parts."[89] He contracted a wireworker to make only the measuring chains, a watchmaker to make the "magnetic needles, with theire pins," a turner to make the boxes that would hold the instruments and the "heads of the stands," a pipe maker to provide the legs of the stands, a founder to do all the brass work, and an especially "versatile head and hand" to set the needles, adjust the sights and cards, and fit "every piece to each other." Tools requiring exacting precision, such as timescales, protractors, and compass cards, were prepared by the "ablest artists of London."

He designed a "perfect forme of a ffeeild book," according to which all the surveyors' books were manufactured. Special large (five or six feet square) sheets of paper were designed to minimize shrinkage. Each sheet was scaled to contain ten acres, with forty Irish perches to the inch. Smaller sheets were lined out into single acres. Books were also prepared for the surveyors that listed all the names of the lands to be measured, along with their old proprietors. "Guesse-plotts" were made of natural, civil, and estate bounds, "whereby not onely to direct the measurers where to beginne, and how to proceed, &c., but alsoe to enable Petty himself how to apportion unto each measurer such scope of land to worke upon, as hee might be able to finish within any assigned tyme."[90] Uniform colored pencils, papers, glues, rulers, and boxes completed the inventory of material culture for the job. Finally, Petty ordered small "Ffrench tents," fold-up tables, and other necessities that would enable "the measurers" to do their business without "house or harbour."

Petty sought out the most knowledgeable persons in each barony and parish in order to secure local knowledge of the bounds and meres of each denomination, the location of convenient quarters and harbors, and the number and location of garrisons, the soldiers of which could be called on to guard the surveyors from "rude persons" who it was expected might oppose their scoping activities. For this last reason also, Petty decided to use soldiers to carry out the bulk of the work. Additionally, he expected that soldiers could endure the hardships of bad lodging, diet, and weather and could "leape hedge and ditch" as required. He thus chose from among the ordinary ranks those who had been "bred to trades" and who could read and write sufficiently. The soldiers were specially trained in how to use the instruments in order to take the bearing of a line, handle the measuring chains (especially in the case of rising and falling ground), make various markings on the land with a spade in order to distinguish "breakings and abutments" and to choose the best "stations" from which to conduct observations with certainty and convenience. Finally, they were instructed how to judge the value of lands in accordance with "beare qualities" and the current conventions for distinguishing profitable from unprofitable land. Another "sort of men," with experience in drawing, painting, or any mode of design, were hired and instructed in the "art of protractinge."[91] These were given the duty of drawing a plot of the land measured, at the scale of forty perches to the inch, on the special paper provided. When they plotted the maps of the baronies, it was necessary to reduce them, since the scale could require a sheet of paper ten feet square. Reduction was achieved by the use of "paralelagrames, of which were made greater numbers, greater variety, and in larger dimensions, then perhaps was ever yet seene upon any occasion."[92]

Petty also employed an auditing system, hiring persons knowledgeable of the manner of fraud in surveying, to check and critique the measurers' field books and to "discover any falsification that might be prejudiciall to the service." Protractions were reprotracted, field books were compared, and checks were made to ensure that no grounds were omitted. The auditors also translated the acres measured into linear feet, according to which the measurers were paid. Petty adopted this method in order to remove any temptation for the measurers to return a higher than justified count of profitable land. By these methods Petty laid enough chain across Ireland to circle the globe close to five times, producing the most detailed and accurate map of Ireland ever. (See figure 7.)

Between his innovations and criticisms of other methods, however, Petty made enemies, some accusing him of fraud. Worsley was never reconciled to Petty after he had condemned Worsely's use of "grosse surrounds" in the Civil Survey. And Petty's rejection of the pretensions to the fine art of surveying more generally cast him as an intervening upstart. The most damning charges came from Sir Hierom Sankey, who accused Petty of accepting bribes, of acquiring land through fraudulent survey, and of using "many foul practices" for his advantage.[93] While there probably was, as Petty claimed, a fair degree of jealousy behind such charges, they did raise questions about the reliability of Petty's measurements, accuracy having profound political relevance in this context. The Council of State looked into the charges, and just after the Restoration, in 1662, the Act of Settlement was passed, which not only confirmed Petty in his properties but also declared his survey the authentic document of reference for the purpose of settling land claims. Dissatisfied claimants would not be entertained in their calls for new surveys unless they could first demonstrate that Petty's figures were off by more than 10 percent. The legislation effectively put an end to challenges against the veracity of the Down Survey, since it was difficult to establish such errors without making a new survey. The first geometric survey of Ireland had thus survived, and it continued to be used in certain counties well into the nineteenth century.[94]

The Down Survey marks a new chapter in the relations between science and government in Ireland. Never before had the country been made so visible in terms of its geography, topography, and its civil and natural boundaries. Though Petty rejected triangulation as being too open to error and not easily subject to check, his standardized methods and materials,[95] his actual perambulation and use of chain measure, and his method of protraction for plotting

FIGURE 7. Petty's cartographic survey of Ireland, the "Down Survey" (c. 1659). Ordnance Survey Ireland Permit No. MP 004805 © Ordnance Survey Ireland and Government of Ireland.

the scaled maps proved effective for distribution of forfeited land. By plotting both civil *and* natural boundaries, as well as estate or "plantation" boundaries, Petty gave the country a new and sharper political definition. His innovation was to avoid confining the survey to barony boundaries, as was first intended, or to the estate boundaries, as was suggested in 1654. Instead, he surveyed every natural and civil boundary: estates, parishes, townlands, baronies, counties, and provinces; rivers, woods, bogs, mountains, rock, and lakes. In relation to the barony division he also made accounts of every intelligence of interest to a planter: the location and condition of ports and the shipping they could accommodate, the location of fortresses, garrisons, and other defenses, the accessibility of the territory, the navigability of rivers, the nature of the soil and its suitability for various crops, the condition of overgrowth, the number of houses and castles (and those burned during the war), the value of fisheries, the extent and condition of woods, the quantity of bog, and the safety of areas in relation to rebels. Thick description raised problems when it came to the Irish names of places, and the Act of Explanation, which followed the survey, set in motion the long tradition of translating Ireland into the English language.[96] The act enabled the colonists to rename their respective lands. English names, "instead of those uncouth, unintelligible ones yet upon them," were recommended. Irish names were to be "interpreted" and translated "where they are not, or cannot be abolished."[97]

The main thing missing from Petty's maps was longitude and latitude,[98] and while Molyneux had hoped to remedy the problem as part of the general atlas of Great Britain, the project never materialized. Francis Lamb republished Petty's maps in 1689, adding longitude, and this edition had wide currency.[99] Lamb's maps were used to adorn surveys and descriptions of the textual form, somewhat like the statistical inquiries of the Royal Dublin Society.[100] Little further mapping of Ireland occurred in cartography until the second half of the eighteenth century. General Charles Vallancey, director of military engineers in Ireland and a key member of the Royal Dublin Society, attempted a military survey between 1776 and 1796, but succeeded in mapping only the southern part of the country.[101] Legislation passed between 1774 and 1796 authorized local government to commission local and county maps. These were conducted by civil engineers and eventually supplied updated maps for each of the thirty-two counties.[102] Ireland saw a large road network created in the eighteenth century, the surveying for which involved more new maps.[103] These road maps brought the first attempt at a triangulated cartography in Ireland.[104] And as a prelude to a major project for drainage and reclamation in the early nineteenth century, the "bogs commission" proposed a national cartography tied to a single trigonomical framework. Though the plan proved impracticable, "the bogs survey did more than anything else to change the face of cartography in early-nineteenth century Ireland."[105] Other cartographic projects were pursued by individuals, for instance, Richard Griffith's topographical survey of southern Roscommon, but none of these efforts could compare with the national Ordnance Survey, conducted between 1824 and 1846.

THE ORDNANCE SURVEY OF IRELAND:
AN EXEMPLARY TERRASCOPE AND SOCIOSCOPE

The Ordnance Survey was the first and indeed only (because of partition in 1922) triangulated cartography of the entire island. Like all matters of great import, development toward the survey was full of vicissitude. Bound up in struggles over resources, political ideologies, professional jealousies and competition, and conflicting opinions on how to proceed, the birth of the survey was preceded by a protracted labor. There were issues concerning who would do the work—Irish civil engineers or the Royal Engineers. At one point the navy made a bid for the project, proposing to extend its hydrographic survey to a combined map of land and sea. The design dragged out with issues concerning scale and method and the possible integration of topographical objects with cadastral ones. Eventually, complaints from Irish members of Parliament concerning land valuations and taxation forced the issue. Their agitations for a revaluation of the soil and a more accurate survey of acreage raised questions about the need for a complex triangulation that would require years to scheme, and parliamentary committees investigated the subject in 1815, 1816, 1822, and 1824.[106] The findings of the last committee can be said to have marked the beginning of the survey.

All of the work was conducted by the Royal Engineer Corps based in Pall Mall in London, the viceroy having expressed the opinion that it could not "be executed by Irish engineers and Irish agents of any description. Neither science, nor skill, nor diligence, nor discipline, nor integrity, sufficient for such a work can be found in Ireland."[107] Determining the extent to which this was true would require research beyond the interest of this work, but there may also have been security and intelligence reasons for the British army taking control of the survey. (See figure 8.) Whatever the reasons, apart from the fact that Irish civil surveyors and engineers were not enlisted to conduct the cartography, no counsel or advice was initially sought from anyone in Ireland, whether local government officials, civil engineers, lawyers, scientists, or mapmakers. When the survey got under way, however, recourse to local intelligences became necessary.[108]

The Ordnance Survey was approved by the parliamentary committee in June 1824 and budgeted at three hundred thousand pounds.[109] The country was to be surveyed on a scale of six inches to the English mile and then reduced and mapped on a scale of one inch to the English mile.[110] The Royal Sappers and Miners carried out the work on the ground under the command of the Royal Engineers, with "county laborers" used for the basic chain work and for hauling equipment. The survey included an enormous

FIGURE 8. British soldiers engaged in the Ordnance Survey. Ordnance Survey Ireland Permit No. MP 004805 © Ordnance Survey Ireland and Government of Ireland.

amount of "filling in" detail on topography, boundaries, roads, rivers, buildings, and so forth, and was designed to allow for an integrated and comprehensive geological survey:

> A great variety of materials towards the formation of statistical and other reports will be collected whilst the work is in progress. The roads and the nature of the materials of which they are composed will be noted, as well as the bridges, fords, ferries and other circumstances which relate to that species of internal communication. The rivers, canals, aqueducts, wharfs, harbours, shipping places and other conveniences for the transport of goods will also be noted in the remark books. These books will also contain a great deal of information respecting the means of conveyance, state of agriculture and manufacture, and in short of almost everything that relates to the resources of the country. The general disposition of the minerals of the country is so important that I have thought it right to direct a very particular attention to this subject. The outline plans of Ireland are the best bases ever given in any country for a geological and mineral survey and the ordnance will, I hope, be able ultimately to accompany their map of Ireland with the most minute and accurate geological survey ever published.[111]

The geological survey was eventually executed, largely under the direction of Richard Griffith, who was also employed on the Ordnance Survey, the boundary survey, and road and bridge building for the Office of Public Works. A "great deal of information" was indeed collected, and the sight of the British army tramping across the countryside with their cartographic engines, marking the land with posts and building triangulation stations, raised suspicions among the people. Indeed, reports survive of posts being torn up and even of attacks on the surveyors.[112] The Ordnance Survey shows that cartography, engineering, and the military went hand in hand in modern state formation.[113] Maps were *ordnance*, objects of military engineering. Petty argued that before one could even begin to know and thereby govern a state, it was necessary first to acquire a map. By the middle of the nineteenth century a complete map of Ireland was finally in the hands of government.[114] But this was not just any map. The map produced by the Ordnance Survey of Ireland was perhaps the most comprehensive and accurate map of the time. The accuracy was achieved using experimental and innovative technologies, and its scope was truly remarkable, embracing almost all aspects of land and people, from natural history to "social economy."

ANATOMY OF THE ORDNANCE SURVEY

Figure 9 captures the basic anatomy of the Ordnance Survey. It was of course a cartography, but it was more than that. It was also an integrating technology, an antiquarian, natural, and social survey, and an engine of translation. The cartography began with the baseline measurement, which was the most accurate baseline measurement ever taken. The accuracy of this key preliminary measurement was achieved by the invention of a compensation engine, known commonly as Colby's Bars, so named after the officer who invented it and who also commanded the survey. Colby's design involved a system of bars made from different metals that were known to expand and contract at different rates at the same temperature. With this mundane science in hand, the bars were marked in order to measure the effects of the temperature on the measurement technology. Colby engineered six microscopes into the instrument so that minute compensations could be made. These minute degrees of accuracy were operative in a baseline measurement of about eight miles. With the baseline measure and through the targeting of innovative limelights with state-of-the-art large-scale theodolites (at the center of which were both telescopes and geometers), huge triangles were projected across Lough Foyle from Derry to Donegal (see figure 1). So began the principal triangulation of Ireland, in

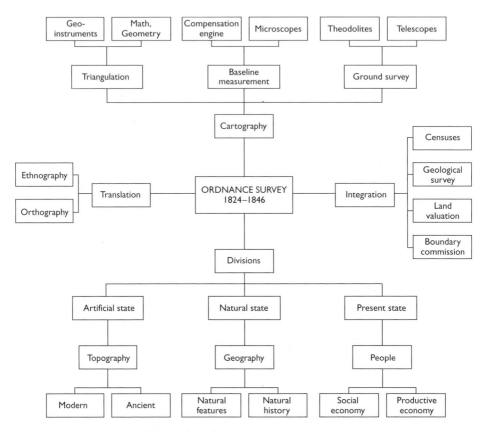

FIGURE 9. Anatomy of the Irish Ordnance Survey.

the course of which, across two decades, some forty thousand miles of tri-
angle would be protracted. (See figure 10.) The triangulated area calculations, performed by an able staff of "computers," became the standard
against which the accuracy of the ground survey was judged.

The importance of the Ordnance Survey as an integrating technology
can hardly be overstated. The census, the land valuation, the boundary
commission, and the geological survey were integrated together through
this extraordinary scope.[115] Governance was grafted to the fibers of the body
politic in precisely the manner that Petty had envisioned. Thus, state and science were co-constructed at the micro- and macrolevels at the same time.
The extent of this co-construction is further revealed in what the engineers
called the "divisions" between the "artificial state, natural state, and present
state," also defined as "topography, geography, and people." The artificial
state was topographically rendered in terms of all "ancient and modern"

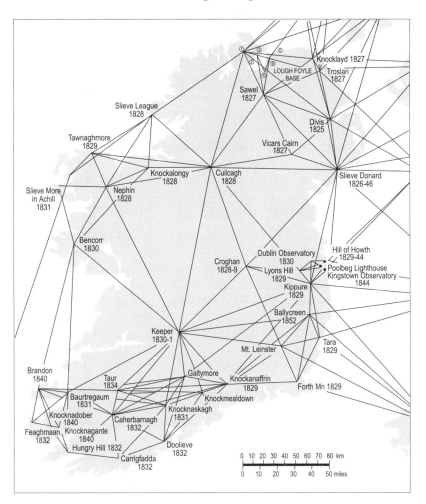

FIGURE 10. The principal triangulation. Ordnance Survey Ireland Permit No. MP 004805 © Ordnance Survey Ireland and Government of Ireland.

transformations of the landscape. The natural state was scoped according to natural features and natural history. And the "present state" was sensed according to both its "productive [political] economy" and its "social [moral] economy." Whole books could be written on any of these aspects of the Ordnance Survey, but it is only by considering them together that one gets a view of the entire design and how it related to the engineering of the data state.

Translation was not a word used by the engine scientists, but it was an important part of the scheme. The practice of translating Ireland into

English began with Petty's survey and was continued in the nineteenth century, when Griffith regularly abolished divisions and incorporated them into new townlands, renaming them in the process. He depended on the police lists for pronunciation and spelling, though sometimes the old names were kept relatively intact so that some referential continuity could be maintained with older surveys. During the Ordnance Survey and under the direction of Thomas Larcom, a qualified linguist was sent into the field to assess the local pronunciations and spellings, and later a new department of the survey was created, "which proceeded to extract a vast number of place-names from the inquisitions, the Down Survey, the books of survey and distribution, and other Irish historical documents and to enter them in the name-books alongside the modern authorities."[116] New "toponymic" field workers and lexicographers were hired: "Ceathramh" became "Carrow," "Baile" became "Bally," "Tyr" became "Tir," and so on. Brian Friel's play *Translations* dramatically captures the ambivalence of the Irish lexicographers who acted as consultants during the anglicization.[117] The translation was based on phonetics, however, so a whole new range of English words was created, some of which made little sense except in terms of pronunciation: for instance, Baile Diarmuid, which translated means Dermot's Town (or home), was rendered instead as Ballyfermot. For this reason the translation sometimes amounted to an erasure of the Irish place-names.

Surveys and censuses were, to use Hartlib's terms, engines for viewing "the frame of a whole state," and whatever the truth of Petty's view of Ireland as a blank page in the late seventeenth century, by the late nineteenth the country had been squared, triangulated, and written over. The integration of these technologies with the engines of police, though particularly evident in the case of colonial Ireland, was not unique. The general parameters, indeed, are as European as anything is. But it was never simply a question of viewing Ireland, of knowing Ireland. On the contrary, it was always a question of working the country over, of engineering Ireland. Meter, graph, and scope engines were the indispensable technologies of this project, and their role as such is what gave the modern state its character as a data state. It was through the use of these engines of statecraft that land and people were transformed into techno-territory and population. But the transformation of a people into a *bio-population* required the employment of what Petty called "political medicine." Chapter 5 discusses how political medicine became public health and how the achievement of public health rested on the practices of medical police.

5 Bio-population

*The Science of Policing Natural
and Political Bodies*

In one of our private conversations, the great savant had seen fit to
tell me of Mr. Oliphant's daring proposal—to employ the Engines
of the police in the scientific exploration of previously hidden
patterns. . . . And surely it was God's will, that the computational
powers of the Engine be brought to bear upon the great commonality,
upon the flows of traffic, of commerce, the tidal actions of crowds—
upon the infinitely divisible texture of His work.
WILLIAM GIBSON and BRUCE STERLING, The Difference Engine

The Medical Council [England] . . . express their satisfaction at
science having at length been recognized by the State as the ally of
civil jurisprudence, and as the guide to a more enlightened code of
Medical Police.
Report of the Medical Council (1855)

Life is confessedly the great object of *police*.
JONAS HANWAY, The Defects of Police, the Cause of Immorality

The population of a modern state, as I suggested in chapter 4, is engineered
through the design and employment of sociometers and socioscopes. The
construction of bio-population, however, requires more than measuring,
sensing, classifying, and defining. The construction of bio-population is
realized through a science that augments life and arrests disease. Petty conceived of this science as "political medicine," and as I seek to show in this
chapter, this and a host of other names were proposed to describe what
eventually became known as public health and safety. One of the most
descriptive names employed during the rise of modern public health, however, was *medical police*. For analytic purposes, this is the name I adopt
from among all those coined. It highlights the fact that health and safety
were secured through policing practices and that these practices were part
of engineering culture and its designs for a life-enhancing political power.
Medical police, in addition, was inextricably bound to the rise of the data
state and the development of socioscopes.

LIFE SECURITY AND THE OBJECTS OF MEDICAL POLICE

There emerged in Europe, from the seventeenth century at least, a discourse of police, variously philosophical and scientific, the center of gravity of which was the exercise of government powers of investigation, regulation, and prosecution in the service of "security." The idea exhibited a remarkable resilience over time and across Europe, despite differences in the way it was practiced in the context of varying discourses of political liberty and the appropriate limits of government power. The role of police in the realization of public health, particularly with respect to the differential targeting of groups or classes, was bound up in struggles over individual liberty and social justice. This is because police involved practices of inspection and surveillance, information and intelligence gathering, and direct intervention (to the point of deadly force) in private, familial, and commercial matters. Medical police did not normally include the deployment of deadly force, but it was nonetheless configured within the general discourse of police. From the beginning of the police idea, state security was tied to "health and safety" through the concern to secure the population.

There are at least seven objects of medical police practice as it developed from the seventeenth to the nineteenth century: (1) the police of the "community," often singling out women and workers for special attention (and prostitutes and the poor even more so); (2) the police of "nuisances," a broad term nonetheless focused on conditions and activities believed to compromise the health and safety of the "public," expressed in the nineteenth century in the language of "sanitary reform," and thereby united with the police of the community; (3) the police of the physical environment, practiced through the science of "sanitary engineering" and united via sanitarianism with the police of the community and nuisances; (4) the police of that which is ingested by bodies, especially in terms of the adulteration and wholesomeness of food, drugs, and water; (5) the police of dangerous materials (e.g., explosives and poisons) and activities directly impacting safety, such as in traffic and at construction sites; (6) the police of occupational hazards; and (7) the police of medical practitioners and suppliers, such as doctors, apothecaries, and "quacks" (and in the eighteenth century, witches). Because these practices were codified in law, medical police overlapped with "medical jurisprudence" and connected with "forensics," "police chemistry,"[1] and the employment of expert witnesses in court. Finally, medical police was designedly a "science" of physical life, though one regularly expressed in a discourse of moral imperative. In this sense medical police was a genuine hybrid of natural and social science. It was a crucial cultural configuration of discourses, practices, and materialities through which science and the state were co-constructed. The development of medical police was, however, a long and politically charged process, one spanning more than two centuries.

POPULATION, POLITICAL MEDICINE, AND METEOROLOGY

Petty argued in the 1670s that the health of the people was crucial to the power and security of the state, an idea that became axiomatic to mercantilism and cameralism. According to Petty, it was "not the Interest of the State to leave Phisitians and Patients (as now) to their own shifts."[2] Direct government regulation of medical practice would not occur, however, until the nineteenth century. In the seventeenth century such power was granted instead to professional organizations. Following established practice in England, Petty involved himself in the establishment of the Dublin College of Physicians, which he described as the "instrument, under God, of reforming the practice of physick in that kingdom."[3] The organization began as the Fraternity of Physicians at the Dublin University (Trinity College) and reorganized in 1667 with a charter from Charles II. The charter endowed the college with police powers similar to its London equivalent, such that no person could practice medicine in or within seven miles of Dublin without the sanction of the college. Reorganized with another new charter in 1692 and titled the King and Queen's College of Physicians in Ireland, the organization's regulative powers were extended further. Practice in the city was restricted to its fellows and licentiates, who were also permitted to practice throughout the country (a privilege also granted to graduates of Oxford and Cambridge). No other person was permitted to practice medicine in Ireland. The college was eventually entrusted with the regulation and supervision of apothecaries, druggists, and midwives, and was given extensive police power to forcibly enter houses where it was suspected that adulterated drugs were present and to confiscate such drugs. In the course of its investigations, the college could examine witnesses under oath and fine and imprison offenders.[4]

Policing medical practice, however, was just one element in Petty's vision of political medicine, which aimed more broadly at removing the causes of disease and premature mortality. In this respect his *Natural and Political Observations on the Bills of Mortality* was as important to the elaboration of political medicine and public health as it was to the development of political arithmetic. It was not only a key early text in the development of statistics; it was also a key text on "vital statistics" and particularly on the enduring medical police question of the relationship between health and the weather. The observations concerned the "Air, Seasons, Fruitfulness, Health, Diseases, Longevity, and the proportions between the Sex and Ages of Mankind."[5] The subject matter was similar to that in Bacon's "Discourses of Life and Death" and was situated by Petty in the field of "natural history."[6]

In this context, representatives of the new science in Ireland sought to employ meters such as thermometers and barometers to record weather conditions in a systematic manner for the first time in the history of the country. Indeed, it was at Locke's prompting that Dr. Charles Willoughby and Dr. Patrick Dun of the Dublin College of Physicians began regularly recording the weather.[7] Thomas Sydenham, Boyle, and Wren all emphasized the importance of metering the weather, Wren engineering a self-registering thermometer, a recording weather clock, and a method of estimating atmospheric moisture so that more standardized records could be constructed.[8] Boyle never lost his interest in meteorology, incorporating relevant observations in his history of cold and writing on the uses of the barometer for inquiries into the relations between atmospheric conditions and health.[9] The same was true of Locke, who kept occasional registers of weather in Oxford and communicated with Paris and Dublin in order to craft comparisons. His register for 1692 was published in the *Philosophical Transactions*, along with an account of his method and the engines he employed.[10]

Dun and Willoughby, both founding members of the Dublin Society, communicated with Locke and Sydenham and were important adherents of medical police in Ireland in the late seventeenth century. Willoughby, in 1691, followed the method of Petty and compared the mortality rates of Dublin from one year to the next over seven years. In addition to his duties as registrar of the college, he crafted his own bills (the raw data being collected at least as early as 1658). But Petty's *Observations upon the Dublin Bills*, published in 1683, were the first to make it into print. In this work, Petty corrected what he believed to be serious deficiencies in the manner in which data was collected, reducing the classification of the causes of death to twenty-four, "being such as may be discovered by commonsense and without Art, conceiving that more will perplex and imbroil the account."[11]

In response to Locke's requests for observations on mortality from a number of European cities, Willoughby provided a detailed account for Ireland, with sections on the extent of small pox, fever, flu, consumption, and convulsions. General mortality was compared for those over and under sixteen years of age; Willoughby also compared burials and christenings and the rate of male versus female mortality. An account of the air and climate was provided, along with observations on agricultural and horticultural production. Information was also provided on building and "improvements" generally, particularly the drainage of bogs, which were viewed as concentrated sources of ill health.

FROM METEOROLOGY TO ENVIRONMENTAL MEDICINE

The "Disposition of the Air" was identified by Petty and others as particularly important for the spread of disease. Shifts in the number of deaths from the plague, from 118 to 927 in a single week, then dropping to 258 and rising again the following week to 852, "must surely be rather attributed to change of the Air, than of the Constitution of Mens Bodies."[12] In this context also the conditions of cities were identified with a unhealthy atmosphere, "the Smoaks, Stinks, and close Air" making urban life less healthful than that of the country. The regulation of the causes of unhealthy urban pollutions remained central to medical police practice and its concern with the quality of air. The miasma theory of disease generation and propagation allowed a special connection to be made between the bogs of Ireland and the state of health. Thus Willoughby reported on the decline in mortality from flu, which he put down to "an amending of the air since the drayning of so many bogs since English Planters and their husbandry came among us."[13]

Willoughby viewed drainage as the necessary preliminary step toward a more complete cultivation of Ireland. He argued that the reclamation of bogs would greatly augment crown lands, on which it would be possible to "maintain a numerous Army out of which greate bodys may be drawn as often as occasion shall require. . . . Ireland will thus be made a nursery of Soldiers for the use of England."[14] Hospitals and workhouses, he proposed, should be built as the "next thing after the improvement of the land." The connections drawn between colonial interests and material culture in Willoughby's survey of political medicine illustrate how deeply embedded power and knowledge were becoming. Willoughby's report on the bills contained more commentary than Petty's, but this can be understood in terms of Petty's fears regarding his natural and political inquiries in the context of the many enemies he made during his meteoric rise in the aristocratic social order. On receiving the report, Locke had it copied into one of his medical commonplace books and a few years later communicated with Dun for further data.[15] Dun, a key figure in the first Dublin Society and president of the College of Physicians, was an especially active advocate of medical police in Ireland in the late seventeenth century, composing a charter for the college, campaigning against "quacks" and "empirics," and writing on adulteration of wine and the political arithmetic of health.

Some important legislation that was passed in the seventeenth and eighteenth centuries set the scene in Ireland for the police of pollutants, trades, adulteration, and traffic. In 1717 a relatively comprehensive health and safety act was passed for Dublin, which among other things prescribed that drivers of carts and wagons walk their horses at the head rather than drive them from behind. The penalty for failure to do so could result in fines, imprisonment, and even a public flogging at the discretion of justices. In 1719 an act was passed to prevent pollution of the River Dodder, which at the time was the main source of water for the city of Dublin. Acts passed during the reign of George III sought to regulate noxious trades, particularly the operation of lime kilns. The act of 11 & 12 Geo. III, went as far as entirely prohibiting the erection of lime kilns within the city. Enforcement of such laws, however, remained a haphazard affair. When major public health legislation was passed for Ireland in 1874, several kilns were located in the most densely populated parts of Dublin. Understanding how a system of modern medical police could emerge from such seemingly ad hoc early measures, however, requires stepping back from practices to consider the coherency of the discourses of medical police across Europe.

CONTINENTAL DISCOURSES OF MEDICAL POLICE

There is little doubt that the great early works in medical police are Continental in origin. Along with the work of Franz Anton Mai, Wolfgang Thomas Rau, and Johann von Justi, Johann Frank's monumental *System of Complete Medical Police* marks the high point of the early literature on government and health. Quoting Joseph von Sonnenfels, one of the earliest police scientists, Frank explained how the "internal security of the State is the aim of the general science of police."[16] Sonnenfels, in *Principles of the Police, Commercial and Financial* (1765), provided the chapter "On the Security of the Person," which dealt with many of the issues subsequently comprehended under medical police.[17] Frank defined medical police, "like all police," as an "art of defense, a model of protection of people and their animal helpers."[18] Like Sonnenfels and Rau, he situated medical police in relation to the wider science of government (or *Polizeiwissenchaft*). Police encompassed government regulation of all entities within the territorial state, including the land, the bodies of the people, trade, factories, morals, entertainments, buildings, roads, and so on. "Life" became the object of police, "the indispensable, the useful, and the superfluous."[19] Thus the *population of a state*, constituted as such through political arithmetic, was located at the heart of a nexus of ideas and practices that defined the "modern art of government, or state rationality: viz., to develop those elements constitutive of individuals' lives in such a way that their development also fosters that of the strength of the state."[20] Frank was a tireless advocate of this new art of government, introducing his opus on medical police through a discussion of the "value of a person and the advantages of the population."[21]

As on the Continent, England's indigenous culture of police in the eighteenth century embraced the health of subjects. Blackstone documented some of the laws against "nusance" and offenses against the "public health" and "public police" that had been elaborated over the previous two centuries.[22] A nuisance was an "annoyance" that "worketh hurt, inconvenience, or damage." He described both public and private nuisances, of which the former were annoyances to all the king's subjects, and the latter, things that caused hurt or damage to an individual's property. Nuisance abatement subsequently became central to medical police practice. As James Black put it in 1844, *nuisance* was a "legal term" that described various sources of "contamination" of the air, water, or environment, whether from chemical processes or manufactures or from any other "annoyance."[23]

The link between charity and police is an important one in English political culture. As Donna Andrews recently put it, eighteenth-century English philanthropists summed up "the social function of charity" under the term *police*.[24] Charity established a link between private benevolent activity and the maintenance of moral and political order.[25] Thus Jonas Hanway explicitly rejected the view that "private actions" stood in opposition to government police, explaining that charity, which sprang from the "impulse of the heart," demanded "regulations as will encourage the industrious; chastise the idle; instruct the ignorant; and punish the profligate." While he insisted that government must rest on the "foundation of religion," he nonetheless argued that "national security and happiness" could be realized only by "the detail of government, or call it *police*."[26] Many philanthropists, like Hanway, promoted the "coercive power" of police as an instrument of charity.[27]

POLICE AS AN ENGLISH DESIGN IN SOCIAL ENGINEERING

As with engine science, it is important to realize that police, and more specifically medical police, was indigenous to England, even if its early experimental deployment occurred in political laboratories such as Ireland.

Using the language of "national security," Hanway practically equated government with police, expressing exactly the meaning the term held on the Continent. Despite mobilizing all the English tropes that set the country in opposition to the Continent, such as liberty, fairness, charity, philanthropy, and private action, Hanway was unambiguous in his view that "without *energy* in government *to enforce*, no well-digested *police* can be established; and that it will never be obtained, unless it is *paid for*."[28] The scope of Hanway's design for police is as wide as any found on the Continent, covering all manner of institutions, the living conditions of the poor, the material structure of cities, education, cleanliness and health, the economy, and the virtues of industriousness and morality. "*Life*" itself, he proclaimed in concert with the greatest police theorists of Continental Europe, is "confessedly the great object of *police*."[29]

That such a cogent conceptualization of police and its relation to health could be articulated in eighteenth-century England is not surprising given that the idea of investigation, regulation, and prosecution in the interests of health was conceived in that country as early as the seventeenth century.[30] The Stuart government, for instance, developed schemes to "preserve the health of the body politic" in the early seventeenth century, particularly the regulation of the practice of medicine in London, the use of royal charters to create hierarchies among the competing medical corporations and societies, and the institution of new plans for securing public health and hygiene. As Harold Cook points out, such actions challenge the "unexamined consensus that the idea of medical police did not exist in England until the later eighteenth century, and that the ideas could not be acted upon until the later nineteenth century."[31] Of course, the translation of discourse into practice was doubtful, especially in the seventeenth century. Nonetheless, the early English schemes are important, because they complicate the proposition that medical police was essentially un-English. Though a board of health with medical policing powers was not created in seventeenth-century England (the Civil War put an end to the scheme), the Privy Council expressed the logic of such a board in a report in the 1630s. The report concluded that the "prevencion of all which inconveniences and many more which tyme and observacion may discover doth especially yea wholy consist in providing a sufficient authoritie both within the libertiyes and without either by waye of Commission or office of health, or other meanes which your Honour shall thincke fitt; to provide officers particularly to look out and discover these misdemeanours, and that they being trulye discovered, ther maye bee in the commission or office of health or other meanes sufficient authoritie and power to punish such as shal be found delinquents."[32] Paul Slack's work on the impact of the plague in Tudor and Stuart England confirms the early development of medical police in England, even if the measures taken were often ad hoc responses to particular crises. Slack shows how, in the second half of the sixteenth century, the Privy Council inched its way toward creating a "large corps of officials" who visited homes with a view to inspection and the enforcement of plague law, particularly in terms of household segregation of the sick.[33] From small and tentative steps initiated by central government, police interventions to prevent the spread of plague "gradually became commonplace and were imposed on the nation."[34] These early moves toward policing the sick involved new interventions into the community as a whole, provoking the kind of controversy that was to become the mark of similar efforts throughout the eighteenth and nineteenth centuries.

The targeting and segregation of the infected initiated a characteristic feature of subsequent medical policing when directed at the community. In the eighteenth century, entire groups were singled out for especially energetic measures, particularly (as is well known) the working classes and the poor. After the poor, perhaps the most consistently targeted group was prostitutes. Indeed, it is remarkable in this respect how concerns about various sexually transmitted diseases were met by similar police strategies, even though those concerns might be expressed in considerably different ideological contexts. Thus, John Fielding, writing in a mid-eighteenth-century discourse of enlightenment rationality and Christian humanitarianism, posited brothels (alongside gaming houses) "to be as material an Object of Police as any whatever."[35] Like Hanway, and indeed John Howard, Fielding articulated a concept of police that linked private benevolence spurred by religious feeling with "rational" government and police design. Police, in this context, was intimately concerned with "prevention," "preservation," and "reformation."[36]

While one of the earliest British uses of the idiom *medical police* occurred in Scotland, it was framed very much in terms of the English discourse of police reform found in Hanway, Fielding, and Howard. Andrew Duncan, professor of medicine at Edinburgh,[37] lectured on medical police throughout the 1790s. He published his *Heads of Lectures on Medical Jurisprudence* as early as 1795 and secured the first British chair of medical police and medical jurisprudence in 1807. In a similar way to Hanway, Duncan argued that patriotism served as the link between private philanthropic action and the need to protect and sustain the community as a national imperative.[38] Duncan was similarly concerned with institutional mechanisms of medical police, such as the construction and management of special hospitals, dispensaries, workhouses, and prisons.[39] While Hanway was more of a policeman than a medical man, and Duncan more of a medical man than a policeman, taken together they illustrate the meeting of the two in eighteenth-century Britain, particularly in terms of the institutional and carceral dimension, which in nineteenth-century Ireland became one of the most elaborate English designs in police.

In the first half of the nineteenth century, the idiom *medical police* looked like it might take greater hold in England, publications appearing with all the scope of their Continental counterparts (though the term itself was already being supplanted by the new German favorite, *state medicine*, and a host of others discussed below). John Roberton's *Medical Police* dealt with the "natural" and "artificial" causes of disease and the types of disease associated with these causes.[40] Under natural causes he covered the soil, climate, and situation (or place); and under artificial, the construction of houses, occupations, "modes of living," and manners. Roberton's book, appearing post-Malthus, is less optimistic regarding the possibility of safely increasing the population, but nonetheless proceeds on the basis of the principle that the "wealth of all nations arises from their quantity of productive labour."[41] In this context he argued for medical police on the grounds that it was the best policy for reducing the proportion of the "inactive population."

Like Frank, Roberton designed a plan of government action on the principle that the "detection and removal of the causes of disease is in reality the true essence of medical police," a definition that just as readily captured the contemporary "essence" of public health.[42] His plan called for the establishment of a "council of health," which would be responsible for appointing "inspectors" who would ensure that the measures for the prevention of disease were adhered to. The inspectors would see to it that soil found to "emit effluvia" be remedied, that "vitiated climate" be purified, and that the size of houses and apartments "be properly regulated," especially in terms of the location of doors, windows, and chimneys, the materials used in construction, and the modes of access for air through lanes, yards, and courts. All occupations where health was likely to be injured were to be "strictly attended to" by the police, and the "modes of living, particularly among the lower orders of society, be in some measure examined, and regulated with that spirit of moderation which would soon put to silence the complaints of those who fell immediately under such scrutiny."[43] According to Roberton, interference with "private property and domestic arrangements" was crucial, and it meant that a plan of medical police could not succeed without the authority of the legislature. Everything for which Chadwick would later become famous was presented by Roberton as medical police, perhaps with the exception of moderation in its execution, an idea not readily associated with the great engineer of health.

Roberton's reference to complaints indicates that the forms of inspection, regulation, information gathering, intervention, and enforcement implied by medical police immediately evoked resistance. But such suspicion was neither unique to England nor specific to the nineteenth century. Frank noted as early as 1783 that "Medical Police is charged with too much curtailment of civic freedom and with aiding legislative despotic power."[44] In relation to the policing of popular entertainments, he was acutely aware of the need for police personnel to be dispatched with good judgment and respect for citizens. The notion that the police officers could "lord it over" the citizens had the result that the public, instead of feeling grateful for the "care" police provided, expressed the "greatest aversion to everything that is called police, and considers as nothing all the good that the police provides against the tyranny of . . . impetuous judgments."[45] Frank compared the "obstinacy of the police superintendent" to stubborn parents who rule their children with an "iron rod." Such a mode of policing, exercised under the "pretense of good order," could only result in the police earning the "hatred of the entire nation."[46]

The development of medical police was thus slower than Roberton, like Frank, would have liked. Indeed, the successful deployment of medical police practice was almost inversely proportional to the extent to which that practice broke free of the idiom *police*. One important consequence of this in England was that rather than police and persuasion becoming opposites, police was packaged in the language of persuasion. Thus Roberton argued that "regulation with . . . [a] spirit of moderation" was the best means of convincing the "lower orders" that it was "not by the iron rod of oppression" that they were to be swayed, but by the "soft and persuasive advices of friendship."[47]

THE POLITICS OF REPRESENTATION AND THE MANY IDIOMS OF MEDICAL POLICING

Because talk of medical police raised the same political fears as police did generally, the first half of the nineteenth century saw a move away from the idiom *medical police* and a proliferation of new labels or the resurrection of older ones. *Sanitary reform* became one of the most prevalent idiomatic nodes in the discourse of health enforcement. While intimately bound to theories about the health of the material environment, and hence the need for "sanitary engineering," the discourse also generated the new idiom *sanitary police* (and even *sanitary sergeants*). Numerous other terms, such as *state medicine, political medicine,* and *public hygiene,* increasingly appeared in the growing literature on science and health. Analysis of the content of these publications demonstrates that they did not constitute a radical break from earlier forms. In 1826, John Gordon Smith published his *Principles of Forensic Medicine,* about a field that had also emerged in the eighteenth century and was sometimes classified as part of medical police. Smith claimed that over two thousand separate works in medical police and almost three thousand in forensic medicine had been published.[48] For Smith, medical police and forensic medicine together constituted "medical jurisprudence," which Michael Ryan defined a decade later as "a science by which medicine and its collateral branches, are rendered subservient to the construction, elucidation, and administration of the laws for the preservation of public health."[49] Ryan suggested that "medical jurisprudence" captured in the "most comprehensive manner, the application of the medical sciences to the purposes of law."[50] Frank had insisted on a strict distinction between forensic medicine and medical police, but the two were grouped together as late as 1879 in, for instance, Aubrey Husband's *Hand-Book of Forensic Medicine and Medical Police.*[51]

Husband separated the two branches within his text, dealing first with forensics and then with medical police, but the connections between them were numerous. Both depended for their practice on officers of police, who went into the field to inspect events or situations with a view to the enforcement of the law. In both branches, samples were collected and analyzed in "police laboratories," and the same methods were used to detect the causes of illness, injury, and death. For instance, in the case of poisoning, both medical police officers and forensic investigators were concerned with identifying and understanding various toxic substances and their indications in (primarily human) bodies, medical police officers in the case of occupational illnesses or death, forensic investigators in the case of deaths in which persons may have been accidentally or deliberately poisoned. Both were concerned with identifying the causes of death and injury of citizens and subjects on behalf of the government, the connection between the two deriving from the earliest sense of general police, the remit of which was to protect the "public safety." As James Black suggested in 1844, the "objects of public hygiene and medical police are not so closely allied and interwoven with those of the medical practitioner as several of those departments of forensic medicine."[52]

Ryan's work on medical jurisprudence began in 1831 with his "analysis of a course of lectures on forensic medicine," expanding in the second edition, in 1836, to encompass "state medicine." Forensic science went through a period of rapid development and differentiation in the nineteenth century. In many respects this gave rise, through its constitution of "poison" as a central epistemic object, to the new science of toxicology, a science that remains a crucial arm of all aspects of the government of life, especially in relation to forensics, environmental protection, occupational safety, the police of human and agricultural contacts with industrial chemicals and biohazards, and of course public health. Ryan's discourse demonstrates the lack of an agreed on demarcation for medical police and highlights the range of terms available through which to designate the practice. According to Ryan, medical police, political medicine, state medicine, public hygiene, "police of health," and medical jurisprudence *together* constituted "the acts of a legislature or government, and magistracy, for the conservation of public health," including (crucially) the regulation of medical practice.[53]

The idiom *state medicine* emerged in the late eighteenth to early nineteenth century in Germany and designated both medical police and forensics. In Britain and Ireland the term became synonymous with medical police, of which forensics might or might not be a subcategory.[54] Frank responded to the new term in the final volume of his work, noting that others had adopted *health police, sanitary police, public health police,* and even *life security police.*[55] He explained that his occasional use of the term *state medicine* was out of "deference" to those who preferred it, and not because it had any particular advantages over *medical police.* Regarding the absence of clarity in the meaning of police more generally, he noted that the jurists still lacked "a philosophical concept of the police which would reduce the variety of it to a common principle," so that its nature could be established and its limits defined.[56]

Ryan explained that "judiciary" or "judicial medicine" related to the presentation of medical evidence in court. "Public hygiene" (or just "hygiene"), on the other hand, was the same as "public medicine."[57] This term became popular toward midcentury and was defined by Ryan as the "laws, morals, and police of the people relating to the preservation of public health."[58] *Political medicine* could also be used interchangeably with *medical police, state medicine,* and *public hygiene,* though at other times it was limited to the theory or philosophy of medical police without reference to the design of administrative agencies.[59] In each case, however, public health was the *objective* of medical police, political medicine, and state medicine, a condition of society to be achieved rather than a practice in and of itself. And like Roberton's, Ryan's account of the objects of medical jurisprudence had the same scope and character as Frank's medical police.[60]

The idiom *public hygiene* emerged in close connection, rather than opposition, to *medical police*. In 1844, James Black published the series of lectures titled "Public Hygiene and Medical Police." For Black, public hygiene was the objective; medical police, the strategy for achieving that objective. Thus Black used the terms *public hygienist* and *medical police director* interchangeably and defined medical police as a practice that investigated what was "injurious to public health," alleviating by "all scientific means, the sum of human misery or unhappiness."[61] A couple of years later William Strange published an article in the *London Medical Gazette* and also a small book, in which he made the case for a comprehensive system of national medical police.[62] Strange argued that almost every position taken by Chadwick in his report on the poor law had been substantiated. He noted that the English Health of Towns Bill, which sought to regulate "all those matters which concern the physical condition of our town population," contained clauses that were "proof" of the legislature's intention to establish "a more or less complete system of medical police."[63] An anonymous article that appeared in 1855 made reference to a recently passed act for "the better Local Management of the Metropolis." The article expressed the view that London had at last its own "system" of medical police through "which the whole of the modern Babylon may be placed under constant scientific sanitary supervision."[64]

Edwin Chadwick is widely remembered for his efforts to sanitize the working classes of England and to use the power of government to force England to be healthy.[65] Remembered less well is Henry Rumsey, whose work on "state medicine" was perhaps the most comprehensive in mid-nineteenth century Britain.[66] His *Essays on State Medicine* (1856) presented a detailed plan for a comprehensive medical police for Britain, organized according to "state investigation," "sanitary regulations," and "administrative machinery." State investigation encompassed all the different types of information necessary for an effective statistical picture of the state of health and for laying out the domains of investigation pertinent to medical policing.[67] Sanitary regulations were distinguished as either preventative, which covered the police of nuisances and all aspects of human environments and activities,[68] or palliative, which included everything related to the provision of health care by doctors and medical institutions, including the regulation of drugs and the appointment of medical officers of state.[69] Administrative machinery dealt on the one hand with

the training of medical police officers and the regulation of medical education generally,[70] and on the other with the organization and police powers
of medical councils and boards of health.[71]

Rumsey's plan of state medicine was quite innovative in its details and
was crafted to fit the specific political demands of the English context. In
key conceptual ways, however, Rumsey's scheme for a system of state medicine was largely homologous—in terms of objects, mechanisms, techniques, purpose, and rationale—with Frank's plan of medical police, and he
used the terms *state medicine* and *medical police*, as well as *public medicine*, interchangeably. Public health was still treated as the goal of medical
police and state medicine rather than as a practice. Rumsey was, however,
acutely aware of English resistance to medical police and went to some
pains to reassure those who cried foul in the name of English liberty at the
first sight of the word *police*. Apart, however, from the specificity of the way
dissent in England was framed within a discourse of the "rights of free-born
Englishmen," the concern about liberty and the proper limits of state power
was not itself unique to England. In any case, I contend that of all the names,
from *political medicine* to *public health, medical police* best captures the
actual practices with which such discourses correlated.

THE DISCOURSE ON MEDICAL POLICE IN IRELAND

In Ireland, a number of works were published dealing with plague and epidemic diseases, and their concern was primarily with preventative measures and control once an epidemic had broken out.[72] Joseph Rogers argued
in 1734 that "fevers" (a broad category in the eighteenth century) resulted
primarily from environmental "poisons," pointing the finger primarily at
badly kept slaughterhouses.[73] The establishment of the new hospitals created microcosms for studying environmental health, and Edward Foster's
Essay on Hospitals, published in 1768, just three years after the Infirmaries
Act, was considered a century later to be a significant contribution to sanitary science.[74]

A small work, "Medical Jurisprudence," was published anonymously by
William Dease circa the 1790s, but it was restricted to the dimension of
medical police that later became forensic medicine, and even in this context
was restricted to the methods for ascertaining causes of injury.[75] A pamphlet on the regulation of the medical profession appeared in 1795.[76] I have
not, however, been able to locate work published in Ireland in the eighteenth century that dealt explicitly with sanitation, though publications

did appear on naval hygiene (an important area for the development of ideas on hygiene generally).[77] These eighteenth-century works could not be said to constitute a coherent body of knowledge, however, and it is difficult to gauge what connection they had to the development of medical police in the nineteenth century, even though some, such as Foster's work, were widely read.

Perhaps the best-remembered author on the environmental aspects of disease in eighteenth-century Ireland was Thomas Rutty. Born in England in 1697 and settled in Dublin in 1724, Rutty was a prolific writer on chemistry, natural history, meteorology, and medicine. He wrote a number of works on the chemical analysis of water, a subject of widespread interest in the eighteenth century.[78] Rutty also published on the natural history of Dublin and on the analysis of milk, though his fame rests most heavily on his *Chronological History of the Weather and Seasons, and of the Prevailing Diseases in Dublin*, published in 1770.[79] In this work Rutty provided forty years of observations and data concerning the relations between weather and disease.[80] The environmental focus necessarily drew attention to the condition of the poor, and all the more so in Ireland because poverty was more extensive there than in England. Rutty made the connection between Irish poverty and disease in the 1770s, and those calling for "social and material improvement" in the nineteenth century regularly cited him and Petty. Thomas Willis, for instance, cited Rutty's claim that "those who know the situation of the poor here can be at no great loss to account for the frequency and the [high] mortality."[81]

Dr. Henry Maunsell, in perhaps the first publication in Ireland under the title of "Political Medicine" (a title he adopted "in default of a better and more precise" one), attacked the medical profession for being concerned only with the treatment of individuals and the "mere cure" of diseases, and for ignoring the "higher object of protecting the public health, and providing for the physical well being of the human race."[82] Maunsell's discourse, which was presented to the Royal College of Surgeons in 1839, marks the beginning of a coherent body of knowledge relating to medical police in Ireland, and was followed two years later by the appointment in the college of the first Irish chair devoted to political medicine.[83] Maunsell's paper was relatively limited in terms of depth, and he acknowledged that to go into the subject at length would "be to write a system of Medical Police." Nonetheless, he briefly addressed eight areas that were important to political medicine: vaccination, the health of seamen, the health of prisoners (which he extended to a more general discussion of epidemic and endemic diseases), quarantine, "unwholesome trades," the treatment of lunatics, the care of the population in sickness, and the sufferings of emigrants in emigrant ships and in new settlements.

Maunsell's essay was published simultaneously by two presses in Dublin and was apparently an important vehicle for putting issues of political medicine, and the direction it was taking in Ireland under the poor law system, before a more general audience. It was reviewed in the *Dublin University Magazine*, where the same argument was made that if "the merest elements of state medicine were understood in this country, it would be utterly impossible to have proposed a scheme [poor law] thus ruinously destructive to the health and lives of those whose only crime is their poverty."[84] Indeed the review fully supported every point made by Maunsell, making the case, more elegantly than even he, that there was "a real and most important connection between medical science and the political well-being of every civilized people," the study of which, it was noted, was more generally known as "state medicine."[85] Political medicine was, the review argued, "the sanatary [sic] guardian of the masses" and of civilization itself. And like Maunsell, the reviewers were unambiguous in apportioning blame for the failures of political medicine, which they asserted was "wholly chargeable on the medical profession itself."[86]

Thomas Willis argued that hospitals could contain disease only once it had already broken out and that the "existence of these institutions prevents the attention which should otherwise necessarily be paid to the comforts, and particularly the state of the dwellings of the poor."[87] Attention to dwellings did not mean simply better housing construction, though that was important, but involved a more general police of living conditions. Willis's solution was a legislative enactment "under which officers of health, or something of a medical police, could be formed."[88] The officers of health were to have the power of enforcing sanitary regulations "under a penalty recoverable in the most summary manner."[89] Residents were to be prevented from keeping animals in their houses, particularly pigs, asses, and poultry. The Irish peasants' tradition of allowing animals to be kept in houses had long been complained of by the Anglo-Irish and regularly served as a point of reference for tirades about Irish degeneracy. It was never acknowledged, however, that such animals (particularly swine) were often the single most important assets possessed by the poor and, as such, a major source of cash, for which they had no other protective accommodations. Willis, claiming that Dublin was subject to epidemic diseases more continually than any other major European city, attributed this ultimately, "to circumstances unhappily deeply laid in the frame of society, and arising from manners and habits generated by ages of civil and moral degradation, which has checked the natural progress of civilization, exhibiting a population increasing, but not improving."[90]

Blaming the manners and habits of the poor for their degraded material condition was not unique to Ireland, yet the poverty of Ireland being greater, the bad habits of the poor were seen as deeper and, in some of the more racist commentary, constitutional to the Irish nature. Thus greater levels of police were easily justified. Yet the advocates of medical police were not entirely partisan, and they were keen to coerce the business and commercial classes into cleaning up their acts. Thus, Willis argued that the officers of health should have the "power to compel owners of all houses" that were rented to thoroughly lime-wash the houses every six months, provide privies connected to sewers, provide dustbins (i.e., trash cans), pave the yards, supply the houses with water, and have the cellars paved, flagged, or bricked. Room keepers with dogs "should be subject to some small police tax." And public authorities, he suggested, should be compelled to provide public urinals, which he thought would best be located in the "immediate neighbourhood of each police station."[91]

An important figure in the development of a body of knowledge relative to medical policing in Ireland was William Stokes. Stokes, though most famed for his use of clinical education in the Meath Hospital, his pamphlet on the use of stethoscope (which was the first to be published in the English language),[92] and his work on diseases of the chest and heart,[93] was also an energetic activist who argued that modern civilization was dependent on a strong relationship between medicine and government. He was an advocate for the creation of the British General Medical Council, on which he served as the crown representative for Ireland in 1858. In 1871, his exertions were key to the creation of the first "Diploma in State Medicine" at Trinity College, candidates for which were expected to be qualified, beyond the general medical arts, in pathology, chemistry, natural philosophy, meteorology, forensics, statistics, and engineering.[94] Stokes was also instrumental in the creation of the Dublin Sanitary Association, on whose behalf he gave a series of lectures to the Royal Dublin Society on epidemics, contagion, sanitary engineering, and sanitary law.[95]

Though the *Dublin Quarterly Journal of Medical Science* occasionally printed reviews relating to English works on medical police and political medicine and on legislation relating to public health, it never published any articles specifically dealing with these subjects. The reviews, however, were always positive. A review of a new journal of public health launched in 1855, for instance, expressed the opinion that "public health and public wealth are justly regarded as synonymous terms," and welcomed with "acclamation" the publication of the new journal.[96] The authors argued that sanitary police and public health law were among "several elements constituting power" that needed to be maintained in order to prevent calamity. The following year the journal reviewed Rumsey's *Essays on State Medicine*, this time sounding a more cautionary note about having "political sentiments" expressed in a journal "devoted to science." Yet, while the authors distanced themselves from the entirety of Rumsey's "medical polity," they fully accepted the "natural and essential connexion that there is between the various branches of state medicine, and also the necessity of legislating with a view of that connexion," and argued that if even a fraction of Rumsey's scheme were "embodied in a system of state medical police, the country would be greatly benefited thereby."[97] The politics of disease, or nosopolitics as Foucault puts it, was particularly powerful in Ireland, where the link was regularly and easily made among poverty, famine, and mortality from disease. Perhaps the most striking example is the exchange between two prominent doctors that became known as the "Corrigan-Graves controversy." Dr. Dominic Corrigan, who along with Stokes was instrumental in the establishment of the Dublin Pathological Association in 1838, sparked the controversy in 1830 with the publication of an article in *Lancet* that claimed that "Famine and Fever are, in Ireland, as cause and effect," and reinflamed it in 1846 by publishing a pamphlet of a similar title at the very onset of the Great Famine, which eventually claimed a million lives during the four years 1846–50.[98]

Corrigan, largely relying on Rutty's observations for the eighteenth century, presented a table of all the major fever epidemics in Ireland between 1728 and 1826, comparing them with changes in the weather and crop failures. He very effectively demonstrated, though not of course to his detractors, that the only sustained correlation with epidemic fever was scarcity of food.[99] Thus he argued that climate or season, absence of cleanliness, overcrowding, intemperance, and contagion, together or alone, were less likely to cause fever than was malnutrition. Without "undervaluing" the advantages of cleanliness, he thought it plain "that all those matters over which the officers of health were given control, had equally existed, for an indefinite period of time, and without being accompanied by any epidemic, and that expending much time and money in their removal, and directing the principal attention to them, was objectionable."[100] Corrigan's solution to the epidemic fever was a "preventative" one, though not in the sanitary sense that the term had come to mean. The solution was "not in medicine, but employment, not in the lancet, but in FOOD, not in raising lazarettos for the reception of the sick, but in establishing manufactories for the employment of the healthy."[101] Corrigan acknowledged the value of infirmaries and fever hospitals, but like Rumsey he was totally opposed to their connection with the poor law and the workhouse. For those who might still suffer from malnutrition, he argued that the dispensaries should provide outdoor relief of food as well as drugs.

Two years later, at the height of the Great Famine, another article appeared claiming that the frequent concurrence of famine and fever made it reasonable to conclude that a "close connexion exists between the two," though the author in this case was much more circumspect regarding the nature of the connection, particularly in terms of whether malnutrition per se was the culprit.[102] By the end of the famine in 1850, however, it was clear that about three-quarters of the one million dead had fallen not to starvation precisely but to disease, and the relationship between hunger and fever was much more widely acknowledged. Such an acknowledgment did not, however, necessarily imply a denial of the value of medical police. Indeed, Stokes, acknowledging the relationship some twenty years later in his lectures on sanitary science at the Royal Dublin Society, made the contrary conclusion. Referring specifically to the prevalence of disease during famine, he asked his audience if "any argument be stronger than this to show the connexion between destitution and disease; any evidence more overwhelming and appalling to prove the want of an enlightened medical police, and to show that the public health must be one of the chief cares of the State?"[103]

"SANITARY INSTITUTIONS" AS INSTRUMENTS OF MEDICAL POLICE

While the discourse of medical police was far more developed in England than in Ireland, the opposite was true of its practice, and this was particularly the case in respect to hospitals and other "sanitary institutions." The new eighteenth-century hospitals, according to Foucault, are to be understood as an institutional experiment that "originates at the point of intersection of a new 'analytical' economy of assistance with the emergence of a general 'police' of health."[104] This is precisely how Jonas Hanway represented the hospital.[105] Hospitals, according to Hanway, were central to the object of police, since they were charged with the "preservation of the lives of fellow-subjects." This charge extended to workhouses and even prisons, since the preservation of life was united with the discipline of subjects and the correction of vice. According to Hanway, it was imperative that the "hospital [be made] tributary to our police, in a much more honourable degree than later times can boast of."[106] Indeed, as late as 1844 it was argued that the "erection of hospitals is intimately connected with the subject of medical police."[107]

Foucault notes that the emergence of the hospital as an element in the political economy of bodies and health cannot be fully understood by either of the extreme and opposed explanations that gravitate around the collectivity and state on the one hand and around the private individual relation between doctor and patient on the other, the latter avowedly "'clinical' in its economic functioning and epistemological form."[108] Rather, one needs to consider the double process of private action within a market economy and a commercialized medical practice, with its individualized epistemology located at the point of intersection between practitioner and patient, and the "concurrent organization of a politics of health, the consideration of disease as a political and economic problem for social collectivities,"[109] a matter of policy that embodies a distinct epistemology of coercive government and environmental alteration in the name of public health.

When writers on medical police dealt with the question of institutional medical provision, they were concerned not only with the general aim of securing the population but also with the related question of the police of medical practice within such institutions. The funding provided by government in Ireland allowed for a degree of regulation unimagined in England. A special board of government officers was created to directly supervise the operation of the grant-aided hospitals, and they issued annual reports on conditions, disease distributions, and mortality rates.[110] By the 1830s, appointments to all seventy-four government-funded fever hospitals were made by the public authorities.[111]

Ireland entered the eighteenth century without a single hospital open to general patients, and no dispensaries or infirmaries.[112] But the country ended the century with a network of general and specialized hospitals, as well as at least one infirmary and fever hospital for each of the thirty-six counties. The infirmaries, supported largely by government funds, numbered seventy-four by the 1830s. Dispensaries also began to be established in the eighteenth century, and with government support since 1807 numbered 650 by the 1840s. The eighteenth century also saw the establishment of some of Ireland's most celebrated hospitals, a few of which exist to this day. Six Dublin doctors opened the first "voluntary hospital" in the "British Isles" in 1718. Though initially no more than a house with accommodation for four patients, it soon became one of Ireland's major hospitals. In 1745, it moved to new premises with capacity for 183 patients. It moved again, in

1786, to an outstanding building on Jervis Street, with capacity for 620 patients, where it remained a major hospital until 1997, when the building was demolished as part of a commercial redevelopment. Three other notable hospitals with a long pedigree are St. Steven's (1733 and still operating), Mercer's (1734, closed in 1983 with staff incorporated into St. James's Hospital), and St. Patrick's mental hospital (1757), the last founded with money bequeathed by Jonathan Swift, today one of Ireland's most important psychiatric hospitals. Given that Swift's piercing satire was often targeted at the great rational formulas of social engineering characteristic of the Enlightenment, a critique exemplified in his "modest proposal" that the babies of Dublin's poor be bought and eaten by the rich as a solution to both poverty and overcrowding, commentators have found it somewhat ironic that he would secure his legacy through the foundation of Ireland's first institution for the "rational" study and treatment of madness. Some suggest that Swift sought to confound, even from the grave, those who wished to understand him, though others suggest that he was more ambivalent toward the designs and engines of rationalist social engineering than his satire suggests.

Specialized hospitals such as Swift's were established alongside general hospitals, and in 1745 Ireland became the site of the first maternity hospital in the world. Moving in 1757 to a lavish new building with a circular hall at the center, it became the Rotunda Maternity Hospital, and it too has remained in operation to this day, in the same building at the north end of O'Connell Street (Sackville Street). The longest continuously operating voluntary hospital in Ireland, the Meath, was opened in 1753, became the Dublin Infirmary in 1774, moved to Heytesbury Street in 1822 and to its present site in Tallagh in 1998. The Meath was at the center of the Dublin School of Medicine, which became world famous under William Stokes and Robert Graves for bringing clinical, or bedside, medical training to the English-speaking world and for the systematic use of the stethoscope (Stokes having published the first English-language treatise on the scope's use). The Meath provided crucial care for the sick poor of the Liberties and received in return an ample supply of living and dead bodies for teaching and research purposes. In 1792, the Westmoreland Lock Hospital was established specifically for the study and treatment of venereal disease. Another eighteenth-century venereal hospital was located on North King Street, though the exact date of its establishment is unclear. Among other eighteenth-century hospitals were the Foundling's, St. Catherine's, St. Nichlolas's, and the Charitable Infirmary. The creation of "Great Hospitals" slowed but continued in the nineteenth century. The Coombe Lying-In Hospital (now a major maternity hospital) was established in 1826, the Adelaide in 1839, the City of Dublin Hospital in 1832, as well as numerous additional fever hospitals. Three hospitals were established in connection with the House of Industry in Dublin, the Richmond Surgical (1811), the Whitworth Chronic (1818), and the Hardwick Fever (1803).

The formation of the Irish hospital network was not unique in the European context during this period. But the pace of its development, the extent of its reach, and its occasional "firsts" give it a relief that aids observation. The country, almost blank of institutional medicine at the beginning of the eighteenth century, was covered by a network of medical institutions in the space of 150 years. But truly unique to Ireland is the extent of government funding, and later, direct involvement, in the hospital, dispensary, and infirmary network. The dispensary system in particular was widely recognized in the mid-nineteenth century as "probably the best in Europe."[113] As early as 1765 the Irish parliament made a statutory grant to Mercer's, the Charitable Infirmary, and the Hospital for Incurables, and took steps to encourage the establishment of county infirmaries.[114] Though the initiative to establish an infirmary was left to private action, legislation made it possible for the grand juries to fund maintenance and to pay a surgeon a salary of one hundred pounds per annum. At the end of the century the Lock Hospital, associated with the House of Industry, received a grant of five thousand pounds. In the early nineteenth century a number of Dublin hospitals, including St. Steven's, the Rotunda, the Cork Street Fever Hospital, and the Meath, secured annual grants from the London parliament. Attempts were made to abolish the government funding on the basis that no like institutions in the entire empire received such support, but these attempts failed. The connection between charity and police was eventually severed with the establishment of general police forces. In the context of that connection, however, the idea of government-funded "charities" was not an oxymoron.[115]

THE POOR LAW AS MEDICAL POLICE

Perhaps the most controversial mode of governing medical institutions in Ireland was that of placing them under the supervision of the poor law commissioners. Unlike in England, where the establishment of workhouses began with the Elizabethan poor laws, Ireland had no national poor law system until 1838, though a number of locally operated "houses of industry" were established. The new Irish workhouses, however, were meant from the start to form part of the medical police system and were built with infirmaries attached and "medical officers" in attendance.[116] This special character of the workhouse system in Ireland set the context through which the poor law commissioners became senior medical police officers. Workhouse infirmaries were rapidly established across the country, and the act empowered the commissioners to "inspect and examine" the administration of the "medical charities" (largely government-funded hospitals). Three years after the establishment of the poor law system, the commissioners issued the elaborate "Medical Charities Report," in which they recommended that the principal supervision and regulation of all the country's infirmaries, dispensaries, and fever hospitals be placed under their management. However, opposition to the poor law officers becoming agents of medical police via the sanitary institutions was strong.

Two parliamentary committees investigated the question: the Commons issued a report in 1843; the Lords, in 1846. Both offered suggestions on how to avoid handing over the sanitary institutions to poor law management. The Medical Charities Bill, brought before Parliament in 1850, sought to create a new, separate board, called the "commissioners of health," but it failed to be heard before the end of the session and was never voted on. The following year a new bill brought all the dispensaries, but not the infirmaries, under poor law police. In 1854, the poor law commissioners made another grab for the infirmaries and fever hospitals, hoping to incorporate them into the poor law–administered fever hospital system, which now consisted of about 150 institutions. They failed in that bid, but perhaps more important, the Medical Charities Act constituted the poor law administration as a medical police in a broad "environmental" sense of the term, such that the poor law commissioners were required to employ "medical inspectors" and a "medical commissioner" charged with the enforcement of public health laws. When comprehensive public health legislation was passed in 1866, it required that all officers connected with the dispensaries were to aid in its execution, and it allowed the poor law commissioners (with the consent of the viceroy) to make their own public health inquiries and issue regulations in accordance with the 1850 Act for the Prevention of Contagious Diseases.[117] When major public health legislation was passed in 1874, every dispensary doctor under poor law administration became a "medical officer of health" for sanitary purposes, and in rural areas and towns of fewer than six thousand people the poor law union became the administrative unit for the mandatory appointment of "inspectors of nuisances." And while the Local Government Board of Ireland was made the highest medical police authority in the country, the members of the newly created board were none other than the poor law commissioners.[118] Thus medical police and the police of the poor were thoroughly integrated in Ireland.

FAMINE AND MEDICAL POLICE

Famine and fever epidemics propelled the creation of a medical police system in Ireland. Indeed, the first major piece of public health legislation passed by the British parliament was forced by the emergency of the 1817–19 famine, which brought about 1.5 million (of a population of 6 million) down with fever, 60,000 of whom were estimated to have died. The legislation, which applied only to Ireland, created the first system of health boards in any part of the United Kingdom of Great Britain and Ireland.[119] Though this was only a temporary measure, boards of health eventually went on to be important elements of the medical police system. The permanent General Board of Health was created in 1820, the first permanent health board in both countries. When famine and epidemic disease struck again in 1826, the board prompted the introduction of legislation that required each parish to appoint "officers of health." The health officers were to ensure that all "nuisances" were removed and that the houses of the poor were whitewashed. Corrigan, while thinking this was for the most part a waste of time, remembered nonetheless how the inspectors had an "imposing effect."[120] The board was composed of unpaid members who provided the viceroy with information and advice, making a number of special reports and supplying a monthly record of mortality from fever in Dublin. It also advised on the creation of local health boards, monitored local expenditures, and evaluated the financial remuneration of medical men performing services on behalf of government.

Another general board of health was created in 1832, this time in response to cholera and with duties similar to those of the 1819 board. This board consisted of four commissioners and employed six medical inspectors. When the Great Famine struck in 1846, a "central" board was created with responsibilities for providing nutritional relief. Since the poor law had already been shaped as a medical police apparatus by this time, however, the role of the central board was limited. For instance, in response to a request that the board enforce the Temporary Fever Act (1847), the poor law commissioners pointed out that sections 9 and 16 of the act explicitly did not authorize the central health board to enforce any measures in relation to cleansing, ventilating, and purifying the habitations of the poor.

Nor were they authorized to remove nuisances or have the dead interred. Such powers lay entirely with the Relief Committees, who ultimately answered to the poor law commissioners. The central board, however, gave plenty of advice, explaining to the Relief Committees the need to rigorously enforce the regulations concerning whitewashing and to prepare the wash precisely as instructed. After whitewashing, the floors were to be sprinkled with freshly made "chloride of lime" solution, and the inhabitants were to be instructed on hygienic precautions. The board even suggested that the relief stations provide washhouses supplied with soap and hot water and that those seeking relief be required to have clean hands, face, and hair.[121] Those already suffering from fever, however, were often reluctant to go to the fever hospitals for fear of being confined, and further legislation was passed that gave the central health board the power to compel them to do so.[122]

Though the range of medical police legislation passed between the 1819 act and the Great Famine was rather ad hoc, thereafter the legislation became more systematic. The legislation can be classified into six types, though their content overlaps quite considerably. First, there was a series of acts for the prevention of disease and the removal of nuisances, which were most often passed at times of famine and epidemics.[123] A second type of legislation, important for establishing the structure and authority of medical police officers, as well as for defining the boundaries of administrative health districts, were the sanitary and public health acts and the local government acts.[124] Another series of acts dealt more explicitly with the built environment, from "town improvement" to sewer construction, paving, and cleansing.[125] A fourth group of laws covered food and drugs in terms of adulteration, handling, and production.[126] A fifth set of laws, including factory and mines acts, dealt with health issues relating to production, whether in terms of occupational illness, the sale, transportation, and handling of dangerous substances, or industrial pollution generally.[127] Finally, there were the various medical charities acts and the poor law acts, which provided for institutional relief and police of the poor and sick.

Apart from the 1851 Medical Charities Act, the most important pieces of legislation were the Local Government Act of 1872 and the Public Health Act of 1874. The significance of these acts can be understood only if viewed together, for the former established the poor law commissioners as the final central government authority in relation to local government and dispensary or infirmary management, and the latter made the officers of those institutions the administrative backbone of the environmentally focused medical police system. Together these acts united all aspects of health and local government and both institutional and environmental medical police under a single centralized board. The board's authority was also extended to supersede other authorities under the various medical police statutes, such as the graveyard boards, the nuisance removal authorities, the sewer authorities, the local authorities as related to bake houses, washhouses, lodgings, and dwellings, and the urban and rural sanitary authorities.[128]

THE NEW SANITARY AUTHORITIES

The everyday authority over medical institutions was given to the poor law guardians, and environmental health was delegated to new urban and rural sanitary authorities. In rural areas, the poor law union became the new sanitary district. Dublin constituted a single district, with the town council being the sanitary authority (though accountable to the Local Government Board). The other corporate towns had a similar setup. In unincorporated towns with more than six thousand inhabitants, which already had commissioners under the Lighting, Cleansing, and Watching of Towns Act, these commissioners became the sanitary authority. The same principle applied in towns with municipal or town commissioners appointed under the municipal authorities or towns improvement acts.[129] Every medical officer of a dispensary became an ex officio "medical officer of health," and the local government board could require local authorities to appoint a "medical superintendent officer of health" or such officers as they believed were required for enforcing the health code. The chief duties of the sanitary authorities were the procurement and supply of "pure water," pollution prevention, building inspection, the prevention of over-crowding, the prevention of the sale of adulterated or diseased food, provision of sewers and drains, street cleaning, maintenance of recreational grounds, erection of baths and washhouses, provision and maintenance of burial grounds, and the institution of general measures to combat contagious diseases, such as carrying out disinfections when required.

If the responsibilities of the now fully coordinated national network of medical police were broad, so were the powers of enforcement. The medical police officers could easily obtain warrants to enter any building or place where it was believed diseased animals or food might be found, whereupon they could search the premises and make seizures. The regular police force could also be mobilized for such purposes. In Dublin, for instance, "the inspectors always call upon the first passing policeman to take charge of any diseased meat that they may have seized until they go in quest of the medical officer."[130] "Passing police" were not too hard to find in Ireland, the country being twice as heavily policed as England and Wales in 1870, with a total of 14,000 officers, or 1 per 425 of population.[131] In Dublin the ratio was almost twice as high. In rural areas regular police officers were particularly responsible for enforcing the sanitary code in relation to animal husbandry, ensuring that every cowshed be constructed for light and ventilation and properly supplied with water, its floor concreted, asphalted, flagged, or bricked, set in cement, and drained. Each animal had to have not less than six by three "superficial feet," exclusive of channel passage, crib, trough, and manger. Any sick animal was to be quickly removed from the healthy cattle "and reported to the police."[132] Indeed, the police were fully credited with arresting foot-and-mouth disease among Irish cattle in the 1860s.[133] And they also performed a range of enforcements under the nuisances acts, the sanitary acts, and the towns improvement acts. The responsibilities of regular police officers were reconfirmed in the new public health legislation, which recognized the extent of their work under section 16 of the Sanitary Act (1866), allowing them to claim expenses from the sanitary authority.[134] The regular police were always thereafter available as backup for the medical police. Both forces need to be understood as part of a general police network that regulated natural and political bodies.

A particularly important police power under the new act was the power to compel parents to vaccinate their children under fourteen years of age for smallpox. The medical police officer could haul the parents up before a justice, and if they subsequently failed to vaccinate the child in question, they could be fined up to twenty shillings.[135] And there were a considerable number of convictions, particularly when compared with rates in England and Wales. Convictions were also secured against those who held wakes for relatives who had died of infectious diseases, who kept pigs or other animals indoors, or who engaged in any activity "so as to cause danger," such as having unmuzzled dogs within fifty yards of a public road, selling animals from the road, carrying loads that projected more than two feet from a cart, and leaving stones, dung, timber, or turf so as to be a hazard.[136]

The coproduction of police, medicine, engineering, and related practices produced a heterogeneous body of knowledge. While each of these areas of knowledge helped to drive the development of the police of natural and political bodies, such police also had its own dynamic. Thus even as the miasma theory of disease began to be challenged by bacteriology, the imperatives of police and the government of natural bodies ensured that the condition of buildings and the supply of fresh air and wholesome food remained central concerns. Where before the dangers from miasma in the atmosphere, in swamps, and in rotting animal and vegetable matter were seen everywhere, soon the dangers from germs were seen everywhere.

The security imperative, which drove the modern police of everything that bore on life, did not diminish in the nineteenth century. In this respect I depart from Foucault and (liberal) governmentality studies. New biomedical knowledge and new political rationalities of self-government shaped the contours but not the advance of the police of life. These were not opposite models. The distinction between discourses and practices is crucial in this respect. In the service of ideology, discourse could easily construct a world in which the public and private were ontologically discrete, the latter by definition free of police. In practice, however, medical police extended across the discursive boundaries between private lives and public life. There is little doubt that an extensive network of (variously organized) practices for the government of natural and political bodies had been engineered, from the general discourse of political medicine to the material detail of the sewer trap and the water filter. The body of Ireland was policed through one of the most striking networks of science and government ever conceived. Johann Frank, who laid out the entire blueprint between 1779 and 1819, would have surely been pleased to see his ideas largely vindicated in practice. Medical police had finally come of age, and *life* would never be the same again.

The police of life produced a system for engineering health and social order that involved not only the police of bodies but also the police of the built environment. Such police implied the transformation of the built environment through the agency of sanitary engineering. Chapter 6 addresses how the built environment was transformed into the infrastructural jurisdiction of a modern state, but because of the close connection between medical police and sanitary engineering, I end chapter 5 with a note on the latter. Sanitary engineering, like medical police, was a confederate science, uniting diverse and autonomous bodies of knowledge in a single coherent practice. As one engineer observed, there was a need to bring the "work of the engineer into closer alliance with medical science."[137] The sanitary engineer required knowledge of chemistry and had to know about the "physical conditions, geological and meteorological, which . . . govern . . . the character of both Air and Water." Part of the job of the sanitary engineer was to ensure that uncontaminated water be conveyed to buildings and that body waste be effectively removed. Diseases were to be prevented through effective systems of ventilation. The geology of the ground had to be known and steps taken to prevent damp and ensure drainage.

Eventually an entire corps of sanitary architects and engineers became networked with the medical police. As one advocate put it, if a "sanitary officer finds premises in a state dangerous to health . . . he is to report the same to the sanitary authority . . . [who] is to refer the report to a surveyor or engineer, who is to consider and to report the cause of the evil and the remedy."[138] Through medical policing and sanitary engineering, every aspect of dwellings came in for government scrutiny and regulation. A discourse of "healthy houses" emerged. Paints were examined for lead content. Wallpaper was analyzed in terms of its porosity and therefore its capacity to absorb "animal effluvium." Furnishings had to be guarded against dust. Thus, the anxieties of purity and danger discussed by Mary Douglas expressed themselves.[139] Dirt and disease were ready to corrupt and attack at every opportunity, disease "seek[ing] an entrance at every unguarded point into our homes."[140] The intimate relations between medical policing, surveying, engineering, and a host of related sciences indicate how the science-state plexus was formed. And medical police was itself an engine science, depending for its practice on meters, scopes, and graphs and involving engineering interventions and material contrivances. By securing life and arresting disease, medical police transformed a people into a bio-population. One might, indeed, describe the modern state as a biopolis, that is, a life-enhancing police state.

6 Engineering Ireland

*The Material Designs
of Modern Statecraft*

In colonial Ireland, a discourse that treated the cultivation of nature and the condition of the physical environment as indices of civilization and moral worth created a theological and ideological legitimization for the English designs of socio-material and political engineering. This chapter focuses on the projects of socio-material engineering through which the body of Ireland was worked over and made an agent of the English social order. The term *agent* is used in the strong sociological sense of agency, for the colonists explicitly viewed their material projects as powerful mechanisms that would act, purposefully, to secure the colonial state. Though diverse in form, including everything from land drainage to the design of houses, the material projects through which the engineering of Ireland was made tangibly real were animated by a discourse of improvement and civilization that exhibited a remarkable consistency across these diverse projects and indeed across the two centuries during which the colonization of Ireland was effected. In this context, the knowledge of engine science was crucial, since it was a form of knowledge pursued through a practice of material engagement with the world. Engine science facilitated the mobilization of natural forces and bodies and their integration through the practice of engineering into social, economic, and political networks of power. The focus of this chapter is the objects of engineering culture—land, roads, buildings, and so on—and their transformation into an infrastructural jurisdiction that, in turn, formed the material basis of the state-country.

THE STATE OF NATURE AND THE
MATERIAL CULTURE OF STATE

The linking together of culture and civility on the one hand and wildness and wilderness on the other, as well as their paired opposition, was not new in the seventeenth century. As Joep Leerssen has shown, this equation was articulated in relation to Ireland as early as the twelfth century.[1] Giraldus Cambrensis, in his topography of Ireland, described the Irish as beastlike forest dwellers, lacking agriculture and village life and thus "civil society." Lacking culture, particularly agriculture, the Irish were "semi-bestial 'naturals.'" What changed by the seventeenth century is that Ireland moved from being on the edge of the world to being near the center of the English orbit.[2] In the context of English colonial expansion across the Atlantic, the Irish who lived beyond the Pale were no longer to be treated as "wild men" outside the English civil domain. They were reconceived as "recalcitrant subjects of the King," who were to be rescued from their wild natural state by fully incorporating them, in the most literal sense of the term, into English civil culture. Taming the land and culturing the environment became central to the practice through which this incorporation was effected. As John Davies put it in his *Discoverie of the True Causes why Ireland was Never Entirely Subdued* (1619), the Irish were not to be left to themselves to live as "wild men"; they were to be made subject to common law, and "if the country is too 'wild' to enforce Common Law, to Forest Law":

> Againe, if King Henry the second, who is said to be the K. that Conquered this Land, had made Forrests in Ireland . . . or if those English Lordes, amongst whom the whole Kingdome was devided, had beene good Hunters, and had reduced the Mountaines, Boggs, and woods within the limits of Forrests, Chases, and Parkes; assuredly, the very Forrest Law, and the Law *De Malefactoribus in parcis*, would in time have driven them into the Plains & Countries inhabited and Mannured, and made them yeeld uppe their fast places to those wild Beastes which were indeede less hurtful and wilde, then they.[3]

Whatever the truth of this representation of the native Irish, Davies's argument, coming just after the Elizabethan conquest and in the wake of the abandonment of Ireland by the last of the native chiefs (the "Flight of the Earls"), marked the beginning of the new policy replacing the supposed Irish state of nature with the planters' culture of state. Subsequently, the eighteenth century became the century of the "Protestant Ascendancy," in both its meanings of a process of ascendancy and as the century of domination by the Protestant aristocracy. It was during this time that the project to incorporate the entire island, to "engineer Ireland," began in earnest.

While not always successful in his grander national schemes, Petty attempted to put them to work in relation to his own property, designing his plantation as a local experiment for projects he envisioned at the level of the state. Having acquired a large estate in Kerry in payment for the

Down Survey, he immediately tried out his experiment for plantation and "improvement." He produced detailed maps of his estate, surveyed the land for resources and agricultural potential, and established an industrial colony, ironworks, and fisheries industry. He reclaimed "wasteland," implemented drainage systems, improved roads, built the first pier in the county, and even founded his own town (Kenmare). In order to acquire the skills he needed (by design of division of labor) and to balance the population so as to secure his holdings (by design of political order), he brought over English craftsmen to settle on the estate.[4]

The experiment ended abruptly during the 1688 "Glorious Revolution." The ironworks and industrial colony were destroyed and the planters driven from the land. But the cultural configuration that spawned this experiment in socio-material engineering would continually reassert itself over the following two centuries. This was so even in the case of Petty's Kerry estate. His great-grandson, Lord Shelburn (who became prime minister of Britain in the 1780s), had Petty's town replanned and rebuilt into an eighteenth-century "model town." Local experimentation with a view to national designs remained a feature of engineering Ireland, and in the nineteenth century crown lands were used for "experimental improvements."[5]

DRAINAGE AND CIVILIZATION

Drainage and reclamation of land emerged from the sixteenth and seventeenth centuries as an enduring project through which to both augment profit and colonize Ireland. The bogs were especially targeted, since they served as an anchor for a series of discourses concerning moral improvement and the relations between civility and culture and between health and environment. The prevalence of bogs in Ireland was taken as further proof of the barbarity of the Irish. Willoughby suggested that "lazyness" and a "neglect of culture" had caused standing water to proliferate, which in turn had undermined woodlands and produced the bogs. The English construction of the "bog Irish" as the exemplification of native degeneracy made it possible to link peasant ill health both to a lack of civilization and culture and to the physical effects of the bog environment.[6] In addition, the miasma theory of disease generation and propagation implied that living in the vicinity of a bog was inherently unhealthy. On these grounds, as well as on the grounds of the economic advantages to be gained from reclamation, the bogs came in for special attention. *Reclamation* in this context carried all its connotations of winning "back or away from vice or error or savagery or waste condition." It meant to "reform, tame or civilize" and "bring under cultivation."[7] By the end of the eighteenth century the bogs had, according to Thomas Newenham, "experienced a very great, and many of the inhabitants will be disposed to add, a very lamentable diminution since the commencement of the last century." This lament for the loss of the bogs was unusual. Newenham explained that turf bogs had "often been improperly confounded with marshes and fens, from which in their effects they are specifically different." Newenham argued that the bogs did not generate disease and that evidence suggested they even possessed "qualities of an antiseptic nature."[8] It was "well known that the inhabitants of those counties, which surround and comprise the great bog of Allen, are as free from peculiar distempers, enjoy as vigorous constitutions, are as long-lived, and at least as well formed for strength and agility as any of the other inhabitants of Ireland."[9] This was, however, a rare dissenting voice concerning the healthfulness of the bogs, which continued to be viewed as indications of a lack of culture and as sources of ill health. *Bog* and *bog Irish* were contemptuous terms signifying a barbarity of land and people and the intimate relation believed to exist between the two. Newenham promoted drainage in general, however, and claimed that the "thick woods which covered the greater part of that country, and necessarily affected the salubrity of its climate, by impeding the current of the air, and retaining the moisture wasted by the westerly winds from the Atlantic ocean, have ceased to exist; and the deep rich soil, which pervades it in various directions, is no longer undrained or in a state of nature."[10]

Drainage work in the eighteenth century was often done through the private action of individual improving landlords, sometimes in connection with essays on the subject published by the Royal Dublin Society. Samuel Madden, for instance, believed that landlords should be the principle force for the improvement of Ireland.[11] But others, such as Willoughby in the seventeenth century, argued that there was such a "greate deale of bog lands yet left in Ireland" that the work of drainage would have to be "reserved for some publick purse," it being "beyond the power of a few private fortunes to undertake so vast an expense."[12] In 1729, Arthur Dobbs argued for the establishment of a government-led "board of trust," which would finance land improvements. Steps in this direction were taken with the introduction of the Bill for Encouragement of Tillage, Draining of Bogs, and Inland Navigation,[13] but the first major government scheme for reclamation of the bogs did not come until the nineteenth century, with the creation of the Bogs Commission.[14] The commission was appointed in 1809 with the mandate to "inquire into the nature and extent of the several bogs in Ireland, and the practicability of draining and cultivating them."[15] Bog surveys were carried out between 1809 and 1813, providing more detailed information on the extent and location of bogs than had ever been collected before and surveying over a million acres. The great Bog of Allen had always been a favorite target for drainage, and it was proposed as the first reclamation project based on the survey.[16] Work on the bogs, however, was just one aspect of a more general drive toward enclosure, the reclamation of "wastelands," the alteration of topsoil, the planting of "artificial grasses," and the construction of an integrated system of drainage.

Although little enclosure, even around Dublin, had been achieved by the beginning of the eighteenth century, it was well underway by the 1750s and continued into the late nineteenth. Once enclosed, the land was cleared of rocks and stones, marled, limed and manured, and either made arable or converted into grassland and pasture.[17] Characteristic Irish Georgian houses were built across the country, and these sometimes served as points for linking new roads. The integrated drainage network involved building ditches around enclosed fields, which were drained into local streams and rivers, then into an arterial system of rivers and canals, and eventually into the sea. The completion (from humble but visionary beginnings) of the arterial drainage system was one of the most important projects of the Office of Public Works, established in 1831.[18] Important government-led initiatives on drainage had been taken in 1822 and 1831,[19] but the drainage acts of 1842 and 1846 provided for the most extensive arterial engineering the country had ever seen.[20] Arterial engineering involved the deepening or widening of rivers, sometimes straightening them where meanders were particularly bad, and the removal of obstacles. Sometimes embankments were built to prevent flooding, and additional ditches and drains were used to link local drainage systems to the main arteries.[21]

OPENING UP THE INTERIOR

Arterial drainage and the development of inland navigation were closely linked, though the latter had seen more significant developments in the eighteenth century, and sometimes the aims of the two clashed, as in the building of weirs for navigational purposes, which could result in a greater propensity for flooding. Engineered inland navigation began with the canals. The Grand and Royal canals, both begun in the eighteenth century, linked the eastern seaboard with the Shannon River in the west.[22] The canals, together with the River Barrow, the middle reaches of which were canalized, formed the core of the inland navigation system that was extended in the nineteenth century by the Board of Public Works.[23] Engineering the inland navigation system was a long, drawn out process and involved many private companies, though the government always stepped in to rescue projects that became financially strapped. Though promoted primarily on economic grounds, these were always linked to the discourse of "improvement," since they opened up the country more effectively to industry and provided arteries for the civilizing mission.

As Mukerji has pointed out, state formation did not simply mean centralization in a bureaucratic structure, but demanded reaching out into the heartland, dispersing government power so as to incorporate the land into the state.[24] The capillary reach of the water system was limited, and thus it was roads more than any other material transportation and communications network—even the railway, which got under way from the 1840s—that permitted a more pervasive net of access into the country. Inland navigation nonetheless brought major civil engineering to Ireland for the first time, building the first major network that mobilized the natural resource of rivers into a communications network. The railway, however, augmented material load capacity exponentially, moving not only large numbers of people but also all sorts of material culture and products of art and engineering.[25]

ROADS AS POLICE

William Greig, a road engineer in the employ of the postmaster general and an advocate of a system of county engineers for building and maintaining roads, published his *Strictures of Road Police* in 1819. Greig chose "road police" for the title because the "care of roads forms so important a branch of the highly interesting and widely extended subject of political economy, or the domestic policy of nations."[26] Roads, as materializations of policy, were themselves agents of police. Rather than addressing how roads might be better policed, Greig discussed how they might be better constructed so that they could serve, in and of themselves, as an engineered infrastructure of police agency.

The eighteenth century brought almost nonstop road building in Ireland, work carried forward in the nineteenth century by the Board of Public Works. In the eighteenth century the postmaster general was responsible for building and maintaining many roads, thus embedding the intelligence capability of the post office in a material network that ran through the country on the ground. There was also extensive construction of what were called county roads, which did not carry tolls. Responsibility for these roads was transferred to the Board of Public Works in 1831.[27] Construction of roads in the eighteenth century entered a new accelerated stage in the 1730s, when legislation provided for the creation of "turn-pike trusts" and the building of toll-roads. An act passed in 1727 stipulated that the existing roads were to be graveled to at least twelve feet in width, the new roads to thirty feet, and legislation passed in 1739 encouraged new roads between "market towns."[28] The Royal Dublin Society published directives on road building in 1736–37, emphasizing the need for solid foundations, layered graveling, and the right materials.[29]

On occasion special "military roads" were built, which linked army barracks with principal towns or cities, such as the north-south road that opened a "direct and easy line of communication between the city of Dublin and the barracks of Glen Crie."[30] The Glen Crie military road and the barracks itself had been built, according to Richard Griffith, "in the times of the rebellions to keep the mountaineers in subjection." Griffith was upset that a colony of soldiers had not been planted on the road, as had originally been planned. He argued that if the plan had been implemented, they "would soon behold a sturdy race of loyal mountaineers, who would not only greatly improve the appearance of the country, but would strengthen the hand of the government by rendering what had lately been considered the shelter of lawless rebels, the residence of a population, grateful to those who had rescued them from a transatlantic emigration."[31] Roads were regularly justified not simply on economic grounds but because they furthered political and cultural penetration into country inhabited by recalcitrant and rebellious subjects. In the wake of the deforestation of the sixteenth and seventeenth centuries and the incorporation of remaining woodlands into managed forests, the mountains and other inaccessible areas were singled out as the hiding places for rebels and outlaws. The commissioners of public works reported that areas without roads had no industry and were dens of "notorious Outlaws and Murderers." By prosecuting the roads into these areas the commissioners had "no doubt that the whole face of the Mountain Country will be improved . . . and that peaceful agricultural industry will supplant that system of lawless outrage which has hitherto been the disgraceful characteristic of the Population."[32]

It is startling the extent to which statements such as these, from as late as the 1830s, resonate with Davies's comments in 1619 or even those of Giraldus Cambresis in the twelfth century. The roads were clearly seen as means to open up the country to industry and material culture. And indeed, they were seen somewhat similarly, if not quite so positively, by the native population, who viewed the road builders with suspicion and were known to attack or sabotage the engineers. Griffith, for instance, reported that the people had a low opinion of them, "and fearing injustice and oppression, regarded [their] operation with distrust and attempted to circumvent [his] plans by every means in their power."[33] Griffith pressed ahead nonetheless and in 1824 could report the successful extension of seventy miles of new road running in a number of different directions into the "wild, neglected country without roads, culture or civilization which extends from the River Shannon to the River Blackwater."[34] The role of these systems in securing state power was most often articulated by engineers and engine scientists, especially those associated with the military.

By invoking the greatness of the ancients, Charles Vallancey, director of military engineering in mid-eighteenth-century Ireland, articulated a vision of the modern state secured in part by inland navigation. Rome, in particular, served to link the modern to the ancient, bypassing the Dark Ages and establishing a lineage of culture and power that could be traced to the classics.[35] This was not simply a discursive activity, however, since the link could be made demonstrably real only by building it into the environment. The second half of the eighteenth century thus sees Ireland rebuilt according to the neoclassical designs and material strategies of Rome. As an ancient engineering power, Rome served as a model for modern engineering culture.

THE BUILT ENVIRONMENT AS DISTRIBUTED CENTERS OF CALCULATION

Rivers, canals, and roads were of little use, however, if they did not connect, in Latour's terms, centers of political, epistemic, and economic calculation.[36] The ports, harbors, fortresses, barracks, court buildings, hospitals, infirmaries, and prisons were nodes in the communications network. The towns grew at a steady pace in the eighteenth century, Dublin gaining its great streets and Georgian buildings, which today give it so much of its character. The Board of Public Works played a central role in the development of public buildings in the nineteenth century, work that was originally under the responsibility of the surveyor general and chief engineer of Ireland and that from 1759 was brought under the Barrack Board and Board of Public Works. In 1802 the maintenance of civil and military buildings was separated, with a barrack inspectorate created to deal solely with military buildings and the "civil buildings commissioners" taking responsibility for nonmilitary buildings.

Complaints in the seventeenth century about the alleged failure of the Irish to build enduring structures added a moral justification to projects already proposed in the name of security and economic development. Dublin Castle, the center of English government in the country, was of primary concern after the Cromwellian conquest, and its rebuilding and renovation were the first responsibility of the surveyor general. A further major renovation was undertaken in the 1830s, when the castle became the headquarters of the new national police force. In the 1840s, the central government took responsibility for the lunatic asylums, including the special Criminal Lunatic Asylum in Dundrum. In the 1850s, a new and in many respects revolutionary system of convict prisons was constructed.[37] Equally important were the workhouses built from the late 1830s on, the infirmaries that were funded from the 1760s on, the dispensaries from the early nineteenth century, and the various levels of support for the hospitals from the mid-eighteenth century on, including the first maternity hospital in the world. About 150 coast guard stations and a network of post offices were built.

Government also maintained the Catholic seminary at Maynooth, the buildings of the Royal Irish Academy, the queen's colleges at Belfast, Cork, and Galway, the National Gallery, and the Natural History Museum. The museum and gallery were part of the complex of buildings around Leinster House, which from 1815 became the headquarters of the Royal Dublin Society.[38] These depositories are of great interest and can be seen as important boundary objects between Irish and English in Ireland.[39] The growth of antiquarianism in eighteenth-century Ireland brought Irish and Anglo-Irish scholars into dialogue. The Anglo-Irish perambulated the country, digging up ancient relics and organizing them in museums. In this context as others, constructing the idea of the modern state in Ireland involved constructing an ancient history. The study of archaeological material culture played an important role in the development of colonial nationalism and patriotism and later also republican nationalism, and therefore the Irish state-idea. Indeed, state-idea, state-system, and state-country were all constructed through material culture.

The level of government involvement in the building and maintenance of permanent structures, whether directly for the purpose of administration and the military or for the wider designs of government through post offices, workhouses, and organizations of practical science, is striking in Ireland between the late seventeenth and the late nineteenth centuries.

FIGURE 11. The General Post Office and Nelson's Pillar, Sackville Street, Dublin, c. 1820. Print attributed to Henry Brocas Jr. after a drawing by S. F. Brocas. Courtesy of the National Library of Ireland.

THE URBANSCAPE AS AGENT OF HEALTH AND ORDER

As ancient Ireland was being constructed in the museum and the library (collecting ancient texts was also crucial), the image of ancient Greece was being engineered into the urban landscape. The development of Georgian Dublin and the creation of the wide streets and intersections of College Green, Dame Street, and Sackville Street (now O'Connell Street) were begun by the Wide Streets Commission, established by act of Parliament in 1757, with the initial project of "making a wide and convenient Way, Street, and Passage, from Essex Bridge, to the Royal Palace or Castle."[40] The commission aimed to bring polite society to the streets through designs that linked ornament, health, and social order in a public and demonstrable way. Parliament Street was subsequently opened in 1762, running from the River Liffey to Dublin Castle. By 1768 Dame Street was opened, and by 1772 a number of new streets running to the River Liffey were completed. The cost of these initial projects, at about forty thousand pounds, was incurred by Parliament and king's letter. Plans were drawn up to make further improvements to Dame Street, South Great George's Street, Henry Street, Sackville Street, Abbey Street, and the westward road from Barrack Street to Islandbridge, Rutland Square, and Cavendish Row. Most of these projects were completed by 1790 and, in conjunction with the great buildings, remade the capital city in the image of the aristocracy. (See figure 11.)

Ornament was not, however, divorced from the practical problems of moving and regulating material traffic. In the nineteenth century a radial road was built from the castle, on the south side of the city, to Frederick Street and Dorset Street, on the north side. A number of new bridges across the river further integrated north and south sides. In 1812 the commissioners reported how their "Public Improvements" in the "Disposition of all Avenues opened in this City" had "successfully promoted Order, Uniformity, and Convenience."[41]

STATE BUILDING THROUGH PUBLIC WORKS

Throughout the country the reorganized Board of Public Works had more impact than any other government agency on the material culture of state in nineteenth-century Ireland. Between 1832 and 1881, almost thirty-three million pounds were advanced under the auspices of the board, most in the form of subsidized loans, but some also in the form of grants.[42] The first report of the Board of Public Works amounted to only three pages but found space to express the discourse of moral improvement through material engineering, explaining how "improvements" in the mountainous parts of the south had resulted in the "manners and conditions of the labouring Classes" being "materially changed for the better."[43] As the works carried out increased, so did the size of the annual reports, reaching over two hundred pages on occasion.[44] In 1841, almost 900,000 pounds were dispensed in loans and a further 125,000 in grants.[45] The money was invested in roads, bridges, harbors and inland navigation, public buildings in Phoenix Park in Dublin, and lunatic asylums. In the first twenty years of the board's existence, over three million pounds were dispensed in grants and over eight million in loans.[46] Almost 130,000 acres were drained in conjunction with the Landed Property Improvement Act.[47] The inspectors of drainage reported that almost 1.5 million acres had been drained or improved in the decade 1842–52.[48]

With the passage of the Sewage Utilization Act in 1865 and the public health acts in the 1870s, the Board of Public Works became much more involved in sanitary engineering. In 1881, apart from the usual works of land improvement, public buildings, transportation (now including trams and railways), and so forth, the commissioners included funds in their budget estimates for a range of works connected with water supply, sewerage, public urinals, paving, and cemetery construction, works covering the entire country. Out of all these mundane materials, apparently so trivial when compared to the discourses of political philosophy and theory, the modern state was engineered.

FIGURE 12. "Map of Ireland Exhibiting the Various Works in
Operation," December 1847, published by the Board of Public Works,
Ireland (*Parliamentary Papers,* 1848, vol. xxxvii). The map shows
drainage projects, roads, land improvement projects, the erection of
public buildings, and other projects. Courtesy of the National Library
of Ireland.

MATERIAL CULTURE, MUD CABINS, AND MORAL STATES

"Town improvement" was facilitated by the passage of lighting, cleansing, and water supply legislation, and beginning in the 1840s and 1850s, the towns improvement acts.[49] The most important of these nationwide was the 1854 Towns Improvement Act. As Arthur Moore put it, the act gave "important and extensive powers for the purposes described in its title, and for various purposes of sanitary and police regulation."[50] The purposes described in the act's title were "to make better Provision for the Paving, Lighting, Draining, Cleansing, Supplying with Water, and Regulation, of Towns in Ireland."[51] The scope of the legislation was wide. It provided for the execution of surveys and plans of towns and the carrying out of public works. It authorized the engineering and maintaining of public sewers, the drainage of houses, the design, paving, and maintenance of streets, and the naming of streets and numbering of houses. It mandated the improvement of the lines of streets and the removal of "obstructions." Sections dealt with "ruinous and dangerous buildings" and measures to be taken for demolition, as well as precautions to be taken during construction. It also contained sections on the cleansing of streets and the prevention of nuisances and smoke pollution. Stipulations on the construction of houses were made in terms of fire prevention and ventilation. The act amended the laws on lodging houses, slaughterhouses, and the sale of unwholesome and adulterated food, and lighting and water supply retained their now familiar significance. The legislation mandated the erection of public clocks, lighted at night. There were clauses relating to the sale of gunpowder, the regulation of beggars and vagrants, the provision of fire engines and firemen, and rules on places of public resort, including pubs and public baths. Hackney carriages, boats, boatmen, porters, fares, and so forth, were all regulated. Provision was made for the erection of public libraries and museums, for the manner of raising money for such projects, and for the procedures of notification concerning works (and the rights of subjects to appeal them). Instructions for constables and watchmen policing the act were articulated, such as reporting buildings in dangerous conditions. Power of entry into private residences was granted for the purpose of enforcing the legislation.

Through these designs the practices of government, science, engineering, and medicine were integrated in organizational systems of health, safety, and security. It was out of these systems that many taken-for-granted institutions of cleanliness and order emerged. The supply of "pure" water was always promoted as part of the project of engineering a "physical" environment capable of securing the twin objects of health and morality, "cleanliness and Godliness." Persons "reared in a filthy, unwhole-some" environment were said to be necessarily "defective in physical development," and "physical wretchedness" in turn "annihilated those mental faculties which are distinctive of the human being," rendering the wants and appetites of those so afflicted no better than those of a "mere animal."[52] The supposed animal condition of the poor, indicated by their physical state, was set in opposition to the civilized condition created by a cultured environment.

The linking of the moral with the physical resonated with the more ancient connection that was drawn between bestiality and the natural state, but the link operated with the added advantage of its applicability to urban conditions, and to housing in particular. As Toby Barnard has noted, "Housing and architecture were part of the English and Protestant mission in Ireland."[53] Petty, in his *Political Anatomy of Ireland*, estimated that of 200,000 houses in Ireland in the 1670s, some 160,000 were "wretched nasty cabins, without chimney, window, or doorshut, and worse than those of the savage Americans."[54] Being "wholly unfit for making merchantable butter, cheese, or the manufactures of woollen, linen, or leather," the cabins of the poor were incapable of sustaining industry and thus partly responsible for the immoral and ungovernable state of the poor.[55] Bishop Berkeley, who described the "wretched and barbaric" conditions in which the Irish peasant lived, made a similar argument in the eighteenth century.[56]

On the eve of the Great Famine the picture was a little better, consider-ably so if one takes account of the massive population increase (at least eightfold since Petty's census), though it was still lamentable by any "modern" standard. Of 1,328,839 houses returned in the 1841 census, almost half a million were mud cabins consisting of a single room without window or chimney, and another half million were cottages of two to four rooms, with windows, though still largely constructed of mud and stone. Only about three hundred thousand houses were built in a permanent manner, of stone and brick.[57] However, what the sanitary reformers had failed to achieve in thirty years, or the "improvers" in over a century (i.e., a substantial reduction of the number of mud cabins), was largely, and in the most terrible way, effected by the Great Famine (1846–49) and its after-math.[58] The famine's devastation was concentrated among the subsistence population, and as this population declined, so did the number of mud cabins. Those consisting of one room and no windows fell from 491,278 in 1841 to 135,589 in 1851, and to 89,374 in 1861, a drop of over 400,000, or 80 percent, in just two decades. The famine permitted the consolidation of farms and the elimination of subdivision, establishing middle-class Catholic farmers as the dominant class in rural Ireland. This class was devoutly Catholic, supplying the ranks of the priests and nuns that spread out across the country. In time they became a new reference point for "respectable Irishness." These developments permitted the country to participate fully in the culture of mid-Victorian respectability.

In 1848, an argument was made before the Royal Dublin Society on the necessity of "model lodging houses" that would promote "not only health but morality . . . among the labouring classes."[59] By the 1880s the idea of a "physical culture of bodies" (to use an expression from the period) was being articulated in terms of "healthy houses," "healthy nurseries and bedrooms," "healthy furniture and decoration," "healthy schools," and so on.[60] The great International Health Exhibition held in London in 1884 led to the publication of no fewer than nineteen volumes of material dealing with these and other subjects related to engineering health. Concern was early expressed about both the "social and moral evils resulting from the practice of one or more families of all ages and sexes sleeping in the same room,"[61] and the health exhibition literature offered numerous designs for healthy houses that were intended to separate children of the opposite sex.[62] In 1877 it was reported that the City of Health was to be constructed in Sussex, England, and advertisements began to appear in a search for partnerships between "sanitary capitalists" and sanitary engineers.[63]

The connection between health and morality in discourses of sanitation was central to the design of an entire range of new organizations in Ireland. Prisons in particular served as the sites through which disciplinary technologies were united with material strategies for constituting governed bodies.[64] Jeremiah Fitzpatrick, a physician and the first inspector general of prisons in Great Britain and Ireland, published an essay in 1784 in which he argued for a rearrangement of "physical appliances" and the imposition of a stricter "regulation" so as to effect a state of "health," "order," and "rationality."[65] Fitzpatrick's essay, especially when viewed in conjunction with his *Thoughts on Penitentiaries*, highlights the significance of material designs for the government of natural bodies. He discussed the nature of air and its function in human bodies and concluded, "No matter is more capable of generating putrid fevers or fluxes, &c. of the most dangerous nature, than the exhalations arising from the discharges of the human body, pent up or stagnated from a want of ventilation."[66] Most of the essay concerned the construction of prisons in terms of the maintenance of health. Indeed, although Foucault focused on Jeremy Bentham's famed

"Panopticon" and historians challenged Foucault by pointing out that it was never built, it was in fact but one example of the way architecture was mobilized from the late eighteenth century on for the more effective observation and government of people. In Bentham's case, the principle of regulation through material design was the key. An article in *The Sanitary Inspector* some hundred years later noted how "construction fills a much larger space in Bentham's correspondence than all his codes put together."[67] Though *his* panopticon design was never built, numerous others certainly were.[68] The historians' critique is nonetheless important, in that it points out the necessity of uniting analyses of ideas, discourses, and designs with actual practices and material culture.

Public buildings were important experimental spaces for sanitary architecture and engineering, and one can easily locate data on their actual construction if one targets the archives of the scientific establishments. John Grey, for instance, presented to the Royal Dublin Society the results of his experiments with a toilet-flushing system at the North Dublin Union Workhouse.[69] Grey began his inquiry with a series of "careful experiments" on a house drain, concluding that a daily flush of twenty-five gallons of water through a six-inch valve and tubular pipe could effectively scour and "thoroughly *cleanse, wash,* and *ventilate*" a drain much more effectively than a constant flow of three thousand gallons over a twenty-four-hour period. Not believing that domestics could be trusted to operate the device, Grey went on to design a "self-acting flusher," which he displayed before both the physicians and surgeons at their respective colleges. He designed a complete system for the workhouse, including a four-seater toilet, reporting how he achieved by these means a "self-cleansing water-closet, that accommodates four visitors at a time, receives about 600 visits in the course of the day, and washes itself every ten minutes, while the drain pipe which receives ejecta of all these visitors is scoured out by a similarly self-acting mechanism once each day."[70]

Mundane and small-scale experiments of this sort were important examples of how social engineering could be achieved through material culture. Small-scale experiments linked the design and construction of material forms with the realization of a certain social order just as effectively as large-scale experiments. It is the latter, however, that tend to receive all the attention, especially engines of institutionalization such as the school and prison systems. By means of hospitals, asylums, schools, workhouses, and penitentiaries, Ireland was covered in the nineteenth century by a highly centralized material system through which health, discipline, and social order were engineered.

SCHOOLS: "A MATTER OF POLICE" AND "REMARKABLE AND EFFICACIOUS ENGINES OF SOCIAL POWER"

The schoolhouse building program was particularly important because it extended (in principle) to the securing, in material spaces that operated like chambers, of all bodies, not just of those who by crime, poverty, illness, or mental affliction were incarcerated. Established in 1831, the Irish National School system was the first national system of government-funded popular education in the world. By 1853 over half a million students were in attendance, and by 1872 over five hundred schools had been built. The system, officially "nondenominational" but increasingly sectarian, worked against the Protestant Ascendancy, which since the seventeenth century had used schools for proselytizing purposes. Authors in the *Dublin University Magazine*, for instance, lamented the decline of the Protestant-controlled Church Education Society's schools in the face of the national system. "Long experience," they complained, "has taught us, that wherever Government makes a grant, it asserts a right of interference and control," and that "no independent action can be asserted by any man, or body of men, which is in any degree dependent on the State."[71] The national schools, the authors claimed, provided the mechanism through which the "Government have . . . overrun the country with a whole army of functionaries," an army "now defended as a matter of police."[72] As well as the national schools, there were factory schools, "ragged" and "feeding" schools (for homeless children), reformatory schools, prison schools, industrial schools, and convent schools.

What needs to be remembered from a material culture perspective is not only the extent of the reach of the school network but also the details of how these material chambers captured and acted on bodies, controlling inputs and outputs in a manner homologous with other chamber engines. Consider, for example, the new government-sponsored and -regulated discipline found in a Dublin national school (1854). Edward M'Gauran, later head schoolmaster at Mountjoy Model Prison, reported on the

> DISCIPLINE: No boy is allowed to speak unless on business and then he holds out his hand as a sign that he wishes permission. Orders, general and particular, are not only obeyed promptly but without the least sign of reluctance. In passing to and from, and also in moving through the school the children march in a single file keeping the step and with their hands behind. The great rule for order and regularity, "a time and a place for everything and everything in its proper time and place" is constantly inculcated and rigidly adhered to. In fact, everything is ready five minutes before the period specified in the "Table", in order that there should not be a moment lost when the proper time has

arrived for commencing the next subject. . . . All confusion is avoided; the children have their books, or writing materials at their hands, classes supplied with instructors, and the whole machinery moves, as it were of itself—no noise—no bustle—no disorder of any kind.[73]

As with the self-acting sanitary flusher, so too with this pedagogical machinery. The system was designed and built in such a way that discipline flowed automatically. This meticulous organization of bodies formed the material engine of discipline and sanitized socio-material space. It is in this context that one can understand the important connection commentators made between "the Irish education system" and the "problem of penal discipline." As the Prussian jurist Franz von Holtzendorff recognized, the forming of characters in schools and their reforming in penitentiaries depended on similar technologies and material designs. Thus while Catholics, Protestants, and government officials clamored for control of the system and the content of the learning, this only confirmed them in their agreement that "in Ireland the educational establishments are remarkable and efficacious engines of social power."[74]

EXPERIMENTAL MODELS AND SOCIAL ENGINEERING

The experimental dimensions of the new establishments for governing natural and political bodies are illustrated by the design of "model" schools, prisons, and training establishments. The prison at the center of the great experiment in penal correctionalism known as the Irish Convict System, for instance, was designed and described as Mountjoy Model Prison.[75] By 1872 there were no fewer than twenty-four "Model Agricultural Schools" throughout Ireland. Seventeen "District Model Schools" were built, as well as six "Minor Model Schools," and a "Central Model School" complex, which was part of the "Model Teacher Training" system.[76] Once a locality secured authorization for its own school, representatives and teachers could be brought to the model schools to see how the government expected them to operate. Special reports were made by the teachers and administrators of the model schools, and alterations were made in their design and organization, including the information technologies that were used to classify and monitor the students.

Material models were organizational experiments in the development of the state system. They did not so much instantiate institutions in organizational form as serve as engines for generating institutional meanings. If institutions are to have a certain taken-for-granted quality, as neo-institutionalists suggest,[77] then these early experiments are in some respects prior to institutionalization. This is an important point, because it implies that a historical analysis must grant that at least some institutions—for instance, disciplinary pedagogy—were literally forged in laboratories for modeling organizational forms. Focusing on these material forms implies a reevaluation of the idea that organizations themselves are secondary to wider "societal" institutions. The historical development of experimental organizational models, crucially material cultural forms, suggests that the directionality of institutionalization from society to organization, or from organization to society, is an empirical issue that cannot be stated in advance of the research. Indeed, one of the most powerful institutions of modern Western culture, "the individual," was deliberately crafted and forced into existence through the material organizational forms of schools, prisons, and so on.[78] The "individual" was a *class* rather than a societal institution, and in this context the institution of self-interest was hammered into people in the new disciplinary organizations.[79] This indicates the importance of developing more effective analyses of the power of organizations qua organizations.[80]

Focusing on the material forms of organizations shows how institutional change sometimes takes place not through a passive and relatively continuous *process* of formation, but through a strategic arrangement and deployment of material forms that crucially fabricate and force institutions into existence. Emphasis on design implies that the institutions of an engineering culture do not "evolve"; rather, they are engineered. Like all engines, however, engineered societies must be governed, regulated, and maintained. How this is to be achieved is a matter of contestation, but one approach in the mid-nineteenth century was that "knowledge" could both generate social power and regulate it. Just as the steam engine made "the power of steam provide, by its expansion, for its own control," so knowledge was "both power and safety; it exercises this self-control; it gives to the mighty social engine both the movement and the governor . . . 'Unmeasured strength with perfect art combined, / Awes, serves, amazes, and—protects mankind!'"[81] Such were the dreams, at least, of nineteenth-century engineering culture. The engine of society, however, was far less harmonious in its working than the steam engine, so recourse was always made to the mechanism of police—the governor of the system.[82]

POLICING MATERIAL PUBLIC SPACES

The great incarceration that occurred in Ireland in the nineteenth century was intimately linked to the constitution of a "moral environment" through the removal of "disorderly" people from the streets. Public order, public safety, and public health together constituted a discourse of police imperative that regularly mobilized the notion of a public nuisance that required removal. A dung heap, stray animal, or drunk person could each be defined as a nuisance and be removed by police officers under the various health and safety codes. Streets that were plumbed, paved, and cleaned, especially major streets, were not to be occupied by ragged and unhygienic bodies. Mid-Victorian Ireland, like Britain, witnessed a clampdown on scenes of "immorality and uncleanliness" in public. What this amounted to was an unprecedented material intervention in the streets that regularly culminated in a physical removal of bodies. F.M.L. Thompson has documented the steps taken in England to clear the streets of hawkers, peddlers, and loiterers: "The effect of such policing was marked. It made the streets, or at least the principal streets more and more into sterile territory on which the public had the right of passage but nothing else, not to meet, assemble, loiter, sit, gossip, trade or play."[83]

The concern to clear the streets of outwardly immoral or irregular behavior was particularly directed against drunks. Thompson has pointed out that, measured by results on charge sheets in England, half or more of police work was concerned with street life or drunks.[84] Popular festivals, particularly in Ireland, came in for special attention.[85] Notorious for their lower-class content of drinking, singing, fighting, sex, and general revelry, the festivals were either suppressed, as in the case of the (infamous) Donnybrook Fair in south Dublin, or transformed into commercial trading fairs. The Donnybrook Fair was defined in the 1830s as an "annual nuisance" and was vigorously policed until finally being banned in the 1850s.[86]

After immoral persons and unlicensed traders, children were identified as requiring special police in the public streets. Many poor children were enticed into the ragged and feeding schools, and thus off the streets, by provision of food and clothes. The English Playground and General Recreation Society complained of the dangers to "youths who are to be the future sinews of our farms, our factories at home and of our army and navy abroad" if they were left "a prey to the vice and contamination [of] unrestrained and unwatched street amusements."[87] The authors, whose article first appeared in the *Philanthropist* (and was later reproduced in the *Irish Quarterly Review*), quoted the *Spectator* to support their call for playgrounds: "The question is how to clear our streets of juvenile vagrants, to allure them to spots where they could play to their hearts' content: but always under a kindly and watchful supervision."[88]

The point here is that while the designs and the construction of a material culture of order, civility, and health needed to be taken seriously in their own right, and that the material forms in particular needed to be granted their power as an agency of order and health, the socio-material spaces so constituted still required the ongoing practices of management and police, organized in the material organization of the state system, if their designs were not to be thwarted. The government of material bodies, for example, demanded both the material culture of sanitary engineering and the regulatory activities of medical police.

In this chapter I have discussed the vast array of material culture through which Ireland was engineered. From topsoil and water closets to hedgerows and healthy houses, the physical condition of land and people was made a target of governing strategies. These strategies involved the incorporation of land, the built environment, and bodies into governed and governing spaces. These spaces ranged from the field and the street to the school and the house. Some, such as the model schools, were material engines for generating institutions and were nodes in a wide-reaching material infrastructure of social power. Others, such as the land, were both economic and political resources and a measure of identity and difference. The cultivated landscape, from ordered forest to manicured field, was an index of moral worth, and the ornament of the Georgian urbanscape constituted an aesthetic of power and cultural superiority.

Ireland provides fertile ground for empirical studies of engineering cultures and states, because it was a crucial site of modern scientific statecraft. From the perspective of this statecraft, "recalcitrant subjects" could be subdued only if they were materially incorporated into the state. A sufficient number of English planters and officials of government followed Davies's advice of 1619.[89] The country was enclosed, drained, and cleared of "debris." It was resoiled and replanted, hedged and trimmed. It was opened up by canals, roads, and railways. The towns were reordered and sanitized, and the bodies of the people were made subject to exacting discipline and police. The infrastructure of workhouses, prisons, and schools was spread across the country. Finally, coast guard stations, police and army barracks, post offices, and courthouses completed the network of governing power. All of these forms are familiar today, but they were not in the eighteenth and nineteenth centuries. Indeed, in every case government looked to science and engineering to provide innovative material designs. While the sociometers and socioscopes discursively incorporated the country into the state-idea and served as technologies of practice for engineering the state-system, the construction of a materially governed environment transformed the built environment into an infrastructural jurisdiction, thereby constructing the state-country as a fully material entity.

Conclusion

The degree to which the Irish case of state formation can be generalized is a question that can be conclusively answered only by additional studies. Some aspects of the Irish case, indeed, are unique to the Irish colonial context, such as a detailed and accurate countrywide cartography as early as the 1650s, a census that recorded individual names in 1821, a highly developed public health and medical police system in the 1850s, and a proactive centralized government throughout the nineteenth century. But the case of state formation in Ireland between the mid-seventeenth and late nineteenth century is not just a historical and local curiosity. Though likely wide variability occurs among the trajectories of particular cases,[1] I suggest that the Irish case brings into relief the role of science in modern state formation generally. This is partly because Ireland was the doorstep colony of England, one of the most powerful and advanced modern engineering states during this period.

Determining the role of science in modern state formation immediately raises the question of how to conceive of the new experimentalism associated with the Royal Society of London in the seventeenth century. The first clue lies in the early insights of Merton, Hessen, and especially Zilsel,[2] all of whom emphasized the centrality of technology and engineering in the new science. With this observation in mind and inspired by the work of Chandra Mukerji,[3] I began by surveying the material culture of experimental inquiry. I aimed to develop an understanding of the new *science as practice* by beginning with the material culture of inquiry rather than with the discourses of theory. The strategy sought to avoid the tendency to see technology as the mere application of science and instead to identify the technologies that were immanent in the research activity itself. Surveying those technologies revealed a vast range of apparatus, but four key forms gradually came into relief. My next problem was to name them in a manner that both respected the categories of the actors and served the purpose of analysis and explanation. Thus I arrived at the idioms *scopes, meters, graphs,* and *chambers.* I am not suggesting that these precise words are always used by actors to describe the type of technologies I am referring to or even that they are necessarily always distinct material forms. For instance, I include scanners and detectors in the category of scopes, and we usually find one or more of them engineered together in a single apparatus of inquiry. I do suggest, however, that these four categories capture relatively distinct practices of inquiry, practices with identifiable centers of gravity that are isomorphic across local settings.

Scopes, such as telescopes, socioscopes, and stethoscopes, augment sense perception. Scopes correlate with the practices of probing, framing, targeting, and surveying phenomena. Meters, on the other hand, suggest another set of practices. Meters measure, but they also order and regulate phenomena. They make possible the permanent generation of quantitative records over time. In addition, by translating the world into number, meters render it available to mathematical and statistical operations. The term *graph,* in distinction, aims to capture the strategies adopted for representing the world writ small, whether in maps, diagrams, pictures, or textual reports. The practice of graphing generates what Latour calls "inscriptions" and "immutable mobiles," representations that endure across time and space and are gathered in "centers of calculation."[4] Chambers, finally, are technologies of material control. They draw attention to the practices of physical manipulation that serve the generation of power and knowledge through the application of force. Thus by focusing on material culture I arrived at a conceptualization of the new science that places the technologies and practices of scoping, metering, graphing, and controlling at the center.

The ingenious design and use of these technologies of representation and intervention (to borrow Ian Hacking's term) set the stage for the extraction of facts about the world. Shapin and Schaffer indicate this character of the new experimentalism in relation to the centrality of Boyle's "pneumatick engine" in the elaboration of matters of fact. Indeed, the centrality of ingenuity and engines in Boyle's vision of experimental inquiry allowed Hobbes to construe the enterprise as an ignoble form of "engine philosophy."[5] Shapin and Schaffer were interested in the rhetorical uses of Hobbes's construal, but I was more interested in the implications that followed if Hobbes was correct in his assessment, and he was indeed correct. The new experimental science did imply a form of inquiry that generated knowledge through the use of ingenious engines. In addition, the four key technologies of inquiry that I identify drive this new research practice, constantly aiding the solution of problems and questions and at the same time generating new ones.

It is these observations that led me to the concept of "engine science." The term points to a form of science that is inherently powerful and is propelled by the use and development of scopes, meters, graphs, and chambers. Two key points need to be made about what I am trying to capture with the language of engine science. First, it is designed to transcend the historiography that views technology as the mere application of science.[6] My terminology emphasizes that science is as much an application of technology as technology is an application of science. Second, the practices of engine science do not originate in natural philosophy so much as in a broader engineering culture found in the military and in statecraft. Engine science was a key center of this engineering culture, because it tied the culture to both the new mechanical philosophy and the new philosophical experimentalism, as well as to the theology that conceived of God as an ingenious architect, engineer, and mathematician. These connections to philosophy and theology importantly distinguish modern engineering culture from that of the ancients.

In addition, it was not simply a case of engine science being applied to statecraft. It is not as though engine science started in the laboratory and then spread to points of implementation. Rather, a mutual traffic was established between science and governance (and as others are now showing, between science and industry, law, etc.). It was a traffic communicated through the shared practices of scoping, metering, graphing, and controlling. In this sense we see a double case of what Sheila Jasanoff and a growing number of STS scholars call coproduction:[7] the coproduction of knowledge and technology, and the coproduction of science and the state. The Irish case exemplifies Jasanoff's observation that "states are made of knowledge, just as knowledge is constituted by states."[8] And states and knowledge are made as such not only through discourses but also through practices and material transformations, key aspects of cultural reality that while ontologically entangled should never be analytically "imploded." It is not the case, as literature scholars are apt to suggest, that "science and literature are more like each other than they are different."[9]

Hobbes was also right when he suggested that experimental politics was the necessary corollary of experimental natural philosophy. About a century later, in the context of the French Revolution and the Terror, the Anglo-Irishman Edmund Burke excoriated the experimental philosopher as the "principle of evil himself: incorporeal, pure, unmixed, dephlegmated, defecated, evil."[10] Sentiment about experimental politics was not so inflamed in the second half of the seventeenth century, but there was plenty of suspicion. Concerns about "Reason of State" in seventeenth-century England encouraged political innovators such as William Petty to find other fields of research. Petty arrived in Ireland to lead the ambition of experimental statecraft in the context of a state broken by the Cromwellian conquest. Petty's construal of Ireland as a "white page," as a tabula rasa, was largely wishful thinking, despite the totality of the military defeat. Nonetheless, the notion of a flattened and emptied space, figuratively if not literally, served the ambition of experimental statecraft in Ireland, as it has in other colonial and postcolonial contexts.

Petty was the quintessential seventeenth-century adventurer-philosopher-capitalist, and he exemplified the new relationship between science and statecraft. While Machiavelli launched the science of (dark) regime-craft, and Hobbes a scientific theory of sovereignty, Petty was the harbinger of the modern engineering state. He was a virtuoso of experimentalism, anatomy, economics, statistics, cartography, and statecraft generally. While his cartography was made law for the purposes of the postconquest land settlement, most of his designs were not immediately implemented. Over the following two centuries, however, Petty's name was invariably cited as others successfully implemented similar projects. The long-term success of engineering statecraft in Ireland is partly explained by the fact that its designs were always wrapped in the discourses of "improvement" and the civilizing mission. The result was a deep interpenetration of science and government and the development of what I call the science-state plexus.

The word *plexus* conveys the complexity of the connections between science and governance in the modern state. With respect to land, for example, we see cartography, geology, natural history, botany, engineering, and experimental agriculture. Every aspect of the government of land becomes welded to engineering practices that inform and are informed by modern science. In terms of the people, we see how public health, medical police, censuses, medicine, education, and other institutional developments integrated bodies into the state, from womb to tomb. The built environment, finally, is incorporated into the state by earthworks, roads, inland navigation, hospitals, postal, police, and coast guard stations, and of course the ubiquitous sanitary engineering. There is little question about the centrality of the culture of engine science in the practices of modern statecraft. The point is that the modern state does not simply use science. Rather, it is crucially constituted by science. Indeed, it is modern science that partly explains the uniqueness of the modern state compared with all other states in the history of the world. The idea of the plexus evokes an image of the state as a network of networks that is discursive, organizational, and material.

The analytic strategy of triangulating culture in terms of discourses, practices, and materiality is deliberately simple, but it reveals a complex image of the modern state. Modern states are socio-technical systems, ingenious contrivances of things human and nonhuman. Viewed in this way, the state as an actor in the image of a (rational) human agent is difficult to comprehend. Governments act of course, but to treat those actions as the actions of a state is to facilitate the discursive and ideological strategy through which particular people at particular times represent their particular actions as the actions of an entire body politic. Yet I am not suggesting, as Foucault did, that we should cut off the king's head in political theory.[11] The sovereign actor state-idea is real to the extent that it is believed to be real and also to the extent that it is constantly iterated and thus institutionalized and taken for granted.[12] My approach has been to show that modern engineering states are, in addition, crucially made from the stuff of land, built environment, and bodies. It is out of these materials that they are artfully, ingeniously, and often quite forcefully contrived, designed, and materially constructed.

After the London government was forced out of Dublin, the state-system was hardly altered. Those who had spoken *as* the state were just one component of it, as easily replaced (once they agreed to leave) as administrations are in elections. Though a civil war occurred, it was over the territorial terms of the treaty rather the internal design of the state. A new state-idea was, however, articulated. It went under the name of the Free State and was represented as a completely new state, a new beginning—indeed, a rebirth. But both the state-system and the material culture of the colonizing government remained. The great buildings were not torn down, nor were they given new facades. The land was not reforested, nor enclosure reversed. Relatively little changed for the vast majority of the people, for when the call was made to "burn everything English but their coal," few took it literally. The statue of Queen Victoria, located outside Leinster House (the seat of the new government) was not removed until 1948. This is symbolic of the profound continuity within the Irish state before and after 1922. Governing institutions and discourses, practices and organizations, and material culture had been so effectively engineered into a modern state in Ireland by 1922 that they could not be undone without great destruction. Thus, while the English failed to secure sovereign rule over the entire island, they succeeded in engineering Ireland in their own likeness.

The implications of the Irish case are important for neocolonial efforts at "nation building" and for sociological understanding of the distinction between states and nations. The notion of nation building *by one people on behalf of another* fails to recognize that nations are, as Anderson so insightfully demonstrates, imagined communities.[13] Nations are first and foremost *peoples* who are bound together through collective memory and consciousness. In the Irish imagination it was church, literature, music, and poetry that formed the center of gravity of the newly imagined cultural nation.[14] Once independence was achieved for three-quarters of the country, science and engineering were excluded from the nation's imagination of itself. Indeed, the image of the nation was rural (understood as not engineered) and antimodern (only recently has Ireland come to formally embrace its engineering and scientific culture).[15] Therein lies the dilemma of all nation-building ambitions and an important reason for the ultimate failure of colonialism: while the "population of a state" can be engineered by one people on behalf of another, the "nation" of a state cannot. And because land is so central to the collective imagination of nation, it is the state-country rather than the state-system that lies at the heart of the nation-state-idea. Thus Irish nationalists use the language of "one land, one nation," while Unionists suggest that the island of Ireland is home to two nations.[16] Of course, there is no *essential* (or "natural") reason why both nations cannot be accommodated in one state, since the relationship between nation and state is itself imagined (granted the Irish would need to do major reimagining for the idea to work). Indeed, the relationship between nation and state shifts considerably in time and space. The United Kingdom, for instance, was forged as a sovereign state composed of four nations. In the contemporary context, the growth of the European state-system is being reimagined in terms of "diversity in unity," of many nations united in one state (though the politics of representation with respect to sovereignty does not permit such an explicit articulation of what is taking place). Thus the equation that is often assumed between "modern state" and "nation-state" fails to grasp the shifting character of the relationship. In addition, the tendency to naturalize the state and nation nexus can be regressive, especially when nation is imagined as a political community entirely defined by shared ethnicity or heritage. As the contemporary debacles of "ethnic cleansing" show, the ethnic nation state-idea exhibits the same tendencies as the racial nation state-idea. My point is that state building and nation building are not equivalent. The former can be imposed on a people from without, but the latter must be imagined from within.

Experimentalism informs political and public action in Western democracies through mechanistic metaphors and instrumental paradigms.[17] But despite the rich source of political and democratic meanings provided by modern science, ideas of self-government, universal franchise, private property, liberty, and freedom are what form the center of gravity of democratic governmentality. The implication of this study is that a deeper and less apparent dimension of modern governance operates at the level of everyday practice and sustains a form of "engineering governmentality." Engineering governmentality undergirds modern statecraft across democratic, totalitarian, colonial, and postcolonial states. It is an index of the modernity of states rather than their levels of democracy. Thus, while the postcolonial Irish context brought an orchestrated imagination of the nation that was decidedly antimodern, engineering governmentality continued to drive state development, evidenced by the ambitious electrification agenda adopted by the new Free State government. It may be true, as Yaron Ezrahi suggests, that in the postmodern world the instrumental paradigms and mechanistic metaphors of modern science are being replaced by the metaphors of art in the broadest sense of the term. But if we focus on the networked practices of science and government, it becomes clear that these practices remain profoundly modern. Scientifically informed government of land, people, and built environment is still broadly continuous with the vision articulated by Petty in the seventeenth century. If Petty could observe government organizations such as the (U.S.) Food and Drug Administration, the National Oceanic and Atmospheric Administration, the Centers for Disease Control, and the United States Geological Survey he would no doubt be fascinated. Yet he would likely see such organizations as consistent with his project of governing political objects according to their natural and artifactual qualities. Little is postmodern about these governing practices. Indeed, the details of the science-state plexus, manifest in the mundane world of agricultural inspectors, public health officials, building codes, sanitary sewers, cartographic surveys, census returns, engineered landscapes, and so on, somewhat bely the material power of the postmodern imagination. There can be little doubt that the (definitively modern) discursive purification of nature and culture has been accompanied by their unprecedented hybridization in practice and materiality.[18] However, because of the modern character of engine science, these practices and materialities are by no means "amodern."

Scientifically informed government is distinct from "scientific government." The latter idea, first articulated by Plato in the idea of the philosopher king, has regularly led to political monstrosity. James Scott, in an insightful contemporary study of engineering and the state, shows precisely how the ambitions of scientific government go awry, especially when an authoritarian high-modern ideology denies the value of local knowledge and triumphs over all other traditions that govern political conduct.[19] Scientifically informed government, on the other hand, sustains an uneasy but nonetheless real boundary between science and government. This is not to suggest that science is apolitical. Rather, a scientifically informed government involves the coproduction of science and government. Science drives the development of governance just as governance drives the development of science. Where the boundary lies between the two is an ongoing matter of boundary work and institutionalization in different historical and political contexts.[20] But the fundamental objects around which the coproduction of science and government occurs remain constant. They are land, people, and the built environment.

Through the combined practices of science and government, land, people, and the built environment are transformed into techno-territoriality, bio-population, and infrastructural jurisdiction. I use the term *techno-territoriality* to emphasize the theoretical point that the issue of territory, in the context of the modern state, is only partly captured by reference to coercive or sovereign dominion within a landmass (which can include territorial waters, islands, and colonies). Modern territoriality involves engineering land *into the state* in a way that extends, through particularizing scientific practices, the depth and reach of state power. The term *bio-population*, likewise, emphasizes that censuses are not simply a case of government counting people. The 1851 Irish census was the most detailed government accounting of life, death, disease, education, economic production, occupations, disabilities, and so on, that the world had ever seen. It even included a history of the causes of death from the earliest records available, through the more detailed accounts beginning in the second half of the seventeenth century, to the extensive records of the first half of the nineteenth century. There is little doubt that the Great Famine was the immediate catalyst for this catalog of life and death, but that does not detract from the character of the Irish censuses as sociometers and nososcopes: they scoped out and quantified everything bearing on life, disease, and death within the state. In addition, the census has to be understood as being connected in complex and heterogeneous ways with medical police and its project of arresting disease and securing health. The idiom *infrastructural jurisdiction* draws attention not only to the power of police officers to enter any building within a territorial domain (a power that is limited, of course, in various ways) but also to the construction of a built environment that is both a governed and a governing agent of health, safety, and social order. This will, of course, be no news to contemporary civil engineers, who learn "the code" in the process of learning their craft, incorporate it into their designs, and materialize it in the structures they build. Nor will the police dimension be lost on building inspectors and fire chiefs, who enforce the code, if with varying degrees of integrity and effort at different times and in different places.

Whether with respect to land, people, or the built environment, the governing practices of police are misunderstood when reduced to the enforcement of criminal law or political repression.[21] This view of police can no more explain the role of the Irish police in the containment of foot and mouth disease in the mid-nineteenth century than it can the role of the police in arresting mad cow disease in Britain at the turn of the twenty-first century. Nor can it capture how the construction of buildings became objects of scientifically informed government inspection, regulation, and enforcement. This is not to deny the many negative aspects of police in relation to struggles for liberty and justice. Rather, it is to point out that the police power of government, informed as it is by science, is also positively productive. It produces safe and secure conditions for human life, protecting it from the worse effects of technoscientific engagements with nature and also from disease and other life-destructive forces. It has always been the case, of course, that scientifically informed police is beset by powerful forces that severely limit life-enhancing government, particularly in the context of business interests that view such police as an impediment to their ability to make a profit.

Foucault noted that it is characteristic of the modern arts of government to improve individual and collective life and at the same time expand the power of the state. James Scott, from a different perspective, arrives at a similar conclusion, that is, that the modern state is the ground for both our freedoms and our unfreedoms.[22] Likewise, the government action that constitutes and secures the population of a state through police power can and often does improve the welfare of the people. For instance, there is no question that the life-security gains of public health and safety are inseparable from the police powers of a governing agency that is assembled, through practices, in the state-system. Vaccination is mandated by government, bodies are medically inspected in schools, safety is enforced in the workplace, builders are coerced to "build to code," and everything the population of a modern state consumes is subject to scientifically informed regulation. The ubiquity of the coproductions of science and government are found in the most mundane details of material life, from the sewer-gas trap under every kitchen sink to the water that comes out of the tap. If any issue is fateful for the average citizens of the modern state, it is the protection of their life-security (in the broadest sense of the term) by government power. In this context the classical liberal ideology of education and persuasion is no more feasible than the so-called neoliberal (now "neoconservative") ideology of antiregulation. The history of medical police shows that without police enforcement there is no public health and safety, an observation increasingly recognized in contemporary discourses of "biosecurity," driven as it is by fears of bioterrorist attack on bodies and anything they ingest.

It is difficult to sustain the idea of a zero-sum relationship between government or police and liberty. Modern liberties were secured in the context of the greatest expansion of government power the world has ever known. The implication is that police states and democratic states are not diametrically opposed. Democratic technoscientific states *are* police states, but ones in which police power is subject to representative and relatively accountable government. It is not a question of whether we are to be policed, but how we are to be policed, and how we are to police the police. The issue of medical police is likely to become more intense in the context of both the permanent technoscientific revolution in which we now live and the increasing threats of bioterrorism and flu pandemic.[23] Scoping and metering technologies extend targeting from the detection of cancer, subatomic particles, and extreme organisms to the detection of plastic explosives at airports, the purchasing patterns of consumers, and the private (now even genomic) lives of citizens, as well as the police exercise of quarantine.[24] In the context of the modern technoscientific order, it is easy to recognize that we live in a scopic regime and a data state.[25] Scopes are technologies of surveillance, just as meters are technologies of information intelligence. In addition, the scientific government of land has gone far beyond its incorporation into the state and the extraction of its resources for economic development. The destructive human and environmental consequences of engineering culture have become a battlefield in which the forces of science, government, and capital accumulation are variously aligned and pitched against one another.[26] The growing centrality of science in politics is the necessary outcome of the development of the science-state plexus. Practically every aspect of life on earth is now simultaneously a scientific and government issue. Indeed, our understanding of the dangers inherent in the coproductions of science and government is framed by those very coproductions.

Modern science as a philosophy of nature has been, at the same time, a philosophy of politics and statecraft. The Enlightenment idea of liberating humanity from the dictates of nature and instinct, and thereby placing reason in the service of human self-understanding and realization, was not *later* corrupted through the colonization of instrumental reason in the service of political domination and economic efficiency. The integrated strategies of scoping, metering, graphing, and controlling have been, since the beginning, directed toward dominating nature *and* society. These practices, at the heart of engine science and engineering culture, are inherently instrumental. To the extent that Enlightenment reason was part and parcel of modern science, it was always instrumental, but it was no less cultural for all that. Engine science was also about substantive understanding of the world, both natural and political, and this indicates that the very distinction between instrumental and substantive reason, between "interest" and "understanding," is theoretically problematic. What Foucault showed with respect to the human sciences is also true of the natural sciences. The will to knowledge and the will to power are inseparable in the modern period. Each directly implies and genuinely co-constructs the other. The modern engineering state is, as a result, a discursive formation of formidable institutional power, a heterogeneously engineered array of organizational practices, and a materially ordered and ordering physical condition of existence. The modern state is, in short, a discursive institution, an organizational system, and a scientifically incorporated country of land, people, and built environment.

Notes

Titles and quotations from primary sources are cited verbatim as published, that is, without modernizing archaic spellings and grammar. Many titles from the seventeenth to the nineteenth century sport expansive subtitles, but unless I considered these to be entirely redundant or irrelevant (which was rare), I reproduce them verbatim. In citations of reproductions or reprints of primary sources, the original date of publication is noted, when possible, in square brackets after the date of the cited version. Finally, legislation cited in the notes is not reproduced in the bibliography, nor are the individual works collected in *The Petty Papers*.

INTRODUCTION

1. Charles Tilly, *Coercion, Capital, and European States, AD 990–1992*, rev. paperback ed. (Malden, MA: Blackwell, 1992).

2. Julia Adams, Elisabeth S. Clemens, and Ann Orloff, "Social Theory, Modernity, and the Three Waves of Historical Sociology," in *Remaking Modernity: Politics, History, and Sociology*, ed. Julia Adams, E. S. Clemens, and A. S. Orloff (Durham, NC: Duke University Press, 2005).

3. I emphasize that I am speaking specifically about analyses of state *formation*, of states as historical processes. The literature has been growing on the *relationship* between science and the state. See, for example, Scott Fricket and Kelly Moore, eds., *The New Political Sociology of Science: Institutions, Networks, and Power* (Madison: University of Wisconsin Press, 2005).

4. For instance, Dietrich Rueschemeyer and Theda Skocpol, eds., *States, Social Knowledge, and the Origins of Modern Social Policies* (Princeton, NJ: Princeton University Press, 1996).

5. For example, see Steven Shapin and Simon Schaffer, *Leviathan and the Air-Pump: Hobbes, Boyle, and the Experimental Life* (Princeton, NJ: Princeton University Press, 1985); and Chandra Mukerji, *Territorial Ambitions and the*

Gardens of Versailles (Cambridge: Cambridge University Press, 1997). Science and modernity have received more attention than state formation per se. See Ming-Cheng M. Lo, *Doctors within Borders: Profession, Ethnicity and Modernity in Colonial Taiwan* (Berkeley: University of California Press, 2002); and James C. Scott, *Seeing Like a State: How Certain Schemes to Improve the Human Condition Have Failed* (New Haven, CT, and London: Yale University Press, 1998).

6. As noted in Adams, Clemens, and Orloff, "Social Theory." See also Julia Adams, *The Familial State: Ruling Families and Merchant Capitalism in Early Modern Europe* (Ithaca, NY: Cornell University Press, 2005); Philip Gorski, *The Disciplinary Revolution: Calvinism and the Rise of the State in Early Modern Europe* (Chicago: University of Chicago Press, 2003); and George Steinmetz, ed., *State/Culture: State Formation after the Cultural Turn* (Ithaca, NY: Cornell University Press, 1999).

7. Sheila Jasanoff, ed., *States of Knowledge: The Co-production of Science and Social Order* (New York: Routledge, 2004), 3.

8. Scott, *Seeing Like a State.*

9. The term *police* is commonly understood to designate the persons who perform the practice of policing. Following historical actors, I use the term in a number of different ways. For instance, the term *medical police* refers to a theory and a strategy for achieving public health as well as an organization of persons. I hope the context in which I use the term will clarify the meaning.

10. Tilly, *Coercion, Capital, and European States,* 2–3. Tilly prefers the term *national states,* but it is difficult to see how this language gets past the nation-state coupling, and the language of nation-state continues to be widely used as though it were unproblematic.

1. SCIENCE, CULTURE, AND MODERN STATE FORMATION

1. Diane Vaughan, *The Challenger Launch Decision: Risky Technology, Culture, and Deviance at NASA* (Chicago: University of Chicago Press, 1996).

2. Thomas F. Gieryn, *Cultural Boundaries of Science: Credibility on the Line* (Chicago: University of Chicago Press, 1999).

3. John Law, ed., *A Sociology of Monsters: Essays on Power, Technology, and Domination* (London: Routledge, 1991); Wiebe Bijker, Thomas Hughes, and Trevor Pinch, eds., *The Social Construction of Technological Systems: New Directions in the Sociology and History of Technology* (Cambridge, MA: MIT Press, 1987); Wiebe E. Bijker and John Law, eds., *Shaping Technology/Building Society* (Cambridge, MA: MIT Press, 1992).

4. Robert Merton, *Science, Technology, and Society in Seventeenth Century England* (New York: Howard Fertig, 2002 [1938]); Boris Hessen, "The Social and Economic Roots of Newton's 'Principia,'" in *Science at the Crossroads: Papers Presented to the International Congress of the History of Science and Technology* (London: Frank Cass & Co., 1971 [1931]); Edgar Zilsel,

"The Sociological Roots of Science," *American Journal of Sociology* 47 (1942): 544–56, repr. in *Social Studies of Science* 30, no. 6 (2000): 935–49.

5. For a discussion of the status anxiety caused by the use of technology in inquiry, see Deborah Jean Warner, "What Is a Scientific Instrument, When Did It Become One, and Why?" *British Journal for the History of Science* 23 (1990): 83–93.

6. Steven Epstein, *Impure Science: AIDS, Activism, and the Politics of Knowledge* (Berkeley: University of California Press, 1996).

7. Tilly, *Coercion, Capital, and European States.*

8. Tilly identifies three types of coercion that a state must engage in: state making, which involves attacking and checking internal rivals; war making, which involves attacking external rivals; and protection, which involves attacking and checking the enemies of allies. All these activities require "extraction" of the means, that is, capital. Tilly, *Coercion, Capital, and European States,* 96.

9. Ibid., 137. He calls these "trajectories of state formation," paths that lead to particular types of state: Russia and Venice, for instance, are examples of states that became coercion-intensive and capital-intensive, respectively. Britain is an example of the capitalized-coercion route, though Tilly notes that this should not be read as simply a compromise or synthesis of the other two forms. See 159.

10. See especially chapter 2 in John Walton, *Western Times and Water Wars: State, Culture, and Rebellion in California* (Berkeley: University of California Press, 1992).

11. The present study is limited to how the new science transformed government and how, in turn, government influenced the development of science, but the implications for issues related to economics will be apparent.

12. Culture has become an important explanatory category in a range of work on the state over the past couple of decades, spawning the first collection of social-scientific essays dealing with the question. See George Steinmetz, ed., *State/Culture: State Formation after the Cultural Turn* (Ithaca, NY: Cornell University Press, 1999).

13. Walton, *Western Times,* 119.

14. Charles Tilly, "Epilogue: Now Where?" in *State/Culture,* ed. Steinmetz, 412.

15. Walton, for instance, states that "the interplay of culture and ideology precede particular mobilization [collective action] strategies, give meaning and purpose to group organization, and determine the interests, organization, and mobilization methods available to a population or community." Walton, *Western Times,* 324. Tilly, on the other hand, treats "culture and identity, not to mention language and consciousness, as changing phenomena to be explained rather than as ultimate explanations of all other social phenomena." Tilly, "Epilogue," 411.

16. Quoted in Steinmetz, "Introduction: Culture and the State," in *State/Culture,* ed. Steinmetz, 6.

17. Mukerji, *Territorial Ambitions and the Gardens of Versailles.*

18. Steinmetz, "Introduction," 5–8.

19. John R. Hall, M. J. Neitz, and M. Battani, "Introduction," in *Sociology on Culture*, ed. John R. Hall, M. J. Neitz, and M. Battani (New York: Routledge, 2003).

20. Paul Lichterman, "'How Culture Matters' and 'Does Culture Matter?'" *Newsletter of the Sociology of Culture Section of the American Sociological Association* 18, no. 2 (Winter 2004): 5. See also Ann Swidler, *Talk of Love: How Culture Matters* (Chicago: University of Chicago Press, 2001); and Ann Swidler, "Culture in Action: Symbols and Strategies," *American Sociological Review* 51 (1986): 273–86.

21. Paul J. DiMaggio and Walter W. Powell, "The Iron Cage Revisited: Institutional Isomorphism and Collective Rationality," *American Sociological Review* 48 (1983): 147–60, repr. in Walter W. Powell and Paul J. DiMaggio, eds., *The New Institutionalism in Organizational Analysis* (Chicago: University of Chicago Press, 1991), 69.

22. Harry Collins, *Changing Order: Replication and Induction in Scientific Practice* (London: Sage Publications, 1985).

23. Lyn H. Lofland, *The Public Realm: Exploring the City's Quintessential Social Territory* (Hawthorne, NY: Aldine de Gruyter, 1998).

24. Mukerji, *Territorial Ambitions.*

25. Susan Davis, *Parades and Power: Street Theatre in Nineteenth-Century Philadelphia* (Philadelphia: Temple University Press, 1986).

26. John W. Meyer, "The Changing Cultural Content of the Nation-State: A World Society Perspective," in *State/Culture*, ed. Steinmetz, 137.

27. Philip Abrams, "Notes on the Difficulty of Studying the State," *Journal of Historical Sociology* 1, no. 1 (1988 [1977]): 58–89.

28. Meyer, "Changing Cultural Content," 138.

29. Peter B. Evans, Dietrich Rueschemeyer, and Theda Skocpol, eds., *Bringing the State Back In* (New York: Cambridge University Press, 1985).

30. Michel Foucault, "The Discourse on Power," in *Remarks on Marx: Conversations with Duccio Trombadori,* ed. R. James Goldstein and James Cascaito (New York: Semiotext[e], 1991), 164.

31. Michel Foucault, "Truth and Power," in *Power/Knowledge: Selected Interviews and Other Writings 1972–1977*, ed. Colin Gordon (New York: Pantheon Books, 1980), 121.

32. Mitchell Dean, *Governmentality: Power and Rule in Modern Society* (London: Sage Publications, 1999), 31.

33. Thomas Osborne, "Security and Vitality: Drains, Liberalism, and Power in the Nineteenth Century," in *Foucault and Political Reason: Liberalism, Neo-liberalism and Rationalities of Government,* ed. Andrew Barry, Nikolas Rose, and Thomas Osborne (Chicago: University of Chicago Press, 1996), 105.

34. Karl Polanyi, *The Great Transformation: The Political and Economic Origins of Our Time,* foreword by Joseph E. Stiglitz, with a new intro. by Fred Block (Boston: Beacon Press, 2001 [1944]), 145.

35. Ibid., 146.

36. T. Johnson, G. Larkin, and M. Saks, *Health Professions and the State in Europe* (New York: Routledge, 1995); Patrick Carroll, "Medical Police and the History of Public Health," *Medical History* 46, no. 4 (2002): 461–94.

37. Patrick Joyce, *The Rule of Freedom: Liberalism and the Modern City* (London: Verso, 2003).

38. Timothy Mitchell, "Society, Economy, and the State Effect," in *State/Culture*, ed. Steinmetz, 76.

39. Jack Goldstone, "The Rise of the West—or Not? A Revision of Socio-economic History," *Sociological Theory* 18, no. 2 (2000): 175–94; Jack A. Goldstone, "Efflorescences and Economic Growth in World History: Rethinking the Rise of the West and the British Industrial Revolution," *Journal of World History* 13 (2002): 323–89.

40. Leigh Star and James R. Griesemer, "Institutional Ecology, Translations and Boundary Objects: Amateurs and Professionals in Berkeley's Museum of Vertebrate Zoology, 1907–39," *Social Studies of Science* 19, no. 3 (1989): 387–420.

41. A conference was held at Cardiff University in 2001 to discuss this question.

42. John Hall, *Cultures of Inquiry: From Epistemology to Discourse in Sociohistorical Research* (Cambridge: Cambridge University Press, 2000).

43. Bruno Latour, *Science in Action: How to Follow Scientists and Engineers Around* (Cambridge, MA: Harvard University Press, 1987), 150.

44. Quoted in Oliver MacDonagh, "Ideas and Institutions, 1830–45," in *A New History of Ireland*, vol. 5, ed. W. E. Vaughan (Oxford: Clarendon Press, 1989), 206.

45. Donald MacKenzie, *Inventing Accuracy* (Cambridge, MA: MIT Press, 1990); Bijker and Law, *Shaping Technology*.

46. Indeed, because the Irish case appears to lie somewhere between colonial contexts and the European context, many Irish historians question whether Ireland can be understood as a colony at all. My own view is that no single model of what a colony should look like exists, and that the Irish case is just one example with its own peculiarities. For an excellent discussion of the debate, see Stephen Howe, *Ireland and Empire: Colonial Legacies in Irish History and Culture* (New York: Oxford University Press, 2000).

2. UNDERSTANDING ENGINE SCIENCE

1. Shapin and Schaffer, *Leviathan and the Air-Pump*, 130.

2. Patrick Carroll-Burke, "Tools, Instruments and Engines: Getting a Handle on the Specificity of Engine Science," *Social Studies of Science* 31, no. 4 (2001): 593–625.

3. William Petty, *The Political Anatomy of Ireland* (London: Brown & Rogers, 1691 [orig. written 1672]), repr. in *A Collection of Tracts and Treatises Illustrative of the Natural History, Antiquities, and the Political and Social State of Ireland*, vol. 2 (Dublin: Thom & Sons, 1861), 29.

4. Robert Boyle, "Some Considerations Touching the Usefulness of Experimental Natural Philosophy, the Second Tome, Containing the Latter Section of the Second Part," in *Robert Boyle: The Works,* 6 vols., ed. Thomas Birch (Hildesheim: Georg Olms Verlagsbuchhandlung, 1966 [1772, orig. written 1671]), 3:435; hereafter cited as *RBW.* The term could also mean "the science of machines." Peter Dear, *Discipline and Experience: The Mathematical Way in the Scientific Revolution* (Chicago: University of Chicago Press, 1995), 169.

5. Michel Foucault, *The Order of Things: An Archaeology of the Human Sciences* (New York: Vintage Books, 1973), 128–30.

6. *Oxford English Dictionary,* ed. James A. H. Murray, Henry Bradley, W. A. Craigie, and C. T. Onions (Oxford: Clarendon Press, 1933); hereafter cited as *OED.*

7. Joseph Beaumont, *The Complete Poems* (Hildesheim: Olms, 1968), quoted in *OED.*

8. John Row, *The History of the Kirk of Scotland* (Edinburgh, 1842), quoted in *OED.*

9. Shapin and Schaffer, *Leviathan and the Air-Pump,* 30. See also M. B. Hall, *Robert Boyle and Seventeenth-Century Chemistry* (Cambridge: Cambridge University Press, 1958), 185.

10. Shapin and Schaffer, *Leviathan and the Air-Pump,* 130.

11. Robert Boyle, "New Experiments Physico-Mechanical, Touching the Spring of the Air, and its Effects, Made, for the most Part, in a New Pneumatical Engine, Written by Way of a Letter To the Right Honourable Charles Lord Viscount of Dungarvan, eldest Son to the Earl of Corke," in *RBW,* 1:10.

12. Ibid., 1:3.

13. Boyle, "Some Considerations Touching the Usefulness of Natural Philosophy, Proposed in a familiar Discourse to a Friend, by way of Invitation to the Study of it," in *RBW,* 2:65. And in the second part of that work: "Man's power over the creatures consists in his knowledge of them; whatever does increase his knowledge, does proportionately increase his power." *RBW,* 3:423.

14. Ibid., 2:64.

15. Ibid., 2:14, emphasis added.

16. Carolyn Merchant, *The Death of Nature: Women, Ecology, and the Scientific Revolution* (London: Wildwood House, 1980).

17. Francis Bacon, *"The Advancement of Learning" and "New Atlantis,"* ed. Arthur Johnson (Oxford: Clarendon Press, 1974; orig. pub. 1605 and 1627, respectively), 244–45.

18. William Petty, *The History of the Survey of Ireland, commonly called The Down Survey,* ed. Thomas Aiskew Larcom (Dublin: Irish Archaeological Society, 1851 [c. 1659]), xiv; hereafter cited as *History of Survey.* In another text he suggested that there was no evidence that Ireland, before "first invaded," possessed any "enginery." Petty, *The Political Anatomy of Ireland,* 29.

19. William Petty, *The Petty Papers: Some Unpublished Writings of Sir William Petty,* 2 vols. Ed. from the Bowood Papers by Marquis of Lansdowne (London: Constable, 1927), 1:261.

20. Edmund Fitzmaurice, *The Life of William Petty 1623–1687* (London: John Murray, 1895), 254.

21. William King, "Concerning Hydraulic Engins," Trinity College, Dublin, MS I.4.18, fols. 105–12. King presented thirteen different designs for water engines to the Society. K. T. Hoppen, *The Common Scientist in the Seventeenth Century: A Study of the Dublin Philosophical Society 1683–1708* (Charlottesville: University Press of Virginia, 1970), 128.

22. Hoppen, *The Common Scientist*, 128.

23. Petty, *The Petty Papers*, 2:268.

24. Ibid., 2:269.

25. William Petty, *The Discourse Made Before the Royal Society Concerning the use of Duplicate Proportion in Sundry Important Particulars: Together with a New Hypothesis of Springing or Elastique Motions* (London: John Martyn, 1674).

26. J. A. Bennett, "Robert Hooke as Mechanic and Natural Philosopher," *Notes and Records of the Royal Society of London* 35 (1980): 33–48.

27. Ibid. Boyle admitted he did little of the experimental labor himself, but he was not adverse to it: "And though my condition does (God be praised) enable me to make experiments by others hands; yet I have not been so nice, as to decline dissecting dogs, wolves, fishes, and even rats and mice, with my own hands. Nor, when I am in my laboratory, do I scruple with them naked to handle lute and charcoal." Boyle, "Some Considerations Touching the Usefulness of Experimental Natural Philosophy," *RBW*, 2:14.

28. Quoted in Michael Hunter, *Science and the Shape of Orthodoxy* (Woodbridge: Boydell Press, 1995), 57.

29. Nicolas Canny suggests that the Hartlib Circle was not the single most important influence upon Boyle, arguing instead that the influence of his father, Richard Earl of Cork, and the experience of the New English planters in Ireland were more important. I see no need to view these influences as competing ones, but agree with Canny that one needs to situate Boyle in the wider context of planter culture and experience. See Nicolas Canny, *The Upstart Earl: A Study of the Social and Mental World of Richard Boyle, First Earl of Cork 1566–1643* (Cambridge: Cambridge University Press, 1982), esp. chap. 7.

30. Michael Hunter, *Science and Society in Restoration England* (Cambridge: Cambridge University Press, 1981), 87.

31. Zilsel, "The Sociological Roots of Science" (1942), 544–52.

32. Ibid., 552–53.

33. Ibid., 552. Examples Zilsel gives are Brunelleschi (1377–1446); Ghiberti (1377–1466); Leone Batista Alberti (1407–72); Leonardo da Vinci (1492–1519); Vanoccio Biringucci (d. 1538); Benvenuto Cellini (1500–1571); and Albrecht Dürer (early sixteenth century).

34. Ibid., 554–55.

35. J. A. Bennett, "The Mechanics' Philosophy and the Mechanical Philosophy," *History of Science* 24 (1986): 1.

36. Zilzel, "The Sociological Roots of Science," 558. Zilzel calls it *the* decisive event, noting that "Galileo's relations to technology, military engineering, and the artist-engineers are often underrated. . . . He established workrooms in his house, where craftsmen were his assistants. This was the first 'university' laboratory in history. He started his research with studies on pumps, on the regulation of rivers, and on the construction of fortresses. His first printed publication (1606) described a measuring tool for military purposes which he had invented" (555).

37. Quoted in Jim Bennett and Stephen Johnston, *The Geometry of War 1500–1750* (Oxford: Museum of the History of Science, 1996), 14. William Petty regularly complained of the niceties of rhetorical flourishes and advocated the "study of things" over the "rabble of words." William Petty, *The Advice of W.P. to Mr. Samuel Hartlib for the Advancement of some particulars parts of Learning* (London, 1648), 12.

38. Quoted in Bennett and Johnston, *The Geometry of War,* 14.

39. Ibid., 16.

40. Bennett, "The Mechanics' Philosophy," 2.

41. Ibid., 3.

42. Ibid., 10.

43. Ibid., 12.

44. Ibid., 13.

45. Ibid., 14.

46. Ibid., 15.

47. Ibid., 18.

48. Ibid., 22.

49. Ibid., 23. See also Bennett, "Robert Hooke as Mechanic and Natural Philosopher."

50. William Molyneux, *Dioptrica Nova: A Treatise of Dioptricks, In Two Parts, Wherein the Various Effects and Appearances of Spherick Glasses, both Convex and Concave, Single and Combined, in Telescopes and Microscopes, Together with Their Usefulness in many Concerns of Humane Life, are Explained.* 2nd ed. (London: Tooke, 1709 [1692]), 7.

51. Dear, *Discipline and Experience,* 223.

52. Petty, *Discourse made before the Royal Society concerning the use of Duplicate Proportion,* 5.

53. For instance, in the advertisements for the first Dublin Society, Petty gave the following "obligation" for aspiring members: "That they provide themselves with the Rules of number, weight and measure; not onely how to measure the plus & minus and the quality and Schemes of matter, but do provide themselves with Scales and Tables, whereby to measure and compute such qualitys and Schemes in their exact proportions." *The Petty Papers,* 2:91.

54. Dear, *Discipline and Experience,* 213.

55. Ibid., 213. Boyle argued that the "empire of man may be promoted by the naturalist's skill in mathematics, (as well pure, as mixed)." Robert Boyle,

"Some Considerations Touching the Usefulness of Experimental Natural Philosophy," in *RBW*, 3:425. He also described mechanics as a mathematical discipline (434).

56. Dear, *Discipline and Experience*, 155.

57. As Bennett, in his "Mechanics' Philosophy," put it: "The experimental method was not merely experiential, but interventionist: it advocated active interference with nature, particularly through the use of instruments of natural philosophy" (1).

58. Dear, *Discipline and Experience*, 155.

59. Dear has given the question of "contrivance" the attention it is due (ibid.).

60. Robert Boyle, "An Examen of Mr. T. Hobbes, his Dialogus Physicus de Natura Aeris; As far as concerns Mr. Boyle's Book of New Experiments touching the Spring of the Air, &c. With an Appendix touching Mr. Hobbes' Doctrine of Fluidity and Firmness," in *RBW*, 1:219. Boyle confirms his initial claims by means of a wholly differently contrived experiment, in which he used weights to hold mice under water until they drowned, observing before they did so the "divers bubbles, which seemed to be the respired air, [that] came out of their mouths, and ascended through the water." Hooke's engines in this context were even more dramatic. Before the gathered members of the Royal Society he conducted vivisection on a dog. After slitting the dog's windpipe, he kept it alive for several minutes using a bellows to pump air into its lungs.

61. Boyle, "Some Considerations Touching the Usefulness of Experimental Natural Philosophy," 3:442.

62. Ibid., 3:443.

63. Ibid.

64. Petty, *The Advice . . . to Mr. Samuel Hartlib*, 26; Boyle, "Some Considerations Touching the Usefulness of Experimental Natural Philosophy," 3:443.

65. Boyle, "Some Considerations Touching the Usefulness of Experimental Natural Philosophy," 3:443.

66. Also included were gardening, glassworks, cooking, dying, casting and founding, distillation, "sublimation, calcination, chrystalization, vitrification, [and] phosphorisation." William Petty, "History of Trades," in *The Petty Papers*, 1:205–7.

67. Thomas Shadwell, *The Virtuoso: A Comedy Acted at the Duke's Theatre* (London: Henry Herringman, 1676), 11.

68. Ibid., 12.

69. Gimcrack was "an enemy to Wit, as all Vertuoso's are." Ibid., 10.

70. Ibid., 49.

71. Ibid., 36.

72. Ibid., 54.

73. On the opposition between the ancient and the modern in this period, see William Temple, "A Defense of the Essay upon Antient and Modern Learning," printed in *Miscellanea: The Third Part* (Dublin: Jonathan Swift & A.M.

Prebendary, 1701): "It is by themselves confest, that till the new philosophy had gotten Ground in these Parts of the World, which is about fifty or sixty Years date, there were but few that ever pretended to exceed or equal the Antients; those that did, were only some Physcians [sic], as *Paracelsus* and His Disciples, who introduced new Notions in Physick, and new Methods of Practice, in opposition to the Galenical; and this chiefly from Chymical Medicines or Operations. But these were not able to maintain their Pretence long; the Credit of their Cures as well as their Reasons soon decaying with the Novelty of them, which had given them Vogue at first" (205–6).

74. Petty, *Discourse made before the Royal Society concerning the use of Duplicate Proportion*, 1–2.

75. Shadwell, *The Virtuoso*, 82.

76. Ibid., 81.

77. He argued that "the due management of divers trades is manifestly of concern to the public" and that this was proved by "those many of our English statute-laws yet in force, for the regulating of the trades of tanners, brick burners, and divers other mechanical professions." Boyle, "Some Considerations Touching the Usefulness of Experimental Natural Philosophy," *RBW*, 3:455. In relation to the society's schemes for agriculture, one yeoman refused to answer its "inquiries on the grounds that 'there is more reason of state in this Royall societie then at first I was aware of.'" Henry Stubbe warned the tradesmen of London of the dangers of the Royal Society's engines. Hunter, *Science and Society in Restoration England*, 125.

78. Boyle, "Some Considerations Touching the Usefulness of Experimental Natural Philosophy," in *RBW*, 3:397.

79. Ibid., 398. Clearly Boyle had an idea of what would later be called "tacit knowledge."

80. Ibid., 398.

81. Ibid., 399.

82. Ibid., 399.

83. Ibid., 451.

84. Ibid., 407.

85. Ibid., 413.

86. Ibid., 414.

87. Ibid., 423.

88. Ibid., 428.

89. Ibid., 438–39.

90. Ibid., 440.

91. Ibid., 446.

92. Ibid., 401.

93. Francis Bacon, "The New Science," in *The Portable Enlightenment Reader*, ed. Isaac Kramnick (New York: Penguin, 1995), 39.

94. In the spirit of Geoffrey Bowker and Susan Leigh Star's argument in their recent book, *Sorting Things Out*, I adopt a "flexible" strategy for distinguishing

the material culture of engine science, reflexively aware of its "political and organizational dimensions" that foreground its construction, and thus the construction of that which it seeks to comprehend. Geoffrey C. Bowker and Susan Leigh Star, *Sorting Things Out: Classification and Its Consequences* (Cambridge, MA: MIT Press, 1999).

95. Hans-Jörg Rheinberger, *Towards a History of Epistemic Things: Synthesizing Proteins in the Test Tube* (Stanford, CA: Stanford University Press, 1997).

96. Ibid.

97. Consider also pH meter, penetrometer, viscometer, watt meter, voltmeter, pyrometer, porometer, insulation meter, manometer, eudiometer, electrometer, photometer, ammeter, gasometer, spectrophotometer, ellipsometer, turbidimeter, calorimeter, polarimeter, magnetometer, interferometer, tachometer, spherometer, microdensitometer, hydrometer, geometer, hemoglobinometer, and so forth.

98. There are also the x-ray, spinthariscope, gastroscope, electroscope, polariscope, hygroscope, helioscope, baroscope, chronoscope, seismoscope, cystoscope, glucose sensor, nephelescope, gyrocompass, ophthalmoscope, tachistoscope, otheoscope, stereoscope, and so forth, and a range of "probes," "detectors," and "scanners."

99. Research into visual representation has constituted one of the most fruitful areas of science studies during the past couple of decades. See, for instance, Martin Rudwick, "The Emergence of a Visual Language for Geological Science, 1760–1840," *History of Science* 14 (1976): 149–95; Michael Lynch, "Discipline and the Material Form of Images: An Analysis of Scientific Visibility," *Social Studies of Science* 15, no. 1 (1985): 37–66; Michael Lynch and Steve Woolgar, eds., *Representation in Scientific Practice* (Cambridge, MA: MIT Press, 1990); James R. Griesemer, "Must Scientific Diagrams Be Eliminable? The Case of Path Analysis," *Biology and Philosophy* 6, no. 2 (1991): 155–80; Jane R. Camerini, "Evolution, Biogeography, and Maps: An Early History of Wallace's Line," *Isis* 84 (1993): 1–28; Ludmilla Jordanova, "Gender, Generation, and Science: William Hunter's Obstetrical Atlas," in *William Hunter and the Eighteenth-Century Medical World*, ed. W. F. Bynum and Roy Porter (New York: Cambridge University Press, 1985); Howard E. Gruber, "Darwin's 'Tree of Nature' and Other Images of Wide Scope," in *On Aesthetics in Science*, ed. Judith Wechsler (Cambridge, MA: MIT Press, 1978); and Mary G. Winkler and Albert Van Helden, "Representing the Heavens: Galileo and Visual Astronomy," *Isis* 83, no. 2 (1992): 195–217.

100. Michael Aaron Dennis, "Graphic Understanding: Instruments and Interpretation in Robert Hooke's *Micrographia*," *Science in Context* 3, no. 2 (1989): 347.

101. The term *virtual witnessing* is Shapin's. Shapin and Schaffer, *Leviathan and the Air-Pump*.

102. Understood in the narrow contemporary sense of an axial plot, graphing in science has been traced to the late eighteenth century. Thomas L. Hankins and Robert J. Silverman, *Instruments and the Imagination* (Princeton, NJ: Princeton University Press, 1995), 117.

103. Michel Foucault, *The Archaeology of Knowledge and the Discourse on Language* (London: Tavistock, 1972); Jacques Derrida, *Writing and Difference* (Chicago: University of Chicago Press, 1978).

104. Bruno Latour, "Drawing Things Together," in *Representation in Scientific Practice*, ed. Lynch and Woolgar.

105. Goldstone, "The Rise of the West—or Not?"

106. On the link between work and virtue and how this was impressed on the young Robert Boyle, see Malcolm Oster, "The Scholar and the Craftsman Revisited: Robert Boyle as Aristocrat and Artisan," *Annals of Science* 49 (1992): 255–76.

107. Boyle, "Some Considerations Touching the Usefulness of Experimental Natural Philosophy," 2:48–51.

108. Ibid., 23.

109. Ibid., 51.

110. Arguing against cameralist and mercantilist doctrine, which held that labor was the *only* source of wealth, Marx cited and paraphrased Petty, stating that nature was itself a source of wealth: "Labour is the Father and active principle of Wealth, as Lands are the Mother." Karl Marx, *Capital: A Critical Analysis of Capitalist Production*, vol. 1 (London: Lawrence and Wishart), 50. See also Petty, *The Petty Papers*, 2:47. Marx describes Benjamin Franklin as "one of the first economists, after Wm. Petty." Marx, *Capital*, 1:47 n. 1. On another occasion he states: "Once for all I may here state, that by classical Political Economy, I understand that economy which, since the time of W. Petty, has investigated the real relations of production in bourgeois society, in contradiction to vulgar economy, which deals with appearances only, ruminates without ceasing on the materials long since provided by scientific economy." Ibid., 85 n. 1. He also states: "Originally, Political Economy was studied by philosophers like Hobbes, Locke, Hume; by business men and statesmen, like Thomas Moore, Temple, Sully, De Witt, North, Law, Vanderlint, Cantillion, Franklin; and especially, and with the greatest success, by medical men like Petty, Barbon, Mandeville, Quesnay." Ibid., 578. William Petty, however, cannot be described simply as a "medical man." He was a virtuoso of experimentalism, engine science, social science, and statecraft. Nonetheless, it is clear that Marx views Petty as one of the most important figures in the foundation of political economy. Other citations of Petty by Marx in vol. 1 are: 57 n. 1; 95 n. 1; 103 n. 3; 124 n. 1; 141 n. 2; 144 n. 4; 297 n. 1; 324; 344 n. 1; and 520 n. 2. The Marquis of Lansdowne stated in 1927 that Petty was "the real founder and inventor of the science of Statistics, and in a more limited sense he may be said to have been the originator of that of Political Economy." "Introduction," *The Petty Papers*, 1:xvii. See also Alessandro Roncaglia, *Petty: The Origins of Political Economy* (Armonk, NY: M. E. Sharpe, 1985).

3. ENGINEERING CULTURE AND THE CIVILIZING MISSION

Epigraph: Petty, *The Petty Papers*, 1:111.

1. John Graunt [and William Petty], *Natural and Political Observations mentioned in a following Index, and made upon the Bills of Mortality. With reference to the Government, Religion, Trade, Growth, Air, Diseases, and the several Changes of the said City*, 3rd ed. (London: Martyn and Allestry, 1665 [1662]). I have studied the debate that has been carried on as to whether Petty or Graunt was the actual author of the observations. I am confidant that the substance of the argument and the style were Petty's and that the design behind it was his. It is likely, however, that Graunt collected and collated the data and also wrote some of the text. There are two reasons why Petty would have published it under Graunt's name. First, it was only two years after the Restoration, and Petty was concerned about publishing his political work and indeed continued to be throughout his life, refusing to publish the *Political Anatomy of Ireland* for fear of the political consequences. In addition, Graunt was his friend, and allowing him to publish the work ensured him entry into the newly founded Royal Society of London. On a more substantive point, Graunt never published, before or after, another piece on political arithmetic, while such is at the center of Petty's life's work. Dr. Willoughby, in his "Enquiries to be Made about the Bills of Mortality, aire, diseases &c.," in Rawlinson MSS, c. 406, fol. 68: Bills of Mortality, Dublin, April 17, 1691, writes: "I cannot pursue a better method than what was begun by the Learned Author of this new way of Observing, Sr. Wm. Petty." Nonetheless, the matter is not conclusively settled. See especially: Charles H. Hull, "Graunt or Petty? The Authorship of the Observations upon the Bills of Mortality," *Political Science Quarterly* 11 (1896): 105–32. Hull found in favor of Graunt, and today it is simply assumed that Graunt was the author.

2. Graunt [and Petty], *Natural and Political Observations*, the Epistle Dedicatory.

3. See, for instance, Fitzmaurice, *Life of Sir William Petty;* and E. Strauss, *Sir William Petty: Portrait of a Genius* (London: Bodley Head, 1954).

4. Quoted in Fitzmaurice, *Life of Sir William Petty*, 2.

5. John Aubrey, "A Brief Life of William Petty, 1623–87," in *Aubrey's Brief Lives*, ed. Oliver Lawson Dick (London: Secker and Warburg, 1949), 237.

6. Quoted in Fitzmaurice, *Life of Sir William Petty*, 4. Fitzmaurice's sources are letters by Petty to his friend Southwell, as well as other manuscripts in Petty's hand (2–3).

7. Quoted ibid., 5.

8. Known more commonly as simply the Dublin Society but also referred to as the Philosophical Society, the Dublin Philosophical Society, and the Philosophical Society of Ireland.

9. Strauss, *Sir William Petty*, 123.

10. Thomas Hobbes, *Leviathan*, with an introduction by A. D. Lindsay (London: Everyman, 1940 [1651]), 391.

11. Thomas Hobbes, "Dialogus Physicus" (1661), translated from the Latin by Simon Schaffer, in Shapin and Schaffer, *Leviathan and the Air-Pump,* 391.

12. On the concept of state legibility, see Scott, *Seeing Like a State.*

13. John T. Gilbert, ed., *A Jacobite Narrative of the War in Ireland 1688–1691,* repr. with an intro. by J. G. Simms (Shannon: Irish University Press, 1971 [1700]), 16–19.

14. William Petty, "The Registry of Lands, Commodities, and Inhabitants (1660–61)" (1661), in *The Petty Papers,* 1:75. The language is Lansdown's. Petty's scheme, modeled on institutions in Holland, but much more extensive in that it went beyond just land, was not to be fully realized until the census of 1841, and the creation of the surveyor and register general for Ireland of the same year.

15. Petty, *The Petty Papers,* 1:90.

16. Ibid., 108.

17. Petty, *The Political Anatomy of Ireland,* 7.

18. On material culture, engineering, and state formation, see Chandra Mukerji, "The Political Mobilization of Nature in Seventeenth Century French Formal Gardens," in *Theory and Society* 23, no. 5 (1994): 651–77; and Mukerji, *Territorial Ambitions.*

19. Edmund Burke, *A Vindication of Natural Society, or, A View of the Miseries and Evils Arising to Mankind from Every Species of Artificial Society. In a letter to Lord****,* ed. with an intro. by Frank N. Pagano (Indianapolis: Liberty Press, 1982), esp. 12–19, 38–45: "But with respect to you ye Legislators, ye Civilizers of Mankind! ye Orpheuses, Moseses, Minoses, Solons, Theseuses, Lycurguses, Numas! with Respect to you be it spoken, your Regulations have done more Mischief in cold Blood, than all the Rage of the fiercest Animals in their greatest Terrors, or Furies, have ever done, or ever could do!" (40).

20. Bruno Latour, *We Have Never Been Modern* (Cambridge, MA: Harvard University Press, 1993).

21. Petty, *Political Anatomy of Ireland,* 7.

22. Petty, *The Advice . . . to Mr. Samuel Hartlib,* 2.

23. Petty, *History of Survey.*

24. Petty, *Political Anatomy of Ireland,* 81.

25. Ibid., 34–36.

26. Ibid., 41.

27. Graunt [and Petty], *Natural and Political Observations,* 146–49.

28. Ibid., 151. Thomas Newenham, *A View of the Natural, Political, and Commercial Circumstances of Ireland* (London: Cadell and Davies, 1809), i–ii.

29. Petty, *The Advice . . . to Mr. Samuel Hartlib,* 4, 12.

30. Quoted in Fitzmaurice, *Life of Sir William Petty,* 11, 181.

31. Petty, *Political Anatomy of Ireland,* 8.

32. William Petty, *Another Essay in Political Arithmetick, concerning the growth of the City of London, with the measures, Periods, Causes, and Consequences thereof, 1682* (London, 1683), 43.

33. Petty, *The Advice . . . to Mr. Samuel Hartlib,* 12.

34. Ibid., 4.

35. Ibid., 5–7.

36. Ibid., 8.

37. Petty, *The Petty Papers*, 2:90. The rules were printed in John Gilbert's *History of the City of Dublin*, 3 vols. (Dublin: McGlashan & Gill, 1854–59), 2:174–76.

38. Petty, *The Discourse made before the Royal Society concerning the use of Duplicate Proportion*, epistle.

39. Aubrey, "Brief Life of William Petty," 241.

40. Petty, *The Petty Papers*, 2:91.

41. Ibid., 2:9 fn. 2.

42. William Petty, *Observations upon the Dublin Bills of Mortality, and the State of that City, 1681* (London: Mark Pardoe, 1683).

43. Petty, *The Petty Papers*, 2:89.

44. William Molyneux, *The Case of Ireland's being bound by Acts of Parliament in England, Stated* (Dublin, 1698). For a discussion of this work see J.G. Simms, *William Molyneux of Dublin 1656–1698*, ed. P.H. Kelly. (Shannon: Irish Academic Press, 1982).

45. The lineage between the two societies has been obscured by the manner in which they have been mapped onto the dichotomy between pure science and applied technology. K. T. Hoppen, in what remains one of the most authoritative sources on the Dublin Society, suggests that the two societies were entirely dissimilar: "Samuel Molyneux died at London in 1728 and with him the spirit of the Philosophical Society and the virtuoso scientists who had supported it. Three years later the Royal Dublin Society was founded, and although Thomas Molyneux was among its earliest members, it was inspired by a new and different attitude towards natural philosophy, being set firmly and exclusively on the rocks of utility and technology. Pure science of the kind that had constituted much of the business of the Philosophical Society made little headway during the first half of the eighteenth century, and comparative domestic stability seemed unable to produce scientists of a quality equal to those who had grown out of internal war and rebellion. Pure scientists were obsessed with the necessity of codifying Newtonian ideas. It was at once the age of thin elegance and of Squire Western. The virtuoso was dead." Hoppen, *The Common Scientist*, 198–99. As shown in chapter 2, the distinction between pure and impure with respect to scientific knowledge is indefensible and, in this instance, makes it difficult for Hoppen to perceive the crucial continuities between the philosophy and culture of the two Dublin societies.

46. *Sciences* was added to the title at the second meeting.

47. Quoted in R. Lloyde Praeger, "The Library," in *Royal Dublin Society Bi-centenary Souvenir 1731–1931*, ed. W.H. Brayden (Dublin, 1931), 46.

48. Ibid., 11.

49. Ibid., 12–16.

50. Quoted ibid., 19.

51. The royal charter was granted in 1820.

52. Jacqueline Hill, *From Patriots to Unionists: Dublin Civic Politics and Irish Protestant Patriotism, 1660–1840* (Oxford: Clarendon Press, 1997), 3.

53. Quoted in Felix Hackett, "The Scientific Activities of the Royal Dublin Society 1731–1931," in *Royal Dublin Society Bi-centenary Souvenir.*

54. Samuel Madden, *A Letter to the Dublin Society on the Improving their Fund and the Manufacture, Tillage &c. in Ireland* (Dublin: G. Ewing, 1736), 29.

55. Quoted in Simms, *William Molyneux*, 105.

56. Ibid., 34.

57. Ibid., 35.

58. Ibid., 39.

59. Quoted in R. F. Foster, *Modern Ireland 1600–1972* (London: Allen Lane, 1990), 212.

60. Hackett, "Scientific Activities of the Royal Dublin Society," 14.

61. Anon., *An Act for Directing the Application of the Sum of Eight Thousand Pounds granted to the Dublin Society, for The Encouragement of such Trades and Manufactures as should be directed by Parliament* (Dublin, 1766). The grant permitted the money to be spent on the encouragement of silk, woolen, leather, iron, steel, copper, brass, paper, glass, and earthenware manufacture, mixed manufactures of silk, wool, cotton, mohair, and liner thread, gold and silver thread, and laces, and printing, stamping, and staining of linens and cottons.

62. John Wade, *An Account of all the Proceedings that have been taken relative to the Management of the Chymical Laboratory in Capel Street, Dublin, from its first Institution to the present Time* (Dublin: James Parker, 1771).

63. Arthur Young, *Arthur Young's Tour in Ireland (1776–1779)*, ed. with intro. by Arthur Wollaston Hutton. 2 vols. (London: Bell and Sons, 1892), 2:131.

64. Quoted ibid., 4.

65. John Rutty, *A Chronological History of the Weather and Seasons, and of the Prevailing Diseases in Dublin. With their various Periods, Successions, and Revolutions, during the Space of Forty Years. With a comparative View of the Difference of the Irish Climate and Diseases, and those of England and other Countries* (London: Robinson and Roberts, 1770).

66. Charles Webster, "New Light on the Invisible College," *Transactions of the Royal Historical Society* 24 (1974): 33.

67. Quoted in Richard Drayton, *Nature's Government: Science, Imperial Britain, and the "Improvement" of the World* (New Haven, CT: Yale University Press, 2000), 55.

68. Oster, "The Scholar and the Craftsman Revisited," 257.

69. Ibid., 258. On nobility and military engineering, see Mukerji, *Territorial Ambitions.*

70. T.C. Barnard, "Improving Clergymen 1660–1760," in *As by Law Established: The Church of Ireland Since the Reformation*, ed. A. Ford, J. McGuire, and K. Milne (Dublin: Lilliput Press, 1995), 136. See also Drayton, *Nature's Government.* In this wonderful book, Drayton shows the full significance of the discourse of improvement as it relates to science and colonialism.

He notes, significantly, that improvement "originally meant to put to profit, and in particular to enclose 'waste' or common land" (51).

71. T. C. Barnard, "Gardening, Diet and 'Improvement' in Later Seventeenth-Century Ireland," *Journal of Garden History* 10, no. 1 (1990): 71.

72. Ibid., 71.

73. Ibid., 72.

74. Ibid., 72. Barnard notes that it is easy to assume, without a counterargument, that the Irish lived as the English claimed but that this would be a mistake. The Irish did engage in gardening and "improvement," and many of the experimental crops and techniques introduced were later abandoned, and indigenous techniques readopted.

75. For instance: Dublin Society, *The Advantages which may arise to the People of Ireland by raising of Flax and Flax-Seed, Considered Together with Instructions for Sowing and Saving the Seed, and Preparing the Flax for the Market* (Dublin: Dublin Society, 1732); and *The Dublin Society's Weekly Observations for the Advancement of Agriculture and Manufactures* (Dublin: Mitchell and Williams, 1763).

76. Madden, *Letter to the Dublin Society,* 40.

77. Anon., *Essays on Agriculture and Planting founded on Experiments made in Ireland, By a Country Gentleman* (Dublin: William Jones, 1790), x, emphasis in original.

78. Walter Wade, *Sketch of Lectures on Artificial or Sown Grasses, as Lucern, Saint-foin, Clovers, Trefoils, Vetches, &c. Delivered in the Dublin Society's Botanical Garden, Glasnevin* (Dublin: Dublin Society, 1808).

79. Joshua Kirby Trimmer, *A Brief Inquiry into the Present State of Agriculture in the Southern Part of Ireland, and its Influence on the Manners and Condition of the Lower Classes of the People: with some considerations upon the Ecclesiastical Establishment of that Country* (London: J. Hatchard, 1809).

80. Gerard Boate, *Ireland's Natural History* . . . (London: John Wright, 1657).

81. Patricia Coughlan, "'Cheap and Common Animals': The English Anatomy of Ireland in the Seventeenth Century," in *Literature and the English Civil War,* ed. Thomas Healy and Jonathan Sawday (Cambridge: Cambridge University Press, 1990), 212.

82. Ibid., 212–13.

83. Ibid., 213.

84. Boate, *Ireland's Natural History,* 89.

85. Edmund Spenser, *A View of the Present State of Ireland* (Oxford: Clarendon Press, 1970 [c. 1598]), 13.

86. Petty, *Political Anatomy of Ireland,* 68.

87. Ibid., 68.

88. See, for instance, George Berkeley, bishop of Cloyne, *A Word to the Wise, or an Exhortation to the Roman Catholic Clergy of Ireland* (Dublin: Faulkner, 1752).

89. Petty, *Political Anatomy of Ireland,* 69.

90. Berkeley, *A Word to the Wise*, 8.

91. The Catholic clergy of Dublin responded with the "highest sense of gratitude" to the bishop's plea.

92. James Tyrrell, "Of the Irish" (1680), in Locke MSS, c. 31, fol. 35, Bodleian Library, Oxford University.

93. Newenham, *A View of the Natural, Political, and Commercial Circumstances of Ireland*, xvii–xviii.

94. Gervase Parker Bushe, "An Essay towards ascertaining the Population of Ireland, In a Letter to the Right Honourable the Earl of Charlemont," in *Transactions of the Royal Irish Academy* (Dublin: Royal Irish Academy, 1790), 153.

95. Patrick Carroll-Burke, *Colonial Discipline: The Making of the Irish Convict System* (Dublin: Four Courts Press, 2000), esp. chap. 4.

96. Hackett, "Scientific Activities of the Royal Dublin Society."

97. In 1900 its administration was returned to Dublin under the Department of Agriculture and Technical Instruction. Ibid., 15.

98. H. Crawford Hartnell, "A Life of Two Hundred Years," in *Royal Dublin Society Bi-centennial Souvenir* (Dublin: Royal Dublin Society, 1931), 22.

99. George Atkinson, "What the Society Has Done for Art," in *Royal Dublin Society Bi-centennial Souvenir*, 38–39.

100. Latour, *We Have Never Been Modern*; Carroll-Burke, "Tools, Instruments and Engines."

101. R. B. McDowell, on the basis of the claim that contributions to the academy's transactions only "occasionally" dealt "with the application of science or scholarship to contemporary practical affairs," concluded that the academy in the nineteenth century "tended more and more to concentrate on pure science." He found support for this notion not in an explanation, justification, or documentation of "pure science," but in a statement from a member of the academy: "The attitude of most members when preparing work to be submitted to the academy could indeed be summed up, with admittedly a touch of exaggeration, in the toast quoted by a future President early in the twentieth century, 'Here's to science, pure and unadulterated, and may it never be of good to anybody.'" R. B. McDowell, "The Main Narrative," in *The Royal Irish Academy: A Bicentennial History 1785–1985*, ed. T. O. Raifeartaigh (Dublin: Royal Irish Academy, 1985), 14. Incredibly, McDowell's presentation of the academy in terms of "science for science's sake" appears in the context of a description of the academy's work that suggests the opposite was the case; that is, engine science was always about dominion over both nature and society.

102. Ibid., 15.

103. The most important award was the Cunningham Medal.

104. Quoted in MacDowell, "The Main Narrative," 16.

105. Ibid., 17.

106. Quoted ibid., 17.

107. Quoted ibid., 17.

108. Quoted ibid., 17.

109. *Transactions of the Royal Irish Academy,* vol. 1 (Dublin: Royal Irish Academy, 1787).

110. Burke, *A Vindication of Natural Society,* 43.

111. Ibid., 54–55.

112. Ibid., 70.

113. Ibid., 76.

114. Ibid., 79.

115. Ibid., 72–73.

116. Edmund Burke, *Reflections on the French Revolution and Other Essays,* intro. by A. J. Grieve, Everyman Series (London: J. M. Dent & Sons; and New York: E. P. Dutton & Sons, 1925 [1790]), 193.

117. Ibid., 169.

118. Ibid., 169.

119. Ken Alder, *Engineering the Revolution: Arms and Enlightenment in France, 1763–1815* (Princeton, NJ: Princeton University Press, 1997), 15.

120. Karl Marx was the next great advocate of the total redesign and engineering of the state. Raising the new edifice from the "ground up" demanded, once again, that the old be razed.

121. Hobbes, *Leviathan,* 90–91.

4. ENGINEERING THE DATA STATE

Epigraphs: O'Neill quoted in Nicholas Canny, *Making Ireland British, 1580–1650* (Oxford: Oxford University Press, 2001), 477. Petty quoted from the preface of his *Discourse on Taxes and Contributions: Shewing the Nature and Measures of Crown Lands etc.* (London, 1662).

1. Petty, *Discourse on Taxes and Contributions,* 487.

2. In one case, about a hundred men, women, and children were subjected to repeated torture, after which "they were 'driven like hogs' 6 miles to the river Bann, with rebels 'pecking them to go fast with swords and pikes thrusting them into their sides.'" They were then stripped and from the bridge forced headfirst into the river, those trying to escape by swimming shot in the water. In another case, a group begging for mercy were locked up in a house and burned to death. Irish men, women, and even children participated in the atrocities. It is likely true, as Canny argues, that subsequent Protestant accounts of the insurrection inflated the number and ferocity of the atrocious attacks. Ibid., 485. But to the extent that such accounts were believed to be true, they were true in their consequences.

3. Ibid., 578.

4. Canny, *The Upstart Earl.*

5. Canny suggests that Petty's map was merely a continuation of what had gone before. Petty's cartography and census, however, represented a significant break with previous efforts, a break that can be understood only in the wider context of the scientific revolution. Nicolas Canny, *Making Ireland British, 1580–1650* (Oxford: Oxford University Press, 2001), 558–59.

6. On the importance of surveying and cartography in the constitution of modern state power, see Mukerji, *Territorial Ambitions*.

7. Philip Corrigan, "Commissioned Cosmologies," discussion paper presented at the Workshop on State Formation in Comparative, Historical, and Cultural Perspectives, St. Peter's College, Oxford, March 1997.

8. Latour, *Science in Action*.

9. T.C. Barnard, *Cromwellian Ireland* (Oxford: Oxford University Press, 1975), 14.

10. Coughlan, "'Cheap and Common Animals,'" 219–20.

11. Samuel Hartlib, *A further Discoverie of The Office of Publick Address for Accommodations* (London, 1648), 26. This text began in 1641 as the "College of Reformation," a scheme for international correspondence among Protestant scholars. The first fully developed proposal appeared in 1646, as *A Brief Discourse Concerning the Accomplishment of our Reformation*. See Charles Webster, ed., *Samuel Hartlib and the Advancement of Learning* (London: Cambridge University Press, 1970).

12. Hartlib, *A further Discoverie of The Office of Publick Address*, 26.

13. Hartlib does not identify whom he is speaking of, but he had a special interest in Holland, which had stopped the advances of the Habsburg armies, chiefly by opening the canals and flooding the lowlands. He makes reference to the country in question as the "onely considerable power of Christendom" (i.e., Protestant) and as England's "neighbour Nation."

14. Hartlib, *A further Discoverie of The Office of Publick Address*, 27.

15. Webster, *Samuel Hartlib and the Advancement of Learning*, 131. The popularity of Hartlib's engine of government in terms of temporal over spiritual matters led John Dury to worry that the idea might be reduced to a bare "Material Engine" without moral or spiritual content. Ibid., 48.

16. Hartlib, *A further Discoverie of The Office of Public Address*, 5–8.

17. Ibid., 8–10.

18. Ibid., 10–11.

19. Ibid., 14–18.

20. Ibid., 19–22.

21. Though not a subject that can be entered into here, the Royal Mail, it can be noted, was centrally a transportation system for such intelligences and interrogatories, scientific, administrative, and military. Hartlib in communication with Boyle, for instance, spoke of his "interrogatories for *Ireland*," including intelligence on surveying, husbandry, and natural history. See Hartlib to Boyle, May 8, 1654; and Hartlib to Boyle, no date, though probably sent some time between 1654 and 1658. A copy of the latter can be found in Boyle, "Letters from Several Persons to Mr. Boyle," *RBW*, 6:89–90.

22. Hartlib, *A further Discoverie of The Office of Public Address*, 24–25, emphasis added.

23. There was also, of course, the problem of "trade secrets" and the theft of designs. Hartlib himself seemed rather suspicious and unhappy with Petty on this score. In a letter to Boyle in which Hartlib discusses the "contrivance of

his [Petty's] great design" for a college teaching Latin by "use and custom" and a history of trades, Hartlib asked Boyle to "handsomely present unto him, how he hath defeated me of two hundred and fifty pounds a year by undermining that more universal design of learning, upon which I have been made to hope these two years." Hartlib to Boyle, August 10, 1658, *RBW*, 6:112–13.

24. Quoted in Petty, *The Petty Papers*, xxix.

25. See, for instance, Arthur Dobbs, *An Essay on the Trade and Improvement of Ireland* (Dublin: Rhames, Smith & Bruce, 1729); anon., *An Abstract of the Number of Protestants and Popish Families in the Several Counties and Provinces of Ireland* (Dublin: Rhames and Gunne, 1736); Richard Price, *Observations on Reversionary Payments . . . ,* 2 vols., 6th ed. (London: Cadell and Davies 1803 [1769]); Thomas Newenham, A *Statistical and Historical Inquiry into the Progress and Magnitude of the Population of Ireland* (London: C. & R. Baldwin, 1805); *The Census of Ireland for the Year 1821 . . .* (Dublin: His Majesty's Stationery Office, 1823), Appendix; and *The Census of Ireland for the Year 1851*, part 5, *Table of Deaths*, vol. 1 (Dublin: Her Majesty's Stationery Office, 1856).

26. See, for instance, ibid., 2:10–15.

27. Ibid., 2:15.

28. All animals, he suggested, possessed such reasoning, but "speech" and "number" advantaged humans.

29. For a discussion of Petty as representing an intersection of Hobbes's and Boyle's philosophy, see Mary Poovey, *A History of the Modern Fact: Problems of Knowledge in the Sciences of Wealth and Society* (Chicago: University of Chicago Press, 1998).

30. Petty, *The Petty Papers*, 2:267.

31. Reprinted in William Petty, *Several Essays in Political Arithmetick* (London: Robert Clavel, 1699).

32. William Petty, *Two Essays in Political Arithmetick, Concerning the People, Housing, Hospitals, &c. of London and Paris* (London, 1687).

33. Petty, *Observations Upon the Dublin Bills of Mortality;* William Petty, *Further Observations upon the Dublin Bills: or, Accompts of the Houses, Hearths, Baptisms, and Burials in that City,* 2nd ed. (London: Mark Pardoe, 1686).

34. William Petty, *Quantulumcunque Concerning Money* (London, 1695); William Petty, *Reflections Upon Some Persons and Things in Ireland* (Dublin, 1660); Petty, *A Discourse on Taxes and Contributions.*

35. Petty, "The Registry of Lands, Commodities, and Inhabitants (1660–61)."

36. Anon., *An Abstract of the Number of Protestants,* 11.

37. *The Census of Ireland for the Year 1861,* part 4: *Report and Tables relating to the Religious Professions, Education, and Occupations of the People* (Dublin: Her Majesty's Stationery Office, 1863).

38. Ibid.

39. A bill to provide for such a count in 1910 was rejected by the House of Commons.

40. George T. Bisset-Smith, *The Census and Some of its Uses: Outlining a plain Philosophy of Population* (Edinburgh: W. Green & Son, 1921), 16.

41. On life insurance, see, for instance, Price, *Observations on Reversionary Payments.*

42. Cited in *The Census of Ireland for the Year 1821.*

43. Ibid. Daniel Beaufort, in his *Memoir of a Map of Ireland; illustrating the Topography of that Kingdom, and containing a short account of its present State, Civil and Ecclesiatical; with a complete index to the map* (Dublin: Slater and Allen, 1792), provided an estimate of four million.

44. Newenham, *A Statistical and Historical Inquiry;* Thomas Newenham, *View of the Natural, Political, and Commercial Circumstances of Ireland.*

45. Newenham, quoting Archdeacon Paley, in *A Statistical and Historical Inquiry,* 223.

46. Ibid., 327.

47. Ibid., 326.

48. See, for instance, Charles Coote, *Statistical Survey of the King's County, Being the Second Volume of the Statistical Surveys of Ireland* (Dublin: Dublin Society, 1801); Joseph Archer, *Statistical Survey of the County Dublin, with Observations on the Means of Improvement; Drawn up for the Consideration, and by Order of the Dublin Society* (Dublin: Dublin Society, 1801); and Robert Fraser, *General View of the Agriculture and Mineralogy, Present State and Circumstances of the County Wicklow, with Observations on the means of their improvement* (Dublin: Dublin Society, 1801). In all, twenty-four of the thirty-two counties were surveyed between 1801 and 1812. For a complete list of the surveys, see Royal Dublin Society, *A Bibliography of the Publications of the Royal Dublin Society from Its Foundation in the Year 1731, together with a List of Bibliographical Material relative to the Society,* 3rd ed. (Dublin: Royal Dublin Society, 1981).

49. Coote, *Statistical Survey of the King's County,* viii.

50. Archer, *Statistical Survey of the County Dublin.*

51. Coote, *Statistical Survey of the King's County,* xi. John Dubourdieu conducted the statistical surveys for Antrim and Down; and Hely Dutton, those for Galway and Clare.

52. An account of the failures was given in the 1821 census report: *The Census of Ireland for the Year 1821,* vi–vii.

53. Ibid., xi.

54. Ibid., xii.

55. Ibid., xii.

56. Ibid., xiii.

57. See, ibid., Appendix I, 383–87.

58. "Ploughlands, Gneeves, or other antiquated and vague terms of measurement" (ibid., xiii).

59. Ibid., xiii.

60. The instructions stated: "No assemblage of Houses is to be considered as a Village, unless it consist of twenty Houses adjoining each other, or nearly

so; and any assemblage (but containing at least five houses) is to be named 'a Hamlet,' and no notice is to be taken of any assemblage of Houses if fewer than five" (ibid., 384).

61. The French conducted some nominal censuses in parts of French North America between 1666 and 1757, though these bear little resemblance to a modern census. A nominal census was conducted in Norway in 1801, though other data was very limited. In England, Scotland, and Wales, the first nominal census was 1841; in Belgium, 1848; in the United States, 1850; in Canada, 1852; and in Italy, 1860. See Bruce Curtis, "Foucault on Governmentality: The Impossible Discovery," *Canadian Journal of Sociology* 27, no. 4 (2002): 505–33; Bruce Curtis, *The Politics of Population: State Formation, Statistics, and the Census of Canada, 1840–1875* (Toronto: University of Toronto Press, 2001).

62. *Census of Ireland for 1821*, ix–x.

63. *Census of Ireland for 1861*, part 1, *Showing the Area, Population, and Number of Houses, by Townlands and Electoral Divisions*, vol. 1, *Province of Leinster* (Dublin: Her Majesty's Stationery Office, 1863).

64. *The Census of Ireland for the Year 1831: Population, Ireland. Abstract of Answers and Returns under The Population Acts* (London: His Majesty's Stationery Office, 1833); *The Census of Ireland for the Year 1841* (London: Her Majesty's Stationery Office, 1843).

65. *Census of Ireland for the Year 1851*, part 6, *General Report* (Dublin: Her Majesty's Stationery Office), xi.

66. Quoted in W. E. Vaughan, "Ireland c. 1870," in *A New History of Ireland*, vol. 5, ed. W. E. Vaughan (Oxford: Clarendon Press, 1989), 767.

67. *Census of Ireland for the Year 1851*, part 6, *General Report*, vii.

68. Ibid., vi.

69. The manner in which the census is divided into parts and then volumes invariably causes confusion for librarians, who regularly deliver volume 4 of part 1 when part 4 is requested. Many libraries believe they have the entire census if they have the four volumes of part 1, and if one requests "part 5," one is told that there are only "four volumes." See the primary sources in the bibliography for the complete references for the 1851 census.

70. Each volume contained about two hundred pages, on the standard size used for parliamentary papers. *Census of Ireland for the Year 1851*, part 1, *Showing the Area, Population, and Number of Houses by Townlands and Electoral Divisions*, vols. 1–4 (Dublin: Her Majesty's Stationery Office, 1852).

71. Anon., "Dr. Maunsell on Political Medicine," *Dublin University Magazine* 13 (May 1839): 556.

72. *Census of Ireland for the Year 1851*, part 6, *General Report*, vi.

73. Anon., "Review of *The Quarterly Journal of Public Health*; including the Transactions of the Epidemiological Society of London," *Dublin Quarterly Journal of Medical Science* 19 (1855): 432.

74. *Census of Ireland for the Year 1851*, part 3, *Report on the Status of Disease* (Dublin: Her Majesty's Stationery Office, 1854).

75. Ibid., 111–14.

76. *Census of Ireland for the Year 1851,* part 5, *Table of Deaths,* vol. 1, 1.

77. Tables are contained in the appendix to part 6 of the 1851 census.

78. *Census of Ireland for the Year 1851,* part 6, *General Report,* xvi. The commissioners reported that all counties bar Dublin saw a population decrease, the highest being Monaghan at 117 per square mile, the lowest being Antrim at 7 per square mile. In the countryside the average decline was 53 per square mile, or 104 per square mile of arable land. Including the towns, the rate was 49. Class differences were very significant: the number of cottiers (holders of under five acres) crashed by almost 75 percent; laborers, by about one-third; and the drop in farmers holding fifteen to thirty acres fell from 310,000 to 192,000. Many farmers with over thirty acres survived very well and even benefited by adding to their consolidated holdings from the land freed up by poorest of the rural population.

79. Robert C. Simington, ed., *The Civil Survey,* AD *1654–1656,* 10 vols. (Dublin: Government Stationery Office, 1931), iii.

80. The oaths to be taken by the surveyor general and the undersurveyors are reproduced in Petty's *History of Survey,* 374–75.

81. Simms, *William Molyneux of Dublin,* 51. Robinson designed and built the great Royal Hospital, in Kilmainham, for retired and sick soldiers.

82. The interrogatory is reprinted in Hoppen, *The Common Scientist in the Seventeenth Century,* 200–201.

83. Ireland first appeared in a map in Ptolemy's world map of the second century AD. It was also represented in the early medieval "diagrammatic mappae mundi" and in the sea charts produced by fourteenth-century Italian and Iberian navigators. Only during the Tudor conquest of the sixteenth century, however, did Ireland come to be effectively represented internally, via the military and political maps produced by the surveyors and engineers of the English army. Exceptional examples in this context are the maps of Robert Lyth (1567–71), the two John Browns (uncle and nephew), Francis Jobson (1587–98), and Richard Bartlett (1601–2). Some of these maps were used for the representations of Ireland by Abraham Ortelius (1573), Gerard Mercator (1564 and 1595), and John Speed (1611). J.H. Andrews and Paul Ferguson, "Maps of Ireland," in *Historians' Guide to Early British Maps: A Guide to the Location of Pre-1900 Maps of the British Isles Preserved in the United Kingdom and Ireland* (London: Royal Historical Society, 1994), 72.

84. Petty, *History of Survey,* 62–63. Petty, however, did not believe Strafford's map of Tipperary was useful, and he considered Worsley's method of surveying to be "absurd."

85. Robert C. Simington, ed., *Books of Survey and Distribution: Being Abstracts of Various Surveys and Instruments of Title, 1636–1703, With Maps* (Dublin: Government Stationery Office, 1956).

86. Ibid., xxi.

87. William Petty, "A Briefe Accompt of the most Material Passages relatinge to the Survey managed by Doctor Petty in Ireland, anno 1655 and 1656" (c. 1659), repr. in Petty, *History of Survey,* xvi.

88. Ibid., xiv.

89. Ibid., xiv.

90. Ibid., xv.

91. Ibid., xv–xvi.

92. Ibid., xvi.

93. William Petty, *A Brief of Proceedings between Sir Hierom Sankey and Dr. William Petty. With The State of the Controversie between them Tendered to all Indifferent Persons* (London, 1659).

94. J. H. Andrews, *A Paper Landscape: The Ordnance Survey in Nineteenth-Century Ireland* (Oxford: Clarendon Press, 1975), 15.

95. Petty, "A Briefe Accompt of the most Material Passages," xvi.

96. Edmund Spenser, *A View of the Present State of Ireland* (Oxford: Clarendon Press, 1970 [c. 1598]), 67–68.

97. The relevant section in the act was noted by Petty in his *Political Anatomy of Ireland*, 73.

98. William Petty, *Hibernia Delineatio: Atlas of Ireland* (Newcastle-upon-Tyne: Frank Graham, 1968 [1685]).

99. Francis Lamb, *A Geographicall Description of ye Kingdom of Ireland. Collected from ye actual Survey Made by Sir William Petty* . . . (London: Francis Lamb, 1689).

100. For instance, see Laurence Eachard, *An Exact Description of Ireland: Chorographically Surveying all its Provinces and Counties After a more Accurate, Plain Eafie, and particular Manner than any before done in this kind* . . . (London: Tho. Salusbury, 1691). A similar textual intelligence publication appeared in the nineteenth century, though it was based on secondary sources: *The Parliamentary Gazetteer of Ireland, adapted to the new poor-law, franchise, municipal and ecclesiastical arrangements, and compiled with a special reference to the lines of railroad and canal communication, as existing in 1843–44; Illustrated by a series of maps, and other plates; and presenting the results, in detail, of the census of 1841, compared with that of 1831*, vol. 1 (Dublin: A. Fullarton & Co., 1844). "The materials out of which the Gazetteer of Ireland is compiled include some rare and unique Documents,—several voluminous results of Engineering Surveys,—almost every book which could be procured on the Topography, either of Ireland alone, or of the United Kingdom,—numerous Agricultural Surveys of Counties,—the productions in the several departments of Antiquities, History, and Science,—a collection of Tours, Sketches, Periodicals, and Serials,—and so large a mass of Parliamentary Reports, as to contain very nearly all the details of the many official investigations which have, within the last thirty-two years, been made into the condition, resources, and statistics, of the country. These materials exhibit Ireland in a comprehensiveness, a minuteness, and a rich variety of views, incomparably greater than could arise from the personal researches—no matter how laborious or prolonged—of a whole corps of special Topographists; and they possess the singular advantage of presenting, through different and even opposite mediums, those numerous features of the country's condition which are so

generally contorted by prejudice, and made the subjects of angry and interminable dispute" (1). The "large . . . mass of Parliamentary Reports" referred to in this quotation were important government engines of intelligence, but they are beyond the scope of this work. On the history of the Royal Commissions of Inquiry, see Hugh McDowall Clokie and J. William Robinson, *Royal Commissions of Inquiry: The Significance of Investigations in British Politics* (Oxford: Oxford University Press, 1937).

101. J.H. Andrews, "Charles Vallancey and the Map of Ireland," *Geographical Journal* 132 (1966): 48–61.

102. J.H. Andrews, *Ireland in Maps: An Introduction* (Dublin: Dolmen Press, 1961).

103. George Taylor, *Taylor and Skinner's Maps of the Roads of Ireland, 1778* (London, 1778).

104. Andrews, *A Paper Landscape,* 5. Andrews suggests that Richard Edgeworth's map of Longford in the 1790s was the first Irish map of "high exactitude."

105. Ibid., 5.

106. Ibid., 5.

107. Ibid., 21.

108. O. J. Vignoles, *The Life of Charles Blacker Vignoles* (Dublin, 1889), 389.

109. Secretary of Board of Ordnance to Colby, June 22, 1824, quoted in Colby to Smyth, August 25, 1828, War Office Records 44/115, London.

110. Ordnance Estimates (1825), item 13, H.C. (35), xviii.

111. Colonel Thomas Colby, *Annual Survey Report* (1826), Larcom Papers, MS 7555, National Library of Ireland, Dublin, quoted in Andrews, *A Paper Landscape,* 145.

112. Lieutenant E. Aldrich to Captain A. Henderson, February 19, 1830, State Papers, Registered Papers, 425, National Archive, Dublin.

113. On the relations among state formation, the military, engineering, and cartography in the case of France, see Mukerji, *Territorial Ambitions.*

114. There also emerged, from the eighteenth century, a tradition of "thematic maps," which linked population numbers to some other criteria of interest. See, for instance, Beaufort, *Memoir of a Map of Ireland;* and Dominic Corrigan, *Cholera Map of Ireland, With Observations* (Dublin: Browne & Nolan, 1866).

115. *Instructions to the Valuators and Surveyors appointed under 15th and 16th Vict., Cap. 63, for the Uniform Valuation of Lands and Tenements in Ireland* (Dublin: Her Majesty's Stationery Office, 1853); *Statutes, as amended, relating to General Valuation and Boundary Survey of Ireland, from the 30th June, 1852, to the 7th August, 1874* (Dublin: Her Majesty's Stationery Office, 1888).

116. Andrews, *A Paper Landscape,* 123.

117. Brian Friel, *Translations* (London: Faber & Faber, 1981). Charles Coote, discussing Irish names in his statistical survey of King's County, noted how the Irish "denominations seem so barbarous to us" but admitted that they did

contain a logic ("Eile iu Cherabuil," for instance, means descriptively "the plain or flat area near the rock") and were thus "undeserving the harsh criticisms, which some authors have bestowed on them." Coote, *Statistical Survey of the King's County*, 3.

5. BIO-POPULATION

Epigraphs: William Gibson and Bruce Sterling, *The Difference Engine* (New York: Bantam Books, 1992). The book is a historical science fiction story that provides an image of what the Victorian world might have looked like if Charles Babbage had managed to build his Difference Engine. *Report of the Medical Council* (1855), quoted in Henry Rumsey, *Essays in State Medicine* (London: John Churchill, 1856), dedication page. Jonas Hanway, *The Defects of Police, the Cause of Immorality* (London: J. Dodsley, 1775), 255.

1. R. A. Wakefield, "Police Chemistry," *Science in Context* 13, no. 2 (2000): 231–67.

2. William Petty, "Anatomy Lecture" (1676), in *The Petty Papers*, 2:176.

3. Quoted in Fitzmaurice, *The Life of William Petty*, 253.

4. Charles Cameron, *History of the Royal College of Surgeons in Ireland, and of the Irish Schools of Medicine* . . . (Dublin: Fannin, 1886), 93.

5. Graunt [and Petty], *Natural and Political Observations*, 1–2.

6. Petty, *The Petty Papers*, 1:187–89.

7. Dr. Charles Willoughby, "Enquiries to be Made about the Bills of Mortality, aire, diseases &c.," in Rawlinson MSS, c. 406, fol. 68: Bills of Mortality, Dublin, and fols. 69–81, 92, and 97, undated, Bodleian Library, Oxford University, quotation from fol. 69.

8. Kenneth Dewhurst, "The Genesis of State Medicine in Ireland," *Irish Journal of Medical Science* 6 (1956): 367–68.

9. Ibid., 368.

10. Locke stated his reasoning thus: "I have often thought that if such a Register as this, or one that were better contriv'd with the help of some Instruments that for exactness might be added, be kept in every County in England and so constantly published, many things relating to the Air, Winds, Health, Fruitfullness etc. might by a sagacious man be collected from them, and several Rules and Observations concerning the extent of Winds and Rains will be in time established to the Great Advantage of Mankind" (quoted ibid., 368).

11. Quoted in C. H. Hull, ed., *Economic Writings of Sir William Petty* (Cambridge: Cambridge University Press, 1899), 4:4. See also Petty, *Further Observations upon the Dublin Bills*.

12. Graunt [and Petty], *Natural and Political Observations*, 71.

13. Quoted in Dewhurst, "Genesis of State Medicine in Ireland," 373.

14. Ibid., 375.

15. Ibid., 381.

16. Johann Frank, *A System of Complete Medical Police*, ed. Erna Lesky (Baltimore, MD: Johns Hopkins University Press, 1976), xvi. Frank conceived

of this work in 1766, and it appeared between 1779 and 1825, the last volumes posthumously.

17. Discussed ibid., xv.

18. Ibid., 12.

19. Michel Foucault, "Omnes et Singulatim: Towards a Criticism of Political Reason," in *Michel Foucault: Politics, Philosophy Culture, Interviews and Other Writings 1977–1984,* ed. Lawrence D. Kritzman (New York: Routledge, 1988), 73.

20. Ibid., 82.

21. Frank, *A System of Complete Medical Police,* ix.

22. William Blackstone, *Commentaries on the Laws of England,* 4 vols. (Oxford: Clarendon Press, 1768), 3:216–22, 4:161–75.

23. James Black, "Lectures on Public Hygiene and Medical Police," *Provincial Medical and Surgical Journal,* part 22 (1844): 327. Blackstone also documented the early quarantine laws, which were confirmed and amended by 29 Geo. II, c. 8, and provided for forty days' confinement of the sick and the employment of "watchmen" for enforcement. The legislation, according to Blackstone, put the law in "a much more regular and effectual order than formerly." Blackstone, *Commentaries on the Laws of England,* 4:162.

24. Donna Andrew, *Philanthropy and Police: London Charity in the Eighteenth Century* (Princeton, NJ: Princeton University Press, 1989), 6.

25. *First report of the Philanthropic Society* (London, 1788).

26. Jonas Hanway, *The Defects of Police, the Cause of Immorality* (London: J. Dodsley, 1775), ii–iii.

27. Ibid., 283.

28. Ibid., emphasis in original.

29. Ibid., 255.

30. Harold J. Cook, "Policing the Health of London: The College of Physicians and the Early Stuart Monarchy," *Social History of Medicine* 2, no. 1 (1989): 1–33.

31. Ibid., 4.

32. Quoted ibid., 25.

33. Paul Slack, *The Impact of Plague in Tudor and Stuart England* (London: Routledge and Kegan Paul, 1985), 207–26. The first plague regulations were promulgated as early as 1518.

34. Ibid., 226.

35. John Fielding, *A plan of a Preservatory and Reformatory for the Benefit of Deserted Girls and Penitent Prostitutes* (London: R. Franklin, 1758), 2.

36. John Fielding, *An Account of the Origin and Effects of a Police set on foot by His Grace the Duke of Newcastle in the year 1753, upon a Plan Presented to His Grace by the late Henry Fielding, esq.* (London: A. Miller, 1758); John Howard, *The State of the Prisons in England and Wales* (London: William Eyres, 1784).

37. Andrew Duncan, *Heads of Lectures on Medical Jurisprudence* (Edinburgh, 1795), published in 1801 as *Heads of Lectures on Medical Jurisprudence and Medical Police* (Edinburgh: Adam Neill).

38. Brenda M. White, "Medical Police, Politics and Police: The Fate of John Roberton," *Medical History* 27 (1983): 408.

39. Ibid., 409.

40. John Roberton, *Medical Police: Or the Causes of Disease, with the Means of Prevention . . . ,* 2 vols., 2nd ed. (London: J. J. Stockdale, 1812).

41. Ibid., 1:xlviii.

42. He explored police in relation to drainage, ventilation, food handling, waste disposal, occupational hazards, diet, and eating utensils. He wrote subsections on the "police of soil," occupations, manners, and so forth, and "police for the construction of houses," "police for climate," and so on. Ibid., 2:351.

43. Ibid., 2:355–57.

44. Frank, *A System of Complete Medical Police,* 11.

45. Ibid., 222.

46. Ibid., 222.

47. Ibid., 357.

48. John Gordon Smith, *The Principles of Forensic Medicine, Systematically Arranged and Applied to British Practice* (London: Underwood, 1828), xvii. Smith relied on Wildberg's *Bibliotheca medicinae publicae* for his figures. I have not been able to locate a copy of this publication.

49. Michael Ryan, *A Manual of Medical Jurisprudence and State Medicine* (London: Sherwood, Gilbert & Piper, 1836), xiii. Ryan used *medical jurisprudence* and *legal medicine* interchangeably.

50. Ibid., xiii.

51. Frank, *A System of Complete Medical Police,* 11; H. Aubrey Husband, *The Students Hand-book of Forensic Medicine and Medical Police,* 3rd ed. (Edinburgh: E & S Livingstone, 1879).

52. Black, "Lectures on Public Hygiene and Medical Police," part 19, 275.

53. Ryan, *A Manual of Medical Jurisprudence and State Medicine,* xiii.

54. See, for instance, Rumsey, *Essays on State Medicine;* Charles Moore, *Remarks on State Medicine* (Dublin, 1888); and anon., "Essays on State Medicine," review article, *Dublin Quarterly Journal of Medical Science* 22 (1856).

55. Frank, *A System of Complete Medical Police,* 285.

56. Ibid., 287.

57. Ryan, *A Manual of Medical Jurisprudence and State Medicine,* xxi.

58. Ibid., xiv–xv.

59. See, for instance, Charles Cameron, *A Manual of Hygiene, Public and Private, and Compendium of Sanitary Laws . . .* (Dublin: Hodges, Foster & Co., 1874). Cameron equated political medicine and state medicine and defined the former as a science for the prevention of the causes of disease (2). He defined hygiene as "the science which relates to the physical condition of man, and the

means by which his health may be sustained, and his life prolonged to old age" (4). See also Henry Maunsell, *Political Medicine* (Dublin, March 1839). John Gordon Smith treated political medicine as the equivalent of state medicine as understood in Germany, defining it as consisting of two branches, forensic medicine and medical police. Smith, *The Principles of Forensic Medicine*, vi.

60. "1. Ages.—Characteristics and import of the several gradations in the period of human life, from the hour of birth to its natural decay, and final extinction; comprehending many circumstances relative to physical education, exercise, and other points of management. 2. Marriage and population.—The proper period and subjects for the former, with the influence of these considerations on the welfare of descendants—fecundity, mortality, &c. as questions of state importance. 3. General or national manners.—Their influence on health. 4. Air, food, and drink.—Importance of their purity and wholesomeness— including the medico-legal consideration of nuisances, adulterations, public cleanliness, ventilation, regulations for markets, slaughter-houses, burial-grounds, &c. 5. Public buildings for numerous inmates.—As manufactories, barracks, prisons, hospitals, ships, &c. as regards ventilation, warmth, economy, discipline, labour, &c. 6. Topography.—Comprehending climate, meteorology, soil, productions, &c. of countries, and particular neighbourhoods. 7. Clothing and dwelling-places. 8. Employment and management of the poor, in order to preserve them from disease. 9. Contagious, epidemic, and endemic diseases.— Enumeration and history of the prevalent varieties; measures to be adopted to prevent their breaking out, or to arrest their progress. Here the important question of Quarantine will fall under consideration. 10. Dangers incident to certain situations.—As mines—during thunder-storms—and from a variety of accidents. Plans and institutions for resuscitating those apparently dead, from drowning, or other causes." Ryan, *A Manual of Medical Jurisprudence and State Medicine*, 477–78.

61. Black, "Lectures on Public Hygiene and Medical Police," part 19, 275. Black presented medical police in terms of general climate; water and fuel; topographical climate and the atmosphere of towns; special "sources of insalubrity, noxiousness and discomfort that may arise from either want of attention to cleanliness or ventilation, or from the deleterious, or even unpleasantness of certain manufactures, chemical and other works, whose drainage or gaseous emanations if not positively injurious to health and property, at least come under the denomination of nuisances and occupational diseases" (part 26, 391).

62. William Strange, "On the Formation of a System of National Medical Police and Public Hygiene," *London Medical Gazette, or Journal of Practical Medicine* 2 (1846): 452–57; William Strange, *The Health and Sickness of Town Populations considered with Reference to Proposed Sanitary Legislation, and to the Establishment of a Comprehensive System of Medical Police . . .* (London: Parker, 1846). The latter source is one of the most widely surviving English books on medical police, with copies in many U.S. libraries and archives.

63. Strange, "On the Formation of a System of National Medical Police," 452–53.

64. Anon., "The Medical Police of London," *Journal of Public Health and Sanitary Review* 1 (1855): 324 (London: Thomas Richards).

65. Edwin Chadwick, *The Health of Nations, a review of the works of Edwin Chadwick, With a Biographical Dissertation by Benjamin Ward Richardson*, 2 vols. (London: Longmans, Green, & Co., 1887). Also the *Report of the Poor Law Commissioners, 1838*, with its two supplementary reports: "Report on the Prevalence of Certain Physical Causes of Fever in the Metropolis which might be removed by Proper Sanatory Measures" (under pen of Neil Arnott and James Kay-Shuttleworth [formerly Philips Kay]); "Report on Some of the Physical Causes of Sickness and Mortality to which the Poor are Particularly Exposed, and which are Capable of Removal by Sanitary Regulations" (under pen of Thomas Southwood Smith) (London: Her Majesty's Stationery Office).

66. See, for instance, Rumsey, *Essays on State Medicine*; Henry Rumsey, *On State Medicine in Great Britain and Ireland* (London: William Ridgway, 1867); Henry Rumsey, *The Educational aspects of State Medicine* (London: W. J. Golbourn, 1868); and Henry Rumsey, *Essays and Papers on Some Fallacies of Statistics concerning Life and Death, Health and Disease, with Suggestions Towards an Improved System of Registration* (London: Smith, Elder and Co., 1875).

67. Rumsey classified the information regarding the state of health according to three divisions. The first dealt with the extent of the population, mortality rates, fertility, rates of sickness and accidents, and the types and condition of dwellings. The second encompassed food and "animal life," physical geography, chemical analysis, and meteorological observations. "Legal" issues relative to jurisprudence, death inquests, and government regulation of medical practitioners formed the third division.

68. Preventative measures included the construction of towns and buildings and the "purification of same viz. nuisances," water supply, drainage, sewerage, paving, and smoke pollution. Preventative measures also included physical education, the sale of food, medicines and poisons, the protection of workers and the public from the hazards of certain trades and occupations, modes of transportation, recreations and places of public resort, and, of course, the handling of dead bodies.

69. Special interventions were required during times of epidemic disease, such as house-to-house visitations, the use of quarantine power, the control of animal diseases, and government-imposed vaccination campaigns.

70. Including the registration and licensing of health professionals and veterinarians.

71. Rumsey, *Essays on State Medicine*.

72. For example, Richard Boulton, *An Essay on the Plague, &c.* (Dublin, 1721).

73. Joseph Rogers, *An Essay on Epidemic Diseases, and more particularly the Endemical Epidemics of the City of Cork, &c.* (Dublin: William Smith, 1734).

74. Edward Foster, *An Essay on Hospitals; or, Succinct Directions for the Situation, Construction, and Administration of Hospitals* . . . (Dublin: W. G. Jones, 1768). Foster claimed that his was the first work to deal with hospital construction and its relations to disease prevention. Infirmaries Act, 36 Geo. III., c. 9 (1765).

75. Anon. [William Dease], *Remarks on Medical Jurisprudence, Intended for the General Information of Juries and Young Surgeons* (Dublin: 1790).

76. Edward Geoghegan, *Observations on the Necessity of Regulating the Medical Profession* (Dublin, 1795).

77. See, for example, Charles Fletcher, *A Maritime State Considered as to the Health of Seamen* (Dublin, 1786).

78. Thomas Rutty, *An Essay towards a Natural, Experimental, and Medicinal History of the Mineral Waters of Ireland* (Dublin, 1757); Thomas Rutty, *The Argument of Sulphur or no Sulphur in Water Discussed* (Dublin, 1762); Thomas Rutty, *A Methodological Synopsis of Mineral Waters* (Dublin, 1762). See also John Burges, *An Essay on the Water and Air of Ballyspillan* (1725); John Smith, *The Curiosities of Common Water; or the Advantages thereof in Preventing and Curing many Distempers* . . . (Dublin: G. Ewing, 1725); Edward Barry, *Wines and Medicinal Waters* (Dublin, 1775); and Henry Kennedy, *An Experimental Enquiry into the Chemical and Medicinal Properties of the Sulphurous Water at Auchnacloy* (Dublin, 1777).

79. Thomas Rutty, *An Essay towards the Natural History of the County of Dublin*, 2 vols. (Dublin: Slater, 1772); Thomas Rutty, *Analysis of Milk and the Different Species thereof* (Dublin, 1762); Rutty, *A Chronological History of the Weather and Seasons*. Also of interest related to the topic of the last work is T. C. Fleury's "Essay on the Epidemic Cold of 1775," which was read before the Medico-philosophical Society and was published in the *Dublin Quarterly Journal of Medical Science* over half a century later. Anon. [Fleury], "The Influenza," *Dublin Quarterly Journal of Medical Science* 5 (1848): 256–58.

80. See also, for instance, Husband, *The Student's Hand-Book of Forensic Medicine and Medical Police*, 432–65; Cameron, *A Manual of Hygiene*, 123–28; and John Moore, "On Meteorology in its Bearing on Health and Disease," in *Lectures on Public Health Delivered in the Lecture Hall of the Royal Dublin Society* (Dublin: Hodges, Foster and Co., 1874).

81. Thomas Willis, *Facts connected with the Social and Sanitary Condition of the Working Classes in the City of Dublin, with tables of sickness, medical attendance, deaths, expectation of life, &c., &c.; Together with some gleanings from the Census Returns of 1841* (Dublin: T. O'Gorman, 1845), 46.

82. Maunsell, *Political Medicine*, 4.

83. John David Henry Widdess, *The Royal College of Surgeons in Ireland and Its Medical School, 1784–1966* (Edinburgh: E. and S. Livingstone, 1967), 71.

84. Anon., "Dr. Maunsell on Political Medicine," 562.

85. Ibid., 552.

86. Ibid., 562.

87. Willis, *Facts connected with the Social and Sanitary Condition of the Working Classes*, 55.

88. Ibid., 48.

89. Ibid., 49.

90. Ibid., 46.

91. Ibid., 49.

92. William Stokes, *A Treatise on the Use of the Stethoscope* (Dublin, 1825). He also published *Two Lectures on the Application of the Stethoscope* (Dublin, 1828).

93. William Stokes, *Diseases of the Chest* (Dublin, 1837); William Stokes, *Diseases of the Heart and Aorta* (Dublin, 1854).

94. William Stokes [Jr.], *William Stokes, His Life and Work (1804–1878)* (London: T. Fisher Unwin, 1898), 168.

95. William Stokes, "Introductory Discourse on Sanitary Science in Ireland," in *Lectures on Public Health Delivered in the Lecture Hall of the Royal Dublin Society* (Dublin: Hodges, Foster and Co., 1874).

96. Anon., "Review of *The Quarterly Journal of Public Health;* including the Transactions of the Epidemiological Society of London," *Dublin Quarterly Journal of Medical Science* 19 (1855): 429.

97. Anon., "Essays on State Medicine," 147–48.

98. Dominic J. Corrigan, *On Famine and Fever as Cause and Effect in Ireland; with Observations on Hospital Location, and the Dispensation in Outdoor Relief of Food and Medicine* (Dublin: J. Fannin & Co., 1846).

99. One of the large-scale effects of malnutrition was diarrhea, and without sanitary conditions typhoid could easily take hold and spread. Indeed, the terms *famine fever* and *famine diarrhea* were widely used, often interchangeably. See Joseph Lalor, "Observations on the late Epidemic Fever," *Dublin Quarterly Journal of Medical Science* 5 (1848): 12–30.

100. Corrigan, *On Famine and Fever as Cause and Effect in Ireland*, 21.

101. Ibid., 26.

102. Lalor, "Observations on the late Epidemic Fever," 27.

103. Stokes, "Introductory Discourse on Sanitary Science," 7.

104. Michel Foucault, "The Politics of Health in the Eighteenth Century," repr. in Paul Rabinow, *The Foucault Reader* (New York: Pantheon Books, 1984), 278.

105. Hanway, *The Defects of Police, the Cause of Immorality*.

106. Ibid., xvii.

107. Black, "Lectures on Public Hygiene and Medical Police," part 26, 391–96, quotation from 395.

108. Foucault, "Politics of Health," 273.

109. Ibid., 274.

110. Dublin Hospitals Regulation Act, 19 & 20 Vict., c. 110 (1856).

111. MacDonagh, "Ideas and Institutions," 209.

112. The most notable hospital in the country before the eighteenth century was the Royal Military Hospital, for "sick, lame and old soldiers." Petty also noted a "hospital for poor children, not yet fully perfected nor endowed."

113. Rumsey, *On State Medicine in Great Britain and Ireland,* 5. Rumsey reported that the Irish system was adopted as the model for reorganization of medical relief in London.

114. R.B. McDowell, *The Irish Administration 1801–1914* (London: Routledge and Kegan Paul, 1964), 166.

115. Rumsey referred to the hospitals as the "noble metropolitan institutions of Ireland" and noted that, while they received private donations, they "always depended, more or less, on grants voted by Parliament" (Rumsey, *Essays in State Medicine,* 226). In 1845, the hospitals and dispensaries within the two Dublin workhouse unions cost forty-eight thousand pounds to maintain, thirty thousand of which was provided by central government. Willis, *Facts Connected with the Social and Sanitary Condition of the Working Classes,* 51. In 1854, 722 dispensaries serviced by 777 medical officers, plus 968 "drug stations," cost almost ninety thousand pounds to maintain, at which point they were under the management of the poor law commissioners.

116. Perhaps it is prophetic that the site of the first Irish poorhouse (initiated in 1667 and established in 1703) is today the site of St. James's Hospital in Dublin, the largest "acute general hospital" in the country.

117. Sanitary Loans Act, 29 & 30 Vict., c. 90 (1866).

118. Sanitary Act, 33 & 36 Vict., c. 69 (1870).

119. An Act to Establish Regulations for the Prevention of Contagious Diseases in Ireland, 39 Geo. III, c. 41 (1819).

120. Corrigan, *On Famine and Fever as Cause and Effect in Ireland,* 21.

121. Circular issued by the Central Board of Health as to precautionary measures in reference to Fever or other Contagious Disease (Dublin, May 17, 1848). See also Circular issued by Central Board of Health concerning Cholera (Dublin, Sept. 1, 1848).

122. The Temporary Fever Act, 9 Vict., c. 6 (1846); and An Act to Amend and Extend the Temporary Fever Act, 10 Vict., c. 22 (1847). See also further amendments by 12 Vict., c. 131 (1848).

123. An Act to Establish Regulations for the Prevention of Contagious Diseases in Ireland, 39 Geo. III, c. 41 (1819); Diseases Prevention Act, 18 & 19 Vict., c. 116 (1855); Nuisances Removal Act, 18 & 19 Vict., c. 121 (1855); Nuisances Removal and Diseases Prevention (amendment) Act, 23 & 24 Vict., c. 77 (1860); Nuisances Removal Act, 26 & 27 Vict., c. 117 (1863).

124. Public Health Act, 11 & 12 Vict., c. 63 (1848); Sanitary Act, 29 & 30 Vict., c. 90 (1866); Sanitary Loans Act, 32 & 33 Vict., c. 100 (1866); Sanitary Act, 31 & 32 Vict., c. 115 (1868); Sanitary Act, 33 & 34 Vict., c. 53 (1870); Public Health (Ireland) Act, 37 & 38 Vict., c. 93 (1874); Local Government Act, 24 & 25 Vict., c . 61 (1858, amended 1861); Local Government Act, 34 & 35 Vict., c. 109, (1871); Local Government Act, 35 & 36 Vict., c. 69 (1872).

125. Common Lodging Houses Acts: 14 & 15 Vict., c. 28 (1851); 16 & 17 Vict., c. 41 (1853); and 23 & 24 Vict., c. 26 (1860); Labouring Classes Lodging Houses and Dwellings (Ireland) Act, 29 & 30 Vict., c. 44 (1866); Artizans and Labourers Dwellings Act, 31 & 32 Vict., c. 130 (1868); Labouring Classes Dwellings Act, 30 Vict., c. 28 (1866); Public Parks (Ireland) Act, 32 & 33 Vict., c. 28 (1869); Gas and Water Works Facilities Act, 33 & 34 Vict., c. 70 (1870); Burial Grounds (Ireland) Act, 19 & 20 Vict., c. 98 (1856); Burial Act, 33 & 34 Vict., c. 98 (1871); Towns Improvement Act, 17 & 18 Vict., c. 103 (1854), which incorporated sections from the Towns Improvement Clauses Act (1847), the Commissioners Clauses Act (1847), and the Lands Clauses Consolidation Act (1845); Lighting, Cleansing, and Watching of Towns Act, 9 Geo. IV, c. 82 (1828); Sewer and Sewage Utilization Acts: 28 & 29 Vict. c. 75 (1865); Amended, 29 & 30 Vict., c. 90 (1866). There is also a series of building acts with clauses relevant to health and safety, some of which were incorporated in the Local Government Act (1858), such as the size of rooms, the thickness of walls, the height of ceilings, the provision of yards, and the safety of roofs and chimneys.

126. E.g., Adulteration of Drugs and Medicines, 9 Geo. II., c. 10 (1735); Adulteration of Food Act, 23 & 24 Vict., c. 84 (1860); Adulteration of Food, Drink and Drugs (amendments), 35 & 36 Vict., c. 74 (1872); and Licensing Act (1872).

127. E.g., Petroleum Acts: 25 & 26 Vict., c. 66 (1862); and 35 & 36 Vict., c. 56 (1872); Sale of Poisons Act, 33 & 34 Vict., c. 26 (1870); Bakehouse Regulation Act, 26 & 27 Vict., c. 44 (1866).

128. Public Health (Ireland) Act, 37 & 38 Vict., c. 93, sects. 7 and 8 (1874).

129. Ibid., sects. 1 and 2.

130. Cameron, *A Manual of Hygiene*, 15.

131. R. V. Comerford, "Ireland 1858–70, Post-famine and Mid-Victorian," in *A New History of Ireland*, vol. 5, ed. W. E. Vaughan (Oxford: Clarendon Press, 1989), 390.

132. Charles Moore, *The Sanitary Condition of Dublin Dairy Yards* (Dublin: Falconer, 1886), 7–8.

133. Vaughan, "Ireland c. 1870," 767. Control of cattle disease was long a function of medical police. The first chair of state medicine in Vienna in 1804, for instance, was filled by someone who had written on the containment and prevention of "cattle plague."

134. Sanitary Act, 29 & 30 Vict., c. 90, sect. 16 (1866); Public Health Act, 37 & 38 Vict., c. 93, sect. 36 (1874).

135. Public Health Act, 37 & 38 Vict., c. 93, sect. 58 (1874).

136. Vaughan, "Ireland c. 1870," 768.

137. This and the following quote are from John Bailey Denton, *Sanitary Engineering: A Series of Lectures given before the School of Military Engineering at Chatham, 1876* (London: E. & F. N. Spon, 1877), dedication page.

138. W. D. Wodsworth, *Digest of the Sanitary Laws in Force in Ireland* (Dublin: Alexander Thom, 1874), 25.

139. Mary Douglas, *Purity and Danger: An Analysis of the Concepts of Pollution and Taboo* (London: Routledge and Kegan Paul, 1966).

140. R.M. Bancroft (president of the Civil and Mechanical Engineers' Society), "Sanitary Engineering," *The Sanitary Inspector: A Monthly Visitor and Advisor,* vol. 1 (London: E.W. Allen, 1877), 76.

6. ENGINEERING IRELAND

1. Joep Leerssen, "Wildness, Wilderness, and Ireland: Medieval and Early-Modern Patterns in the Demarcation of Civility," *Journal of the History of Ideas* 56 (1995): 25–39.

2. Ibid., 32.

3. Quoted ibid., 34. John Davies, *A Discoverie of the True Causes why Ireland was Never Entirely Subdued, and Brought under the Obedience of the Crowne of England, un till the Beginning of His Majesties Happy Raigne* (London, 1619), 114–15. It is important to note here that the term *forests* now designates woodlands under government, such as the king's forests; they are a form of park. Hence mountains, bogs, and woods are to be reduced and confined within the limits of forests, chases, and parks.

4. See Petty's last will and testament, in Fitzmaurice, *The Life of Sir William Petty,* 318–24.

5. *Papers respecting Experimental Improvements on the Crown Lands at Kingwilliams Town, in the Barony of Duhallow in the County of Cork; and to the New Lines of Public Roads constructed in County Cork and Kerry,* H.C. 1834 (173), LI.

6. Dr. Willoughby, "Enquiries to be Made about the Bills of Mortality, aire, diseases &c.," in Rawlinson MSS, c. 406, fol. 68: Bills of Mortality, Dublin, April 17, 1691. See also, Boate, *Ireland's Natural History.*

7. *OED* (1933 ed.).

8. Newenham, *Statistical and Historical Inquiry,* 29. Newenham cited Petty to back up the claim.

9. Ibid., 30.

10. Ibid., 29–30.

11. Madden, *A Letter to the Dublin Society etc.,* 30.

12. Willoughby, "Enquiries to be Made about the Bills of Mortality, aire, diseases &c."

13. Dobbs, *An Essay on the Trade and Improvement of Ireland,* 167.

14. 49 Geo. III, c. 102. See also *Reports of the Commissioners Appointed to enquire into the Nature and Extent of the Several Bogs in Ireland* (London: His Majesty's Stationery Office, 1810–14).

15. Quoted in Gordon L. Herries Davies and R. Charles Mollan, eds., *Richard Griffith, 1784–1878* (Dublin: Royal Dublin Society, 1980), 33.

16. The project was led by Richard Griffith, who also participated in the ordnance and geological surveys and was an important player in relation to roads, railways, and inland navigation.

17. L. M. Cullen, "Economic Development, 1750–1800," in *A New History of Ireland*, vol. 4, ed. T. W. Moody and W. E. Vaughan (Oxford: Clarendon Press, 1986), 180.

18. An Act for the Extension and Promotion of Public Works in Ireland, 1 & 2 Will. IV, c. 33 (1831).

19. Poor Employment Act , 3 Geo. IV, c. 34 (1822); More O'Terrall's Act, 1 & 2 Will. IV, c. 57 (1831).

20. Drainage (Ireland) Act, 5 & 6 Vict., c. 89 (1842); Drainage (Ireland) Act, 9 Vict., c. 4 (1846).

21. When government turned to labor schemes as a way of providing relief during the Great Famine, 140 drainage districts were created, and works were carried out in 121 of them. Over a quarter million acres were effected by the work, at a cost of almost two million pounds (in 1840s values), of which close to 90 percent was borne by central government. Further legislation in 1863 saw about another half million spent draining about seventy-eight thousand acres over a period of twenty-five years.

22. The Grand Canal was initiated in the mid-eighteenth century by the newly created commissioners of inland navigation. The Grand Canal Company was formed in 1772, which took over construction and ran the canal, providing a passenger service until 1852. The Royal Canal was initiated by a private company but was subsequently taken over by the commissioners of inland navigation, which completed the project in 1822. Anon., *An Account of the Rise and Progress of the Royal Canal in Ireland, and also of the Opposition Thereto* (Dublin: N. Kelly, 1797), 6.

23. The Barrow Navigation connected the Grand Canal, which ran west on the south side of Dublin, with Waterford Harbour. The Boyne Navigation linked Slane, northwest of Dublin, with Drogheda, on the eastern seaboard. The Lough Corrib Navigation in Galway connected the lake with Lough Mask. The Maigue Navigation linked Adare in Limerick with the Shannon. And the Ballinamore, Ballyconnell, and Ulster canals served the north. Rena Lohan, *Guide to the Archives of the Office of Public Works* (Dublin: Government Stationery Office, 1994).

24. Mukerji, *Territorial Ambitions.*

25. The material stuff that traveled through the material infrastructure needs to be studied in itself as well as in terms of the discourses about it. A comprehensive analysis would consider closely the fabrics, machines, paper, and so on, for these reveal the world of skill and craft that carried meaning throughout the country. See Chandra Mukerji, *From Graven Images: Patterns of Modern Materialism* (New York: Columbia University Press, 1983).

26. William Greig, *Strictures of Road Police, Containing Views of the Present Systems, by which Roads are Made and Repaired, together with Sketches of its Progress in Great Britain and Ireland, from the earliest to the present times* (Dublin: Archer, Cumming, Milliken, Dugdale, Keene, Hodges & McArthur, and Larkin, 1819), xii.

27. Lohan, *Guide to the Archives*, 4.

28. 1 Geo. II, c. 13 (1727); 13 Geo. II, c. 10 (1739). See also David Broderick, *An Early Toll-Road: The Dublin-Dunlear Turnpike, 1731–1855* (Dublin: Irish University Press, 1996), 48.

29. Royal Dublin Society, "Directions for Making Roads," in *Dublin Society . . . Essays and Observations* (Dublin, 1736–37). The Royal Dublin Society expressed the view that the turnpike roads already built according to these specifications were recognized as "the finest in Europe." In the 1760s, legislation allowed roads to be financed by county cess, which was levied on each barony by the grand jury. Cullen, "Economic Development," 184.

30. Peter O'Keeffe, "Richard Griffith: Planner and Builder of Roads," in *Richard Griffith 1784–1878*, ed. Gordon Davies and R. C. Mollan (Dublin: Royal Dublin Society, 1980), 59.

31. Quoted ibid., 59.

32. Board of Public Works, *Public Works: First Report of the Commissioners of Public Works in Ireland, Upon the State of several Roads and Bridges placed under their care by the Act 1 & 2 Will. IV, c. 33; pursuant to the Act of Parliament, 6 Geo. IV, c. 101, s. 9* (Dublin: His Majesty's Stationery Office, 1833), 1–2.

33. Quoted in O'Keeffe, "Richard Griffith," 61.

34. *Report on the Southern District*, H.C. 1824 (352) M.

35. Charles Vallancey, *A Treatise on Inland Navigation or the Art of Making Rivers Navigable, Of making Canals in all sorts of Soils, and of Constructing Locks and Sluices* (Dublin: G. and A. Ewing, 1763).

36. Latour, *Science in Action*.

37. Carroll-Burke, *Colonial Discipline*.

38. After 1850, government funded the maintenance of Leinster House, and in 1868 the Science and Art Commission recommended an expansion of the complex to include a public library, a science and art museum, an agricultural museum, a museum of Irish antiquities, and a school of art. In 1916 the nationalist rebels evicted the Royal Dublin Society from Leinster House, making it the seat of the new government, which it remains to this day. It is flanked on one side by the National Library and the National Museum and on the other by the National Gallery and Natural History Museum.

39. Star and Griesemer, "Institutional Ecology, Translations and Boundary Objects."

40. Dublin Wide Streets Commission, *Extracts from the Minutes of the Commissioners appointed by Act of Parliament, for Making Wide and Convenient Ways, Streets, and Passages, in the City of Dublin: Containing the copy of a Memorial to His Excellency the Lord Lieutenant; Together with a General Statement of their Proceedings, Engagements, and Funds from the Commencement of the Institution in 1757, to January 1802* (Dublin, 1812).

41. Ibid., 16.

42. Board of Public Works, *Public Works: Fiftieth Annual Report from the Commissioners of Public Works in Ireland: with Appendices, for the Year 1881–82* (Dublin: Her Majesty's Stationery Office, 1882).

43. Board of Public Works, *First Report of the Commissioners of Public Works in Ireland*, 1.

44. Board of Public Works, *Public Works: Twentieth Annual Report from the Board of Public Works in Ireland* (1852).

45. Board of Public Works, *Public Works: Tenth Annual Report from the Board of Public Works in Ireland* (1842), 5.

46. About twenty-five hundred individual loans were made for land improvement, costing almost two million pounds. Thirty-eight of these loans permitted expenditure on farm buildings. Board of Public Works, *Twentieth Annual Report*, 8. The report includes maps of all the piers and harbors (over forty) erected in Ireland under the acts of 9 Vict., c. 3, and 10 & 11 Vict., c. 75.

47. In 1851 over twenty thousand acres benefited from the more effective method of "thorough draining, and a considerable proportion of this land was also "subsoiled." Ibid., 11.

48. Ibid., 41.

49. Among these were the Towns Improvement Clauses Act (1847), the Commissioners Clauses Act (1847), the Lands Clauses Consolidation Act (1845), the Towns Improvement Act (1854), and the Dublin (amended 1864), Cork (1855), Belfast, Limerick and Derry improvement acts.

50. Arthur Moore, *The Towns Improvement (Ireland) Act, 1854, 17 & 18 Vict. Cap. 103: with Provisions of Acts Incorporated therewith, and Acts amending the same* (Dublin: Alex. Thom, 1856), iii.

51. Ibid., iii.

52. William Hogan, "On the Necessity for Model Lodging Houses in Dublin," paper read before the Royal Dublin Society, 1848, published in William Hogan, *The Dependence of National Wealth on the Social and Sanatory Condition of the Labouring Classes; [and] On the Necessity for Model Lodging Houses in Dublin, and the Advantages they would confer on the community* (Dublin: Hodges and Smith, 1849), 11.

53. Barnard, "Improving Clergymen," 144.

54. Petty, *The Political Anatomy of Ireland*, 77.

55. Ibid., 77.

56. See Berkeley, *A Word to the Wise* (previously discussed in chapter 3).

57. Thomas Willis, *On the Social and Sanatory Condition of the Labouring Classes in Dublin* (Dublin, 1845), 28.

58. Jonathan Pim, *An Address Delivered at the Opening of the Thirtieth Session of the Statistical Society of Ireland, being a Review of the Economic and Social Progress of Ireland Since the Famine* (Dublin: Richard D. Webb, 1876).

59. Hogan, "On the Necessity for Model Lodging Houses in Dublin," 10–19.

60. See International Health Exhibition, *The Health Exhibition Literature*, 19 vols. (London: William Clowes and Sons, 1884), and particularly the following from volume 1: Catherine Gladstone, "Healthy Nurseries and Bedrooms"; Henry Acland, "Health in the Village"; William Eassie, "Healthy and Unhealthy Houses in Town and Country"; Robert Edis, "Healthy Furniture

and Decoration"; Charles Paget, "Healthy Schools"; and James Lakeman, "Health in the Workshop."

61. Hogan, "On the Necessity for Model Lodging Houses," 10.

62. See for instance, in *The Health Exhibition Literature* (19 vols.), H. H. Collins, "What Conditions are Essential for a Healthy Dwelling and how far is it desirable that they Should be Rendered Compulsory by Legislation" (vol. 2); Henry Acland's "Health in the Village" provides a design that designates the locations for the bedrooms for boys, girls, and parents, the boys and girls separated by a landing (1:33).

63. *The Sanitary Inspector*, vol. 1 (London: E. W. Allen, 1877), reported that the City of Health was to be erected to the west of Worthing, on the Sussex coast, to be named Courtlands, and to be built by the Sanitary Estates Association, Limited (26).

64. Michel Foucault, *Discipline and Punish: The Birth of the Prison* (New York: Penguin Books, 1977).

65. Jeremiah Fitzpatrick, *An Essay on Gaol-Abuses, and on the Means of Redressing them: Together with the General Method of Treating Disorders to which Prisoners are most Incident* (Dublin: P. Byrne, 1784).

66. Ibid., 27–28.

67. "Indeed, among the numerous wrongs, great and small, on which the philosopher in his old age used to dilate with a kind of cheerful acrimony peculiar to himself, there was none which roused so much resentment as the suppression of his Panopticon, which he always attributed to a personal grudge on the King's part." *The Sanitary Inspector*, 91.

68. Carroll-Burke, *Colonial Discipline*.

69. John Gray, *Observations on House and General Sewerage, and on an Improved Plan for Cleansing and Ventilating House Drains by a Self-acting Mechanism: with a Description of the Apparatus, as applied in the North Dublin Union Workhouse, under the Superintendence of the Poor-law Commissioners: Being the substance of a paper read at the Royal Dublin Society* (Dublin: Hodges and Smith, 1855).

70. Ibid., 30.

71. Anon., "A Glance at Irish Statistics," *Dublin University Magazine* 45 (1855): 251 (Dublin: James McGlashan).

72. Ibid., 251.

73. Anon., "Our Juvenile Criminals: the Schoolmaster and the Gaoler," *Irish Quarterly Review* (1854): 27. Quoted in Carroll-Burke, *Colonial Discipline*, 151.

74. Franz von Holtzendorff, *Reflections and Observations on the present condition of the Irish Convict System* (1863), 7.

75. Designed by Joshua Jebb, who also designed "Pentonville" in London (1842). Mountjoy was opened in 1850. See Carroll-Burke, *Colonial Discipline*.

76. Lohan, *Guide to the Archives*, 38–39.

77. See the introduction by Powell and DiMaggio in *The New Institutionalism in Organizational Analysis*, ed. Walter W. Powell and Paul

J. DiMaggio (Chicago: University of Chicago Press, 1991), 14–15, and the chapters by Ronald Jepperson ("Institutions, Institutional Effects, and Institutionalism") and Lynne Zucker ("The Role of Institutionalization in Cultural Persistence").

78. Carroll-Burke, *Colonial Discipline,* esp. chapter 4.

79. Ibid.

80. These issues are now more central to institutionalism. See Roger Friedland and Robert R. Alford, "Bringing Society Back In: Symbols, Practices, and Institutional Contradictions," in *The New Institutionalism in Organizational Analysis,* ed. Powell and DiMaggio, 232–63.

81. Lord Brougham's opening address to the first congress of the National Association for the Promotion of Social Science, Birmingham, 1857, in *Transactions of the National Association for the Promotion of Social Science, 1857* (London: John W. Parker and Son, 1858). The verse is Darwin describing the steam engine.

82. Carroll-Burke, "Medical Police."

83. F. M. L. Thomson, *The Rise of Respectable Society: A Social History of Victorian Britain, 1830–1900* (Cambridge, MA: Harvard University Press, 1988), 332. W. E. Vaughan has documented the same process in Ireland in the mid-Victorian period. Vaughan, "Ireland c. 1870."

84. Thomson, *Rise of Respectable Society,* 331.

85. Elizabeth Malcolm, "Popular Recreation in Nineteenth Century Ireland," in *Irish Culture and Nationalism, 1750–1950,* ed. Oliver MacDonagh, W. F. Mandle, and Pauric Travers (London: Palgrave Macmillan, 1983).

86. John Flint, *The Dublin Police and the Dublin Police System* (Dublin: James McCormick, 1847), 43.

87. Anon., "Playground and General Recreation Society," *Irish Quarterly Review* (July 1859): xxxvi.

88. Ibid., xxxvii.

89. Davies, *A Discoverie of the True Causes why Ireland was Never Entirely Subdued.*

CONCLUSION

1. For instance, in the context of what I call medical police, a recent work demonstrates the different trajectories of drug regulation in the United States and Germany: Arthur A. Daemmrich, *Pharmacopolitics: Drug Regulation in the United States and Germany* (Chapel Hill: University of North Carolina Press, 2004).

2. Merton, *Science, Technology, and Society in Seventeenth Century England;* Hessen, "The Social and Economic Roots of Newton's 'Principia'"; Zilsel, "The Sociological Roots of Science."

3. Mukerji, *Territorial Ambitions.*

4. Latour, "Drawing Things Together."

5. Shapin and Schaffer, *Leviathan and the Air-Pump.*

6. For a recent example of this historiography, see Margaret C. Jacob and Larry Stewart, *Practical Matter: Newton's Science in the Service of Industry and Empire, 1687–1851* (Cambridge, MA: Harvard University Press, 2004). Despite this shortcoming, this book makes the best case I have seen for the centrality of the new science to the rise of modern industrial production. Of course, it will be no surprise to practitioners of science studies that technology is not the mere application of science.

7. Jasanoff, ed., *States of Knowledge.*

8. Ibid., 3.

9. Susan Merrill Squier, *Liminal Lives: Imagining the Human at the Frontiers of Biomedicine* (Durham and London: Duke University Press, 2004), 31.

10. Quoted in Jacob and Stewart, *Practical Matter,* 109.

11. Michel Foucault, "Truth and Power," in *Power/Knowledge,* 121. For a response to those who have followed Foucault's suggestion, see Bruce Curtis, "Taking the State Back Out: Rose and Miller on Political Power," *British Journal of Sociology* 46, no. 4 (1995): 575–97.

12. Meyer, "The Changing Cultural Content of the Nation-State," 123–43.

13. Benedict Anderson, *Imagined Communities: Reflections on the Origin and Spread of Nationalism* (New York: Verso, 1991).

14. For an expansive history of the Irish nation as an imagined community, see R. V. Comerford, *Ireland: Inventing the Nation* (London: Arnold Publishers, 2003).

15. Charles Mollen, who until recently was the arts officer of the Royal Dublin Society, has worked tirelessly to reclaim Ireland's scientific heritage. See, for instance, David Attis and Charles Mollen, eds., *Science and Irish Culture: Why the History of Science Matters in Ireland* (Dublin: Royal Dublin Society, 2004).

16. Comerford, *Ireland,* 1.

17. Yaron Ezrahi, *The Descent of Icarus: Science and the Transformation of Contemporary Democracy* (Cambridge, MA: Harvard University Press, 1990).

18. Latour, *We Have Never Been Modern.*

19. Scott, *Seeing Like a State.*

20. On boundary work in science, see Gieryn, *Cultural Boundaries of Science.*

21. I wish to thank Mark Neocleous for sending me his work on police in the wake of reading my article "Medical Police and the History of Public Health." Neocleous's research demonstrates better than any the expansiveness of police in the production of modern social order. See Mark Neocleous, *The Fabrication of Social Order: A Critical Theory of Police Power* (London: Pluto Press, 2000); Mark Neocleous, "Social Police and the Mechanisms of Prevention: Patrick Colquhoun and the Condition of Poverty," *British Journal of Criminology* 40 (2000): 710–26; and Mark Neocleous, "Policing and Pin-Making: Adam Smith, Police and the State of Prosperity," *Policing and Society* 8 (1998): 425–49.

22. Scott, *Seeing Like a State,* 7.

23. It is important to note that government centralization is not a measure of police power in a state. For instance, the United States of America, despite its highly localized structures of government and police, is arguably one of the most exemplary cases of a modern democratic police state. This was shown early in the twentieth century in the infamous case of "Typhoid Mary," the Irish immigrant cook who was imprisoned for life because she was deemed a healthy carrier of typhoid but refused to cease working with food. The New York medical police officer who arrested Mary (in the company of two regular police officers) later reflected on how there is "little a Board of Health cannot do in the way of interfering with personal and property rights for the protection of public health." Quoted in J. Andrew Mendelsohn, "'Typhoid Mary' Strikes Again: The Social and Scientific in the Making of Modern Public Health," *Isis* 86, no. 2 (1995): 268–77, 275. A recent news article on a new Centers for Disease Control (CDC) rule that steps up surveillance of travelers because of concern about a flu pandemic noted that CDC "documents supporting the rule emphasize that the courts have long found that public health concerns can trump individual rights, including certain expectations of privacy and freedom of movement." "CDC Seeking New Rules to Keep Tabs on Travelers," *Washington Post,* reprinted in the *Sacramento Bee,* November 23, 2005.

24. For instance, the first credible report of cold fusion (now called room-temperature fusion because of the politics of representation) appeared in the journal *Nature* on April 28, 2005, and was immediately imagined as a means to "peer easily into luggage or cargo containers." *New York Times,* reprinted in the *Sacramento Bee,* April 28, 2005. As of 2005, the world has come to face a new flu strain that has already moved from birds to humans, a widespread outbreak of which would severely test state and interstate medical police and could involve mortality rates greater than those caused by the 1918 global flu pandemic.

25. The protection and security of persons are now dependent on their integration into the data state. For instance, a 1998 UNICEF report entitled "The Progress of Nations" described the "right" to an official identity as "the first right." Without an official identity in the form of a birth certificate, one-third of all newborns could be barred from state services such as education and health care, and tracking mortality rates and the exploitation of children also becomes impossible. As the director of UNICEF put it: "If a third of the children who are born every year are in essence non-existent in the eyes of the state, then it puts them at risk. . . . Not having a birth certificate is the functional equivalent of not having been born." "Third of Births Aren't Registered, UNICEF Says," *New York Times,* July 8, 1998.

26. See, for instance, Sheila Jasanoff, *The Fifth Branch: Science Advisors as Policy Makers* (Cambridge, MA: Harvard University Press, 1990); Sheila Jasanoff, *Risk Management and Political Culture* (New York: Russell Sage, 1986); and Thomas Beamish, *Silent Spill: The Organization of an Industrial Crisis* (Cambridge, MA: MIT Press, 2002).

Bibliography

PRIMARY SOURCES

Acland, Henry. 1884. "Health in the Village." In *Health Exhibition Literature,* vol. 1. London: William Clowes and Sons.

Aldridge, John. 1847. *Review of the Sanitary Condition of Dublin.* Dublin: Hodges and Smith.

Anon. 1642. *The State of Dublin: As it stood the 27 of December, And of other parts of Ireland. Being the copy of a letter sent from a good hand to an Alderman of this City. By reading which you will finde the vanity and falsehood of those vaine foolish Pamphlets invented and published of late.* London: Nath. Butler.

Anon. 1651. *The Reformed Husband-Man; Or A Brief Treatise of the Errors, Defects, and Inconveniences of our English Husbandry, in Ploughing and Sowing for Corn; with The Reasons and general Remedies; and a large, yet faithful Offer or Undertaking for the benefit of them that will joyn in this good and publick work; Imparted some years ago to Mr. Samuel Hartlib, and now by him re-imparted to all ingenuous Englishmen, that are willing to advance the Prosperity, Wealth and Plenty of their Native Countrey.* London.

Anon. 1662. *A Collection of some of the Murthers and Massacres Committed on the Irish in Ireland since the 23d. of October 1641, with some observations and falsifications on a late printed abstract of murthers said to be committed by the Irish.* London.

Anon. 1689. *The Sad and Lamentable Condition of the Protestants in Ireland, being an Account of the Barbarous Proceedings of the Natives against the English, as also of the facility of rescuing those distressed protestants out of the hands of the bloody papists provided there be a speedy supply from England.* London.

Anon. 1736. *An Abstract of the Number of Protestants and Popish Families in the Several Counties and Provinces of Ireland.* Dublin: Rhames and Gunne.

Anon. 1749. *The State of the Nation, with a general balance of the Publick Accounts*. Dublin: Faulkner.

Anon. 1754. *The State of Ireland, Laid open to the View of His Majesty's Subjects*. London.

Anon. 1766. *An Act for Directing the Application of the Sum of Eight Thousand Pounds granted to the Dublin Society, for The Encouragement of such Trades and Manufactures as should be directed by Parliament*. Dublin.

Anon. 1771. *A View of the Schemes at present under Consideration of the Governors of the Lying-in Hospital*. Dublin.

Anon. 1790. *Essays on Agriculture and Planting founded on Experiments made in Ireland, By a Country Gentleman*. Dublin: William Jones.

Anon. [William Dease]. 1790. *Remarks on Medical Jurisprudence, Intended for the General Information of Juries and Young Surgeons*. Dublin.

Anon. 1797. *An Account of the Rise and Progress of the Royal Canal in Ireland, and also of the Opposition Thereto*. Dublin: N. Kelly.

Anon. 1800. *A Short Description of the Dublin Society's Botanical and Agricultural Garden at Glasnevin*. Dublin.

Anon. 1820. *The State of The Poor of Ireland briefly considered and Agricultural Education recommended, to check Redundant Population and to Promote National Improvement*. Carlow: Richard Price.

Anon. 1825. "Review: Abstract of the Answers and Returns made pursuant to 'An Act to provide for taking an Account of the Population of Ireland, and for ascertaining the Increase or Diminution thereof.'" *Dublin Philosophical Journal and Scientific Review* 1. Dublin: Hodges and M'Arthur.

Anon. 1837. *Papers on subjects connected with the duties of the Corps of Royal Engineers*, vol. 1. London: Barker.

Anon. 1839. "Dr. Maunsell on Political Medicine." *Dublin University Magazine* 13 (May): 551–65.

Anon. 1846. Review of "Corrigan's 'On Famine and Fever, as Cause and Effect, in Ireland: with Observations on Hospital Location, and the Dispensation, in Out-Door Relief, of Food and Medicine.'" *London Medical Gazette, or Journal of Practical Medicine* 2: 385–87.

Anon. 1846. "Review of Taylor's *A Manual of Medical Jurisprudence*." *Dublin Quarterly Journal of Medical Science* 2: 157–64.

Anon. 1846. "Review of The Potato Disease, its Origin, Nature, and Prevention; with a Chemical and Microscopical Analysis of the Sound and Diseased Tubers." *London Medical Gazette, or Journal of Practical Medicine* 2: 384–85.

Anon. 1846. "Review of William Baly's *On the Mortality in Prisons, and the Diseases most frequently fatal to Prisoners*." *London Medical Gazette, or Journal of Practical Medicine* 2: 345–47.

Anon. 1846. "Symtoms Produced by Eating Diseased Potatoes." *London Medical Gazette, or Journal of Practical Medicine* 2.

Anon. 1847. "Irish Astrologers." *Dublin Quarterly Journal of Medical Science* 4: 271–72.

Anon. 1847. "Review of Kennedy on Epidemic Cholera." *Dublin Quarterly Journal of Medical Science* 4: 193–98.

Anon. 1847. "Review of Marsh, Aldridge, and Board of Health on Food and Nutrition." *Dublin Quarterly Journal of Medical Science* 4: 146–56.

Anon. [T. C. Fleury]. 1848. "The Influenza." *Dublin Quarterly Journal of Medical Science* 5: 256–58.

Anon. 1848. "Review of Clymer and Bartlett on Fever." *Dublin Quarterly Journal of Medical Science* 5: 129–41.

Anon. 1848. "Review of Milroy, Sigmund, and Parkes on Cholera." *Dublin Quarterly Journal of Medical Science* 5: 141–44.

Anon. 1854. "Our Juvenile Criminals: the Schoolmaster and the Gaoler." *Irish Quarterly Review.* Dublin.

Anon. 1855. "Epidemic Diseases Present in all Ireland on the Night of March 30th, 1851." *Journal of Public Health and Sanitary Review* 1: 171–73. London: Thomas Richards.

Anon. 1855. "A Glance at Irish Statistics." *Dublin University Magazine* 45: 243–52. Dublin: James McGlashan.

Anon. 1855. "The Medical Police of London." *Journal of Public Health and Sanitary Review* 1: 324–25. London: Thomas Richards.

Anon. 1855. "Review of *The Quarterly Journal of Public Health;* including the Transactions of the Epidemiological Society of London." *Dublin Quarterly Journal of Medical Science* 19: 429–32.

Anon. 1856. "Essays on State Medicine." Review article. *Dublin Quarterly Journal of Medical Science* 22.

Anon. 1856. "The Progress of Preventive Medicine and Sanitary Measures." *Dublin Quarterly Journal of Medical Science* 22, no. 5.

Anon. 1859. "Playground and General Recreation Society." *Irish Quarterly Review* (July): xxxv–xxxix.

Anon. 1874. "Public Health in Ireland." Review Essay. *Dublin Quarterly Journal of Medical Science* 58.

Antisell, Thomas. 1847. *Suggestions Towards the Improvement of the Sanatory Condition of the Metropolis.* Dublin: James McGlashan.

Archer, Joseph. 1801. *Statistical Survey of the County Dublin, with Observations on the means of Improvement; Drawn up for the Consideration, and by Order of the Dublin Society.* Dublin: Dublin Society.

Ashe, Isaac. 1875. *Medical Politics: Being the Essay to which was awarded the First Carmichael Prize, of £200, by the Council of the Royal College of Surgeons, Ireland, 1873.* Dublin: Fannin.

Atkinson, William. 1843. *Principles of Political Economy; or the Laws of the Formation of Wealth, Developed by Means of the Christian Law of Government.* New York: Greeley & McElrath.

Aubrey, John. 1949. *Aubrey's Brief Lives.* Ed. Oliver Lawson Dick. London: Secker and Warburg.

Bacon, Francis. 1974 [1605, 1627]. *"The Advancement of Learning" and "New Atlantis."* Ed. Arthur Johnson. Oxford: Clarendon Press.

————. 1995. "The New Science." In *The Portable Enlightenment Reader,* ed. Issac Kramnick. New York: Penguin.

Baker, Henry. 1742. *The Microscope Made Easy: or, I. The Nature, Uses, and Magnifying Powers of the best Kinds of Microscopes Described, Calculated, and Explained: for the Instruction of such, particularly, as desire to search into the Wonders of the Minute Creation, tho' they are not acquainted with Optics. Together with Full Directions how to prepare, apply, examine, and preserve all Sorts of Objects, and proper Cautions to be observed in viewing them. II. An Account of what surprizing Discoveries have been already made by the Microscope: With useful Reflections on them, and also a great Variety of new Experiments and Observations, pointing out many uncommon Subjects for the Examination of the Curious.* London: R. Dodsley.

Bancroft, R. M. 1877. "Sanitary Engineering." *The Sanitary Inspector: A Monthly Visitor and Advisor,* vol. 1. London: E. W. Allen.

Barry, Edward. 1775. *Wines and Medicinal Waters.* Dublin.

Beaufort, Daniel. 1792. *Memoir of a Map of Ireland; illustrating the Topography of that Kingdom, and containing a short account of its present State, Civil and Ecclesiatical; with a complete index to the map.* Dublin: Slater and Allen.

Beck, John. 1835. *Researches in Medicine and Medical Jurisprudence.* 2nd ed. New York: E. Bliss.

Berkeley, George. 1752. *The Querist, Containing Several Queries Proposed to the Consideration of the Public.* Dublin: Faulkner.

————, bishop of Cloyne. 1752. *A Word to the Wise, or an Exhortation to the Roman Catholic Clergy of Ireland.* Dublin: Faulkner.

Bisset-Smith, George T. 1921. *The Census and some of its Uses: Outlining a plain Philosophy of Population.* Edinburgh: W. Green & Sons, Ltd.

Black, James. 1844. "Lectures on Public Hygiene and Medical Police." *Provincial Medical and Surgical Journal* 19, 275–80; 22, 327–32; 24, 359–64; 26, 391–96; 36, 551–57.

Blacker, William. 1837. *An Essay on the Improvement to be made in the Cultivation of Small Farms by the introduction of green crops, and house-feeding the stock thereon.* 5th ed. Dublin: William Curry, Jun. & Company.

————. 1837. *Prize Essay, Addressed to the Agricultural Committee of the Royal Dublin Society on the management of Landed Property in Ireland; the consolidation of small farms, employment of the poor, etc, etc.* Dublin: William Curry and Company.

Blackstone, William. 1768. *Commentaries on the Laws of England.* 4 vols. Oxford: Clarendon Press.

Board of Public Works. 1833. *Public Works: First Report of the Commissioners of Public Works in Ireland, Upon the State of several Roads and Bridges placed under their care by the Act 1 & 2 Will. IV, c. 33; pursuant to Act of Parliament, 6 Geo. IV c. 101, s. 9.* Dublin: His Majesty's Stationery Office.

————. 1842. *Public Works: Tenth Annual Report from the Board of Public Works in Ireland.* Dublin: Her Majesty's Stationery Office.

————. 1852. *Public Works: Twentieth Annual Report from the Board of Public Works in Ireland*. Dublin: Her Majesty's Stationery Office.

————. 1862. *Public Works: Thirtieth Report from the Board of Public Works, Ireland, with the Appendices*. Dublin: Her Majesty's Stationery Office.

————. 1872. *Public Works: Fortieth Report from the Board of Public Works, Ireland, with the Appendices*. Dublin: Her Majesty's Stationery Office.

————. 1882. *Public Works: Fiftieth Annual Report from the Commissioners of Public Works in Ireland: with Appendices, for the Year 1881–82*. Dublin: Her Majesty's Stationery Office.

Boate, Gerard. 1657. *Ireland's Natural History. Being a true and ample Description of its Situation, Greatness, Shape, and Nature; Of its Hills, Woods, Heaths, Bogs; Of its Fruitfull Parts and profitable Grounds, with the Severall ways of Manuring and Improving the same: With its Heads or Promontories, Harbours, Roads and Bays; Of its Springs and Fountains, Brooks, Rivers, Loghs; Of its Metalls, Mineralls, Freestone, Marble, Sea-coal, Turf, and other things that are taken out of the ground. And lastly, of the Nature and temperature of its Air and Season, and what diseases it is free from, or subject unto. Conducing to the Advancement of Navigation, Husbandry, and other profitable Arts and Professions. For the Common Good of Ireland, and more especially, for the benefit of the Adventurers and Planters therein*. London: John Wright.

Boulton, Richard. 1721. *An Essay on the Plague, &c*. Dublin.

Boyle, Robert. 1966 [1772]. "An Examen of Mr. T. Hobbes, his Dialogus Physicus de Natura Aeris; As far as concerns Mr. Boyle's Book of New Experiments touching the Spring of the Air, &c. With an Appendix touching Mr. Hobbes' Doctrine of Fluidity and Firmness" (1662). In *Robert Boyle: The Works*, vol. 1 of 6, ed. Thomas Birch. Hildesheim: Georg Olms Verlagsbuchhandlung.

————. 1966 [1772]. "Letters from Several Persons to Mr. Boyle." In *Robert Boyle: The Works*, vol. 6 of 6, ed. Thomas Birch. Hildesheim: Georg Olms Verlagsbuchhandlung.

————. 1966 [1772]. "New Experiments Physico-Mechanical, Touching the Spring of the Air, and its Effects, Made, for the most Part, in a New Pneumatical Engine, Written by Way of a Letter To the Right Honourable Charles Lord Viscount of Dungarvan, eldest Son to the Earl of Corke" (1672). In *Robert Boyle: The Works*, vol. 1 of 6, ed. Thomas Birch. Hildesheim: Georg Olms Verlagsbuchhandlung.

————. 1966 [1772]. "The Origin of Forms and Qualities, According to the Corpuscular Philosophy; Illustrated by Considerations and Experiments, Written formerly by Way of Notes upon an Essay from Nitre. Augmented by a Discourse of Subordinate Forms" (1666). In *Robert Boyle: The Works*, vol. 3 of 6, ed. Thomas Birch. Hildesheim: Georg Olms Verlagsbuchhandlung.

————. 1966 [1772]. "Some Considerations Touching the Usefulness of Experimental Natural Philosophy, Proposed in a familiar Discourse to a Friend, by way of Invitation to the Study of it" (1663). In *Robert Boyle:*

The Works, vol. 2 of 6, ed. Thomas Birch. Hildesheim: Georg Olms Verlagsbuchhandlung.

———. 1966 [1772]. "Some Considerations Touching the Usefulness of Experimental Natural Philosophy. The Second Tome, containing the latter Section of the Second Part" (1671). In *Robert Boyle: The Works*, vol. 3 of 6, ed. Thomas Birch. Hildesheim: Georg Olms Verlagsbuchhandlung.

———. 1685. *Of the Reconcileableness of Specific Medicines to the Corpuscular Philosophy, To which is Annexed a Discourse about the Advantages of the Use of Simple Medicines.* London: Samuel Smith.

———. 1696. *Medicinal Experiments: Or, A Collection of Choice and Safe Remedies, for the most part Simple and easily prepared: Very useful in Families and fitted for the Service of Country People.* London: Samuel Smith.

———. 1991. *The Early Essays and Ethics of Robert Boyle.* Ed. John Harwood. Carbondale, IL: Southern Illinois University Press.

Brady, Cheyne. 1854. *The Practicability of Improving the Dwellings of the Labouring Classes, with Remarks on the Law of Settlement and Removal of the Poor.* London: Edward Stanford.

Brazill, Thomas. 1854. *Report to the Corporation of Dublin on the Proposed supply of the City and Suburbs with Pure Water at High Pressure.* Dublin: John Falconer.

Burges, John. 1725. *An Essay on the Water and Air of Ballyspillan.*

Burke, Edmund. 1925 [1790]. *Reflections on the French Revolution and Other Essays.* Introduction by A. J. Grieve, Everyman Series. London: J. M. Dent & Sons, and New York: E. P. Dutton & Sons.

———. 1982. *A Vindication of Natural Society, or, A View of the Miseries and Evils Arising to Mankind from Every Species of Artificial Society. In a Letter to Lord ****.* Ed. with an intro. by Frank N. Pagano. Indianapolis: Liberty Press.

Burrowes, Rev. Robert. 1787. "Preface." *Transactions of the Royal Irish Academy.* Dublin: Royal Irish Academy.

Bushe, Gervase Parker. 1790. "An Essay towards assertaining the Population of Ireland, in a Letter to the Right Honourable the Earl of Charlemont." In *Transactions of the Royal Irish Academy.* Dublin: Royal Irish Academy.

Cameron, Charles. 1874. "Half-Yearly Report on Public Health." *Dublin Quarterly Journal of Medical Science* 58: 410–48.

———. 1874. *A Manual of Hygiene, Public and Private, and Compendium of Sanitary Laws, for the information and guidance of public health authorities, officers of health, and sanitarians generally.* Dublin: Hodges, Foster & Co.

———. 1886. *History of the Royal College of Surgeons in Ireland, and of the Irish Schools of Medicine, including numerous biographical sketches, also a medical bibliography.* Dublin: Fannin.

Catalogue of Articles of Irish Manufacture, Produce, and Invention, exhibited at the Royal Dublin Society's House, 8 June, 1841, and following days. Dublin: Graisberry & Gill, 1841.

Census of Ireland. 1939 [1659]. Ed. Seamus Pender. Dublin: Stationery Office.

Census of Ireland for the Year 1821: Abstract of the Answers and Returns Made pursuant to an Act of the United Parliament, passed in the 55th Year of the Reign of His Late Majesty George the Third, intituled [sic] "An Act to provide for taking an Account of the Population of Ireland, and for ascertaining the Increase or Diminution thereof." Preliminary Observations, Enumeration Abstract, Appendix. 1823. Dublin: His Majesty's Stationery Office.

Census of Ireland for the Year 1831: Population, Ireland. Abstract of Answers and Returns under The Population Acts. 1833. London: His Majesty's Stationery Office.

Census of Ireland for the Year 1841. 1843. London: Her Majesty's Stationery Office.

Census of Ireland for the Year 1841, Addenda to. Showing the Number of Houses, Families, and Persons, in the Several Townlands and Towns of Ireland. 1843. London: Her Majesty's Stationery Office.

Census of Ireland for the Year 1851. Part 1, *Showing the Area, Population, and Number of Houses by Townlands and Electoral Divisions.* Vol. 1, *Province of Leinster.* Vol. 2, *Province of Munster.* Vol. 3, *Province of Ulster.* Vol. 4, *Province of Connaught.* 1852. Dublin: Her Majesty's Stationery Office.

———. Part 2, *Returns of Agricultural Produce in 1851.* 1852. Dublin: Her Majesty's Stationery Office.

———. Part 3, *Report on the Status of Disease.* 1854. Dublin: Her Majesty's Stationery Office.

———. Part 4, *Report on Ages and Education.* 1855. Dublin: Her Majesty's Stationery Office.

———. Part 5, *Table of Deaths.* Vol. 1, *Containing the Report, Tables of Pestilences, and Analysis of the Table of Deaths, Prepared by William Wilde.* Vol. 2, *Hospitals and Sanitary Institutions.* 1856. Dublin: Her Majesty's Stationery Office.

———. Part 6, *General Report.* 1856. Dublin: Her Majesty's Stationery Office.

———. Part 7, *General Alphabetical Index to the Townlands and Towns, Parishes and Baronies of Ireland, Showing the number of the sheet of the Ordnance Survey Maps in which they appear; the areas of the Townlands, Parishes, and Baronies; the County, Barony, Parish, and Poor Law Union in which the Townlands are situated; and the volume and page of the Townland Census of 1851, which contains the Population and Number of Houses in 1841 and 1851, and the Poor Law Valuation in 1851.* 1861. Dublin: Her Majesty's Stationery Office.

Census of Ireland for the Year 1861. Part 1, *Showing the Area, Population, and Number of Houses, by Townlands and Electoral Divisions.* Vol. 1, *Province of Leinster.* Vol. 2, *Province of Munster.* Vol. 3, *Province of Ulster.* Vol. 4, *Province of Connaught.* 1863. Dublin: Her Majesty's Stationery Office.

———. Part 2, *Report and Tables of Ages and Education.* 2 vols. 1863. Dublin: Her Majesty's Stationery Office.

———. Part 3, *Vital Statistics*. Vol. 1, *Report and Tables relating to the Status of Disease*. Vol. 2, *Report and Tables relating to Deaths*. 1863. Dublin: Her Majesty's Stationery Office.

———. Part 4, *Report and Tables relating to the Religious Professions, Education, and Occupations of the People*. 1863. Dublin: Her Majesty's Stationery Office.

———. Part 5, *General Report*. 1864. Dublin: Her Majesty's Stationery Office.

Census of Ireland for the Year 1871. Part 1, *Area, Houses, and Population: Also the Ages, Civil Condition, Occupations, Birthplaces, Religion, and Education of the People*. Vol. 1, *Province of Leinster*. Vol. 2, *Province of Munster*. Vol. 3, *Province of Ulster*. Vol. 4, *Province of Connaught*. 1875. Dublin: Her Majesty's Stationery Office.

———. Part 2, *Vital Statistics*. Vol. 1, *Reports and Tables relating to the Status of Disease*. Vol. 2, *Report and Tables relating to Deaths*. 1873. Dublin: Her Majesty's Stationery Office.

———. Part 3, *General Report with Illustrative Maps and Diagrams, Summary Tables, and Appendix*. 1876. Dublin: Her Majesty's Stationery Office.

Census of Ireland for the Year 1881. Part 1, *Area, Houses, and Population: Also the Ages, Civil or Conjugal Condition, Occupations, Birthplaces, Religion, and Education of the People*. Vol. 1, *Province of Leinster*. Vol. 2, *Province of Munster*. Vol. 3, *Province of Ulster*. Vol. 4, *Province of Connaught*. 1882. Dublin: Her Majesty's Stationery Office.

———. Part 2, *General Report, with Illustrative Maps and Diagrams, Tables, and Appendix*. 1882. Dublin: Her Majesty's Stationery Office.

Central Board of Health. 1847. *Fever: Circular issued by the Central Board of Health as to precautionary measures in reference to Fever or other Contagious Disease*. Dublin.

———. 1848. *Cholera: Circular issued by the Central Board of Health*. Dublin.

———. N.d. *Extracts from Letters from the Central Board of Health to the late Relief Commissioners respecting Rations proposed for the Destitute Poor under the Temporary Relief Act; circulated by the late Commissioners for the guidance of Relief Committees and others*. Dublin.

Chadwick, Edwin. 1887. *The Health of Nations, a review of the works of Edwin Chadwick, With a biographical dissertation by Benjamin Ward Richardson*. London: Longmans, Green, and Co.

Chapman, Henry. 1903. *A Manual of Medical Jurisprudence, Insanity, and Toxicology*. Philadelphia: W. B. Saunders.

Clark, Henry. 1852. *Superiority of Sanitary Measures over Quarantines: An Address Delivered before the Suffolk District Medical Society at its Third Anniversary Meeting*. Boston: Thurston, Torry and Emerson.

Clark, Joseph. 1790. "An Account of a Disease which, until lately, proved fatal to a great Number of Infants in the Lying-in Hospital of Dublin, with Observations on its Causes and Prevention." *Transactions of the Royal Irish Academy 1789*. Dublin: Royal Irish Academy.

Collins, H. H. "What Conditions are Essential for a Healthy Dwelling and how far is it Desirable that they Should be Rendered Compulsory by Legislation." In *Health Exhibition Literature*, vol. 2. London: William Clowes and Sons.

Collins, Robert. 1848. *Observations on the Prevention of Contagious Diseases, by the Effectual Ventilation of the Houses of the Lower Classes.* Dublin: Hodges and Smith.

Colquhoun, Patrick. 1800. *A Treatise on the Commerce and Police of the River Thames.* London: J. Mawman.

———. 1969 [1806]. *A Treatise on the Police of the Metropolis.* 7th ed. Montclair, NJ: Patterson Smith.

Coote, Charles. 1801. *Statistical Survey of the King's County, Being the Second Volume of the Statistical Surveys of Ireland.* Dublin: Royal Dublin Society.

Corfield, W. H. 1880. *Dwelling Houses, Their Sanitary Construction and Arrangements.* London: H. K. Lewis.

Corrigan, Dominic J. 1846. *On Famine and Fever as Cause and Effect in Ireland; with Observations on Hospital Location, and the Dispensation in Outdoor Relief of Food and Medicine.* Dublin: J. Fannin & Co.

———. 1866. *Cholera Map of Ireland, With Observations.* Dublin: Browne & Nolan.

Culpeper, Nicholas. 1649. *A Physicall Directory, or a translation of the London dispensatory made by the College of Physicians in London.* London.

Curran, J. O. 1847. "Observations on Scurvy as it has lately appeared throughout Ireland, and in several Parts of Great Britain." *Dublin Quarterly Journal of Medical Science* 4: 83–134.

Cusack, James William. 1847. "On the Mortality of Medical Practitioners from Fever in Ireland." *Dublin Quarterly Journal of Medical Science* 5: 134–45.

———. 1848. "On the Mortality of Medical Practitioners in Ireland" (2nd article). *Dublin Quarterly Journal of Medical Science* 5: 111–28.

Davies, John. 1619. *A Discoverie of the True Causes why Ireland was Never Entirely Subdued, and Brought under the Obedience of the Crowne of England, un till the Beginning of His Majesties Happy Raigne.* London.

Davy, Humphry. 1814. *Elements of Agricultural Chemistry, in a Course of Lectures for The Board of Agriculture.* 2nd ed. London: Longman, Hurst, Rees, Orme, and Brown.

Denton, John Bailey. 1877. *Sanitary Engineering: A Series of Lectures given before the School of Military Engineering at Chatham, 1876.* London: E. & F. N. Spon.

———. 1885. *Sewage Disposal: Ten Years Experience in works of Intermittent Downward Filtration, Separately and in Combination with Surface Irrigation; with notes on the practice of and results of Sewage Farming.* 2nd ed. London: E. & F. N. Spon.

Dobbs, Arthur. 1729. *An Essay on the Trade and Improvement of Ireland.* Dublin: Rhames, Smith, & Bruce.

Druitt, Robert. 1855. "Short Notes on some of the Details of Sanitary Police." *Journal of Public Health and Sanitary Review* 1: 15–22; 359–63. London: Thomas Richards.

Dublin Corporation. 1860. *Minutes of Correspondence between the Pipe Water Committee of the Corporation of Dublin, and the Directors of the Grand Canal Company, with reference to a supply of water for the City and Neighbourhood of Dublin.* Dublin: J. Porter.

Dublin Philosophical Journal and Scientific Review. 1825–26. Vols. 1 and 2. Dublin: Hodges and McArthur.

Dublin Sanitary Association. 1849. *Report of the Transactions of the Dublin Sanitary Association.* Dublin: James McGlashan.

———. 1873–99. *Reports of the Executive Committee of the Dublin Sanitary Association.* Dublin: R. D. Webb & Son.

Dublin Society. 1732. *An Account of Saffron: The Manner of its Culture and saving for Use, with the Advantages it will be of to this Kingdom.* Dublin: Dublin Society.

———. 1732. *The Advantages which may arise to the People of Ireland by raising of Flax and Flax-Seed, Considered Together with Instructions of Sowing and Saving the Seed, and Preparing the Flax for the Market.* Dublin: Dublin Society.

———. 1733. *Instructions for Planting and Managing Hops, and for Raising Hop-Poles.* Dublin: Dublin Society.

———. 1763. *The Dublin Society's Weekly Observations for the Advancement of Agriculture and Manufactures.* Dublin: Mitchell and Williams.

———. 1805. *Abstracts of Acts for Encouraging the Cultivation, and for the better preservation of Trees, Shrubs, Plants, & Roots.* Dublin: Dublin Society.

Dublin Water Works. 1859. *Report from Committee No. Two, to the Municipal, February, 1859.* Dublin: Dollard.

Dublin Wide Streets Commission. 1812. *Extracts from the Minutes of the Commissioners appointed by Act of Parliament, for Making Wide and Convenient Ways, Streets, and Passages, in the City of Dublin: Containing the copy of a Memorial to His Excellency the Lord Lieutenant; Together with a General Statement of their Proceedings, Engagements, and Funds from the Commencement of the Institution in 1757, to January 1802.* Dublin.

Duncan, Andrew. 1801 [1795]. *Heads of Lectures on Medical Jurisprudence and Medical Police.* Edinburgh: Adam Neill.

Eachard, Laurence. 1691. *An Exact Description of Ireland: Chorographically Surveying all its Provinces & Counties After a more Accurate, Plain Eafie, and particular Manner than any before done in this kind. Shewing the exact STATE of the Kingdom, and all the Principal Things that are Necessary to be known. And 5 Maps relating thereto.* London: Tho. Salusbury.

Eassie, William. 1875. *Cremation of the Dead: Its History and bearings upon Public Health.* London: Smith, Elder, & Co.

———. 1884. "Healthy and Unhealthy Houses in Town and Country." In *Health Exhibition Literature*, vol. 1. London: William Clowes and Sons.

Edis, Robert. 1884. "Healthy Furniture and Decoration." In *Health Exhibition Literature*, vol. 1. London: William Clowes and Sons.

Editor's Preface. 1848. *Dublin Quarterly Journal of Medical Science* 5: i–iv.

Farming Society of Ireland. 1815. *Charter of the Farming Society of Ireland*. Dublin.

Fielding, John. 1758. *An Account of the Origin and Effects of a Police set on foot by His Grace the Duke of Newcastle in the year 1753, upon a Plan Presented to His Grace by the late Henry Fielding, esq.* London: A. Millar.

———. 1758. *A Plan of a Preservatory and Reformatory for the Benefit of Deserted Girls, and Penitent Prostitutes*. London: R. Franklin.

First report of the Philanthropic Society. 1788. London.

Fitzpatrick, Jeremiah. 1784. *An Essay on Gaol-Abuses, and on the Means of Redressing them: Together with the General Method of Treating Disorders to which Prisoners are most Incident*. Dublin: P. Byrne.

———. 1790. *Thoughts on Penitentiaries*. Dublin: H. Fitzpatrick.

Fletcher, Charles. 1786. *A Maritime State Considered as to the Health of Seamen*. Dublin.

Flint, John. 1847. *The Dublin Police, and the Police System*. Dublin: James McCormick.

Foster, Edward. 1768. *An Essay on Hospitals; or, Succint Directions for the Situation, Construction, and Administration of County Hospitals, With An Appendix, wherein the Present Scheme for establishing Public County Hospitals in Ireland, is impartially considered*. Dublin: W. G. Jones.

Frank, Johann. 1976. *A System of Complete Medical Police*. Ed. Erna Lesky. Baltimore, MD: Johns Hopkins University Press.

Fraser, Robert. 1801. *General View of the Agriculture and Mineralogy, Present State and Circumstances of the County Wicklow, with Observations on the means of their improvement*. Dublin: Dublin Society.

Geoghegan, Edward. 1795. *Observations on the Necessity of Regulating the Medical Profession*. Dublin.

Gerhard, Willam Paul. 1898. *Sanitary Engineering*. New York: Wm. P. Gerhard.

Giffen, G. H. 1901. *Students' Manual of Medical Jurisprudence and Public Health*. Edinburgh: Bryce.

Gilbert, John. 1854–59. *History of the City of Dublin*. 3 vols. Dublin: McGlashan and Gill.

Gilbert, John T., ed. 1971 [1700]. *A Jacobite Narrative of the War in Ireland 1688–1691*. Repr. with an intro. by J. G. Simms. Shannon: Irish University Press.

Girdlestone, Rev. C. 1855. "On the Scientific Investigation of Sanitary Questions." *Journal of Public Health and Sanitary Review* 1: 29–31.

Gladstone, Catherine. 1884. "Healthy Nurseries and Bedrooms." In *Health Exhibition Literature*, vol. 1. London: William Clowes and Sons.

Grattan, Richard. 1820. *Remarks on the Importance of the Medical Profession, and on the Present State of Medical Practice in Ireland.* Dublin: John Jones.

Graunt, John [and William Petty]. 1665 [1662]. *Natural and Political Observations, mentioned in the following Index, and made upon the Bills of Mortality. With reference to the Government, Religion, Trade, Growth, Air, Diseases, and the Several Changes of the Said City.* 3rd ed. London: Martyn and Allestry.

Gray, John. 1855. *Observations on House and General Sewerage, and on an Improved Plan for Cleansing and Ventilating House Drains by a Self-acting Mechanism: with a Description of the Apparatus, as applied in the North Dublin Union Workhouse, under the Superintendence of the Poor-law Commissioners: Being the substance of a paper read at the Royal Dublin Society.* Dublin: Hodges and Smith.

Greig, William. 1819. *Strictures of Road Police, Containing Views of the Present Systems, by which Roads are Made and Repaired, together with Sketches of its Progress in Great Britain and Ireland, from the earliest to the present times.* Dublin: Archer, Cumming, Milliken, Dugdale, Keene, Hodges & McArthur, and Larkin.

Griffith, Richard. 1814. *Geological and Mining Report on the Leinster Coal District.* Dublin: Graisberry and Campbell.

Grimshaw, Thomas. 1874. "On Zymotic and Preventable Diseases." In *Lectures on Public Health Delivered in the Lecture Hall of the Royal Dublin Society.* Dublin: Hodges, Foster & Co.

———. 1883. "On Some Important Relations Between Census Statistics and Sanitary Statistics." *Transactions of the Academy of Medicine in Ireland,* vol. 1. Dublin: Fannin.

Hanway, Jonas. 1775. *The Defects of Police, the Cause of Immorality.* London: J. Dodsley.

Harrel, David. 1889. *Standing Orders and Regulations for the Government and Guidance of the Dublin Metropolitan Police as approved by His Excellency the Lord Lieutenant.* Dublin: Alex. Thom. & Co.

Hartlib, Samuel. 1648. *A further Discoverie of The Office of Publick Addresse for Accommodations.* London.

———. 1970. *Samuel Hartlib and the Advancement of Learning.* Ed. Charles Webster. Cambridge: Cambridge University Press.

Henderson, George. 1874. "On the Construction of Dwelling Houses with Reference to their Sanitary arrangement." In *Lectures on Public Health Delivered in the Lecture Hall of the Royal Dublin Society.* Dublin: Hodges, Foster & Co.

Hobbes, Thomas. 1940 [1651]. *Leviathan.* With an introduction by A. D. Lindsay. London: Everyman.

———. 1985 [1661]. "Dialogus Physicus." Trans. from the Latin by Simon Schaffer. In Steven Shapin and Simon Schaffer, *Leviathan and the Air-Pump: Hobbes, Boyle, and the Experimental Life.* Chicago: University of Chicago Press.

Hogan, William. 1848. "On the Necessity for Model Lodging Houses in Dublin." Paper read before the Royal Dublin Society. Published in William Hogan, *The Dependence of National Wealth on the Social and Sanatory Condition of the Labouring Classes; [and] On the Necessity for Model Lodging Houses in Dublin, and the Advantages they would confer on the community.* Dublin: Hodges and Smith, 1849.

———. 1849. *The Dependence of National Wealth on the Social and Sanatory Condition of the Labouring Classes.* Dublin: Hodges and Smith.

Howard, John. 1784. *The State of the Prisons in England and Wales.* London: William Eyres.

Hull, Charles H. 1896. "Graunt or Petty? The Authorship of the Observations upon the Bills of Mortality." *Political Science Quarterly* 11: 105–32.

Husband, H. Aubrey. 1879. *The Students Hand-Book of Forensic Medicine and Medical Police.* 3rd ed. Edinburgh: E & S Livingstone.

Instructions to the Valuators and Surveyors appointed under 15th and 16th Vict., Cap. 63, for the Uniform Valuation of Lands and Tenements in Ireland. 1853. Dublin: Her Majesty's Stationery Office.

International Health Exhibition. 1884. *The Health Exhibition Literature.* 19 vols. London: William Clowes and Sons.

Johnson, Samuel. 1775 [1773]. *A Dictionary of the English Language.* London: W. Strachan, J. and F. Rivington.

Johnstone, John. 1801. *An Account of the Mode of Draining Land, according to the system practised by Mr. Joseph Elkington.* 2nd ed. London: B. McMillan.

Kennedy, Henry. 1777. *An Experimental Enquiry into the Chemical and Medicinal Properties of the Sulphurous Water at Auchnacloy.* Dublin.

King, William. N.d. "Concerning Hydraulic Engins." MS I.4.18, fols. 105–12, Trinity College, Dublin.

Knox, William. 1768. *The Present State of the Nation: Particularly with respect to its Trade, Finances, &c. &c. addressed to The King and both Houses of Parliament.* London: J. Almon.

Lakeman, James. 1884. "Health in the Workshop." In *Health Exhibition Literature,* vol. 1. London: William Clowes and Sons.

Lalor, Joseph. 1848. "Observations on the late Epidemic Fever." *Dublin Quarterly Journal of Medical Science* 5: 12–30.

Lamb, Francis. 1689. *A Geographicall Description of ye Kingdom of Ireland. Collected from ye actual Survey made by Sir William Petty, Corrected & amended by the advice & assistance of severall Able Artists, late Inhabitants of that Kingdom. Containing one General Mapp of ye whole Kingdom, with four Provincial Mapps, & 32 County Mapps, divided into Baronies, where in are described ye Cheife Cities, Townes, Rivers, Harbors, and Head-lands, &c. To which is added a Mapp of Great Britain and Ireland, together with an Index of the whole, Being very usefull for all Gentlemen, and Military Officers, as well for Sea, as Land Service.* London: Francis Lamb.

Lardner, Dionysius. 1826. *Syllabus of the first part of a Course of Lectures on Mechanical & Experimental Philosophy, to be delivered at the Cork Mechanics Institute.* Cork: I. Hennessy.

Law, Robert. 1848. "Letter of Dr. Law on the Subject of the Board of Health." *Dublin Quarterly Journal of Medical Science* 5.

Locke, John. 1667. *Table of Weather for London.* Locke MSS. file 19, fol. 394. Bodleian Library, Oxford University.

———. N.d. "The Towing Engine." Locke MSS. c. 31, fol. 48. Bodleian Library, Oxford University.

Macdonnell, Robert. 1874. "On Antiseptics and Disinfection." In *Lectures on Public Health Delivered in the Lecture Hall of the Royal Dublin Society.* Dublin: Hodges, Foster and Co.

Madden, Samuel. 1736. *A Letter to the Dublin Society on the Improving their Fund and the Manufacture, Tillage &c. in Ireland.* Dublin: G. Ewing.

Malthus, T.M. 1803. *Remarks on a Late Publication entitled, "An Essay on the Principle of Population; or, A View of its Present and Past Effects on Human Happiness."* London: R. Bickerstaff.

Mapother, Edward. 1867. *Lectures on Public Health delivered at the Royal College of Surgeons.* 2nd ed. Dublin: Fannin.

———. 1874. "The Prevention of Artisans' Diseases." In *Lectures on Public Health Delivered in the Lecture Hall of the Royal Dublin Society.* Dublin: Hodges, Foster & Co.

Matheson, Robert. 1908. *A Review of the Anti-Tuberculosis Campaign in Ireland.* Paper read before the Meeting of the British Association for the Advancement of Science, held in Dublin, September 1908. Dublin: Alex. Thom.

Maunsell, Henry. 1839. *Political Medicine.* Dublin.

Miller, Philip. 1732. *The Gardeners Dictionary: Containing the Methods of Cultivating and Improving the Kitchen, Fruit and Flower Garden. As also the Physick Garden, Wilderness, Conservatory, and Vineyard, according to the Practice of the Most Experienc'd Gardeners of the Present Age. Intersperss'd with the History of the Plants, the Characters of each Genus, and the Names of all particular Species, in Latin and English; and an Explanation of all the Terms used in Botany and Gardening. Together with Accounts of the Nature and Use of Barometers, Thermometers, and Hygrometers proper for Gardeners; And of the Origin, Causes, and Nature of Meteors, and the particular Influences of Air, Earth, Fire, and Water upon Vegetation, according to the best Natural Philosophers.* Dublin: Richard Gunne.

Molyneux, William. 1698. *The Case of Ireland's being bound by Acts of Parliament in England, Stated.* Dublin.

———. 1709 [1692]. *Dioptrica Nova. A Treatise of Dioptricks, In Two Parts. Wherein the Various Effects and Appearances of Spherick Glasses, both Convex and Concave, Single and Combined, in Telescopes and Microscopes, Together with Their Usefulness in many Concerns of Humane Life, are Explained.* 2nd. ed. London: Tooke.

Moore, Arthur. 1848. *Sanitary Acts for Ireland, passed in 1846, 1847, & 1848, comprising the Temporary Fever Acts, together with an abstract of the provisions of 58 Geo. III cap. 47 and 59 Geo. III cap. 41, relating to Infectious or Contagious and Epidemic Diseases, Officers of Health, and local Boards of Health; and of the Nuisances Removal and Diseases Prevention Act, 11 & 12 Vic. cap 123; order in council under that act, suggestions of Central Board of Health, &c. with notes and index.* Dublin: Alex. Thom.

———. 1856. *The Towns Improvement (Ireland) Act, 1854, 17 & 18 Vict. Cap. 103: with Provisions of Acts Incorporated therewith, and Acts amending the same.* Dublin: Alex. Thom.

Moore, Charles. 1854. *Suggestions for Improvements in the Sewerage of Cities and Towns.* Dublin: Hodges & Smith.

———. 1874. *A Glance at Preventive Medicine in 1769 and in 1874.* Dublin: Fannin & Co.

———. 1886. *The Sanitary Condition of Dublin Dairy Yards.* Dublin: Falconer.

———. 1888. *Remarks on State Medicine.* Dublin.

Moore, John. 1874. "On Meteorology in its Bearing on Health and Disease." In *Lectures on Public Health Delivered in the Lecture Hall of the Royal Dublin Society.* Dublin: Hodges, Foster and Co.

Moore, William. 1847. *An Outline of the History of Pharmacy in Ireland.* Dublin: Hodges and Smith.

Morris, J. A. 1838. *Complete Abstract of the New Irish Poor Law Act.* Dublin: Lorenzo F. Shaw.

Neville, Parke. 1854. *Report on the Capabilities of the River Dodder to afford a Supply of Water for the Use of the City of Dublin and the Suburbs.* Dublin: O'Neill & Duggan.

———. 1855. *Report to the Right Hon. the Lord Mayor, Aldermen and Councilors of the City of Dublin, on the Progress made in the Sewerage, and on the State of the Public Works of the City for years 1853 & 1854.* Dublin: O'Neill & Duggan.

Newenham, Thomas. 1805. *A Statistical and Historical Inquiry into the Progress and Magnitude of the Population of Ireland.* London: C. & R. Baldwin.

———. 1809. *A View of the Natural, Political, and Commercial Circumstances of Ireland.* London: Cadell and Davies.

O'Brien-Furlong, Robert. 1874. "On Sanitary Legislation." In *Lectures on Public Health Delivered in the Lecture Hall of the Royal Dublin Society.* Dublin: Hodges, Foster and Co.

Paget, Charles. 1884. "Healthy Schools." In *Health Exhibition Literature*, vol. 1. London: William Clowes and Sons.

Papers respecting Experimental Improvements on the Crown Lands at Kingwilliams Town, in the Barony of Duhallow in the County of Cork, and to the New Lines of Road of Public Roads constructed in County Cork and Kerry. 1834. H.C. (173), LI.

Parliamentary Gazetter of Ireland, adapted to the new poor-law, franchise, municipal and ecclesiastical arrangements, and compiled with a special reference to the lines of railroad and canal communication, as existing in 1843–44; illustrated by a series of maps, and other plates; and presenting the results, in detail, of the census of 1841, compared with that of 1831. 1844. Vol. 1. Dublin: A. Fullarton and Co.

Peirson, Sam. 1725. The Present State of the Tillage in Ireland Considered, and Some Methods offered for its Improvement. Dublin: George Grierson.

Pemble, William. 1675. A Brief Introduction to Geography. Containing a Description of the Grounds and General Part thereof. Oxford: Forrest.

Percival, Edward. 1807. Memoirs of the Life and Writings of Thomas Percival, M.D., F.R.S. London: J. Johnson.

———. 1817. Medical Reports on the Epidemic Fevers of Dublin, on Insanity and on Several Miscellaneous Subjects. Dublin: Hibernia Press Office.

Percival, Thomas. 1773. Essays Medical and Experimental. London: Joseph Johnson.

———. 1776. Philosophical, Medical, and Experimental Essays. London: Joseph Johnson.

Perry, John. 1721. An Answer to Objections against the making of a Bason, with reasons for the bettering of the Harbour of Dublin. Dublin: S. Powell.

Petty, William. 1648. The Advice of W.P. to Mr. Samuel Hartlib for the Advancement of some particular parts of Learning. London.

———. 1659. A Brief of Proceedings between Sir Hierom Sankey and Dr. William Petty. With The State of the Controversie between them Tendered to all Indifferent Persons. London.

———. 1660. Reflections Upon Some Persons and Things in Ireland. Dublin.

———. 1662. A Discourse on Taxes and Contributions: Shewing the Nature and Measures of Crown Lands etc. London.

———. 1674. The Discourse made before the Royal Society concerning the use of Duplicate Proportion in Sundry Important Particulars: Together with a New Hypothesis of Springing or Elastique Motions. London: John Martyn.

———. 1682. A further Assertion of the Propositions concerning the Magnitude, &c. of London, contained in two Essays in Political Arithmetick; mentioned in Philos. Transact. Numb. 183; together with a Vindication of the said Essays from the Objections of some Learned Persons of the French Nation. London.

———. 1683. Another Essay in Political Arithmetick, concerning the growth of the City of London, with the measures, Periods, Causes, and Consequences thereof, 1682. London.

———. 1683. Observations upon the Dublin Bills of Mortality, and the State of that City. 1681. London: Mark Pardoe.

———. 1686. An Essay concerning the Multiplication of Mankind: Together with another Essay in Political Arithmetick, Concerning the Growth of the City of London: with the Measures, Periods, Causes, and Consequences thereof. 1682. 2nd. ed. London: Mark Pardoe.

————. 1686. *Further Observations upon the Dublin Bills: or, Accompts of the Houses, Hearths, Baptisms, and Burials in that City.* 2nd ed. London: Mark Pardoe.

————. 1687. *Five Essays in Political Arithmetick.* London: Mortlock.

————. 1687. *Two Essays in Political Arithmetick, Concerning the People, Housing, Hospitals, &c. of London and Paris.* London.

————. 1695. *Quantulumcunque Concerning Money.* London.

————. 1699. *Political Arithmetick, or a Discourse concerning The Extent and Value of Lands, People, Buildings; Husbandry, Manufacture, Commerce, Fishery, Artizans, Seamen, Soldiers; Publick Revenues, Interest, Taxes, Superlucration, Registries, Banks; Valuation of Men, Increasing of Seamen, of Militia's Harbours, Situation, Shipping, Power at Sea, &c. As the same relates to every Country in general, but more particularly to the Territories of His Majesty of Great Britain, and his Neighbours of Holland, Zealand, and France.* London: Clavel.

————. 1699. *Several Essays in Political Arithmetick.* London: Robert Clavel.

————. 1851 [c. 1659]. "A Briefe Accompt of the most Material Passages relatinge to the Survey managed by Doctor Petty in Ireland, anno 1655 and 1656." Repr. in William Petty, *The History of the Survey of Ireland, Commonly Called The Down Survey,* ed. Thomas Aiskew Larcom. Dublin: Irish Archaeological Society.

————. 1851 [c. 1659]. *The History of the Survey of Ireland, commonly called The Down Survey.* Ed. Thomas Aiskew Larcom. Dublin: Irish Archaeological Society.

————. 1861 [1691]. *The Political Anatomy of Ireland.* (Orig. written 1672.) London: Brown & Rogers. Repr. in *A Collection of Tracts and Treatises Illustrative of the Natural History, Antiquities, and the Political and Social State of Ireland,* vol. 2. Dublin: Thom & Sons.

————. 1927. *The Petty Papers: Some Unpublished Writings of Sir William Petty.* 2 vols. Ed. from the Bowood Papers by the Marquis of Lansdowne. London: Constable.

————. 1967 [1928]. *The Petty-Southwell Correspondence 1676–1687.* Ed. the Marquis of Lansdowne. New York: Augustus M. Kelley.

————. 1968 [1685]. *Hibernia Delineatio: Atlas of Ireland.* Newcastle-upon-Tyne: Frank Graham, 1968.

Pim, Frederic. 1890. *The Health of Dublin, being three addresses to the Dublin Sanitary Association bound and published together.* Dublin: R. D. Webb and Son.

Pim, Jonathan. 1876. *An Address Delivered at the Opening of the Thirtieth Session of the Statistical Society of Ireland, being a Review of the Economic and Social Progress of Ireland Since the Famine.* Dublin: Richard D. Webb.

Pooler, Robert. 1887. *The Irish Farmer's Manual being A Practical Compendium of the most improved Systems of Husbandry; comprehending the various subjects of manures, draining, soiling, rotation of crops; managements of* bees; the culture of clover, turnips, mangel wurzel, lucerne, and the other crops cultivated in Ireland; together with various rural subjects, of importance to the small farmer and others. Dublin: Milliken & Son.

Preston, William. 1803. Essay on the natural advantages of Ireland, the manufactures to which they are adapted and the best means of improving those manufactures. Dublin: Royal Irish Academy.

Price, Richard. 1803 [1769]. Observations on Reversionary Payments; on Schemes for Providing Annuities for Widows, and for Persons in Old Age; on the Method of Calculating the Values of Assurances on Lives; and on the National Debt. Also Essays on different Subjects in the Doctrine of Life-Annuities and Political Arithmetic; A Collection of New Tables, and a Postscript on the Population of the Kingdom. 2 vols. 6th ed. London: Cadell and Davies.

Prior, Thomas. 1729. A List of the Absentees of Ireland, and the Yearly Value of their Estates and Incomes Spent Abroad. With Observations on the Present Trade and Condition of that Kingdom. 2nd ed. Dublin: Gunne.

Report of a Committee of the Dublin Society respecting the Merino Factory, Co. Kilkenny. 1819. Dublin: Graisberry.

Report of the Commissioners Appointed to enquire into the Conduct and Management of the Corporation for Paving, Cleansing, and Lighting the Streets of Dublin. 1806. Dublin: His Majesty's Stationery Office.

Report of the Poor Law Commissioners. 1838. With supplementary reports: "Report on the Prevalence of Certain Physical Causes of Fever in the Metropolis which might be removed by Proper Sanatory Measures" (under pen of Neil Arnott and James Kay-Shuttleworth [formerly Philips Kay]); "Report on Some of the Physical Causes of Sickness and Mortality to which the Poor are Particularly Exposed, and which are Capable of Removal by Sanitary Regulations" (under pen of Thomas Southwood Smith). London: Her Majesty's Stationery Office.

Report of the Royal Commissioners appointed to inquire into the Sewerage and Drainage of the City of Dublin, and other matters connected therewith, together with minutes of evidence, appendix, index, &c. 1880. Dublin: Alex. Thom.

Reports of the Commissioners Appointed to enquire into the Nature and Extent of Several Bogs in Ireland. 1810–14. London: His Majesty's Stationery Office.

Resolutions of the "Special Committee on Registration and Sanitary Police." 1860. In Transactions of the National Association for the Promotion of Social Science. London: John W. Parker.

Return of Royal Sappers and Miners employed under the command of Captain Cameron, Royal Engineers, upon the Ordnance Survey of Ireland. 1847. Dublin.

Reynolds, Emerson. 1874. "On the Discrimination of Unadulterated Food." In Lectures on Public Health Delivered in the Lecture Hall of the Royal Dublin Society. Dublin: Hodges, Foster and Co.

Roberton, John. 1812. *Medical Police: or the Causes of Disease, with the Means of Prevention; and Rules for Diet, Regimen, &c. Adapted particularly to the cities of London and Edinburgh, and generally to all large towns.* 2 vols. 2nd ed. London: J. J. Stockdale.

Rogers, Jasper. 1854. *Two Lectures on the Sanitary Improvement of Dublin, delivered in the Board Room of the Royal Dublin Society.* Belfast: John Anderson.

Rogers, Joseph. 1734. *An Essay on Epidemic Diseases, and more particularly the Endemical Epidemics of the City of Cork, &c.* Dublin: William Smith.

Royal Botanic Gardens. 1818. *Prospectus of the Arrangements in the Dublin Society's Botanical and Agricultural Garden, at Glasnevin.* Dublin: Graisberry and Campbell.

Royal Dublin Society. 1736–37. "Directions for Making Roads." In *Dublin Society . . . Essays and Observations.* Dublin.

———. 1740. *Essays and observations on the following subjects, viz On trade, directions for making roads, instructions for making syder, observations on the linen manufactory.* Dublin.

Rumsey, Henry. 1856. *Essays on State Medicine.* London: John Churchill.

———. 1860. "On Certain Departments of Medico-Sanitary Police and Medico-Legal Inquiry, in Connexion with the Scientific Superintendence of Mortuary Registration." In *Transactions of the National Association for the Promotion of Social Science.* London: John W. Parker and Son.

———. 1867. *On State Medicine in Great Britain and Ireland.* London: William Ridgway.

———. 1868. *The Educational Aspects of State Medicine.* London: W. J. Golbourn.

———. 1875. *Essays and Papers on Some Fallacies of Statistics concerning Life and Death, Health and Disease, with Suggestions Towards an Improved System of Registration.* London: Smith, Elder and Co.

Russell, Patrick. 1791. *A treatise of the plague: containing an historical journal, and medical account, of the plague, at Aleppo, in the years 1760, 1761, and 1762. Also remarks on quarantines, lazarettos, and the administration of police.* London: G. G. & J. Robinson.

Rutty, Thomas. 1757. *An Essay towards a Natural, Experimental, and Medicinal History of the Mineral Waters of Ireland.* Dublin.

———. 1762. *Analysis of Milk and the Different Species thereof.* Dublin, 1762.

———. 1762. *The Argument of Sulphur or no Sulphur in Water Discussed.* Dublin.

———. 1762. *A Methodological Synopsis of Mineral Waters.* Dublin.

———. 1770. *A Chronological History of the Weather and Seasons, and of the Prevailing Diseases in Dublin. With their various Periods, Successions, and Revolutions, during the Space of Forty Years. With a comparative View of the Difference of the Irish Climate and Diseases, and those of England and other Countries.* London: Robinson and Roberts.

————. 1772. *An Essay towards the Natural History of the County of Dublin.* 2 vols. Dublin: Slater.

Ryan, Michael. 1836. *A Manual of Medical Jurisprudence, and State Medicine.* London: Sherwood, Gilbert & Piper.

The Sanitary Inspector. 1877. Vol. 1. London: E. W. Allen.

The Sanitary Review: A Monthly Record of Sanitary Science, and devoted to all Subjects which affect the Health and Welfare of the People. 1875. Vol. 1. London: Model Houses Association.

Shadwell, Thomas. 1676. *The Virtuoso: A Comedy, Acted at the Duke's Theatre.* London: Henry Herringman.

Simington, Robert C., ed. 1931. *The Civil Survey, AD 1654–1656.* 10 vols. Dublin: Government Stationery Office.

————, ed. 1956. *Books of Survey and Distribution: Being Abstracts of Various Surveys and Instruments of Title, 1636–1703. With Maps.* Dublin: Her Majesty's Stationery Office.

Smith, Adam. 1896. *Lectures on Justice, Police, Revenue and Arms.* Ed. Edwin Cannan. Oxford: Clarendon Press.

Smith, John. 1725. *The Curiosities of Common Water; or The Advantages thereof in Preventing and Curing many Distempers. Gather'd from the writings of several Eminent Physicians; and also from more than Forty Years Experience. To which are added Some Rules for preserving Health by Diet.* 8th ed. Dublin: G. Ewing.

Smith, John Gordon. 1828. *The Principles of Forensic Medicine, Systematically Arranged and Applied to British Practice.* London: Underwood.

Spenser, Edmund. 1970 [c. 1598]. *A View of the Present State of Ireland.* Oxford: Clarendon Press.

Statutes, as amended, relating to General Valuation and Boundary Survey of Ireland, from the 30th June, 1852, to the 7th August, 1874. 1888. Dublin: Her Majesty's Stationery Office.

Stokes, William. 1825. *A Treatise on the Use of the Stethoscope.* Dublin.

————. 1828. *Two Lectures on the Application of the Stethoscope.* Dublin.

————. 1837. *Diseases of the Chest.* Dublin.

————. 1854. *Diseases of the Heart and Aorta.* Dublin.

————. 1874. "Introductory Discourse on Sanitary Science in Ireland." In *Lectures on Public Health Delivered in the Lecture Hall of the Royal Dublin Society.* Dublin: Hodges, Foster and Co.

Stokes, William, [Jr.]. 1898. *William Stokes, His Life and Work (1804–1878).* London: T. Fisher Unwin.

Strange, William. 1846. *The Health and Sickness of Town Populations considered with Reference to Proposed Sanitary Legislation, and to the Establishment of a Comprehensive System of Medical Police, and District Dispensaries, with appendices and statistical tables.* London: Parker.

————. 1846. "On the Formation of a System of National Medical Police and Public Hygiene; with Observations on those Clauses of the Health of Towns

Bill which refer to the Appointment of District Medical Officers." *London Medical Gazette, or Journal of Practical Medicine* 2: 452–57.

Studdert, Lancelot, and Thomas Abbott. 1873. *Analyses of Water Supplied to Dublin and Neighbouring Townships, Made at the Royal College of Science, Dublin.* Dublin: Office of The Medical Press and Circular.

Sullivan, William. 1852. *Facts and Theories; or, the Real Prospects of the Beet-Sugar Manufacture in Ireland.* Dublin: James McGlashan.

Taylor, Alfred S. 1850. *Medical Jurisprudence.* Philadelphia: Lea and Blanchard.

Taylor, George. 1778. *Taylor and Skinner's Maps of the Roads of Ireland.* London.

Temple, William. 1701. "A Defense of the Essay upon Antient and Modern Learning." In *Miscellanea: The Third Part.* Dublin: Jonathan Swift & A. M. Prebendary.

Thomson, William, ed. 1883. *Transactions of the Academy of Medicine in Ireland*, vol. 1. Dublin: Fannin.

Transactions of the Epidemiological Society of London for the Year 1855. 1856. London: T. Richards.

Transactions of the Royal Agricultural Improvement Society, and Annual Report and Proceedings of the Council, for the Year 1844. 1845. Dublin: William Curry, Jun. and Co.

Trimmer, Joshua Kirby. 1809. *A Brief Inquiry into the Present State of Agriculture in the Southern Part of Ireland, and its Influence on the Manners and Condition of the Lower Classes of the People: with some Considerations upon the Ecclesiastical Establishment of that Country.* London: J. Hatchard.

Tyrrell, James. 1680. "Of the Irish." In Locke MSS, c. 31, fol. 35. Bodleian Library, Oxford University.

Vallancey, Charles. 1763. *A Treatise on Inland Navigation or the Art of Making Rivers Navigable, Of Making Canals in all sorts of Soils, and of Constructing Locks and Sluices.* Dublin: G. and A. Ewing.

Vignoles, O. J. 1889. *The Life of Charles Blacker Vignoles.* Dublin.

von Holtzendorff, Franz. 1863. *Reflections and Observations on the present condition of the Irish Convict System.*

Wade, John. 1771. *An Account of all the Proceedings that have been taken relative to the Management of the Chymical Laboratory in Capel Street, Dublin, from its first Institution to the present Time.* Dublin: James Parker.

Wade, Walter. 1808. *Sketch of Lectures on Artificial or Sown Grasses, as Lucern, Saint-foin, Clovers, Trefoils, Vetches, &c. Delivered in the Dublin Society's Botanical Garden, Glasnevin.* Dublin: Dublin Society.

Warburton, George. c. 1693. *These are to give notice that from the 25th of this instant June the post will pass thrice a week betwixt England and Ireland: and in like manner betwixt Dublin and the several post-stages in the country.* Dublin.

Willis, Thomas. 1845. *Facts connected with the Social and Sanitary Condition of the Working Classes in the City of Dublin, with tables of sickness, medical attendance, deaths, expectation of life, &c., &c.; Together with some glean-ings from the Census Returns of 1841.* Dublin: T. O'Gorman.

———. 1845. *On the Social and Sanatory Condition of the Labouring Classes in Dublin.* Dublin.

Willoughby, Charles. 1691. "Enquiries to be Made about the Bills of Mortality, aire, diseases &c." In Rawlinson MSS, c. 406, fol. 68: Bills of Mortality, Dublin; and fols. 69–81, 92, and 97. Bodleian Library, Oxford University.

———. N.d. "Proposals for an Improvement in Ireland." In Rawlinson MSS, c. 406, fol. 91. Bodleian Library, Oxford University.

Wodsworth, W.D. 1874. *Digest of the Sanitary Laws in Force in Ireland.* Dublin: Alex Thom.

Young, Arthur. 1892. *Arthur Young's Tour in Ireland (1776–1779).* Ed. with an intro. by Arthur Wollaston Hutton. 2 vols. London: Bell and Sons.

SECONDARY SOURCES

Abrams, Philip. 1988 [1977]. "Notes on the Difficulty of Studying the State." *Journal of Historical Sociology* 1, no. 1: 58–89.

Adams, Julia. 1999. "Culture in Rational-Choice Theories of State-Formation." In *State/Culture: State-Formation After the Cultural Turn,* ed. George Steinmetz. Ithaca, NY: Cornell University Press.

———. 2005. *The Familial State: Ruling Families and Merchant Capitalism in Early Modern Europe.* Ithaca, NY: Cornell University Press.

Adams, Julia, Elisabeth S. Clemens, and Ann Orloff. 2005. "Social Theory, Modernity, and the Three Waves of Historical Sociology." In *Remaking Modernity: Politics, History, and Sociology,* ed. Julia Adams, E.S. Clemens, and A.S. Orloff. Durham, NC: Duke University Press.

Adas, Michael. 1989. *Machines as the Measure of Men: Science, Technology, and Ideologies of Western Dominance.* Ithaca, NY: Cornell University Press.

———. 1997. "Review Essay: A Field Matures: Technology, Science, and Western Colonialism." *Technology and Culture* 38, no. 2: 478–87.

Alcott, Linda, and Elizabeth Porter, eds. 1993. *Feminist Epistemologies.* New York: Routledge.

Alder, Ken. 1997. *Engineering the Revolution: Arms and Enlightenment in France, 1763–1815.* Princeton, NJ: Princeton University Press.

———. 1999. "French Engineers Become Professional." In *The Sciences of Enlightened Europe,* ed. William Clark, Jan Golinski, and Simon Shaffer. Chicago: University of Chicago Press.

Allen, Michael Thad, and Gabrielle Hecht, eds. 2001. *Technologies of Power: Essays in Honor of Thomas Parke Hughes and Agatha Chipley Hughes.* Cambridge, MA: MIT Press.

Alter, Peter. 1987. *The Reluctant Patron: Science and the State in Britain 1850–1920.* Oxford: Berg.

Althusser, Louis. 1994 [1969]. "Ideology and Ideological State Apparatuses." In *Mapping Ideology,* ed. Slavoj Žižek. London: Verso.

Anderson, Benedict. 1991. *Imagined Communities: Reflections on the Origin and Spread of Nationalism*. New York: Verso.

Andrew, Donna. 1989. *Philanthropy and Police: London Charity in the Eighteenth Century*. Princeton, NJ: Princeton University Press.

Andrews, J. H. 1961. *Ireland in Maps: An Introduction*. Dublin: Dolmen Press.

———. 1966. "Charles Vallancey and the Map of Ireland." *Geographical Journal* 132: 48–61.

———. 1975. *A Paper Landscape: The Ordnance Survey in Nineteenth-Century Ireland*. Oxford: Clarendon Press.

———. 1994. "Meaning, Knowledge and Power in the Map Philosophy of J. B. Harley." *Trinity Papers in Geography* 6.

Andrews, J. H., and Paul Ferguson. 1994. "Maps of Ireland." In *Historians' Guide to Early British Maps: A Guide to the Location of Pre-1900 Maps of the British Isles Preserved in the United Kingdom and Ireland*. London: Royal Historical Society.

Arnold, David. 1993. *Colonizing the Body: State Medicine and Epidemic Disease in Nineteenth-Century India*. Berkeley: University of California Press.

———. 1994. "The Colonial Prison: Power, Knowledge, and Penology in Nineteenth Century India." *Subaltern Studies VIII: Essays in Honour of Ranajit Guha*. Delhi: Oxford University Press.

Ashworth, William B. 1990. "Natural History and the Emblematic World View." In *Reappraisals of the Scientific Revolution*, ed. David C. Lindberg and Robert S. Westman. Cambridge: Cambridge University Press.

Atkinson, George. 1931. "What the Society Has Done for Art." In *Royal Dublin Society Bi-centennial Souvenir*. Dublin: Royal Dublin Society.

Attis, David, and Charles Mollen, eds. 2004. *Science and Irish Culture: Why the History of Science Matters in Ireland*. Dublin: Royal Dublin Society.

Baber, Zaheer. 1996. *The Science of Empire: Scientific Knowledge, Civilization, and Colonial Rule in India*. Albany, NY: State University of New York Press.

Barnard, T. C. 1975. *Cromwellian Ireland*. Oxford: Oxford University Press.

———. 1990. "Gardening, Diet and 'Improvement' in Later Seventeenth-Century Ireland." *Journal of Garden History* 10, no. 1: 71–85.

———. 1993. "The Political, Material and Mental Culture of the Cork Settlers, c. 1650–1700." In *Cork History and Society: Interdisciplinary Essays on the History of an Irish County*, ed. P. O'Flanagan and C. G. Buttimer. Dublin: Geography Publications.

———. 1994. "The Hartlib Circle and the Cult and Culture of Improvement in Ireland." In *Samuel Hartlib and University Reformation: Studies in Intellectual Communication*, ed. M. Greengrass, M. Leslie, T. Raylor. Cambridge: Cambridge University Press.

———. 1995. "Improving Clergymen, 1660–1760." In *As by Law Established: The Church of Ireland since the Reformation*, ed. A. Ford, J. McGuire, and K. Milne. Dublin: Lilliput Press.

Barry, Andrew. 1993. "The History of Measurement and the Engineers of Space." *British Journal for the History of Science* 26: 459–68.

Beamish, Thomas. 2002. *Silent Spill: The Organization of an Industrial Crisis.* Cambridge, MA: MIT Press.

Bennett, J.A. 1980. "Robert Hooke as Mechanic and Natural Philosopher." *Notes and Records of the Royal Society of London* 35: 33–48.

———. 1986. "The Mechanics' Philosophy and the Mechanical Philosophy." *History of Science* 24: 1–28.

Bennett, Jim, and Stephen Johnston. 1996. *The Geometry of War 1500–1750.* Oxford: Museum of the History of Science.

Biernacki, Richard. 1995. *The Fabrication of Labor: Germany and Britain, 1640–1914.* Berkeley: University of California Press.

Bijker, Wiebe E., 1995. "Sociohistorical Technology Studies." In *Handbook of Science and Technology Studies,* ed. Sheila Jasanoff et al. Thousand Oaks, CA: Sage.

Bijker, Wiebe E., and John Law, eds. 1992. *Shaping Technology/Building Society.* Cambridge, MA: MIT Press.

Bijker, Wiebe, Thomas Hughes, and Trevor Pinch, eds. 1987. *The Social Construction of Technological. Systems: New Directions in the Sociology and History of Technology.* Cambridge, MA: MIT Press.

Block, Fred. 1987. *Revising State Theory: Essays in Politics and Postindustrialism.* Philadelphia: Temple University Press.

Block, Fred L. 1996. *The Vampire State: And Other Myths and Fallacies about the U.S. Economy.* New York: New Press.

Bowker, Geoffrey C., and Susan Leigh Star. 1999. *Sorting Things Out: Classification and Its Consequences.* Cambridge, MA: MIT Press.

Bowler, Peter J., and Nicholas Whyte. 1997. *Science and Society in Ireland: The Social Context of Science and Technology in Ireland, 1800–1950.* Belfast: Queens University Belfast and the Institute of Irish Studies.

Boyce, D. George, and Alan O'Day, eds. 1996. *The Making of Modern Irish History: Revisionism and the Revisionist Controversy.* London: Routledge.

Bradshaw, Brendan. 1993. *Representing Ireland: Literature and the Origins of Conflict, 1534–1660.* New York: Cambridge University Press.

Bradshaw, Brendan, Andrew Hadfield, and Willy Maley, eds. *Representing Ireland: Literature and the Origins of Conflict, 1534–1660.* Cambridge: Cambridge University Press.

Broderick, David. 1996. *An Early Toll-Road: The Dublin-Dunlear Turnpike, 1731–1855.* Dublin: Irish University Press.

Brown, Theodore M. 1982. "J. P. Frank's 'Medical Police' and Its Significance for Medicalization in America." In *The Use and Abuse of Medicine,* ed. M.W. de Vries, R.L. Berg, and M. Lipkin Jr. New York: Praeger.

Buchanan, R.A. 1989. *The Engineers: A History of the Engineering Profession in England, 1750–1914.* London: J. Kingsley.

Bud, Robert, and Susan E. Cozzens, eds. 1992. *Invisible Connections: Instruments, Institutions, and Science.* Bellingham, WA: SPIE Optical Engineering Press.

Bud, Robert, and Deborah Warner, eds. 1998. *Instruments of Science: An Historical Encyclopedia.* New York: The Science Museum [London] and the National Museum of American History [Smithsonian Institution, Washington, DC] in association with Garland Publishing.

Burchell, Graham, C. Gordon, and P. Miller, eds. 1991. *The Foucault Effect: Studies in Governmentality, with Two Lectures by and an Interview with Michel Foucault.* Chicago: University of Chicago Press.

Burke, John. 1983. *The Use of Science in the Age of Newton.* Berkeley: University of California Press.

Bynum, W.F., and Roy Porter, eds. 1987. *Medical Fringe and Medical Orthodoxy, 1750–1850.* London: Croom Helm.

Callon, Michel, John Law, and Arie Rip, eds. 1986. *Mapping the Dynamics of Science and Technology: Sociology of Science in the Real World.* London: Macmillan.

Camerini, Jane R. 1993. "Evolution, Biogeography, and Maps: An Early History of Wallace's Line." *Isis* 84: 1–28.

Canny, Nicolas. 1982. *The Upstart Earl: A Study of the Social and Mental World of Richard Boyle, First Earl of Cork 1566–1643.* Cambridge: Cambridge University Press.

———. 2001. *Making Ireland British, 1580–1650.* Oxford: Oxford University Press.

Carins, David. 1988. *Writing Ireland: Colonialism, Nationalism, and Culture.* New York: Manchester University Press.

Carroll, Patrick. 1996. "Science, Power, Bodies: The Mobilization of Nature as State Formation." *Journal of Historical Sociology* 9, no. 2: 139–67.

———. 2002. "Medical Police and the History of Public Health." *Medical History* 46, no. 4: 461–94.

Carroll-Burke, Patrick. 2000. *Colonial Discipline: The Making of the Irish Convict System.* Dublin: Four Courts Press.

———. 2001. "Tools, Instruments and Engines: Getting a Handle on the Specificity of Engine Science." *Social Studies of Science* 31, no. 4: 593–625.

———. 2002. "Material Designs: Engineering Cultures and Engineering States—Ireland 1650–1900." *Theory and Society* 31: 75–114.

Cassell, R. 1977. "Medical Charities Act of 1851 and the Growth of State Medicine in Mid-Victorian Ireland." PhD diss., University of North Carolina.

Cassell, Ronald D. 1997. *Medical Charities, Medical Politics: The Irish Dispensary System and the Poor Law, 1836–1872.* London: Royal Historical Society.

Cetina, Karin Knorr. 1999. *Epistemic Cultures: How the Sciences Make Knowledge.* Cambridge, MA: Harvard University Press.

Christoffel, Tom. 1982. *Health and the Law: A Handbook for Health Professionals.* New York: Free Press.

Clarke, Adele E., and Joan H. Fujimura, eds. *The Right Tools for the Job: At Work in Twentieth-Century Life Sciences.* Princeton, NJ: Princeton University Press.

Clokie, Hugh McDowall, and J. William Robinson. 1937. *Royal Commissions of Inquiry: The Significance of Investigations in British Politics*. Oxford: Oxford University Press.

Coakley, Davis. 1988. *The Irish School of Medicine: Outstanding Practitioners of the Nineteenth Century*. Dublin: Townhouse.

Cohen, Bernard S. 1996. *Colonialism and Its Forms of Knowledge*. Princeton, NJ: Princeton University Press.

Collier, Bruce, and James MacLachlan. 1998. *Charles Babbage and the Engines of Perfection*. Oxford: Oxford University Press.

Collins, Harry. 1985. *Changing Order: Replication and Induction in Scientific Practice*. London: Sage Publications.

Collins, Harry, and Trevor Pinch. 1998. *The Golem: What You Should Know about Science*. Cambridge: Cambridge University Press.

Comerford, R. V. 1989. "Ireland 1850–70, Post-famine and Mid-Victorian." In *A New History of Ireland*, vol. 5, ed. W. E. Vaughan. Oxford: Clarendon Press.

———. 2003. *Ireland: Inventing the Nation*. London: Arnold Publishers.

Connell, K. H. 1950. *The Population of Ireland, 1750–1845*. Oxford: Clarendon Press.

Cook, Geoffrey. 1986. "Britain's Legacy to the Irish Social Security System." In *Ireland and Britain since 1922*, vol. 5, ed. P. J. Drudy. Cambridge: Cambridge University Press.

Cook, Harold J. 1989. "Policing the Health of London: The College of Physicians and the Early Stuart Monarchy." *Social History of Medicine* 2, no. 1: 1–33.

Corrigan, Philip. 1990. *Social Forms/Human Capacities: Essays in Authority and Difference*. London: Routledge.

———. 1997. "Commissioning Cosmologies." Discussion paper presented at the Workshop on State Formation in Comparative, Historical, and Cultural Perspectives, St. Peter's College, Oxford, March.

Corrigan, Philip, and Derek Sayer. 1991. *The Great Arch: English State Formation as Cultural Revolution*. Oxford: Blackwell.

Coughlan, Patricia. 1990. "'Cheap and Common Animals': The English Anatomy of Ireland in the Seventeenth Century." In *Literature and the English Civil War*, ed. Thomas Healy and Jonathan Sawday. Cambridge: Cambridge University Press.

Critchley, T. A. 1967. *A History of Police in England and Wales, 1900–1966*. London: Constable.

Cronin, Denis A. 1995. *A Galway Gentleman in the Age of Improvement: Robert French of Monivea, 1716–79*. Dublin: Irish Academic Press.

Cullen, L. M. 1986. "Economic Development, 1750–1800." In *A New History of Ireland*, vol. 4, ed. T. W. Moody and W. E. Vaughan. Oxford: Clarendon Press.

Curtis, Bruce. 1995. "Taking the State Back Out: Rose and Miller on Political Power." *British Journal of Sociology* 46, no. 4: 575–97.

———. 1996. "Studying the State as Process: Domain, Capacity, Project." Paper presented at the colloquium État de nouvelles perspectives en histoire canadienne (The State: New Perspectives in Canadian History). Université de Montréal.

———. 1998. "From Moral Thermometer to Money: Metrological Reform in Pre-confederation Canada." *Social Studies of Science* 28, no. 4: 547–70.

———. 2001. *The Politics of Population: State Formation, Statistics, and the Census of Canada, 1840–1875.* Toronto: University of Toronto Press.

———. 2002. "Foucault on Governmentality: The Impossible Discovery." *Canadian Journal of Sociology* 27, no. 4: 505–33.

Daemmrich, Arthur A. 2004. *Pharmacopolitics: Drug Regulation in the United States and Germany.* Chapel Hill: University of North Carolina Press.

Davis, Susan. 1986. *Parades and Power: Street Theatre in Nineteenth-Century Philadelphia.* Philadelphia, PA: Temple University Press.

Dean, Mitchell. 1999. *Governmentality: Power and Rule in Modern Society.* London: Sage Publications.

Dear, Peter. 1995. *Discipline and Experience: The Mathematical Way in the Scientific Revolution.* Chicago: University of Chicago Press.

Dennis, Michael Aaron. 1989. "Graphic Understanding: Instruments and Interpretation in Robert Hooke's *Micrographia*," *Science in Context* 3, no. 2: 309–64.

Derrida, Jacques. 1978. *Writing and Difference.* Chicago: University of Chicago Press.

Dewhurst, Kenneth. 1956. "The Genesis of State Medicine in Ireland." *Irish Journal of Medical Science* 6: 365–84.

DiMaggio, Paul J., and Walter W. Powell. 1991 [1983]. "The Iron Cage Revisited: Institutional Isomorphism and Collective Rationality." *American Sociological Review* 48: 147–60. Repr. in Walter W. Powell and Paul J. DiMaggio, eds., *The New Institutionalism in Organizational Analysis.* Chicago: University of Chicago Press.

Douglas, Mary. 1966. *Purity and Danger: An Analysis of the Concepts of Pollution and Taboo.* London: Routledge and Kegan Paul.

Downey, Gary L., and Juan C. Lucena. 1995. "Engineering Studies." In *Handbook of Science and Technology Studies,* ed. S. Jasanoff, G. E. Mrekle, J. C. Petersen, and T. Pinch. Thousand Oaks, CA: Sage Publications.

Drayton, Richard. 2000. *Nature's Government: Science, Imperial Britain, and the "Improvement" of the World.* New Haven, CT: Yale University Press.

Edge, David, and Michael Mulkay. 1976. *Astronomy Transformed.* New York: Wiley.

Emsley, Clive. 1991. *The English Police: A Political and Social History.* New York: Addison Wesley Longman.

Epstein, Steven. 1996. *Impure Science: AIDS, Activism, and the Politics of Knowledge.* Berkeley: University of California Press.

Evans, Peter B., Dietrich Rueschemeyer, and Theda Skocpol, eds. 1985. *Bringing the State Back In.* New York: Cambridge University Press.

Ezrahi, Yaron. 1990. *The Descent of Icarus: Science and the Transformation of Contemporary Democracy*. Cambridge, MA: Harvard University Press.

Fanning, Ronan. 1986. "Britain's Legacy: Government and Administration." In *Ireland and Britain Since 1922*, ed. P. J. Drudy. Cambridge: Cambridge University Press.

Fitzmaurice, Edmund. 1895. *The Life of William Petty 1623–1687*. London: John Murray.

Fleisher, Steven M. 1980. "The Law of Basic Public Health Activities: Police Power and Constitutional Limitations." In *Legal Aspects of Health Policy: Issues and Trends*, ed. R. Roemer and G. McKray. Westport, CT: Greenwood Press.

Forsyth, Gordon. 1966. *Doctors and State Medicine: A Study in British Health Service*. London: Pitman Medical.

Foster, R. F. 1990. *Modern Ireland, 1600–1972*. London: Allen Lane.

———. 1993. *Paddy & Mr. Punch: Connections in Irish and English History*. London: Penguin Books.

Foucault, Michel. 1972. *The Archaeology of Knowledge and the Discourse on Language*. London: Tavistock.

———. 1973. *The Order of Things: An Archaeology of the Human Sciences*. New York: Vintage Books.

———. 1977. *Discipline and Punish: The Birth of the Prison*. New York: Penguin Books.

———. 1980. *Power/Knowledge: Selected Interviews and Other Writings 1972–1977*, ed. Colin Gordon. New York: Pantheon Books.

———. 1982. "The Subject and Power." In *Beyond Structuralism and Hermeneutics*, 2nd ed., ed. Hubert L. Dreyfus and Paul Rabinow. Chicago: University of Chicago Press.

———. 1984. "The Politics of Health in the Eighteenth Century." Repr. in Paul Rabinow, *The Foucault Reader*. New York: Pantheon Books.

———. 1988. "Omnes et Singulatim: Towards a Criticism of Political Reason." In *Michel Foucault: Politics, Philosophy Culture, Interviews, and Other Writings 1977–1984*, ed. Lawrence D. Kritzman. New York: Routledge.

———. 1989. *Foucault Live: Interviews, 1966–84*. New York: Semiotext(e).

———. 1990. *The History of Sexuality*. Vol. 1, *An Introduction*. New York: Vintage Books.

———. 1991. *Remarks on Marx: Conversations with Duccio Trombadori*, ed. R. James Goldstein and James Cascaito. New York: Semiotext(e).

———. 1992. *Michel Foucault: Philosopher*. New York: Routledge.

———. 1994. *The Birth of the Clinic: An Archaeology of Medical Perception*. New York: Vintage.

Frangsmyr, Tore, J. L. Heilbron, and Robin E. Rider, eds. 1990. *The Quantifying Spirit in the Eighteenth Century*. Berkeley: University of California Press.

Friedland, Roger, and Robert R. Alford. 1991. "Bringing Society Back In: Symbols, Practices, and Institutional Contradictions." In *The New Institutionalism in Organizational Analysis*, ed. Walter W. Powell and Paul J. DiMaggio. Chicago: University of Chicago Press.

Friel, Brian. 1981. *Translations*. London: Faber & Faber.

Galison, Peter. 1997. *Image and Logic: A Material Culture of Microphysics*. Chicago: University of Chicago Press.

Gatenby, P. A. 1996. *A History of the Meath Hospital*. Dublin: Townhouse.

Gibson, William, and Bruce Sterling. 1992. *The Difference Engine*. New York: Bantam Books.

Giere, Ronald N. 1999. *Science without Laws*. Chicago: University of Chicago Press.

Gieryn, Thomas F. 1999. *Cultural Boundaries of Science: Credibility on the Line*. Chicago: University of Chicago Press.

Goldstone. Jack. 1991. *Revolutions and Rebellion in the Early Modern World*. Berkeley: University of California Press.

———. 2000. "The Rise of the West—or Not? A Revision of Socio-economic History." *Sociological Theory* 18, no. 2: 175–94.

———. 2002. "Efflorescences and Economic Growth in World History: Rethinking the Rise of the West and the British Industrial Revolution." *Journal of World History* 13: 323–89.

Goldstrom, J. M., and L. A. Clarkston, eds. 1981. *Irish Population, Economy, and Society: Essays in Honour of the Late K. H. Connell*. Oxford: Clarendon Press.

Golinski, Jan. 1998. *Making Natural Knowledge: Constructivism and the History of Science*. Cambridge: Cambridge University Press.

———. 1999. "Barometers of Change: Meteorological Instruments as Machines of Enlightenment." In *The Sciences of Enlightened Europe*, ed. William Clark, Jan Golinski, and Simon Shaffer. Chicago: University of Chicago Press.

Gooding, David, Trevor Pinch, and Simon Schaffer, eds. 1989. *The Uses of Experiment: Studies in the Natural Sciences*. Cambridge: Cambridge University Press.

Gorski, Philip. 2003. *The Disciplinary Revolution: Calvinism and the Rise of the State in Early Modern Europe*. Chicago: University of Chicago Press.

Griesemer, James R. 1991. "Must Scientific Diagrams Be Eliminable? The Case of Path Analysis." *Biology and Philosophy* 6, no. 2: 155–80.

Grimshaw, Allen D., ed. 1990. *Conflict Talk: Sociolinguistic Investigations of Arguments in Conversation*. Cambridge: Cambridge University Press.

Gruber, Howard E. 1978. "Darwin's 'Tree of Nature' and Other Images of Wide Scope." In *On Aesthetics in Science*, ed. Judith Wechsler. Cambridge, MA: MIT Press.

Gummett, Philip. 1980. *Scientists in Whitehall*. Manchester: Manchester University Press.

Hackett, Felix. 1931. "The Scientific Activities of the Royal Dublin Society 1731–1931." In *Royal Dublin Society Bi-centenary Souvenir 1731–1931*, ed. W. H. Brayden. Dublin: Royal Dublin Society.

Hacking, Ian. 1983. *Representing and Intervening: Introductory Topics in the Philosophy of Natural Science*. Cambridge: Cambridge University Press.

————. 1990. *The Taming of Chance*. Cambridge: Cambridge University Press.

Hackmann, Willem D. 1989. "Scientific Instruments: Models of Brass and Aids to Discovery." In *The Uses of Experiment: Studies in the Natural Sciences*, ed. David Gooding, Trevor Pinch, and Simon Schaffer. Cambridge: Cambridge University Press.

Hall, John. 2000. *Cultures of Inquiry: From Epistemology to Discourse in Sociohistorical Research*. Cambridge: Cambridge University Press.

Hall, John R., M. J. Neitz, and M. Battani, eds. 2003. *Sociology on Culture*. New York: Routledge.

Hall, M. B. 1958. *Robert Boyle and Seventeenth-Century Chemistry*. Cambridge: Cambridge University Press.

Hamlin, Christopher. 1990. *A Science of Impurity: Water Analysis in Nineteenth-Century Britain*. Berkeley: University of California Press.

————. 1998. *Public Health and Social Justice in the Age of Chadwick: Britain 1800–1854*. Cambridge: Cambridge University Press.

Hankins, Thomas L. 1999. "Blood, Dirt, and Nomograms: A Particular History of Graphs." *Isis* 90: 50–80.

Hankins, Thomas L., and Robert J. Silverman. 1995. *Instruments and the Imagination*. Princeton, NJ: Princeton University Press.

Hannaway, Caroline. 1981. "From Private Hygiene to Public Health: A Transformation in Western Medicine in the Eighteenth and Nineteenth Centuries." In *Public Health: Proceedings of the 5th International Symposium on the Comparative History of Medicine—East and West*, ed. Teizo Ogawa. Tokyo: Saikon Publishing.

Haraway, Donna. 1991. "Situated Knowledges: The Science Question in Feminism and Privilege of Partial Perspective." In *Simians, Cyborgs, and Women: The Reinvention of Nature*. New York: Routledge.

Haraway, Donna J. 1997. *Modest_Witness@Second_Millennium. Female-Man©_Meets_OncoMouse™: Feminism and Technoscience*. New York: Routledge.

Hardiman, Tom. 1983. "Science Policy." In *A Profit and Loss Account of Science in Ireland*, ed. Phyllis E. M. Clinch and R. Charles Mollan. Dublin: Royal Dublin Society.

Harkness, Deborah E. 1997. "Managing an Experimental Household: The Dees of Mortlake and the Practice of Natural Philosophy." *Isis* 88: 247–62.

Harrison, Rachel, and Frank Mort. 1980. "Patriarchal Aspects of Nineteenth Century State Formation: Property Relations, Marriage and Divorce, and Sexuality." In *Capitalism, State Formation and Marxist Theory: Historical Investigations*, ed. Philip Corrigan. London: Quartet Books.

Hartnell, H. Crawford. 1931. "A Life of Two Hundred Years." In *Royal Dublin Society Bi-centennial Souvenir*. Dublin: Royal Dublin Society.

Harwood, John T., ed. 1991. *The Early Essays and Ethics of Robert Boyle*. Carbondale: Southern Illinois University Press.

Herries Davies, Gordon L. and R. C. Mollan, eds. 1980. *Richard Griffith, 1784–1878*. Dublin: Royal Dublin Society.

Hessen, Boris. 1971 [1931]. "The Social and Economic Roots of Newton's 'Principia.'" In *Science at the Crossroads: Papers Presented to the International Congress of the History of Science and Technology.* London: Frank Cass & Co.

Higgs, Edward. 2004. *The Information State in England.* New York: Palgrave Macmillan.

Hill, Jacqueline. 1997. *From Patriots to Unionists: Dublin Civic Politics and Irish Protestant Patriotism, 1660–1840.* Oxford: Clarendon Press.

Hobsbawm, E. J. 1981. "The Contribution of History to Social Science." *International Social Science Journal* 33, no. 4: 624–40.

Hoppen, K. T. 1970. *The Common Scientist in the Seventeenth Century: A Study of the Dublin Philosophical Society 1683–1708.* Charlottesville: University Press of Virginia.

Howe, Stephen. 2000. *Ireland and Empire: Colonial Legacies in Irish History and Culture.* New York: Oxford University Press.

Hull, C. H., ed. 1899. *Economic Writings of Sir William Petty.* Cambridge: Cambridge University Press.

Hunter, Michael. 1981. *Science and Society in Restoration England.* Cambridge: Cambridge University Press.

———. 1995. *Science and the Shape of Orthodoxy.* Woodbridge: Boydell Press.

Ihde, Don, and Evan Selinger, eds. 2003. *Chasing Technoscience: Matrix for Materiality.* Bloomington: Indiana University Press.

Jacob, Margaret C., and Larry Stewart. 2004. *Practical Matter: Newton's Science in the Service of Industry and Empire, 1687–1851.* Cambridge, MA: Harvard University Press.

Jacobsen, John Kurt. 2000. *Technical Fouls: Democratic Dilemmas and Technological Change.* Boulder, CO: Westview Press.

Jasanoff, Sheila. 1986. *Risk Management and Political Culture.* New York: Russell Sage.

———. 1990. *The Fifth Branch: Science Advisors as Policy Makers.* Cambridge, MA: Harvard University Press.

———, ed. 2004. *States of Knowledge: The Co-production of Science and Social Order.* New York: Routledge.

Jepperson, Ronald. 1991. "Institutions, Institutional Effects, and Institutionalism." In *The New Institutionalism in Organizational Analysis,* ed. Walter W. Powell and Paul J. DiMaggio. Chicago: University of Chicago Press.

Johnson, T., G. Larkin, and M. Saks. 1995. *Health Professions and the State in Europe.* New York: Routledge.

Jordanova, L. J. 1981. "Policing Public Health in France 1780–1815." In *Public Health: Proceedings of the 5th International Symposium on the Comparative History of Medicine—East and West,* ed. Teizo Ogawa. Tokyo: Saikon Publishing.

Jordanova, Ludmilla. 1985. "Gender, Generation, and Science: William Hunter's Obstetrical Atlas." In *William Hunter and the Eighteenth-Century*

Medical World, ed. W. F. Bynum and Roy Porter. New York: Cambridge University Press.

Joyce, Patrick. 2001. "Maps, Blood and the City: The Governance of the Social in Nineteenth Century Britain." In *The Social in Question: New Bearings in History and the Social Sciences,* ed. Patrick Joyce. New York: Routledge.

———. 2003. *The Rule of Freedom: Liberalism and the Modern City.* London: Verso.

Kaplan, Steven L. 1976. *Bread, Politics and Political Economy in the Reign of Louis XV.* 2 vols. The Hague: Martinus Nijoff.

Katz, Barry M. 1997. "Review Essay: Technology and Design—a New Agenda." *Technology and Culture* 38, no. 2: 452–66.

Kearney, Richard. 1997. *Postnationalist Ireland: Politics, Culture, Philosophy.* New York: Routledge.

Kiberd, Declan. 1996. *Inventing Ireland: The Literature of the Modern Nation.* Cambridge, MA: Harvard University Press.

Kline, Ronald. 1995. "Construing Technology as Applied Science: Public Rhetoric of Scientists and Engineers in the United States 1880–1945." *Isis* 86: 194–221.

Konvitz, Josef W. 1987. *Cartography in France, 1600–1848: Science, Engineering, and Statecraft.* Chicago: University of Chicago Press.

Koyré, Alexandre. 1943. "Galileo and the Scientific Revolution of the Seventeenth Century." *Philosophical Review* 52, no. 4: 333–48.

Kramnick, Isaac. 1995. *The Portable Enlightenment Reader.* New York: Penguin Books.

Kudlick, Catherine J. 1996. *Cholera in Post-revolutionary Paris: A Cultural History.* Berkeley: University of California Press.

Latour, Bruno. 1984. *The Pasteurization of France.* Cambridge, MA: Harvard University Press.

———. 1987. *Science in Action: How to Follow Scientists and Engineers Around.* Cambridge, MA: Harvard University Press.

———. 1990. "Drawing Things Together." In *Representation in Scientific Practice,* ed. Michael Lynch and Steve Woolgar. Cambridge, MA: MIT Press.

———. 1992. "The Costly Ghastly Kitchen." In *The Laboratory Revolution in Medicine,* ed. Andrew Cunningham and Perry Williams. Cambridge: Cambridge University Press.

———. 1993. *We Have Never Been Modern.* Cambridge, MA: Harvard University Press.

———. 1999. "Give Me a Laboratory and I Will Raise the World." In *The Science Studies Reader,* ed. Mario Biagioli. New York: Routledge.

———. 1999. *Pandora's Hope: Essays on the Reality of Science Studies.* Cambridge, MA: Harvard University Press.

———. 2004. *Politics of Nature: How to Bring the Sciences into Democracy.* Cambridge, MA: Harvard University Press.

———. 2004. "Why Has Critique Run Out of Steam? From Matters of Fact to Matters of Concern." *Critical Inquiry* 30: 225–48.

Latour, Bruno, and Steve Woolgar. 1986. *Laboratory Life: The Construction of Scientific Facts.* Princeton, NJ: Princeton University Press.

Law, John. 1974. "Theories and Methods in the Sociology of Science: An Interpretive Approach." *Social Science Information* 13: 163–71.

———, ed. 1991. *A Sociology of Monsters: Essays on Power, Technology, and Domination.* London: Routledge.

———. 1993. *Modernity, Myth, and Materialism.* Oxford: Blackwell.

Law, John, and Michael Lynch. 1990. "Lists, Field Guides, and the Descriptive Organization of Seeing: Birdwatching as an Exemplary Observational Activity." In *Representation in Scientific Practice,* ed. Michael Lynch and Steve Woolgar. Cambridge, MA: MIT Press.

Law, John, and Annemarie Mol. 1995. "Notes on Materiality and Sociality." *Sociological Review* 43: 274–94.

———, eds. 2002. *Complexities: Social Studies of Knowledge Practices.* Durham, NC, and London: Duke University Press.

Lawrence, Christopher. 1981. "Sanitary Reformers and the Medical Profession in Victorian England." In *Public Health: Proceedings of the 5th International Symposium on the Comparative History of Medicine—East and West,* ed. Teizo Ogawa. Tokyo: Saikon Publishing.

Leavitt, Judith Walzer. 1992. "'Typhoid Mary' Strikes Back: Bacteriological Theory and Practice in Early Twentieth-Century Public Health." *Isis* 83: 608–29.

———. 1996. *Typhoid Mary: Captive to the Public's Health.* Boston: Beacon Press.

Lee, W. L. Melville. 1971. *A History of Police in England.* Montclair, NJ: Patterson Smith.

Leerssen, Joep. 1995. "Wildness, Wilderness, and Ireland: Medieval and Early-Modern Patterns in the Demarcation of Civility." *Journal of the History of Ideas* 56: 25–39.

Lenoir, Timothy. 1988. "Practice, Reason, Context: The Dialogue Between Theory and Experiment." *Science in Context* 2, no. 1: 3–22.

Lindberg, David C., and Robert S. Westman, eds. 1990. *Reappraisals of the Scientific Revolution.* Cambridge: Cambridge University Press.

Lindemann, M. 1980. "Producing Policed Man: Poor Relief, Population Policies and Medical Care in Hamburg." PhD diss., University of Cincinnati.

Lo, Ming-Cheng M. 2002. *Doctors within Borders: Profession, Ethnicity, and Modernity in Colonial Taiwan.* Berkeley: University of California Press.

Lofland, Lyn H. 1998. *The Public Realm: Exploring the City's Quintessential Social Territory.* Hawthorne, NY: Aldine de Gruyter.

Lohan, Rena. 1994. *Guide to the Archives of the Office of Public Works.* Dublin: Government Stationery Office.

Long, Pamela O. 1997. "Power, Patronage, and the Authorship of Ars: From Mechanical Know-How to Mechanical Knowledge in the Last Scribal Age." *Isis* 88: 1–41.

Lynch, Michael. 1985. "Discipline and the Material Form of Images: An Analysis of Scientific Visibility." *Social Studies of Science* 15, no. 1: 37–66.

———. 1986. *Art and Artifact in Laboratory Science.* London: Routledge and Kegan Paul.

Lynch, Michael, and Steve Woolgar, eds. 1990. *Representation in Scientific Practice.* Cambridge, MA: MIT Press.

MacDonagh, Oliver. 1989. "Ideas and Institutions, 1830–45." In *A New History of Ireland*, vol. 5, ed. W. E. Vaughan. Oxford: Clarendon Press.

MacKenzie, Donald. 1990. *Inventing Accuracy.* Cambridge, MA: MIT Press.

MacKenzie, Donald, and Judy Wajcman, eds. 1999. *The Social Shaping of Technology.* Milton Keynes: Open University Press.

MacKinnon, Catharine A. 1989. *Toward a Feminist Theory of the State.* Cambridge, MA: Harvard University Press.

MacLeod, Roy. 1967. "The Frustration of State Medicine, 1880–1899." *Medical History* 11: 15–40.

———. 1968. "The Anatomy of State Medicine: Concept and Application." In *Medicine and Science in the 1860s*, ed. F. N. L. Poynter. London: Wellcome Institute for the History of Medicine.

———, ed. 1988. *Government and Expertise.* Cambridge: Cambridge University Press.

———. 1996. *Public Science and Public Policy in Victorian England.* Aldershot: Variorum.

Maguire, Mark. 1998. "Socialists, Savages and Hydroelectric Schemes: A Historical Anthropological Account of the Construction of Ardnacrusha." *Irish Journal of Anthropology* 3: 60–77.

Malcolm, Elizabeth. 1983. "Popular Recreation in Nineteenth Century Ireland." In *Irish Culture and Nationalism, 1750–1950*, ed. Oliver MacDonagh, W. F. Mandle, and Pauric Travers. London: Palgrave Macmillan.

Manwaring-White, Sarah. 1983. *The Policing Revolution: Police Technology, Democracy, and Liberty in Britain.* Brighton: Harvester Press.

Marx, Karl. *Capital: A Critical Analysis of Capitalist Production*, vol. 1. London: Lawrence and Wishart.

McDowell, R. B. 1964. *The Irish Administration 1801–1914.* London: Routledge and Kegan Paul.

———. 1985. "The Main Narrative." In *The Royal Irish Academy: A Bicentennial History 1785–1985*, ed. T. O. Raifeartaigh. Dublin: Royal Irish Academy.

McGinn, Robert E. 1991. *Science, Technology, and Society.* Englewood Cliffs, NJ: Prentice Hall.

McGucken, William. 1984. *Scientists, Society, and State: The Social Relations of Science Movement in Great Britain 1931–1947.* Columbus: Ohio State University Press.

McLoughlin, Thomas. 1999. *Contesting Ireland: Irish Voices against England in the Eighteenth Century.* Dublin: Four Courts Press.

Mehan, Hugh. 1993. "Beneath the Skin and between the Ears: A Case Study in the Politics of Representation." In *Understanding Practice: Perspectives on Activity and Context*, ed. Seth Chaiklin and Jean Lave. New York: Cambridge University Press.

Mendelsohn, J. Andrew. 1995. "'Typhoid Mary' Strikes Again: The Social and the Scientific in the Making of Modern Public Health." *Isis* 86: 268–77.

Merchant, Carolyn. 1980. *The Death of Nature: Women, Ecology, and the Scientific Revolution.* London: Wildwood House.

Merton, Robert. 2002 [1938]. *Science, Technology, and Society in Seventeenth Century England.* New York: Howard Fertig.

Merton, Robert K. 1996. *On Social Structure and Science,* ed. Piotr Sztompka. Chicago: University of Chicago Press.

Meyer, John. 1999. "The Changing Cultural Content of the Nation-State: A World Society Perspective." In *State/Culture: State-Formation after the Cultural Turn,* ed. George Steinmetz. Ithaca, NY: Cornell University Press.

Meyer, John, and Brian Rowan. 1977. "Institutionalized Organizations: Formal Structure as Myth and Ceremony." *American Journal of Sociology* 84: 340–63.

Mitchell, D. A. 1989. *A Peculiar Place: A History of the Adelaide Hospital.* Dublin: Blackwater.

Mitchell, Timothy. 1999. "Society, Economy, and the State Effect." In *State/Culture: State Formation after the Cultural Turn,* ed. George Steinmetz. Ithaca, NY: Cornell University Press.

———. 2002. *Rule of Experts: Egypt, Techno-Politics, Modernity.* Berkeley: University of California Press.

Mohr, James C. 1993. *Doctors and the Law: Medical Jurisprudence in Nineteenth-Century America.* New York: Oxford University Press.

Morley, David, and Kuan-Hsing Chen, eds. 1996. *Stuart Hall: Critical Dialogues in Cultural Studies.* New York: Routledge.

Mukerji, Chandra. 1983. *From Graven Images: Patterns of Modern Materialism.* New York: Columbia University Press.

———. 1989. *A Fragile Power: Scientists and the State.* Princeton, NJ: Princeton University Press.

———. 1990. "Reading and Writing with Nature: Social Claims and the French Formal Garden." *Theory and Society* 19, no. 6: 651–79.

———. 1994. "The Political Mobilization of Nature in Seventeenth Century French Formal Gardens." *Theory and Society* 23, no. 5: 651–77.

———. 1994. "Toward a Sociology of Material Culture: Science Studies, Cultural Studies, and the Meanings of Things." In *The Sociology of Culture,* ed. Diana Crane. Cambridge: Blackwell.

———. 1997. *Territorial Ambitions and the Gardens of Versailles.* Cambridge: Cambridge University Press.

———. 1998. "Unspoken Assumptions: Voice and Absolutism at the Court of Louis XIV." *Journal of Historical Sociology* 11, no. 3: 283–315.

Mulkay, Michael. 1969. "Some Aspects of Cultural Growth in the Natural Sciences." *Social Research* 36, no. 1: 22–52.

Neocleous, Mark. 1988. "Policing and Pin-Making: Adam Smith, Police and the State of Prosperity." *Policing and Society* 8: 425–49.

———. 2000. *The Fabrication of Social Order: A Critical Theory of Police Power.* London: Pluto Press.

————. 2000. "Social Police and the Mechanisms of Prevention: Patrick Colquhoun and the Condition of Poverty." *British Journal of Criminology* 40: 710–26.

O'Brien, Joseph V. 1982. *Dear, Dirty Dublin: A City in Distress, 1899–1916.* Berkeley: University of California Press.

O'Connell, Joseph. 1993. "Metrology: The Creation of Universality by the Circulation of Particulars." *Social Studies of Science* 23, no. 1: 129–73.

Oestreich, Gerhard. 1982. *Neostoicism and the Early Modern State.* New York: Cambridge University Press.

O'Grada, Cormac. 1989. *The Great Irish Famine.* Basingstoke: Macmillan.

O'Keeffe, Peter. 1980. "Richard Griffith: Planner and Builder of Roads." In *Richard Griffith 1784–1878,* ed. Gordon Davies and R. C. Mollan. Dublin: Royal Dublin Society.

Osborne, Thomas. 1996. "Security and Vitality: Drains, Liberalism, and Power in the Nineteenth Century." In *Foucault and Political Reason: Liberalism, Neo-liberalism and Rationalities of Government,* ed. Andrew Barry, Nikolas Rose, and Thomas Osborne. Chicago: University of Chicago Press.

Oster, Malcolm. 1992. "The Scholar and the Craftsman Revisited: Robert Boyle as Aristocrat and Artisan." *Annals of Science* 49: 255–76.

Palmer, Stanley H. 1988. *Police and Protest in England and Ireland 1780–1850.* Cambridge: Cambridge University Press.

Pannabecker, John R. 1998. "Representing Mechanical Arts in Diderot's *Encyclopédie.*" *Technology and Society* 39, no. 1: 33–73.

Petrow, Stephan. 1994. *Policing Morals: The Metropolitan Police and the Home Office, 1870–1914.* Oxford: Clarendon Press.

Pickering, Andrew, ed. 1992. *Science as Practice and Culture.* Chicago: University of Chicago Press.

————. 1995. *The Mangle of Practice: Time, Agency, and Science.* Chicago: University of Chicago Press.

Pickstone, John. 1992. "Fever Epidemics and British 'Public Health,' 1780–1850." In *Epidemics and Ideas: Essays on the Historical Perception of Pestilence,* ed. Terence Ranger and Paul Slack. Cambridge: Cambridge University Press.

Pinch, Trevor J. 1985. "Towards an Analysis of Scientific Observation: The Externality and Evidential Significance of Observation Reports in Physics." *Social Studies of Science* 15, no. 1: 3–36.

Polanyi, Karl. 2001 [1944]. *The Great Transformation: The Political and Economic Origins of Our Time.* Foreword by Joseph E. Stiglitz, with a new intro. by Fred Block. Boston: Beacon Press.

Poovey, Mary. 1995. *Making a Social Body: British Cultural Formation, 1830–1864.* Chicago: University of Chicago Press.

————. 1998. *A History of the Modern Fact: Problems of Knowledge in the Sciences of Wealth and Society.* Chicago: University of Chicago Press.

Porter, Dorothy, ed. 1994. *The History of Public Health and the Modern State.* Amsterdam: Rodopi.

————. 1996. "Social Medicine and the New Society: Medicine and Scientific Humanism in Mid-twentieth Century Britain." *Journal of Historical Sociology* 9, no. 2: 168–87.

————. 1999. *Health, Civilization, and the State: A History of Public Health from Ancient to Modern Times.* London: Routledge.

Porter, Dorothy, and Roy Porter, eds. 1993. *Doctors, Politics and Society: Historical Essays.* Atlanta, GA: Rodopi.

Porter, Theodore M. 1995. *Trust in Numbers: The Pursuit of Objectivity in Science and Public Life.* Princeton, NJ: Princeton University Press.

Powell, Walter W., and Paul J. DiMaggio, eds. 1991. *The New Institutionalism in Organizational Analysis.* Chicago: University of Chicago Press.

Praeger, R. Lloyde. 1931. "The Library." In *Royal Dublin Society Bi-centenary Souvenir 1731–1931,* ed. W.H. Brayden. Dublin: Royal Dublin Society.

Procacci, Giovanni. 1991. "Social Economy and the Government of Poverty." In *The Foucault Effect: Studies in Governmentality,* ed. Graham Burchell, Colin Gordon, and Peter Miller. Chicago: Chicago University Press.

Rabinow, Paul. 1983. *Social Science as Moral Inquiry.* New York: Columbia University Press.

Raeff, Marc. 1983. *The Well-Ordered Police State: Social and Institutional Change through Law in the Germanys and Russia, 1600–1800.* New Haven, CT: Yale University Press.

Ranger, Terence, and Paul Slack, eds. 1992. *Epidemics and Ideas: Essays on the Historical Perception of Pestilence.* Cambridge: Cambridge University Press.

Reid, Donald. 1991. *Paris Sewers and Sewermen: Realities and Representations.* Cambridge, MA: Harvard University Press.

Reynolds, Elaine A. 1998. *Before the Bobbies: The Night Watch and Police Reform in Metropolitan London, 1720–1830.* London: Macmillan.

Rheinberger, Hans-Jörg. 1997. *Towards a History of Epistemic Things: Synthesizing Proteins in the Test Tube.* Stanford, CA: Stanford University Press.

Robertson, George, Melinda Mash, Lisa Tickner, Jon Bird, Barry Curtis, and Tim Putnam, eds. 1996. *Future Natural: Nature/Science/Culture.* New York: Routledge.

Rose, Nikolas. 1990. *Governing the Soul: The Shaping of the Private Self.* New York: Routledge.

Rosen, George. 1953. "Cameralism and the Concept of Medical Police." *Bulletin of the History of Medicine* 27: 21–42.

————. 1957. "The Fate of the Concept of Medical Police 1780–1890." *Centaurus* 5, no. 2: 97–113.

————. 1993. *A History of Public Health.* Baltimore, MD: Johns Hopkins University Press.

Rothman, Brian. 1999. "Thinking Dia-Grams: Mathematics and Writing." In *The Science Studies Reader,* ed. Mario Biagioli. New York: Routledge.

Rouse, Joseph. 1987. *Knowledge and Power: Toward a Political Philosophy of Science.* Ithaca, NY: Cornell University Press.

Royal Dublin Society. 1981. *A Bibliography of the Publications of the Royal Dublin Society from Its Foundation in the Year 1731, together with a List of Bibliographical Material relative to the Society.* 3rd ed. Dublin: Royal Dublin Society.

Rudwick, Martin. 1976. "The Emergence of a Visual Language for Geological Science, 1760–1840." *History of Science* 14: 149–95.

Rueschemeyer, Dietrich, and Theda Skocpol, eds. 1996. *States, Social Knowledge, and the Origins of Modern Social Policies.* Princeton, NJ: Princeton University Press.

Rusnock, Andrea A. 1999. "Biopolitics: Political Arithmetic in the Enlightenment." In *The Sciences of Enlightened Europe,* ed. William Clark, Jan Golinski, and Simon Shaffer. Chicago: University of Chicago Press.

Sailer, Susan Shaw, ed. 1997. *Representing Ireland: Gender, Class, Nationality.* Gainesville: University Press of Florida.

Sayer, Derek. 1987. *The Violence of Abstraction.* Oxford: Basil Blackwell.

Schaffer, Simon. 1994. "Babbage's Intelligence, Calculating Engines, and the Factory System." *Critical Inquiry* 21, no. 1: 203–27.

———, ed. 2000. "Modernity and Metrology." In *Science and Power: The Historical Foundations of Research Policies in Europe,* ed. Luca Guzzetti. Luxembourg: European Union Publication.

Scott, James C. 1998. *Seeing Like a State: How Certain Schemes to Improve the Human Condition Have Failed.* New Haven, CT, and London: Yale University Press.

Seidman, Steven, ed. 1989. *Jurgen Habermas on Society and Politics: A Reader.* Boston: Beacon Press.

———. 1997. "Sociology and Cultural Studies." In *From Sociology to Cultural Studies: New Perspectives,* ed. Elizabeth Long. Malden, MA: Blackwell.

Seymour, W. A., ed. 1980. *A History of the Ordnance Survey.* Folkstone, Kent: Dawson.

Shapin, Steven. 1989. "The Invisible Technician." *American Scientist* 77, no. 6: 554–63.

———. 1990. "History of Science and its Sociological Reconstructions." *History of Science* 20: 157–211.

———. 1994. *A Social History of Truth: Civility and Science in Seventeenth-Century England.* Chicago: University of Chicago Press.

———. 1996. *The Scientific Revolution.* Chicago: University of Chicago Press.

Shapin, Steven, and Barry Barnes. 1976. "Head and Hand: Rhetorical Resources in British Pedagogical Writing, 1770–1850." *Oxford Review of Education* 2: 231–54.

———. 1977. "Science, Nature and Control: Interpreting Mechanics' Institutes." *Social Studies of Science* 7, no. 1: 31–74.

Shapin, Steven, and Simon Schaffer. 1985. *Leviathan and the Air-Pump: Hobbes, Boyle, and the Experimental Life.* Princeton, NJ: Princeton University Press.

Shapiro, Michael. 1988. *The Politics of Representation*. Madison: University of Wisconsin Press.

Sigerist, Henry E. 1943. *Civilization and Disease*. Ithaca, NY: Cornell University Press.

Simms, J.G. 1982. *William Molyneux of Dublin, 1656–1698*, ed. P.H. Kelly. Dublin: Irish Academic Press.

———. 1986. *War and Politics in Ireland, 1649–1730*. London: Hambledon Press.

Simon, Bart. 2002. *Undead Science: Science Studies and the Afterlife of Cold Fusion*. New Brunswick, NJ: Rutgers University Press.

Sismondo, Sergio. 2004. *An Introduction to Science and Technology Studies*. Oxford: Blackwell Publishing.

Skempton, A.W. 1987. *British Civil Engineering, 1640–1840: A Bibliography of Contemporary Printed Reports, Plans, and Books*. New York: Mansell Publishing.

———. 1996. *Civil Engineers and Engineering in Britain, 1600–1830*. Brookfield, VT: Variorum.

Skocpol, Theda. 1979. *States and Social Revolutions: A Comparative Analysis of France, Russia, and China*. New York: Cambridge University Press.

———. 1994. *Social Revolutions in the Modern World*. New York: Cambridge University Press.

Slack, Paul. 1985. *The Impact of Plague in Tudor and Stuart England*. London: Routledge and Kegan Paul.

Sladovich, Hedy E. 1991. *Engineering as a Social Enterprise*. Washington, DC: National Academy Press.

Smelser, Neil J. 1992. "The Rational Choice Perspective." *Rationality and Society* 4: 380–410.

Smith, Crosbie, and M. Norton Wise. 1989. *Energy and Empire: A Biographical Study of Lord Kelvin*. Cambridge: Cambridge University Press.

Smith, David A., Dorothy J. Solinger, and Steven C. Topik, eds. 1999. *States and Sovereignty in the Global Economy*. London: Routledge.

Squier, Susan Merrill. 2004. *Liminal Lives: Imagining the Human at the Frontiers of Biomedicine*. Durham, NC, and London: Duke University Press.

Stacey, Margaret. 1992. *Regulating British Medicine: The General Medical Council*. Chichester: John Wiley.

Stapleton, Darwin H. 1986. *The History of Civil Engineering since 1600: An Annotated Bibliography*. New York: Garland.

Star, Leigh, and James R. Griesemer. 1989. "Institutional Ecology, Translations and Boundary Objects: Amateurs and Professionals in Berkeley's Museum of Vertebrate Zoology, 1907–39." *Social Studies of Science* 19, no. 3: 387–420.

Starr, Paul. 1982. *The Social Transformation of American Medicine*. New York: Basic Books.

Stead, Philip John. 1985. *The Police of Britain*. New York: Macmillan.

Steedman, Carolyn. 1984. *Policing the Victorian Community: The Formation of English Provincial Police Forces, 1856–80.* Boston: Routledge and Paul.

Steinmetz, George, ed. 1999. *State/Culture: State Formation after the Cultural Turn.* Ithaca, NY: Cornell University Press.

Strauss, E. 1954. *Sir William Petty: Portrait of a Genius.* London: Bodley Head.

Swidler, Ann. 1986. "Culture in Action: Symbols and Strategies." *American Sociological Review* 51:273–86.

———. 2001. *Talk of Love: How Culture Matters.* Chicago: University of Chicago Press.

Thomas, George M., J. W. Meyer, F. O. Ramirez, and J. Boli. 1987. *Institutional Structure: Constituting State, Society, and the Individual.* Newbury Park, CA: Sage Publications.

Thompson, E. P. 1964. *The Making of the English Working Class.* New York: Pantheon Books.

Thomson, F. M. L. 1988. *The Rise of Respectable Society: A Social History of Victorian Britain, 1830–1900.* Cambridge, MA: Harvard University Press.

Tilly, Charles, ed. 1975. *The Formation of National States in Western Europe.* Princeton, NJ: Princeton University Press.

———. 1992. *Coercion, Capital, and European States, AD 990–1992.* Rev. paperback ed. Malden, MA: Blackwell Publishers.

———. 1999. "Epilogue: Now Where?" In *State/Culture: State Formation after the Cultural Turn,* ed. George Steinmetz. Ithaca, NY: Cornell University Press.

Traweek, Sharon. 1988. *Beamtimes and Lifetimes: The World of High Energy Physicists.* Cambridge, MA: Harvard University Press.

Turner, Gerard L. E. 1998. *Scientific Instruments 1500–1900: An Introduction.* Berkeley: University of California Press.

Valverde, Mariana. 2000. "Some Remarks on the Rise and Fall of Discourse Analysis." *Histoire sociale/Social History* 33, no. 65: 59–77.

Van Helden, Albert. 1983. "The Birth of the Modern Scientific Instrument, 1550–1700." In *The Use of Science in the Age of Newton,* ed. John Burke. Berkeley: University of California Press.

Vaughan, Diane. 1996. *The Challenger Launch Decision: Risky Technology, Culture, and Deviance at NASA.* Chicago: University of Chicago Press.

Vaughan, W. E. 1989. "Ireland c. 1870." In *A New History of Ireland,* vol. 5, ed. W. E. Vaughan. Oxford: Clarendon Press.

Vickers, Brian, ed. 1987. *English Science, Bacon to Newton.* New York: Cambridge University Press.

Vincent, Andrew. 1987. *Theories of State.* New York: Basil Blackwell.

Wakefield, R. A. 2000. "Police Chemistry." *Science in Context* 13, no. 2: 231–67.

Walton, John. 1992. *Western Times and Water Wars: State, Culture, and Rebellion in California.* Berkeley: University of California Press.

Warner, Deborah Jean. 1990. "What Is a Scientific Instrument, When Did It Become One, and Why?" *British Journal for the History of Science* 23:83–93.

Wayman, Patrick A. 1987. *Dunsink Observatory, 1785–1985*. Dublin: Dublin Institute for Advanced Studies.

Webster, Charles, ed. 1970. *Samuel Hartlib and the Advancement of Learning*. London: Cambridge University Press.

———. 1974. "New Light on the Invisible College." *Transactions of the Royal Historical Society* 24: 33.

Weindling, Paul. 1994. "Public Health in Germany." In *The History of Public Health and the Modern State*, ed. Dorothy Porter. Amsterdam: Rodopi.

Westfall, Robert S. 1977. *The Construction of Modern Science: Mechanisms and Mechanics*. New York: Cambridge University Press.

Whelan, Kevin. 1996. "The Region and the Intellectuals." In *On Intellectuals and Intellectual Life in Ireland: International, Comparative and Historical Contexts*, ed. Liam O'Dowd. Dublin: Royal Irish Academy.

White, Brenda M. 1983. "Medical Police, Politics and Police: The Fate of John Roberton." *Medical History* 27: 407–22.

White, Terence de Vere. 1955. *The Story of the Royal Dublin Society*. Tralee: Kerryman.

Widdess, John David Henry. 1967. *The Royal College of Surgeons in Ireland and Its Medical School, 1784–1966*. London: E. and S. Livingstone.

Wing, Kenneth R. 1985. *The Law and the Public's Health*. Ann Arbor, MI: Health Administration Press.

Winkler, Mary G., and Albert Van Helden. 1992. "Representing the Heavens: Galileo and Visual Astronomy." *Isis* 83, no. 2: 195–217.

Winner, Langdon. 1986. "The State of Nature Revisited." In *The Whale and the Reactor: A Search for Limits in an Age of High Technology*. Chicago: University of Chicago Press.

Wise, Norton. 1988. "Meditating Machines." *Science in Context* 2, no. 1: 77–113.

Zilsel, Edgar. 2000 [1942]. "The Sociological Roots of Science." *American Journal of Sociology* 47: 544–52. Repr. in *Social Studies of Science* 30, no. 6: 935–49.

Žižek, Slavoj, ed. 1994. *Mapping Ideology*. New York: Verso.

Zucker, Lynne. 1991. "The Role of Institutionalization in Cultural Persistence." In *The New Institutionalism in Organizational Analysis*, ed. Walter W. Powell and Paul J. DiMaggio. Chicago: University of Chicago Press.

Index

Text:	10/13 Aldus
Display:	Aldus
Compositor:	International Typesetting and Composition
Printer and binder:	Thomson-Shore, Inc.
Illustrator:	Bill Nelson
Indexer:	Andrew Joron